Disciplined Programming

Using Pascal

Disciplined Programming

Using Pascal

Samuel E. Rhoads
Honolulu Community College

Michael V. Gearen
Punahou School

 Wm. C. Brown Publishers

Book Team

Editor *Earl McPeek*
Developmental Editor *Theresa Grutz*
Production Editor *Linda M. Meehan*
Art Editor *Janice M. Roerig*

 Wm. C. Brown Publishers

President *G. Franklin Lewis*
Vice President, Editor-in-Chief *George Wm. Bergquist*
Vice President, Director of Production *Beverly Kolz*
Vice President, National Sales Manager *Bob McLaughlin*
Director of Marketing *Thomas E. Doran*
Marketing Communications Manager *Edward Bartell*
Marketing Manager *David F. Horwitz*
Executive Editor *Edward G. Jaffe*
Production Editorial Manager *Colleen A. Yonda*
Production Editorial Manager *Julie A. Kennedy*
Publishing Services Manager *Karen J. Slaght*
Manager of Visuals and Design *Faye M. Schilling*

Cover Image: The Nest of Dragons, © Samuel E. Rhoads.
A dragon curve is a recursively generated series of line segments that
form a path from one point to another. The "Nest of Dragons" consists
of four dragon curves, each starting at the same point but ending at four
points on a spiral. The program that produced the image was written in
Pascal, and is available from the authors upon request.

Turbo Pascal is a registered trademark of Borland International.

Library of Congress Catalog Card Number: 88–64092

ISBN 0–697–06336–4

Printed in the United States of America by Wm. C. Brown Publishers,
2460 Kerper Boulevard, Dubuque, IA 52001

10 9 8 7 6 5 4 3 2 1

To the loving memory
of our mothers:

Eleanore Searle Rhoads
Virginia Burke Gearen

Contents

Preface

In the last ten years or so we have witnessed a virtual explosion of computers. Near the end of the 1970s only a few people had access to a microcomputer and computers were thought of as those huge machines used by universities, large businesses and the military. Today there are computers everywhere. A large segment of the population has access to one or more computers and uses them on a daily basis. Our lives are filled with computers, from the tiny computers in our cars and microwave ovens, to the desktop computers at home and in the office, to the huge computers used by banks, schools, government agencies, research agencies and the military. Personal computers are used for word processing, number processing, desktop publishing and game playing, as well as many other functions.

These computers would not do anything if they weren't *programmed*. It is the program that the computer runs that causes it to do whatever it does. Furthermore, these programs would not exist if they weren't written by someone, a *computer programmer*.

This book is a text on computer programming; i.e., it is designed for those who wish to learn how to program computers. It is written for a beginning programmer; no previous experience with computers or computer programming is assumed.

It is important to understand that, even though we use the computer language Pascal in this book, it is not just a book on Pascal. The programming process is much more than the process of typing in a program at a computer keyboard, and we have tried to emphasize this distinction. Many people think that learning a computer language, such as Pascal, is the same as learning to program. We try very hard to show that this is not the case.

On the other hand, the programs in this book are written in Pascal, so the reader will learn a great deal about Pascal by using the book. We do not claim or attempt to cover all of the elements of Pascal; that is not our goal. We cover the large majority of the language; the only major feature that is not included is pointers. The book uses what is known as "Standard Pascal" throughout. Appendix C discusses the differences between the Pascal used in the book and some well-known Pascal compilers.

The Level of the Course

The text is designed for use at the college level in the introductory computer programming class and covers the Association of Computing Machinery (ACM) recommended curriculum for CS1. It is also designed for use in the Advanced Placement Computer Science course and covers the material recommended for the first semester, i.e., Computer Science A.

Overview

The first two chapters provide a general introduction to the conceptual fundamentals, history, and jargon of computing machines and computing. At the very least, you should read these two chapters quickly to get a feel for what computing is and an understanding of the programming process.

Stop and Think

At various places in the book you will see a little computer character holding a stop sign.

This indicates a place for you to pause in your reading and either think extra carefully about what is being said at that point or take a few moments and do some sort of calculation before reading on. Please stop and do whatever the text suggests before reading further whenever you see this character. It will help in your understanding of the material.

Chapters 3–8 introduce and develop essential programming concepts and methods, followed by the corresponding Pascal vocabulary and syntax. In these chapters, the complete programming process is followed step by step, resulting in complete Pascal programs.

Chapters 9–14 present more advanced programming concepts and implementation details, including various searching and sorting algorithms, character string manipulation, database maintenance, file handling, two-dimensional arrays and recursion.

Beginning with chapter 3, each of the chapters focuses on one or two specific problems to be solved with the computer. At first, alternate chapters cover the development of an algorithm for the solution of the problem and the implementation of that algorithm in Pascal. Later, these two steps are both done in a given chapter, but never at the same time. Chapter 3 is particularly important in that it introduces fundamental programming concepts that are used throughout the book.

Real computer programs never consist of just one fundamental concept; i.e., every real program uses most, if not all, of these fundamental concepts. Therefore, we do not treat the fundamental concepts of programming in isolation. Rather, we introduce assignment, input, output, selection and repetition together in chapter 3. While this might seem like a lot to cover in one chapter, rest assured that these concepts are constantly reviewed in subsequent chapters.

You will get plenty of practice using these fundamental concepts throughout the remainder of the text.

Assignment

When we introduce the concept of assignment, we use the word "*store*" to indicate the process of having the computer find the value of an expression and put that value into a variable. This results in steps such as:

store First + Second in Third

which works from left to right—the same order that we are accustomed to reading.

Those readers already familiar with programming might know that assignment is done "right to left" rather than "left to right" in many programming languages. We like the word *store* and we like visualizing the concept of assignment as a left to right operation. While this can cause minor problems—it has to be turned around in order to get coded correctly—we have found that the word *store* and the left-to-right thinking that it produces far outweigh any problems with the coding step.

"Once Again"

At the suggestion of several reviewers, we have included a "Once Again" section in each of chapters 3 through 13. In these sections we briefly review the new ideas introduced in the chapter by sketching these ideas with another problem or example.

Gender References

We do not like using the words "he" and "him" to refer to a member of a general audience; surely the readers of this book are both women and men. While we agree with the intent, we also do not like the use of "he or she" and "her or him"; this use becomes annoying after a while. To solve the problem, we have decided, arbitrarily, that the programmer we are talking to is a woman, and the user of the programs is a man. Thus, whenever we are referring to a programmer, we'll use "she" and "her," and whenever we are referring to a user, we'll use the words "he" and "him." The illustrations that appear throughout the book reflect this convention: the programmer in the illustrations is a young woman, the user is a young man.

Exercises

We include many carefully selected exercises. For those chapters that focus on algorithm development, the exercises for that chapter allow the student to develop algorithms for different problems which are at about the same level of complexity. For those chapters focusing on Pascal implementation, the exercises emphasize the implementation of similar algorithms.

Covering the Entire Book

While this book is designed for a one semester course, it might turn out that there is insufficient time to cover all the material in one semester. If that is the case, many of the topics in chapters 11–14 can be covered independently of the others, so, with a bit of planning, the teacher can pick and choose among them.

Acknowledgments

We would like to acknowledge those that have assisted in the preparation of the book.

First, our students and colleagues. We owe our thanks to the many students over the years who have helped us formulate our thoughts on how computer programming should be taught. These students have suffered through various drafts of this book and have added considerably to its final form. As the book neared completion, we were helped by a number of students and colleagues who offered specific suggestions or found errors in the text. We recognize their help by using their names throughout the text in the examples. In particular, we'd like to thank Tim Wilson and Doug Fernandez. Tim has read several drafts of the manuscript, taught the course using the text in early forms and offered many useful suggestions. Doug checked all the examples of code in the book by typing in and running each program. He found several errors that we would not have found otherwise.

Second, we would like to recognize the support of the schools where we teach. Honolulu Community College and Punahou School have both allowed us the use of their facilities while the text has been in preparation and have been understanding about the number of hours we have spent on its preparation.

Third, we would like to thank the reviewers who have offered their thoughts and suggestions: John W. Jamison, Jr., Intergraph Corp.; Sean P. McGowan, University of Lowell; Ron McCarty, Behrend College; John Hawley, Wright State University; Anne Oney, De Anza College; Neil Murray, North Country Community College; and, especially, J. Evan Noynaert, Missouri Western State College. Their careful reading of the text and many suggestions have aided us a great deal in preparing the manuscript. It is a much better textbook as a result of their help.

Special thanks go to our editors, Earl McPeek and Theresa Grutz, and the rest of the people at Wm. C. Brown Publishers. It has been a pleasure working with Earl and his staff. They provided the moral support when it was needed and believed in the idea from the beginning.

The manuscript for this book has been prepared with TeX and LaTeX. We want to thank Donald E. Knuth and Leslie Lamport for producing these wonderful aids. One of the unanticipated joys of writing the book has been learning TeX and LaTeX, and in reading *The TeXbook*.

The illustrations were drawn by Katie Ralston. They add a light touch to the text that we like very much; we hope you like them too. Thanks, Katie.

Finally, to Pui Hin and Barbara: thanks for putting up with us during the months when we surely spent more time thinking about this than you would have liked.

Chapter 1

Programming Fundamentals

> My favorite way to describe computer science
> is to say that it is the study of algorithms.
> An algorithm is a precisely defined sequence
> of rules telling how to produce specified
> output information from given input information
> in a finite number of steps.
> — Donald E. Knuth

1.1   Introduction

This text is concerned with computer programming. Our chief goal is to help you become a good programmer. The difference between *programming* and *coding* will be stressed throughout the book. *Programming* implies the entire process from defining a problem through testing the resulting program that implements the solution. Computer programs today are normally written in what have come to be called *programming languages*. The programming language we will use in this book is known as *Pascal*. Pascal was designed by Niklaus Wirth in the late 1960s and has become a very popular language to use in a beginning programming class. The primary reasons Pascal is so popular for a beginning course in programming are its simplicity and elegance. Wirth did not attempt to design a powerful language that could be used by everyone to solve any problem; rather, he wanted to design a language that made the fundamental concepts of programming easy to see and to implement.

There are hundreds of computer languages in use today. Knowing how to program is not the same as knowing one of these computer languages. In this book we will help you to learn how to write computer programs and to learn Pascal. Once you learn good programming skills, you will be able to pick up other computer languages and use these skills while writing programs in the other languages.

While we will concentrate on programming, we feel that beginning programmers should be aware of some of the history of computing; therefore, this chap-

1

ter contains a very brief history of the development of computers and computer programs.

1.2   Problem Solving

Think of computer programming as problem solving with a computer. Experts in problem solving consider a problem as consisting of three parts: a *given*, a *goal* and a set of *guidelines*. The given is where you are, the goal is where you want to get, and the set of guidelines is the collection of rules that determine what you can do to get from the given to the goal. In computer programming, problems are solved with a computer; therefore, the set of guidelines is limited to those things a computer can do. The given can be thought of as the data the computer program has to work on; that is, the input. The goal is the data that the program is to produce, or the output. Neither the input nor the output is limited to what can be typed in at the computer's keyboard. The input could come from an external source such as a file or some sort of instrumentation attached to a machine. The output could be saved in an external file or used to drive another machine. The purpose of this book is to help you learn how to make a computer take a given amount of data and produce a particular result.

While it seems that the number of problems a computer can solve is growing, there are still many problems in the world today that are not appropriate for solution by computer. In this book we'll only be concerned with the sort of problems a computer can help solve, and we'll only be able to take an introductory look at those.

Computer programming is much more than simply writing a bunch of lines of computer code in some computer language. Programming actually consists of several steps, only one of which is the step where code is written (we'll call this the *coding* step).

Good programming requires that before coding is begun, the programmer first carefully defines the problem. It is necessary that you know what you want the program to do before you start writing it. Although it seems obvious that one has to know what the program is to do before it can be written, it isn't always done that way. Careless programmers sometimes jump right into writing the program before they are sure what it's supposed to do. Furthermore, by writing a careful definition of the problem to be solved, one often gains additional insight into the solution.

The second step is to work out a solution to the problem. This step also needs to be completed before the coding can start. Good programmers never try to solve a problem while they are writing code. If you do, you'll discover than the entire process becomes confused and takes even longer than it would have if you had spent the time up front finding a good solution to the problem.

Even after a solution is found, there is another step that has to be completed before coding can begin. The solution has to be expressed precisely in a step-by-step fashion, i.e., as an *algorithm*. The algorithm should be *language*

1. Define the problem.
2. Find a solution to the problem.
3. Design and write an algorithm for the solution.
4. Code the algorithm in some computer language.
5. Test and debug the program.

+ Document continuously.

Figure 1.1 The FIVE + STEPS of Programming

independent; that is, it should focus on the steps of the solution rather than on the syntax of any particular language.

When the solution is clearly expressed algorithmically, the coding begins. The coding step should be little more than simply translating the steps of the algorithm into the syntax of a particular language. We'll see several examples of this in this text.

After the coding step, the program must be tested thoroughly to make sure it does what is intended; when it doesn't, it must be corrected.

Each stage in the programming process should be described—in writing—so that someone other than the programmer can fully understand it.

In this book, we'll call these the FIVE + STEPS of programming. Figure 1.1 contains the FIVE + STEPS.

You should understand that these steps build upon one another. If you get into the middle of one particular step and realize that an earlier step was not completed or was done incorrectly, you must be willing to discard what you have done and start over at the step that was incomplete. After spending a lot of time on coding a group of steps and then realizing that the algorithm or the solution is wrong, it is often difficult to throw away all that code and start over. Nevertheless, you must be willing to do just that to become a good programmer. Good programmers know that if they do the first three steps properly, it is much less likely that they will have to throw away code and start over.

This is not the entire story either. After a program is finished, or seems to be finished, there may be more to do. The algorithm itself may be improved upon—much of the research that is done in computing science is directed toward the improvement of existing algorithms. In fact, many professionals regard computing science as the study of algorithms.

You could test an algorithm over and over again on a variety of cases, but you would not be sure it will work in all cases until it has been proven correct. The study of the proof of the correctness of algorithms is not much different from mathematics; indeed, there is a great deal of overlap between mathematics and computing science.

Furthermore, good programming requires that the programs be easy to use by other programs and by humans. When computers were new to us, we were willing to bend to their needs and limitations. People were sometimes forced to change the spelling of their names to satisfy the computer—actually the computer programmer—and people had to be very careful to supply the computer with the data it needed in just the right way or chaos would result. We've come a long way since then. Today it is the computer—actually, the computer program and the programmer—that must be flexible.

The programming process needs to be carefully documented, and not just during the coding step. Professional programmers spend a significant amount of time writing the *specifications* for a program (a description of *what* the program is to do, rather than *how*). These specifications must be approved by the one for whom the program is being written before the algorithm is designed.

No program that solves a significant problem is ever really finished. It is often the case that some new twist is added, or some new technique to solve the problem is discovered—a better algorithm is found. Perhaps it is realized that a larger or different problem needs to be solved with the same program. In short, real computer programs always need to be maintained. This is why the code must contain internal comments that explain what the program is doing and why. If they do not, programs that seem perfectly clear to a programmer one day can seem very mysterious the next day, and totally unclear to someone other than the programmer.

1.3   The Top-Down Approach

Perhaps you have heard the terms *top-down approach* or *stepwise refinement* in connection with the programming process. Actually, these terms refer to a disciplined method of problem solving that's useful in situations other than computer programming. In fact, the most important thing you learn in a programming course is how to think about complex problems, not how to write computer programs.

In using the top-down approach for programming, one describes the function of the program in several broad strokes, and then takes each of these broad strokes separately and regards it as a *subprogram*. These subprograms are further refined in smaller strokes, and this process is continued until the remaining problems are simple enough to be solved directly. These lowest-level modules are written first and tested. Modules should have single purposes and should be tested to insure that they perform their functions correctly. They are then used to build the next level modules, and these are, in turn, tested to insure that they work correctly. When the entire collection of modules is finally put together, the program is completed.

The main advantage of this method is that it can be used to solve all kinds of problems, from simple to complex. There are other advantages, however. The modular structure of the resulting algorithms and programs make them far easier to understand, and often the modules are useful in situations other than those for which they were originally written.

Another advantage of this method is that the development of each module can be assigned to different programmers or teams of programmers. As long as each group knows exactly what data their module will be given and what function their module is to perform, they can write their module independently of the remaining modules.

The modular approach is also important in the testing and debugging phase. The more complex a program is, the harder it is to think of all the possible ways it could go wrong. The only way to build reliable programs is to use simple, single-purpose modules as basic building blocks, test them thoroughly, and then combine them to build larger blocks, which are also tested thoroughly as the program is built.

1.4 Brief History of Computing

It is difficult to write a short history of computing. The difficulty lies in deciding where to start and what and whom *not* to mention. We have selected highlights of the fascinating history of computing, and have left out much more than we included.

Early History

People have been "computing" and using computing aids for ages. There's no way to know for sure when it all started. Early shepherds surely used stones to keep track of the number of sheep they owned. In 500 B.C. the Chinese started using a computing aid known as an *abacus*. This device is sometimes still used in China.

Pascal and Leibniz

Blaise Pascal—the man that Niklaus Wirth named the computer language Pascal for—invented a computing device something like an adding machine in the 1640s. His *numerical wheel calculator*, as he called it, never caught on: people were afraid that it might cost them their jobs if they used a machine to do the calculations, and some feared the machine could be modified to yield answers that would benefit the person doing the modifying. Gottfried Wilhelm von Leibniz took Pascal's design a little further and invented a mechanical calculator in the 1670s. It also was never widely used but its design influenced the design of mechanical calculators for the next 200 years.

Babbage and Lady Lovelace

In the early 1820s, Charles Babbage and John Herschel were working on a problem in astronomy and continued to run into errors in astronomical tables that had been prepared by hand. Babbage is quoted to have said, "I wish to God these calculations had been executed by steam!" In those days steam was the principal source of energy; Babbage's remark meant that he wished the calculations had been done by some sort of machine. After making the remark, he started to think about the problem and invented a machine that would do just what he wanted. He made a model of the machine—he called it a *Difference Engine*—and persuaded the British government to give him a grant to build a working model.

The Difference Engine was never completed for two main reasons: Babbage's ideas required mechanical parts working together to tolerances that could not be constructed at the time, and, while working on the Difference Engine, Babbage thought of an even better computing device, the *Analytical Engine*. The government refused to give Babbage any more money to build his new invention and it also was never completed.

While he was working on the designs of his computing machines, he came to know Lady Augusta Ada Byron, Countess of Lovelace. Lady Lovelace was a liberated woman for her time. She was a gifted mathematician, one of very few women in a field of study long thought to be solely the province of men. Lady Lovelace worked with Babbage and understood his ideas better than anyone else; she even corrected several mistakes in his calculations. She added several pages of notes to those prepared by others about the machine. Included in her notes was a series of instructions on how to use the machine. These instructions are today considered the first computer program and she is considered to be the world's first computer programmer. A modern computer language, somewhat similar to Pascal, has been named in her honor: *Ada*.

Several years later, Babbage's designs were shown to have been correct. Had the mechanical know-how been available at the time, his computers would have worked.

1.5   Twentieth Century

The principal efforts in computing in the United States in the latter half of the 1800s and the first 30 years in the 1900s were concerned with conducting the U.S. census. It became an enormous task to count all the people in the U.S. by hand. Herman Hollerith designed a tabulating machine that reduced the time it took from several years to a few weeks. He formed a company that later merged with other companies to become International Business Machines (IBM).

First Generation

In the early 1940s, Howard G. Aiken was developing the *MARK I* at Harvard University. He was given $1 million by Thomas J. Watson of IBM to develop it. IBM at the time was still primarily concerned with conducting the U.S. census but the hope was that the MARK I would aid with tabulating the number of people in the country and also help with the calculations needed in the war effort. The MARK I was the closest machine to Babbage's Analytical Engine ever built.

In the late 1930s John V. Atanasoff, a professor of mathematics at Iowa State University, and his student Clifford Berry, designed and built a vacuum tube computer, called the *ABC* (*Atanasoff-Berry Computer*). Their design influenced John W. Mauchley and J. Presper Eckert at the University of Pennsylvania, who built the *ENIAC* (*Electronic Numerical Integrator And Computer*) just at the end of the war.

The ENIAC was the first large scale computer; it was two stories high, and contained 1900 vacuum tubes and 70,000 resistors. It generated huge amounts of heat and required enormous cooling systems to keep it running. It was theoretically capable of about 5,000 calculations per second, which means it could theoretically do in one hour about what 100 people with adding machines could accomplish in six months.

The brilliant mathematician John von Neumann was responsible for several theoretical breakthroughs in the mid-1940s that affected the designs of the early computers and these effects are still felt today. Von Neumann and Atanasoff were two of the first to suggest that the binary number system be used in the design of computers rather than base ten numbers.

Mauchley and Eckert formed their own company to build and sell a computer that was essentially the same design as the ENIAC, the UNIVAC. The UNIVAC was the first computer sold commercially. The U.S. Government used a UNIVAC for the census in 1950 and used it continuously through 1963. A great deal of news and controversy about the ability of a computer was generated in 1952 when a UNIVAC was used to predict the outcome of the presidential election between Eisenhower and Stevenson. With only 5% of the vote recorded, Eisenhower was correctly predicted to have won the election.

We speak of different "generations" of computers. These earliest computers—MARK I, ENIAC and UNIVAC—with their vacuum tubes are considered *first generation computers*.

The United States was not the only country trying to develop computers in the 1930s and 1940s. There was a group in Germany working on a design but never completed it due to Hitler's rejection of their ideas. Alan Turing in Great Britain did some theoretical work that is still being used in computer science. Turing also proposed a definition of computer intelligence, called the Turing test, that is still considered by many computer scientists to be the best working definition of Artificial Intelligence. At about the same time, a group of scientists in Great Britain designed a special purpose computer called *Colossus* to break code during World War II.

First Examples of Programming

One of the biggest problems faced by the earliest computers was their inflexibility. They were not "programmable" by today's definition. They would perform only one task, and to change that task required rewiring them. This "rewiring" amounted to programming them. And it's worth noting that the first programmers on both the MARK I and the ENIAC were women. Grace Hopper programmed the MARK I and Adele Goldstein programmed the ENIAC.

Mathematician John von Neumann also gets credit for being the first to publish the *stored program concept*. This concept says that rather than rewiring the computer each time a new task is to be performed, let the program be stored inside the computer itself. The program then becomes part of the data the computer uses. Von Neumann wrote his programs in what today would be called *machine language*. The data stored in a computer is stored in the form of thousands of 1s and 0s. Each instruction to the computer had to be in the same form, so programs were long lists of 1s and 0s.

Machine language is very difficult to program in. It wasn't very long before people realized that they could write their instructions in a pseudo-language a little closer to English and have the computer itself translate them into machine language. Languages like this are called *assembly languages*.

Hardware vs. Software

We should introduce the terms *hardware* and *software*. "Hardware" refers to any physical part of the computer, i.e., the computer itself. "Software" refers to the programs that the computer runs. If we use an analogy from music, the hardware of a computer corresponds to the record player, the amplifier and the speakers; the software corresponds to the music itself.

During the 1940s a computer expert was an expert in both hardware and software. The two fields began to separate in the 1950s. People began to specialize in one area or the other. Today most computer experts are experts in either hardware or software—usually in a narrower sub-area. Few people are considered experts in both areas. There have been times when progress in hardware has led the way and equivalent progress in software has lagged behind. At other times, software developments have outpaced developments in hardware.

Second Generation

The invention of the transistor marks the beginning of the *second generation* of computers. Besides the savings in size due to the transistor replacing the vacuum tube, second generation computers also used new techniques for storing data. Magnetic core memory was used for memory; indeed, even today many people use the word "core" when they refer to the memory of a computer even though magnetic core memory has not been used in the new computers for years.

Higher Level Languages

The 1950s also saw the development of the first *higher level languages*. Writing a program in a higher level language amounts to writing instructions in an English-like set of commands and then having the computer itself translate these instructions into machine language that it understands.

Two very important languages got their start in the 1950s: *Fortran*[1] and *LISP*. IBM oversaw the development of Fortran (for *FOR*mula *TRAN*slation) in 1954. The earliest versions of Fortran were awful and were quickly replaced by Fortran II in 1957. John McCarthy developed LISP (for *LIS*t *P*rocessing) in 1957. Both Fortran and LISP have changed a great deal over the last 30 years and both are still in wide use today. LISP is still the language of choice of the majority of people doing Artificial Intelligence programming today.

A language that was designed to meet the needs of business, *COBOL* (for *CO*mmon *B*usiness-*O*riented *L*anguage), was developed in 1960. As with Fortran, COBOL was developed by a team of people, each having his or her own idea as to what the language should be like. One of the people who worked on COBOL was Grace Hopper, mentioned previously as the programmer for the MARK I.

Third Generation

The inclusion of an integrated circuit (IC) in a computer marks the beginning of the *third generation* of computers. Where one tube in a first generation computer and one transistor in a second generation computer each amounted to one circuit, just one of these tiny silicon wafers, called *chips*, could hold hundreds of circuits. Computers that previously took up entire rooms were reduced to large boxes. One of the first large mainframe computers using integrated circuits was the IBM/360 introduced in 1964. For several years, the IBM/360 was a model

---

[1]Fortran used to be spelled in all uppercase letters, i.e., "FORTRAN"; however, today the recommended spelling is "Fortran".

for other large computers. Other manufacturers produced minicomputers, like Digital Equipment's PDP-4.

Operating Systems

The first operating systems were developed in the late 1950s and early 1960s. "Operating system" does not mean a "system that's operating." An operating system is software, not hardware. An operating system is a *program* that serves as an interface between the computer and any other software that is running on the computer. When different software developers are able to count on a computer running a particular operating system, they don't have to write their programs with the peculiarities of the different computers in mind, only with the properties of the operating system. Then each computer manufacturer can develop a version of the operating system in question for their own machines and be confident that software written for that operating system will run.

UNIX, a multi-user multitasking operating system and one of today's most popular operating systems in academic circles, got started in the late 1960s.

Fourth Generation

Fourth generation computers used Large Scale Integration (LSI) and Very Large Scale Integration (VLSI) technology. Where hundreds of circuits could be put on one IC, thousands could be put on one of the new chips. The IBM/370 became the model of a fourth generation computer.

The first microprocessor using VLSI technology (the 4004) was developed by Intel in 1971 and the microcomputer boom soon followed. Steve Jobs and Steve Wozniak formed the Apple Computer Company and started selling complete microcomputers in 1976.

By 1980 people had computers on their desks that were much more powerful than the most powerful computers in the world in the 1950s. Computers that used to cost millions of dollars were surpassed in power and flexibility by computers that cost a few thousand dollars.

The evolution of languages continued too. Fortran was upgraded and many features were added to the language in attempts to keep pace with the changes that were taking place. But since everyone wanted to keep Fortran upward compatible (i.e., programs written in older versions of Fortran should still run under the newer versions), Fortran retained many of the weaknesses inherent in the original design.

John Kemeny and Thomas Kurtz from Dartmouth developed what was designed to be a simpler language than Fortran in the mid-1960s, called *BASIC* (for *B*eginners *A*ll-purpose *S*ymbolic *I*nstruction *C*ode). Microcomputer manufacturers started packaging BASIC with their computers and, as a result, BASIC has become a very popular language. Unfortunately the early versions of BASIC contained many of the same shortcomings as Fortran. Each manufacturer attempted to overcome these shortcomings by adding features to the language that would make BASIC more modern. This resulted in so many different versions of the language that if a person learned BASIC in one environment, he or she could not use those same techniques on another computer. The common core of all the different versions is not a "structured" language, and as a result, BASIC is no longer considered a good language with which to start a study of programming.

Many people studied the science of programming during the 1960s. Edsger Dijkstra was one of the first to criticize the use of a "GOTO" statement and point out the advantages of *structured programming*. The language *ALGOL* was one of the first languages designed to provide structure to the programming process. ALGOL never quite caught on—perhaps because it never got the support of IBM, which was still promoting Fortran and COBOL. In the last half of the 1960s, Niklaus Wirth, using many of the ideas introduced with ALGOL, developed Pascal and, as mentioned earlier, Pascal has become the most popular language for a beginning course in programming. While Pascal is a very popular language, it has its own weaknesses, which will be mentioned at various points in this text.

There were, of course, many other languages developed over the years. As far as structured languages are concerned, the languages that one hears about the most today are Modula-2, C and Ada. Modula-2 was also designed by Wirth; it is much like Pascal but without some of the weaknesses (of course, some people think Modula-2 has its own weaknesses). The C programming language is a powerful, compact language that is becoming more and more popular in scientific programming. The United States Department of Defense has supported the development of Ada in an attempt to design a language that has many purposes. There is no one best language; every language has strengths and weaknesses. Rather than arguing about which language is the best, programmers should be concerned with choosing a language that is appropriate to the job at hand.

Besides languages, other software has been developed and these programs have become immensely popular. In the late 1970s Dan Bricklin and Bob Franklin wrote VisiCalc, the first electronic spreadsheet. VisiCalc was largely responsible for the increased sales of the Apple computers. People were now able to use their computers without having to write their own programs.

Gary Kildall wrote *CP/M*, an operating system for the Intel 8080, in 1977. This made it possible for people with different computers (not too different, as they all had to use the 8080 but did not have to be made by the same manufacturer) to run the same programs. The flood of personal computer software began.

1.6 The 1980s and Beyond

In 1981 IBM finally introduced their microcomputer, the IBM PC. It used an operating system, called PC-DOS (for *Personal Computer-Disk Operating System*) acquired from Microsoft, Inc. PC-DOS was somewhat similar to CP/M but used the Intel 8088 processor instead. The IBM PC was the computer that

really started the microcomputer revolution. Many software developers started
developing software for the IBM PC and an avalanche of hardware and software
began. Hundreds of companies tried making "IBM compatible" computers
and thousands of software developers started writing programs for the "PCs."
Programs like WordStar, Lotus 1-2-3 and dBASE revolutionized how people
wrote letters and did business. Microsoft sold another version of PC-DOS to
developers of compatible computers under the name MS-DOS. IBM released the
IBM AT in 1984 based on the Intel 80286, and other companies started making
AT "clones." In 1987 IBM released the PS/2, a new series of microcomputers.
OS/2, a powerful multi-user operating system, has been developed for personal
computers.

Apple Computer has released several models of the Apple II over the years
that have become very popular, especially in education. They have developed
the Macintosh as well. The Macintosh is designed to be very "user friendly"; a
user can control the computer without having to learn operating system commands. The newest "Mac," as of this writing, is the Mac II. The Mac II is a
very powerful microcomputer, as powerful as some of the minicomputers on the
market.

Several other companies have developed their own microcomputers, that
have also had considerable influence on the microcomputer explosion; we do
not have space to mention them all.

UNIX has continued to grow and develop. It is the operating system of
choice of most university computer science departments today. Even though it
is a very large system, microcomputers are getting larger and more powerful
and there are now versions of UNIX that will run on microcomputers, making
microcomputers capable of serving more than one user and performing more
than one job.

The 1980s have seen not only advances in microcomputers; computers in
general are getting more powerful and, at the same time, less expensive and
smaller. Advances in software have been equally impressive. Today we can
purchase a computer, equip it with the appropriate software, add a peripheral
or two (like a laser printer), put it all on a desktop, and perform what would
have been considered miracles just a few years ago.

An interesting relationship between the power and price of computing devices has been noticed. The approximate costs of computing devices have
dropped by a factor of about ten every seven years. A huge supercomputer
costing $100 million in 1973 could be purchased for about $10 million in 1980.
A scientific calculator cost about $500 in 1973. By 1980 you could buy one for
about $50 and today you can get a calculator that will do about the same thing
for around $5. If this trend continues—and experts see no reason to think it
won't—the supercomputer will be available for about $10 thousand in 2001.

The Fifth Generation?

The *fifth generation* of computers may have begun; we do not have the necessary
perspective to tell yet. Fifth generation computers will come even closer to

bridging the gap between computing and thinking. Only a few years ago it was easy to say that no computer will ever be capable of original thought; computers can only do what they are programmed to do and so will not be able to think, or compose music or poetry, or solve unsolved problems of mathematics. Well, computers—actually, computer programs—now play better chess than almost every human, they do compose music and poetry (perhaps not "good" music or poetry, yet), and they have been used to solve some of the greatest unsolved problems of mathematics. While we are not prepared to claim that someday computers will be capable of original thought, we are willing to state that today computers are indispensable to our modern way of life. We simply cannot do without them anymore. The future will see a continuing partnership between humans and computers; perhaps if we cannot travel to the stars, our partners will be able to go in our place.

We'll end our brief history here. It's too close to the present to have a good perspective on what's happening. The tremendous change that we have witnessed during the last five years will be history in another five years. Then we'll be able to look back and see the changes that are taking place today more clearly. In another five years, we will likely see today's changes as minor compared to the changes then taking place.

1.7 Summary and Review

- In this chapter we have outlined the programming process in what we call the FIVE + STEPS:

  1. Define the problem.
  2. Find a solution to the problem.
  3. Design and write an algorithm for the solution.
  4. Code the algorithm in some computer language.
  5. Test and debug the program.

  + Document continuously.

- We have described the top-down, modular approach to this process and discussed some of its advantages.

- We have given a brief history of the development of computers (hardware) and the programs run on them (software) as well as some of the people who made the advances possible. We discussed four generations of computers and the technological advances that separated the generations. We've tried to give an idea as to what might be expected in the future generations of computers and computer software.

1.8   New Terms Introduced

Ada A modern computer language named after Lady Augusta Ada Byron, Countess of Lovelace.

ALGOL One of the first structured languages; designed to make program development and maintenance more logical.

algorithm A step-by-step description of the solution to a problem.

assembly languages Low-level computer languages in which each step in the program closely compares to a step performed by the computer.

BASIC A popular language designed to make programming easier for beginners.

C A modern compact computer language that allows both low and high-level instructions.

chip An integrated circuit; a wafer of silicon capable of holding hundreds or thousands of circuits.

COBOL A computer language designed and widely used for business applications.

coding The fourth step of the programming process—that of translating an algorithm into a particular computer language.

CP/M An early operating system for microcomputers.

documentation Written descriptions of what a program does and/or how to use it.

first generation computers The earliest computers; designed and built in the 1940s.

fifth generation computers Computers that really "think." At the present time, many people are attempting to build computers that think like humans but it is too early to say how well they will succeed.

FIVE + STEPS The five steps of the programming process including documentation.

Fortran One of the first "high-level" computer languages; designed for scientific programming.

fourth generation computers Computers using chips that contain thousands of circuits, (LSI and VLSI technology).

hardware The physical parts of a computer.

LISP A language designed for list processing; used widely for Artificial Intelligence programming.

LSI Large Scale Integration of circuits on chips.

machine language A programming language in which the steps of the program are written directly in the actual code executed by the computer.

Modula-2 A modern computer language designed by the designer of Pascal and intended to eliminate some of its perceived weaknesses.

MS-DOS The operating system used on IBM PC and IBM PC-compatible computers.

operating system The program that the computer runs at all times and that controls the operation of the computer.

OS/2 A multi-user operating system designed for the IBM AT, IBM AT-compatible, IBM PS/2, and other personal computers.

Pascal A programming language designed for teaching programming.

programming The process of using a computer to solve a problem.

second generation computers The first computers using transistors.

software The programs run by a computer.

stored program concept The concept that a computer program can be stored in the computer's memory as data.

subprogram A self-contained portion of a larger program that accomplishes a particular task.

third generation computers The first computers using integrated circuits.

top-down programming A problem solving approach where bigger jobs are successively broken down into smaller and smaller jobs.

UNIX A powerful operating system becoming more and more widely used in academia and business.

VLSI Very Large Scale Integration of circuits on chips.

1.9   Suggested Reading

For further reading on the topics introduced in this chapter, consult:

- *The First Electronic Computer: The Atanasoff Story*, Alice R. Burks and Arthur W. Burks, University of Michigan Press, 1988.

- *Structured Programming*, O. J. Dahl, E. Dijkstra and C. A. R. Hoare, Academic Press, 1972.

- *The Computer from Pascal to von Neumann*, H. H. Goldstine, Princeton University Press, 1972.

- *The Mythical Man-Month*, F. Brooks, Addison-Wesley, 1974.

- "GOTO Statement Considered Harmful," E. Dijkstra (letter to the editor), *Communications of The ACM*, 1968.

Chapter 2

Bits, Bytes, Hardware and Software

2.1 Introduction

In this chapter we will introduce you to some of the "jargon" used today while talking about computers. Many of these words are used today in casual conversations, conversations that would have sounded like they were in a foreign language just a few years ago. While it's nice to be able to join these conversations and it's useful to know the jargon when you're talking to a salesperson at the local computer shop, the primary reason for discussing them in this chapter is to give you an understanding of what's going on inside the computer. Knowing something about the design of a computer will give you a better appreciation of how it can be used to solve problems.

2.2 Bits and Bytes

A binary computer (and due to the genius of people like John V. Atanasoff and John von Neumann, virtually all computers today are binary) is a machine that manipulates high and low voltages, which are arbitrarily represented as 1s and 0s. We call these 1s and 0s *bits*, a contraction of *binary digits*. We can represent any positive integer as a string of 1s and 0s using the binary, or base 2, number system. Whereas the decimal (base 10) system uses ten digits (0 through 9), the binary system uses two digits (0 and 1).

When we increase a base 10 number by one, we simply replace the rightmost digit by the next higher one in the sequence, except when

17

Decimal	Binary
0	0
1	1
2	10
3	11
4	100
5	101
6	110
7	111
8	1000
9	1001
10	1010
11	1011
⋮	⋮

Figure 2.1 Decimal and Binary Representations

it's a 9, in which case it's replaced by a 0 and the next digit to the left is increased by one.

Now reread the previous sentence, replacing the 10 with a 2 and the 9 with a 1.

That's how we count in the binary system.

Figure 2.1 illustrates the first few integers expressed in decimal and binary.

In base 10, a number consists of a string of digits from 0 to 9, each holding a place. The rightmost digit is in the 1s place, the next place to the left is in the 10s place, then the 100s place, and so on. Each time we move left one place the value increases by a factor of 10. So, for example, the number 734 means seven 100s, three 10s and four 1s. Similarly, in binary notation, each digit holds a place. The rightmost is the 1s place, the next place to the left is the 2s place, then the 4s place and so on. Each time we move left one place, the value goes up by a factor of 2. Thus the binary number 10110 represents one 16, no 8s, one 4, one 2 and no 1s, which is 22.

It's convenient to combine these binary digits into groups of various sizes. One such useful size is a group of eight bits, called a *byte*. It's easy to see that if we count in binary and use a maximum of eight places, we can count from 0 to 11111111, which is 255 in decimal. Eight bits in a row are hard to read so it is customary to put a small space between the first four bits and the second four; the byte representing 255 would usually be written 1111 1111. To summarize, with one byte we can represent any integer from 0 to 255.

2.3 Hexadecimal Numbers

As we count in binary we can see that even small numbers require lots of bits to represent them. To make things much shorter, we can use yet another number system, a base 16 system, which is called *hexadecimal* or simply *hex*. To represent numbers in base 16 we need 16 digits. We already have the ten from 0 through 9, so we need 6 more. Since it's convenient to use characters available on a keyboard that have a natural sequence to them, people decided to use the letters A through F. Thus the hexadecimal digit A represents the decimal number 10, and the hexadecimal digit F represents the decimal number 15. With this in mind we can see how to count and read numbers in hex: Read that sentence a few paragraphs back again, this time replacing the 10 with a 16 and the 9 with an F. The sentence becomes:

> When we increase a base 16 number by one, we simply replace the rightmost digit by the next higher one in the sequence, except when it's an F, in which case it's replaced by a 0 and the next digit to the left is increased by one.

That's how we count in hex. In base 16, a number consists of a string of digits from 0 to F, each holding a place. The rightmost digit is in the 1s place, the next to right is in the 16s place, then the 256s place, and so on.

Figure 2.2 illustrates the first few integers expressed in decimal, binary and hexadecimal.

Each time we move left one place, the value increases by a factor of 16. So, for example, the hex number 52D means five 256s, two 16s and thirteen 1s. In decimal this would be 1325. The nice thing about hex is that one hexadecimal digit represents four bits, so one byte can be represented by two hexadecimal

Decimal	Binary	Hexadecimal
0	0	0
1	1	1
2	10	2
3	11	3
4	100	4
5	101	5
6	110	6
7	111	7
8	1000	8
9	1001	9
10	1010	A
11	1011	B
12	1100	C
13	1101	D
14	1110	E
15	1111	F
16	1 0000	10
17	1 0001	11
⋮	⋮	⋮
254	1111 1110	FE
255	1111 1111	FF
256	1 0000 0000	100
⋮	⋮	⋮

Figure 2.2 Decimal, Binary and Hexadecimal Representations

digits. For example, 1011 in binary is (let's see, that's one 8, no 4s, one 2 and one 1) 11 in decimal, which is B in hex. The binary 0110 is (you do it too!) 6 in decimal, which is also 6 in hex. So the binary 1011 0110 is B6 in hex, while the binary 0110 1011 is 6B in hex.

2.4   ASCII

If all we wanted the computer to do was to work with numbers from 0 to 255, we could represent them by one byte each. Clearly, there are many other kinds of things that computers work with: bigger numbers, negative numbers, fractions, words and sentences, and even graphics. Each of these kinds of data can be represented using some scheme involving bytes.

Words and sentences are built from basic building blocks, which are the letters from A to Z and a to z, the numeric digits 0 to 9, and various punctuation marks and symbols. Each of these characters can be assigned a code; one of the most common coding systems is the *American Standard Code for Information Interchange (ASCII)* pronounced "ask-ee." The ASCII coding scheme uses combinations of seven bits to represent 128 different characters. For example, the 7-bit code 1000001, which is 41 in hex or 65 in decimal, stands for the letter A. You'll find an ASCII table in appendix D.

You will notice that ASCII uses only seven bits while a byte has eight. The eighth bit was used for parity checking at one time—parity checking is a method of error checking—but is not used that way much today. As a consequence, there are extended ASCII schemes in use today that utilize the eighth bit, yielding coding for another 128 characters.

2.5 The Organization of a Computer

The information in a computer is in the form of bits, which represent both numeric and non-numeric data. What is the environment in which these bits live? The parts of a computer fall into three general categories: the CPU, the memory and the peripheral devices.

The CPU

The term *CPU* is a term that you may be familiar with. It stands for "Central Processing Unit" and refers to what could be considered the heart and brain of the computer. The CPU is normally thought of as consisting of two parts, the Control Unit and the Arithmetic/Logic Unit *(A/LU)*.

The Control Unit is responsible for pumping information to and receiving information from the various other parts of the computer. It is also responsible for carrying out some instructions and giving other instructions to the A/LU. One instruction that the Control Unit might execute would involve moving some bits from one place in memory to another. One might think of the Control Unit as the heart of the computer.

The *A/LU* is the unit that does the actual calculations in the computer. It receives instructions and data from the Control Unit, and executes the instructions on the data. One such instruction might involve adding two numbers together. The A/LU is the part of the computer that actually carries out the arithmetic instructions in a program; it could be considered the brain of the computer.

The kind of program a CPU can understand consists of a sequence of very specific, simple instructions taken from a collection called the *instruction set* for that CPU. Even though the instructions themselves are simple, a computer is considered powerful because of the speed with which it can perform these instructions. A typical CPU might carry out hundreds of thousands or even millions of instructions each second.

Our characterization of the Control Unit as the heart of the computer and the A/LU as the brain is not accurate; the Control Unit does more than the human heart does, while the human heart and lungs together are responsible for pumping vital fluids and oxygen through the body. Further, we normally think of the human brain as having the capacity of thinking and remembering. In our breakdown of the computer, we have put its memory in a separate category.

The Memory

Computer memory comes in several varieties, but each is a collection of places where the computer can store strings of bits and recall them later. Depending on the computer, these strings of bits may come in lengths of 8, 16, 32 or even 64. The length of the string is known as the *word length* of the computer.

In fact, this used to be the way to tell whether the computer was a *microcomputer*, a *minicomputer* or a *mainframe*. Microcomputers had a word length of 8 bits, minicomputers 16, and mainframes 32 or more. Today this distinction doesn't work at all; the newest microcomputers are 32-bit machines and they're still considered micros.

Dollar figures and the number of users served are better in drawing the lines. A micro costs between one hundred and ten thousand dollars and usually serves a single user. A mini costs between that and a few hundred thousand dollars and usually serves less than one hundred users. A mainframe can cost millions of dollars and can serve hundreds of users. Even these distinctions are not precise. There are versions of UNIX and other operating systems available for microcomputers that allow several users and several processes at the same time. It can also be the case that a large mainframe computer is used by one user on one job, although in such a case the job would be one requiring an enormous amount of computing power.

Fast Access Memory

Computer memory can be either quick access or relatively slow access. The quickest access memory might not be thought of as memory at all. The CPU has sections called *registers* in which strings of bits are placed while they are being processed. Data stored in a register can be accessed more quickly than data stored anywhere else. Typically a CPU will have a limited number of registers.

There are two types of quick access memory that are external to the CPU: RAM and ROM. Most people think *RAM* stands for "Random-access Memory" and it does, but it shouldn't. To make its function more clear, RAM should be thought of as "Read and Write Memory." Data can be written to and read from RAM very quickly, and every location in RAM can be accessed at the same speed. Actually, the "random" is inappropriate too. Accessing the data stored in memory "randomly" would mean that there is no way of predicting which data item will be retrieved. What is meant is that every item of data can be accessed directly without having to access all the others; i.e., "direct access," not "random access." So, what should come to your mind when you see the acronym RAM is "Direct Access, Read and Write Memory." You can form your own conclusions as to why the acronym RAM was chosen over the more informative DAM.

RAM is usually *volatile*, which means that when the power is turned off, the contents are lost. You can think of RAM as a large chalkboard in the computer where numbers can be written and read, and which is erased every night.

ROM stands for "Read-only Memory." ROM is different from RAM in that it can't be written to. One can think of ROM as a book; the data in ROM has been put there by someone else and we can read it. The information in ROM is permanent; even when the computer is turned off, the ROM retains its information. This is referred to as *nonvolatile* memory. Usually the ROM stores low-level program instructions for the CPU. Typically, the computer will read its own ROM when it is turned on and find enough instructions there to know what to do next. This has come to be called *booting up* and comes from the expression "to pull yourself up by your bootstraps."

The size of a computer's memory is usually expressed in kilobytes. The prefix *kilo* usually means 1000, except with reference to computers. The language of computers is the binary system, and the closest we can come to 1000 using powers of 2 is 1024 (2^{10}), so it has become customary to use K for kilo to mean multiples of 1024. Thus, if you hear that a computer has 640K bytes of RAM, it means that it has 640 times 1024 bytes, or 655,360 bytes.

The big shortcoming of RAM is that the information it holds is lost when the computer is turned off. This is the cause of a lot of heartache for everyone new to computing. Anyone who has some computer experience has a tale of losing data. No matter how many times a person new to computing is told of this, it always seems to happen at least once before the lesson "takes." To avoid losing the data, you can "save" a copy of what's in RAM into some form of secondary memory, which is like RAM in that it can be written to and read from directly, but like ROM in that when the power goes off, the information is still there. The most common form of secondary memory is disk storage.

Slower Access Memory

Most microcomputers now use floppy disks, which hold from about 100,000 to about one million characters—that is, from 100K bytes to 1M bytes. As indicated above, 1K bytes is 1024 bytes; 1M (for mega) bytes is the closest we can come to one million using powers of 2, which is 2^{20} or 1,048,576. Some microcomputers, most minicomputers, and all larger computers use some sort of hard disk storage. A micro might have a hard disk with 10, 30 or maybe up to 70 megabytes capacity. Large computers can have millions of megabytes of storage.

Computers can access the information stored on disks quickly (hard disk access is considerably faster than on a floppy), but not as quickly as RAM. Whereas the data in RAM is stored in integrated circuits (chips) made of semiconductor material, the data stored on disks is in the form of magnetized areas spread out on the disk surface in an organized fashion. All of the information written to or read from a disk must pass through the "read-write head," which is similar to the record-play head on a tape recorder. One thing that makes disk access slower is the time it takes for the right area of the disk to spin around and come under the read-write head.

Not all disks store information magnetically. Some store data as tiny pits burned into a metal surface by a laser beam. This pattern of pits can be read later by another, much less powerful laser. This technology has been made popular in the form of audio compact disks, or CDs. The big advantage of this method is that much more information can be stored in the same area of the disk. The disadvantage is that it's difficult to erase information once it's written. In this sense, this type of "optical" disk storage is more like ROM.

Peripheral Devices

A computer would be perfectly happy with its CPU moving bits around from main memory to the disk drives and so forth, but it wouldn't do anyone any good without some way for it to communicate with the outside world. This is done through various input and output devices, collectively known as peripherals.

When we say *input*, we refer to information flowing in to the memory; that is, sending data to the computer. The usual way for this to happen is by means of a keyboard, but there are other input devices such as bar-code readers and *OCRs* (Optical Character Readers).

Output refers to information flowing out from the memory; i.e., receiving data from the computer. Most output is displayed on a TV-style screen or monitor—often called a *CRT* for cathode ray tube or *VDT* for video display terminal, fancy names for a TV tube—or printed on some sort of printer.

In the case of microcomputers, the common setup consists of a monitor, keyboard, and two disk drives connected to the CPU, and in most cases a printer is connected as well. Minicomputers and mainframes are multi-user machines, which means that several people can share the same CPU and its resources. The users interact by means of a terminal, which basically consists of a keyboard and monitor, cabled in some way to the main CPU.

It is becoming increasingly common to have computers *networked*. Essentially this means that a group of computers are connected together in some manner or another and can share each other's data as well as use common peripherals, such as laser printers. Often the computers on the network don't have their own mass storage capability; in such cases, the computers are called *workstations*.

2.6 Software

The CPU, the memory, both RAM and ROM, the disk drives and the peripheral devices are all examples of *hardware*. The actual instructions that the computer carries out are in the form of a program. Programs are known as *software*.

Remember the analogy from chapter 1: the record or tape player, the amplifier and the speakers hooked up to your music system are all hardware. The music that you are playing is software.

Lower-Level Languages

The instructions in a CPU's instruction set are coded in bytes, usually one byte for the simple instructions like "stop" and two or more for instructions like "move what's in register #1 to memory location 45,910." Such a list of bytes can itself be stored in memory somewhere, as von Neumann first noticed, and the CPU can be told to read the first such byte, interpret it as an instruction and do what it says, and continue until one of the instructions says to stop. This is a program at the lowest level, called a machine language program. If the program is written at a slightly higher level, using English-like abbreviations called *mnemonics* for each step, the program is in *Assembly Language*.

For example, figure 2.3 shows a few lines of assembly language code for a microprocessor and the resulting machine language code, in hex.

Operating Systems

One program that is usually (but not necessarily) written in assembly language is the *operating system* of the computer. This is the program that controls or manages the other programs run on the computer as well as its various resources. When you want to run a higher-level program on a computer, you ask the operating system to do so. The commands to read data from a disk into memory, or copy data from one disk to another are operating system commands. When higher-level programs want to read or write data on a disk, or send data to the printer, they call on the operating system. On a multi-user system, the

```
 . . .
   11          LXI D,0800H
   00
   80
   21          LXI H,0FFOH
   F0
   0F
   06          MVI B,00H
   00
 . . .
```

Figure 2.3 Machine and Assembly Language Code

operating system also keeps track of the many tasks running at the same time, so that they don't interfere with each other.

Higher-Level Languages

The only language that a CPU really understands is machine language—a list of instructions from its instruction set. These instructions are very elementary, and it takes a lot of them to do something simple, like display `Hello world!` on the screen. If you were to see such a program, it would probably not be clear to you what the program was designed to do.

Higher-level languages—like Fortran, LISP, COBOL, BASIC, ALGOL and Pascal—provide ways to express instructions like this, and much more complicated ones, so that they can be understood by people, but not by the computer. In order for the computer to be able to carry out an instruction in a higher-level language, it must first be translated into machine language. Given a list of higher-level instructions, this translation can take place in one of two ways: one instruction at a time, or all at once. And what do you suppose does the translating? Another program!

Interpreters and Compilers

A program that does the translation one instruction at a time is called an *interpreter*. It translates one instruction into machine language instructions, then calls on the CPU to perform those instructions. It then translates the next higher-level instruction, and so on. The user has the impression that the higher-level program itself is running.

A program that translates the whole program all at once is called a *compiler*. It takes the entire list of higher-level instructions, which is called the *source code*, and translates it into a machine-language program, which is called the *object code*. The compiler doesn't run the program, it just translates it. Running the object code program is usually a separate step in the process.

The advantage of an interpreter is that you can run it immediately after it is written, and if you make a change you can run it immediately after the change. The disadvantage is that it runs more slowly because each instruction has to be translated every time the program is run. The advantage of a compiler, on the other hand, is that it runs much faster, because the translation is done only once. If you make a change, however, the entire program has to be recompiled before it is run.

Compiling

When you write a program in a compiled language—and henceforth we'll assume that the version of Pascal you're using is compiled—you first need to write the source code, using some sort of text editor or word processor. The editor is itself a program—a program that allows you to type things at a keyboard and puts what you type into a file.

You then run the compiler to generate the object code. The compiler takes your source code (actually the file containing your source code) and attempts to create another file containing the machine language version of your program— the *object code*. Notice that we said "attempts to create." Frequently the source code contains errors when it is first typed; errors that prevent the compiler from successfully doing the translation. As the compiler does its work, it will handle the discovery of errors in a number of different ways, depending on the type of error and the particular compiler.

Three Types of Error

We will briefly discuss three basic types of error: *syntax errors*, *run-time errors*, and *logic errors*. We'll have more to say about errors in later chapters.

A syntax error is an error in the use of the higher-level language. The compiler is working according to very strict rules while translating. If the source code contains mistakes like missing punctuation marks, misspelled words or words that are out of place, the compiler gets confused and can't continue translating; the object code is not generated.

Run-time errors are those that the compiler never finds but that cause the program to crash as it is running. One example would be attempting to divide a number by zero; another would be trying to take the square root of a negative number. Neither of these uses illegal syntax, but the combined result is impossible for the computer to perform.

Logic errors are the most subtle and the hardest to find and correct. The program compiles and runs with no apparent problem, but the output it produces is simply wrong because the method of producing it is wrong. A logic error is usually the result of using a faulty algorithm. Paying attention to the first three steps of the programming process will tend to reduce the number of logic errors.

The usual course of events is that the compiler reports on any and all syntax errors that it locates and displays some sort of error message indicating what it thinks the error was. These error messages may or may not point to the real problem in the source code, but the programmer must find and correct every syntax error before she can go on. After all the syntax errors have been eliminated, the object code is generated and run. If there are run-time errors present, the program crashes (that is, it stops running and displays some sort of error message) when it gets to the first one. After this error is found and corrected, the program is compiled again and run again. If there are still run-time errors, the program crashes again. This process repeats until the programmer is satisfied that all of the run-time errors have been found and eliminated.

Sometimes these errors are off in segments of the program that get executed only rarely; a good programmer will thoroughly test the program, trying to think of ways to make it fail. Of course, the best way to rid your program of these errors is to avoid them in the first place, but that is often easier said than done.

After the syntax and run-time errors have been dealt with, the testing process must continue and locate any logic errors that might be present. The complete testing and debugging process may take longer than the other steps combined, *especially if the programmer rushes through the earlier steps.* The testing and debugging process is discussed in some detail in a separate chapter.

We've heard beginning programmers happily exclaim, "My program compiled, it's finally done!" They are often disappointed to then learn that there are still errors in the program, either run-time errors or logic errors. The programming process is by no means complete when the source code has been found free of syntax errors. Testing and debugging of programs is a normal part of the whole process, not additional techniques to be used only when the program doesn't seem to work.

By the way, one of the first recorded uses of the word "debugging" in reference to computers was made by Grace Hopper, whom we mentioned in chapter 1. One day while she and others were working on the MARK II computer back in the 1940s, it started acting strangely. They traced the problem to a giant moth being beaten to death by one of the computer's mechanical relays. Hopper pulled the moth from the relay with a pair of tweezers and put it in the log book. One of the first computer "bugs" was a real bug!

2.7 Summary and Review

- In this chapter we have discussed the elements of computer architecture. We have seen that computers can be thought of as housing and managing strings of 1s and 0s called bits, and that groups of these bits can best be understood using binary and hexadecimal number systems. Strings of eight bits are called bytes; strings of seven bits, via the ASCII coding scheme, represent all of the characters on the familiar typewriter keyboard, and some others as well.

- As far as hardware is concerned, the computer consists of three main components: the CPU, the memory and the peripherals. The CPU is the hub of activity in the computer, controlling the flow of bits between itself and the memory and peripherals, according to a limited number of instructions that it understands. The memory consists of main memory and secondary memory. Main memory is semiconductor-based and access to it is very fast. Secondary memory is usually stored on magnetic media and is somewhat slower. The computer communicates with the outside world through its peripheral devices, such as the keyboard, screen or printer.

- We discussed software, i.e., the programs that are run on a computer, and various kinds of software that you might use. The operating system of the computer is the program that manages the interaction among the various components.

- The code for a computer program is written in a computer language. Computer languages differ in, among other respects, their level of complexity. Machine language programs are at the lowest level—they are understood by the CPU directly. Higher-level languages, such as Pascal, must be translated, either by a compiler or an interpreter, into machine language instructions.

- Programs must be thoroughly tested and debugged after they are written to eliminate run-time and logic errors, which the compiler or the interpreter isn't designed to see.

2.8 New Terms Introduced

A/LU The Arithmetic/Logic Unit; the part of the CPU that performs the arithmetical and logical calculations.

ASCII The American Standard Code for Information Interchange. A coding system widely used on computers.

bit The smallest piece of data manipulated by a computer; mathematically a 0 or 1. From *binary digit*.

byte A group of eight bits.

compiler A program that translates another program written in a high-level computer programming language, such as Pascal, into machine language.

control unit The part of the CPU that moves the data from one place in the computer to another and controls what happens in the computer.

CPU The computer's Central Processing Unit, the heart and brain of the computer.

debugging The process of removing errors from a program.

disk memory Slower access but large and relatively inexpensive and permanent memory.

hexadecimal Base 16 numeration system.

input Data moving towards a computer's memory.

interpreter A program that runs another program written in a high-level computer programming language, such as BASIC, one statement at a time without translating the entire program.

logic error An error caused by telling a computer to do the wrong thing but something that it can do.

mainframe A large computer, serving hundreds of users.

microcomputer The smallest type of computer, typically serving a single user.

minicomputer A mid-size computer, typically serving 10-50 users.

networking Linking several computers together so that they can share data and equipment.

object code A file containing a machine language version of a program; produced by a compiler.

output Data moving away from a computer's memory.

peripheral An input or output (or both) device connected to the CPU.

RAM Direct access, read/write memory.

ROM Read-only memory.

run-time error An error caused by telling a computer to do something that it cannot do.

source code A file containing a program written in a high-level computer programming language.

supercomputer The largest and fastest computers.

syntax error An error caused by not using a language according to its definition.

2.9 Exercises

1. Perform the conversions necessary to fill in the blanks below.

Decimal	Binary	Hexadecimal
		6F
	1101 0010	
124		
		B3
	0011 1100	
38		

2. Rewrite the sentence on page 17 so that it tells how to count in *octal*, which is base 8. Add a column to figure 2.2 to include octal representations of the same numbers. Add a column to the table in exercise 1 for octal and fill in the column with the octal representation of each number.

3. A coding system used on some computer systems instead of ASCII is EBCDIC, which stands for "Extended Binary Coded Decimal Interchange Code." Find a table of EBCDIC codes and compare it with the ASCII table in appendix D. Do you see any advantages or disadvantages to the EBCDIC system?

4. Learn about the computer system you will be using to code and run your Pascal programs. In particular, learn about the type of system (micro, mini or mainframe), the amount of memory, the disk storage capacity and the operating system. Learn enough about your text editor so that you can type in the following Pascal program, and save it:

```
program First(input, output);
begin
   writeln('Hello world!')
end.
```

Type it in exactly as it appears here, character for character. Don't leave out the period after **end**.

5. If you completed the previous exercise successfully, then find out how to compile and run a program and do so. The program may not be very exciting, but you'll learn a great deal about the programming environment in which you'll be working.

Chapter 3

Problem Solving and Algorithms

> It has often been said that a person doesn't
> really understand something until he teaches it to
> someone else. Actually a person doesn't really
> understand something until he can teach it to a
> *computer*, i.e., express it as an algorithm.
> — Donald E. Knuth

3.1 Overview of the Chapter

In this chapter we will use the FIVE + STEPS from chapter 1 (page 3) to write a complete algorithm for a guessing game that the computer will play with a user. The first three steps of the FIVE + STEPS will be covered. (Step 4, coding the algorithm, will be done in the next chapter.) We will begin to discuss some of the basic elements of our algorithmic language and will introduce the elementary concepts of assignment, input and output, selection and repetition.

3.2 Introduction

Let's start with a sample problem. We'll use the problem as an example of the first three of the FIVE + STEPS and will use it to develop the basic building blocks of our algorithmic language. According to the FIVE + STEPS, the first thing we have to do is define the problem.

3.3 Step 1: Define the Problem

Write a program that will play a number guessing game with a person sitting at the terminal.

If that were the statement of the problem, wouldn't you agree that it is not very well defined? Lots of questions have not been answered. If you were given this as an assignment, you would have to ask your teacher a lot of questions before you could complete the assignment. The problem definition step is the step that gets these answers. Before you attempt to go on to the step of solving the problem, you have to know what the problem is. Try to think of some of the questions that need to be answered.

Some of the obvious ones are:

- What kind of numbers are to be guessed? In what range?

- Who is going to do the guessing?

- How many guesses are allowed?

- Where do the numbers come from?

In the real world, you would have to get these answers from the person who is giving you the job of writing the program. In the real world, a programmer must ask these sorts of questions before she is ready to start thinking about the solution. In books like this one you are not able to ask someone else these questions but nevertheless, they need to be asked and answered. That's one of the difficulties of giving problems in textbooks: the problems are usually carefully stated and the author usually has spent a considerable amount of time thinking about problems that can be solved by the students at that point in the course. As a result, students get the impression that all problems are stated clearly. This is surely not the way things are in the real world. Most of the time the person who is asking you to write a program has a limited insight into the world of computers and a limited insight into what the problem really is. Some people think you can just tell the computer the problem and the computer will figure out a solution.

In any case, we need to be able to continue with this example, so let's assume we asked someone the above questions and received answers to them and to other questions. Let's assume that the answers we got to our questions would clarify the problem to say:

> Write a program that will cause the computer to play a guessing game with a person sitting at the terminal. The person can think of a number between 1 and 1000 and the computer will try to guess it.

That's a little better and maybe you are tempted to proceed to the next step and try to solve the problem. Whether you go on now to step two or think about it some more, you soon will realize that you need to ask still more questions to clarify the problem. For example, you would not be happy, we hope, with a program that started guessing at 1, and if that was wrong, would guess 2, and if that was wrong, would guess 3, etc. Nobody would think much of such a program and surely we would want to do a better job than that.

Somewhere along the way, you would ask a question something like:

"Can the computer get a hint if the guess is wrong?"

Let's suppose the answer to this question is "yes." Then we would probably have the computer start guessing at 500 and if that was wrong, have the computer ask the user if the next guess should be higher or lower before making the next guess. For example, let's suppose the person was thinking of the number 635. The following series of questions and answers would be one example of a dialogue between the computer and the user that could result:

```
          ⋮
Computer: My guess is 500.  Is that right?
User:     No.
Computer: Should I guess higher or lower?
User:     Higher.
Computer: My guess is 750.  Is that right?
User:     No.
Computer: Should I guess higher or lower?
User:     Lower.
Computer: My guess is 625.  Is that right?
          ⋮
```

This series of questions and answers would continue until the computer finally guessed the number 635. Do you agree that it would finally get the right number? Finish the series of questions and answers until the computer guesses 635.

How many guesses did the computer need?

The definition of the problem then becomes:

Write a program that will cause the computer to play a guessing game with a person sitting at the terminal. The person will think of a number between 1 and 1000 and the computer will try to guess it. The computer will make a guess, display the guess and ask if it is right or wrong. If the guess is right, the computer will print some sort of self-congratulatory message and the program will end. If the guess is wrong, the computer will ask if it should guess higher or lower before making the next guess. The computer should continue making guesses until it gets the number right.

Three Personalities

It is important that at this point you start thinking of the three different personalities involved with the program. One of these three personalities is you, the programmer. You are responsible for developing a program that will make the computer do what you want. You will have to write the algorithm and program in a manner that you can understand.

A second personality is the computer. The computer is supposed to act like it's talking to the user. You need to give the computer a personality so that when it carries on the conversation with the user, the user will feel that he is really talking to the computer.

The third is that of the user. Do not think of yourself as the user. If you do, you will tend to develop a program that you understand but that no one else will be able to use. Think of the user as a complete stranger to you and to computer programming. Let's pretend that when you finish this program, you are going to go outside, grab the first person you see, drag that person back to the computer, set him down in front of it, and press the RETURN key. From that point on, you should not have to do anything else. The computer will tell the user everything that he needs to know.

There may be other personalities involved with the problem at hand; for example, there is usually someone else presenting you with the problem and you may need to consider that person's wishes. Still other people may read your programs after they are finished and we will see that programs need to be written in a way that they can easily be understood by others.

Let's return to our problem. We should be ready to start thinking about the solution.

3.4   Step 2: Find a Solution to the Problem

Think about the problem the other way around for a minute. Suppose that you are doing the guessing and someone else is thinking of a number between 1 and 1000. Wouldn't your first guess be 500?

Surely, if you were to do the guessing, you would start by guessing 500 and so we want the computer to start that way. And, as indicated above, if the first guess is too low, we would want to make the next guess higher than the first. If you were to continue guessing, you would continue guessing about halfway in the middle of the remaining numbers until you get the right number. Let's solve the problem by making the computer do just that. That is, the first shot at our solution becomes:

> Make a guess right in the middle of the possible numbers and if that's not right, eliminate half of the numbers by asking if the next guess should be higher or lower. Make another guess in the middle of the remaining numbers and continue the process until the user says the guess is right.

This method has lots of names; the most common is *binary search*. We will use this method again and again in this book and indeed it is one of the most widely used methods of searching for a particular value in an ordered list of values.

The above so-called solution is really only a description of the solution, and while it might serve as a description, it is not explicit enough to make it easy to turn into a computer program. When we see the description of the solution, we have a good feeling about how to do it but it is still too vague to program.

What we need is a step-by-step description of the solution, steps which are simple and exact that we can tell the computer to execute. Such a step-by-step description is called an *algorithm*.

So, now that we have a solution in mind, we are ready to describe that solution in a step-by-step manner. That is, we are ready to develop an algorithm that describes the solution.

3.5   Step 3: Write an Algorithm

In order to develop the algorithm, we need to be aware of what the computer will understand. (Actually, the computer doesn't understand anything, but there are simple instructions that we can give it that it can follow. It is easier to pretend that the computer "understands" these simple instructions.) We cannot, in one step, tell the computer to solve a complicated series of expressions, but we can get it to do so by telling it to do a bunch of small steps that together constitute the big step. In the following pages we will discuss some of these small steps that we can assume the computer will understand.

Variables

Much of what the computer can do involves *variables*. Before we continue to discuss the algorithm, we need to talk a little about variables.

The easiest way to think of a variable is to think of a small place in the computer's memory where something can be stored, and to understand that we can give a name to that place in memory. Some people think of variables as little post office boxes in memory. Each little box is able to hold one piece of information at a time and each little box has a name. Figure 3.1 illustrates how you can think of variables in RAM.

The important thing to understand is that the programmer can tell the computer to put different values in these mail boxes—also called "pigeonholes"—at different times. Remember also that the location in memory is referred to by name. We, as programmers, get to choose the names, and thereafter the computer will remember what has been stored in that location. The computer can also be instructed to look at the value stored in a particular box and either print the value, use the value to calculate another value, or make a decision based on what the value is. From now on, we'll refer to these pigeonholes as *variables*.

Assignment

One of the most common things that we need to do with a variable is to put something in it. This is called *assigning a value to a variable*, or, more simply, *assignment*. To do this we need to know the name of the variable and the value that we want to store there. Let's talk about names first.

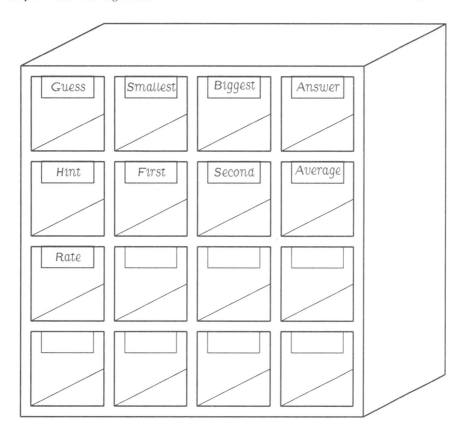

Figure 3.1 Variables

We will be careful when we choose names for variables. Rather than use names like X or R1, we will use names that clearly indicate what the values they contain represent, names like *Rate* or *Answer*.

A concrete example would be useful. Suppose that in the algorithm we are developing, we want to use a variable to hold the value of the computer's most recent guess. Remember that the guess will probably start at 500 and then change as the program continues. Wouldn't you agree the best name to choose for this variable is *Guess*? Of course, so let's just assume that there is a place in memory that can hold a number and the name of this place is *Guess*.

We need to have some way to indicate that we are storing some value in a variable. There are any number of ways that you could indicate this in an algorithm.

Suppose, for example, that you wanted to put the value 500 in the variable *Guess*. You could write any one of the following in your algorithm:

> store 500 in Guess
> put 500 in Guess
> let Guess be 500
> make Guess equal to 500
> move 500 into Guess
> set Guess to 500
> assign 500 to Guess

The important thing is not which of these ways you choose. It is important that you see this as a fundamental thing you can tell the computer to do and that you choose some way of expressing the operation. It will also be easier to follow your own algorithms if you adopt a consistent way of expressing the assignment. In this text, we will consistently use the first of the choices above, that is, we will use:

> store $\langle something \rangle$ in $\langle variablename \rangle$

to indicate assignment to a variable. You, of course, do not have to use this way of expressing it in your algorithms but you need to choose some way of expressing assignment and you should be consistent.

Back to variables. We said: store $\langle something \rangle$ in ... . You will often want to do something besides store a simple number in a variable. Sometimes you will want to do some arithmetic and store the result of the arithmetic in a variable. You might have other variables that currently have values, and you might want to use them to calculate new values, and want to store the new values in another variable. As we will see, there will also be times when you want to store things other than numbers in variables. These values, whatever they are, will be the values of what we will call *expressions*.

Suppose you have variables *First* and *Second* each holding some value. If you wanted to find the average of these values and store the average in another variable, say *Average*. You could write:

> Add the values of First and Second together, divide the result by two and store this result in the variable called Average.

But it would be easier to write:

> store (First + Second) divided by 2 in Average

Since this is so easy to understand, we will adopt the convention of writing something like:

> store $\langle expression \rangle$ in $\langle variablename \rangle$

in our algorithms, and will mean that the computer is to find the value of the
⟨*expression*⟩ and store that value in the variable with name, ⟨*variablename*⟩.
(Note: the name of the variable is *not* ⟨*variablename*⟩. We italicize the word
⟨*variablename*⟩ to indicate that you are expected to choose a name for the
variable and to put that name here.)

Expressions are things that have values. We assume that the computer can
evaluate the expressions and store the result where we indicate. We also assume
that when we use the name of a variable in an expression, the computer will
know it is supposed to use the value stored in that variable. It's no coincidence
that computer languages do exactly this.

Now that we know about variables, we can use them to make some more
progress on the algorithm. We can see that the first guess the computer should
make is 500 because this is halfway between 1 and 1000. But, how do we make
the second guess? Repeat the example dialogue we had before. Remember that
the user is thinking of 635.

```
          ⋮
Computer: My guess is 500.  Is that right?
User:     No.
Computer: Should I guess higher or lower?
User:     Higher.
Computer: My guess is 750.  Is that right?
User:     No.
Computer: Should I guess higher or lower?
User:     Lower.
Computer: My guess is 625.  Is that right?
          ⋮
```

We get the computer to make the second guess of 750 by throwing away
all the numbers less than (and including) 500 and then choosing the number
halfway between 501 and 1000. How do we get the computer to make the third
guess of 625? At this point we know the number is between 501 and 749 so we
throw away all the numbers bigger than 749 and choose the number halfway
between 501 and 749 for our next guess. This can be accomplished easily by
using variables for the largest and the smallest numbers left in the collection of
numbers to be guessed. What we want to do is start off with a variable that
contains the smallest number (1) and another variable that contains the largest
number (1000) and then adjust these two variables as guesses are made and
hints given.

Before we can continue, we need to choose names for these variables. Don't
choose names that are too short, like L and S. Don't choose names that are too

long, like *UpperBoundForValuesLeft*. Good names for these variables might be simply *Biggest* and *Smallest*.

When the program starts, we would want *Biggest* to contain 1000 and *Smallest* to contain 1, and we can assign these values at the beginning of the program. As the user responds to the questions, our algorithm will adjust the values of *Biggest* and *Smallest*. Let's see how the values will be changed, again using the example dialogue above. Consider the dialogue in figure 3.2 and take note of how the values of *Biggest*, *Smallest* and *Guess* change.

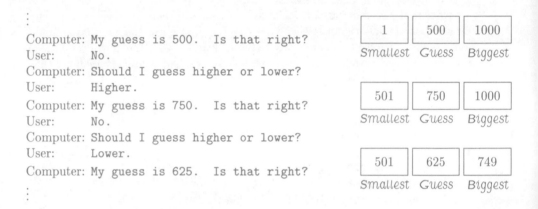

```
   ⋮
Computer: My guess is 500.  Is that right?
User:     No.
Computer: Should I guess higher or lower?
User:     Higher.
Computer: My guess is 750.  Is that right?
User:     No.
Computer: Should I guess higher or lower?
User:     Lower.
Computer: My guess is 625.  Is that right?
   ⋮
```

| 1 | 500 | 1000 |
| Smallest | Guess | Biggest |

| 501 | 750 | 1000 |
| Smallest | Guess | Biggest |

| 501 | 625 | 749 |
| Smallest | Guess | Biggest |

Figure 3.2 Dialogue between Computer and User

To accomplish this, we will have to write the algorithm so that it will cause the values of *Smallest*, *Biggest* and *Guess* to change in this manner. We will do just that in a few pages.

First, we have to worry about how to describe the ways to get the computer to ask the user questions and let the user answer.

Input and Output

Two of the elementary things that computers can do are *input* and *output*. These two concepts go together like opposite sides of a coin. Collectively they are known as I/O.

Input refers to data moving into the computer's memory from some outside source, and *output* means the reverse, that is, data moving from memory to someplace outside the computer's memory.

Contrast these two concepts with the concept of assignment mentioned above. When we say to *store* something in a variable, we are really moving the data from memory to memory—and perhaps making some calculations along the way. I/O is data moving to memory from outside and from memory to outside.

Input

If assignment were the only way to change the value stored in a variable, then every time a program was run, it would do exactly the same thing. All decisions about what is to be stored in the variables would have to be made before the program was executed. That would severely limit the usefulness of a computer. It is critical that we be able to change what is stored in a variable *as* the program is running. We must be able to get data into the computer's memory *at run time*.

The most elementary example of how this can be done—and the only example that we'll deal with for now—is input from the keyboard; that is, input from the user. In the problem we are working on, we will want the user to be able to supply information to the computer as the program is running. Put another way, we want to be able to have the computer ask the user a question and want the user to have a way to answer the question. When the user types an answer on the keyboard and the computer takes that answer and stores it a variable in memory, that's what we mean by input.

From now on, in our algorithms, we'll write:

> *accept ⟨variablename⟩*

and that will mean:

> Pause and wait for the user to type something at the keyboard. Take whatever the user types and store it in the variable called ⟨*variablename*⟩.

Once again there are other words that could be used. You might want to use either *input* or *get* rather than *accept*. Whatever you choose, be sure that you see this as an instruction to the computer. Don't confuse the steps in the algorithm with instructions for the user. The steps in the algorithm explain what we want the *computer* to do, not the user.

When you do want the computer to tell the user what to do, you have to program the computer to put some instructions on the screen for the user to read. That becomes output and that's the next elementary operation to be discussed.

Output

Recall that we said output is moving data from the computer's memory to some outside location. For now let's only worry about moving things from memory to the monitor screen. In our solution, we need to ask the user some questions, like:

    Should I guess higher or lower?

This constitutes output since what we want the computer to do is to put these characters—the letters in the sentence—on the screen for the user to read.

When we want something displayed on the screen, we'll simply say *display*, and indicate what we want the computer to display. For example, if we want the computer to ask the question mentioned earlier, we'll say:

> display "Should I guess higher or lower?"

When this step appears in the algorithm, we will understand that we want the computer to print the message on the screen.

We can do more than just messages, of course. In the solution to the problem that we've selected, we want to display the current guess at several places. This too is straightforward. When we write:

> display ⟨variablename⟩

we will mean that we want the computer to display the value currently stored in that variable.

We can also use the two ideas together: if we want to display a message and a value, we simply put the message in quotes and the value not in quotes. Using our current problem again as an example, we could write the following line in the algorithm:

> display "My guess is", Guess, "Is that right?"

In general we can think of the display step as:

> display ⟨expressionlist⟩

where the expressions to be displayed may be variables, messages, or even more complicated expressions, like $(First + Second) / 2$.

It's important to emphasize that *display* is *our* choice for a word to use to indicate the concept of output. There's no law that says *you* have to use *display*. An algorithm is a concise method of expressing your solution to a problem. You are free to use any words you want in writing an algorithm. The important thing is for each step to be an indication of what you want the computer to do. The same is true for *store* and *accept*. You decide what words you want to use for these concepts. If you want to use the same words we use in the text, that's fine, but you don't have to.

You must also be careful to only include steps that the computer can actually accomplish. The steps must be *effective*. For example, you could not include a step like:

> store 17/0 in First

Division by zero is mathematically undefined so a step like this would cause the computer to crash.

A step like:

Determine whether or not God exists.

is surely not effective today. (If a computer is ever able to accomplish this step, the reply will likely be "I do now!")

We now have quite a bit of power. We can indicate when we want the computer to perform some calculations and where to store the results (assignment); we can indicate when we want the computer to accept something from the user (input) and we can indicate when we want the computer to display something on the screen (output).

We are ready now to go on to another fundamentally important thing that we need to be able to get the computer to do. We need to be able to get the computer to do different things at different times depending on circumstances. This is called either *selection* or *branching*.

Selection

We have been assuming, so far, that the steps in our algorithm are to be followed by the computer one after another. That is, that the computer will execute one step—somehow—and then go on and execute the next step. This is rather like driving along a long, straight, country road. Sometimes, however, we come to a place where there is a fork in the road, and we need to take one road or the other. As we write algorithms and programs we will often need to include places where we will want the computer to choose one of two or more roads to follow.

We have the need for such an ability in our current problem. We plan to have the computer ask the user if its *Guess* is correct and accept the user's answer. What the computer does next depends on the user's answer. If the user indicates that the guess is not correct, we want the computer to ask the user whether the next guess should be higher or lower. On the other hand, if the user indicates that the computer's guess is the right number, we aren't going to ask whether it should guess higher or lower because there won't be any more guesses.

Similarly, when we have the computer ask the user whether the next guess should be higher or lower, we will adjust the value of *Biggest* if the user indicates the next guess should be lower, and will adjust the value of *Smallest* if the next guess should be higher.

Both of the above require the ability to choose between two steps or series of steps.

Figure 3.3 shows a flowchart that illustrates this situation quite clearly. In the figure, the diamond indicates some sort of decision or test. If the result of the test turns out to be *true*, then the steps on one side are executed. If the test is *false*, the steps on the other side are executed. This is the classic situation where selection is done.

To indicate this situation in our algorithms, we'll use an *if...then...else*. The *if...then...else* will consist of the word *if* followed by some sort of test or

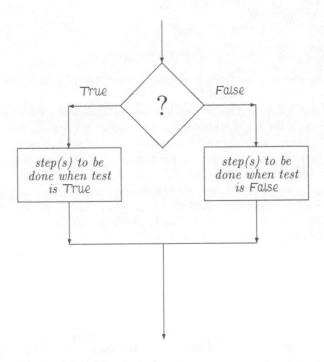

Figure 3.3 Flowchart for a Simple Branch

condition, followed by the word *then*, followed by a step or series of steps to be done when the test is *true*. If desired, we will include an *else part*. The else part will consist of the word *else* followed by a step or series of steps to be executed when the test is *false*.

Consider our problem and the solution we've been working on. When the computer makes a guess, it will display a message asking if the guess is right or not. The user is expected to answer the question either "Yes" or "No." If the user says "No," *then* we want the computer to ask the user if the next guess should be higher or lower. *If* the user indicates the next guess should be higher, *then* we want the computer to eliminate those numbers less than or equal to the guess, *otherwise* to eliminate those numbers greater than or equal to the guess.

Remember we are going to accomplish this elimination by changing the values of the variables *Smallest* and *Biggest*. We can indicate this in our algorithm by writing:

```
display "My guess is", Guess, "Is that right?"
accept Answer
if Answer is "No"
     then
          display "Should I guess higher or lower?"
          accept Hint
          if Hint is "Higher"
               then
                    store Guess + 1 in Smallest
          else
                    store Guess − 1 in Biggest
```

These points are not trivial and there are many ways to write the algorithm. If you see another way to do it, you should feel free to write your own algorithm. Of course, you want to develop the most efficient and elegant algorithm you can.

Notice that these steps provide just what we wanted earlier when we were looking at the values of *Smallest* and *Biggest*. After each wrong guess, either *Smallest* is changed to the value of *Guess* plus one, or *Biggest* is changed to the value of *Guess* minus one.

Selection is one of the basic techniques used in programming at all levels. We'll have lots more to say about selection throughout the remainder of the text. This introduction to the idea will be sufficient for us to continue with our current algorithm.

By the way, you will encounter situations where the computer should do something only if some condition does *not* hold. In such a situation it is much better to write:

```
if not ⟨condition⟩
     then
          do something
```

than to write:

```
if ⟨condition⟩
     then
          don't do anything
     else
          do something
```

Repetition or Looping

The next idea we want to introduce allows the computer to execute the same series of steps over and over. This is known as *looping* or *repetition*. Many solutions to problems require some steps to be executed over and over.

In the real world, there are numerous examples of repetition. A very simple example might be, "Beat the egg whites until stiff." No one has any problem understanding that the cook is supposed to beat the egg whites over and over until they become stiff.

For an example a little closer to programming, it would not seem strange to say something like, "Examine each name in this list of names until you find the name you are looking for," if you were explaining how to search a list of names for a particular name. The procedure is a *loop*; you want to examine a name in the list and compare it to a given name and continue doing this over and over again until you find the name you are searching for. Actually, a more accurate statement might be, "Examine each name in this list of names until you either find the name you are looking for or come to the end of the list." When we are telling a computer what to do—i.e., when we are writing a computer program—we must be careful to consider situations like this; we have to be sure to cover all the possibilities. By the way, this example assumes the names in the list are in no particular order. If they are ordered, the process is different. How would you explain to someone how to look up a name in a phone book?

We will develop three different kinds of loop in this book and discuss each as it is introduced. We start by using our guessing game problem as an example of one kind of loop.

It is clear in our solution for the guessing game problem that we want the computer to make a guess and ask if it's right or not; if it's wrong, ask for a hint and make another guess; and to continue doing this again and again until it guesses the right number. We would not want to write these same steps over and over—in fact we would not know how many times to write them because we don't know in advance how many guesses the computer is going to have to make. The answer lies in the use of a loop. The series of steps that the computer is to execute again and again is called the *body of the loop*. We instruct the computer to execute the body of the loop again and again. Naturally, we need to have some way to get the looping to end.

All this is accomplished with something called a *loop until*. Figure 3.4 shows a flowchart for a *loop until*.

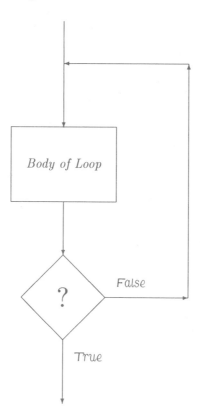

Figure 3.4 Flowchart for a *loop until*

In our algorithms we'll write:

loop
    ⟨*step*⟩
    ⟨*step*⟩
    ⟨*step*⟩
    ⋮
until ⟨*condition*⟩

This means that we want the computer to execute the steps in the loop until
⟨*condition*⟩ becomes true.

For a more concrete example, consider what we want our algorithm to accomplish. We want the computer to make a guess and ask the user if the guess is
right or wrong; if it's wrong, get a hint and make another guess. The computer
should continue to do this until the guess is right.

Using the steps we developed earlier, we can build the loop as follows:

```
loop
    store the number halfway between Smallest and Biggest in Guess
    display "My guess is", Guess, "Is that right?"
    accept Answer
    if Answer is "No"
        then
            display "Should I guess higher or lower?"
            accept Hint
            if Hint is "Higher"
                then
                    store Guess + 1 in Smallest
            else
                    store Guess − 1 in Biggest
until Answer is "Yes"
```

In the following chapters we'll introduce other kinds of loops: loops that continue while a certain condition is true and loops that are executed a fixed number of times. Since we don't need these kinds of loops to solve the guessing game problem, we won't spend any time on them now.

Initialization

The *initialization* steps are the steps that give initial values to any variables used in the program later. In the steps below, notice that the variables *Smallest* and

Biggest have to be initialized but the variable *Guess* does not. The first time we refer to *Guess*, we are storing the average of *Smallest* and *Biggest* there. If we did not initialize *Smallest* and *Biggest* before coming to this step, they would contain undefined values, which would result in *Guess* containing an undefined value. All variables must be given values somehow—with either an input step or an assignment—before they are used in an expression.

A value can be given to the variable either by allowing a user to input the value or by assigning a value to the variable. A simple example will help. Consider the following algorithm, which is designed to compute the sum of the integers from 1 to 100:

```
store 0 in Counter
loop
    add 1 to Counter
    add Counter to Sum
    until Counter = 100
```

This will not work! The algorithm failed to initialize *Sum*. Whatever value was stored in *Sum* when the algorithm began would be included in the result, and the result would be garbage! The correct algorithm is:

```
store 0 in Counter
store 0 in Sum
loop
    add 1 to Counter
    add Counter to Sum
    until Counter = ·100
```

A small but very important difference.

Introduction and Conclusion

The steps following the loop are those steps that get done after the computer finally guesses the user's number. In the problem definition, we indicated that we wanted the computer to display some self-congratulatory message—something like:

```
I got it, aren't I smart?
```

We should also have the computer display some sort of good-bye message, like:

```
Thank you for playing with me.
```

A good rule of thumb for an interactive program is to always include an introduction for the user to see as well as a conclusion. The introduction should alert the user to what is about to happen and the conclusion should provide a graceful exit from the program. The details are often left for the coding step, which we discuss in chapter 4.

The Complete Algorithm

Putting these steps in, we obtain a complete algorithm:

```
START OF Guessing Game

display an introductory message for the user
store 1 in Smallest
store 1000 in Biggest
loop
     store the number halfway between Smallest and Biggest in Guess
     display "My guess is", Guess, "Is that right?"
     accept Answer
     if Answer is "No"
          then
               display "Should I guess higher or lower?"
               accept Hint
               if Hint is "Higher"
                    then
                         store Guess + 1 in Smallest
                    else
                         store Guess − 1 in Biggest
     until Answer is "Yes"
display "I got it, aren't I smart?"
display "Thank you for playing with me."

END OF Guessing Game
```

Indentation

We should emphasize our conventions regarding writing algorithms, in particular, the way that we indent. Indentation makes it clear just which steps are done at which time. Those steps that are done only when a condition is *true*, as in an *if...then*, should be indented. Those steps that are in a loop should be indented. One more skeleton of an algorithm might help.

START OF ALGORITHM

⟨*step*⟩
⟨*step*⟩
loop
   ⟨*step*⟩
   ⟨*step*⟩
  if ⟨*condition*⟩
     then
        ⟨*step*⟩
        ⋮
        ⟨*step*⟩
    else
      loop
        ⟨*step*⟩
        ⋮
        ⟨*step*⟩
        until ⟨*condition*⟩
   ⟨*step*⟩
   ⟨*step*⟩
  until ⟨*condition*⟩
⟨*step*⟩

END OF ALGORITHM

The above algorithm consists of four main steps. The first two and the last are unspecified. The third step is a loop until. Inside the loop there are five steps, the third of which is an if...then...else. In the *then part*, there is an unspecified number of steps. In the *else part*, there is one step, a loop until.

3.6 The First Three Steps—Once Again

This section will be used in chapters 3 through 13 to briefly review the new ideas introduced in the chapter with a different problem or example. Let's retrace the first three steps on another problem. We won't present the detail of the previous sections; just the main points of applying steps 1–3 of the programming process on the problem.

Define the Problem

The problem is a game, called "21 Matches." In this case we will have the computer play the game with a user. Suppose there are 21 matches laying on a table and two players each pick up some number of matches until no matches are left. The player who picks up the last match loses the game. At each turn, a player must pick up at least 1 and not more than 4 matches. Assume that the user goes first. Write a program that will play the game with a user and write it so that the computer will win whenever possible.

Solve the Problem

The problem as stated is not fair to the user. If the computer plays the game intelligently, and the human plays according to the rules, the computer cannot lose. Let's see why. All the computer has to do is make sure there is only one match left at some point in the game. To this, the computer needs to insure that there are 6 matches left on the user's next-to-last turn. Then if the user picks up 1 match, the computer will pick up 4, leaving the last one for the user. If the user picks up 2, the computer will pick up 3. Whatever the user picks up, the computer picks up 5 minus that number; in each case leaving the user the last match.

In general, the computer can always win if whenever it has finished picking up some matches, the number of matches left is one more than a multiple of 5; that is, 1 or 6 or 11 or 16, etc. Since 21 is such a number and the user has to go first, the computer can always win.

The solution to the problem becomes: let the user pick up some number of matches between 1 and 4 inclusive, have the computer pick up 5 minus the number of matches picked up by the user, and continue until there are no matches left, announcing that the computer won the game.

Turn the Solution Into an Algorithm

An algorithm for this solution is easy to develop. It uses the same fundamental concepts developed in this chapter. We'll have a big *loop until* that continues until there are no matches left; we'll have assignment steps that keep track of the number of matches on the table, and we'll have an *if...then* that only asks the user how many matches he wants to pick up if there are matches left. Naturally there will be steps that do output when we want to *display* a message for the user to read, and there will be input steps which *accept* the user's responses.

Look at the following algorithm and see if you don't agree that it turns our solution into a step-by-step description of what we want the computer to do. We chose the variable names *MatchesLeft* and *UserPicksUp*. Is it clear what these variables are being used for?

START OF 21 Matches

display an introduction to the game for the user
store 21 in MatchesLeft
loop
    display "There are", MatchesLeft, "matches left, how many do you pick up?"
    accept UserPicksUp
    subtract UserPicksUp from MatchesLeft
    if MatchesLeft > 0
        then
            display "I pick up", 5 − UserPicksUp, "matches."
            subtract 5 − UserPicksUp from MatchesLeft
    until MatchesLeft = 0
display "I won, ha ha!"

END OF 21 Matches

One improvement that really should be made is a check on the user's input. The algorithm should not allow the user to pick up less than one or more than four matches. A loop that forces the user to enter a valid number of matches should be added. It's not very hard to do, so let's add it. Compare the algorithm above with the one on the next page.

```
START OF 21 Matches

display an introduction to the game for the user
store 21 in MatchesLeft
loop
    display "There are", MatchesLeft, "matches left, how many do you pick up?"
    accept UserPicksUp
    if UserPicksUp < 1 or > 4
        then
            loop
                display "Sorry, you must choose between 1 and 4 matches."
                accept UserPicksUp
            until 1 ≤ UserPicksUp ≤ 4
    subtract UserPicksUp from MatchesLeft
    if MatchesLeft > 0
        then
            display "I pick up", 5 − UserPicksUp, "matches."
            subtract 5 − UserPicksUp from MatchesLeft
    until MatchesLeft = 0
display "I won, ha ha!"

END OF 21 Matches
```

Notice that since the game is not a fair game, we didn't have to check to see who won, we knew already who was going to win.

But wait! On the last pick by the user there will only be one match left. What if the user enters the number 3? As it stands, the algorithm will allow this. We will have to make sure that the user picks up at least one match but not more than 4 and not more than the number of matches left. Look at the algorithm on the next page to see how it will look with these changes.

START OF 21 *Matches*

display an introduction to the game for the user
store 21 in MatchesLeft
loop
    display "There are", MatchesLeft, "matches left, how many do you pick up?"
    accept UserPicksUp
    if UserPicksUp < 1 or > 4 or more than MatchesLeft
      then
        loop
          display "Sorry, you must choose between 1 and 4 matches"
          display "but not more than", MatchesLeft, "matches."
          accept UserPicksUp
        until $1 \leq UserPicksUp \leq 4$ and $\leq$ MatchesLeft
    subtract UserPicksUp from MatchesLeft
    if MatchesLeft > 0
      then
        display "I pick up", 5 − UserPicksUp, "matches."
        subtract 5 − UserPicksUp from MatchesLeft
    until MatchesLeft = 0
display "I won, ha ha!"

END OF 21 *Matches*

It goes without saying that this problem can be made more interesting by either changing the number of matches that are on the table to start with or by letting the user decide whether the user or the computer should pick first. In the latter case, the algorithm could be written so that if the user lets the computer go first, the user would always win if he never makes a mistake. If, however, the user does make a mistake and picks up a number of matches that gives the computer a chance to win, the computer should take advantage of this and play to win from that point on. We'll leave these modifications for the exercises.

3.7 Summary and Review

- In this chapter we gave two examples of the first three steps of the programming process, a complete example and a quick one. In both cases, we started with a simple definition of a problem to be solved. In the complete example we illustrated how important it is to make sure the definition is clear before going on to the second step of the process.

- We demonstrated how a solution to a problem is found. We saw how a refinement of the definition of the problem helped with the solution and that the process of solving the problem led into the step of writing the algorithm.

- We introduced some of the basic building blocks of computer algorithms. The basic concepts introduced in this chapter, and the terms we decided to use to express them in our algorithms, are:

    1. **Assignment:** to perform calculations and store the result in a place where it can be used. We'll use:

       store ⟨*expression* ⟩ in ⟨*variablename* ⟩

    2. **Input and output:** to move data to and from the computer's main memory. We'll use:

       accept ⟨*variablename* ⟩ for input, and

       display ⟨*expressionlist* ⟩ for output.

    3. **Selection:** to test a condition and execute one step or series of steps if the condition is *true*, and, optionally, another step or series of steps if it's *false*. We'll write:

       if ⟨*condition* ⟩
           then
               ⟨*step*⟩
               ⟨*step*⟩

                 ⋮

               ⟨*step*⟩
           else
               ⟨*step*⟩
               ⟨*step*⟩

                 ⋮

               ⟨*step*⟩

    4. **Repetition or Looping:** to perform a series of steps repeatedly until a certain condition is met. We've only discussed the loop until, which we'll express:

       loop
           ⟨*step*⟩
           ⟨*step*⟩

             ⋮

           ⟨*step*⟩
           until ⟨*condition* ⟩

3.8 New Terms Introduced

accept The word used in an algorithm to indicate input.

assignment The act of evaluating an expression and storing the value in a variable.

binary search A technique used to search an ordered list. First, the item in the middle of the list is examined. If it's not the item being sought, either the lower or upper half of the list is discarded and the item in the middle of what remains is examined. The process continues until the desired item is found or the list is exhausted.

branching Another term for selection.

display The word used in an algorithm to indicate output.

effective A term describing the fact that the steps in an algorithm must be capable of being carried out by a computer.

if...then...else The words used in an algorithm to indicate selection.

initialization The act of executing a series of steps that must be executed at the beginning of a routine.

loop until The words used in an algorithm to indicate repetition.

looping Another term for repetition.

repetition Performing a series of steps over and over.

selection Executing one or another series of steps based on the truth or falsity of some condition.

store The word used in an algorithm to indicate assignment.

variable A named place in memory where something can be stored.

3.9   Exercises

1. Explain in your own words what the following steps in an algorithm mean for the computer to do:

       store 8 in Time
       accept Rate
       store Rate times Time in Distance
       display "The distance is", Distance, "miles."

2. Consider the following algorithm:

       display "Here we go!"
       store 10 in Counter
       loop
            display Counter
            subtract 1 from Counter
            until Counter is less than 0
       display "Blast Off!"

   What is the intent of this algorithm? Would it work?

   If we added the following line at the end, what would it display?

       display "The counter is", Counter

3. Write an algorithm for a program that would allow a user to enter a number and would then have the computer tell the user whether the number entered is positive, negative or zero.

4. Rewrite the guessing game algorithm in the chapter to include a counter that keeps track of the number of guesses the computer took. The concluding message should then tell the user how many guesses it took.

5. The guessing game algorithm has a fixed range of numbers—from 1 to 1000. Modify the algorithm to let the user choose the range of numbers.

6. The guessing game algorithm provides no way for a user to play the game more than once. Modify the algorithm using a *loop until* so that the user can play multiple games until he wants to stop.

7. The "21 Matches" game is not fair since the computer will always win. Modify the definition of the problem to allow the user to decide who is going to go first and how many matches will be on the table to start with. Then modify the solution to the problem to allow whomever the user chooses to go first. Let the computer play in such a manner that it

might lose if the user never makes a mistake, but so that it will win if the user ever gives it a chance. Write an algorithm for this solution.

For exercises 8–10, suppose that someone else is suggesting a problem to be solved with a computer program. The problems are *not* defined well enough to begin writing an algorithm. For each exercise, first write a complete problem definition, and then write an algorithm for a solution to the problem. You need to play both roles: that of the problem poser and that of the programmer—you should think of questions that a programmer would think of and then decide what answers the problem poser would come up with. You are *not* supposed to actually write the programs.

8. "Employees at my factory are paid time and a half for working overtime. I need a program that calculates the pay for each employee for one pay period."

9. "I wish I had a program that would convert feet to meters and meters to feet."

10. "Please write a program for me that finds the average of a list of numbers."

Chapter 4

Introduction to Pascal

> The sooner you start coding your program,
> the longer it's going to take.
> — Henry Ledgard

4.1 Overview of the Chapter

While writing an algorithm, one has to concentrate on the solution to the problem at hand. However, once the algorithm is finished, you can concentrate instead on the syntax of whatever language you are using to implement the algorithm. With this chapter, we begin our discussion of the language Pascal. You will see the general form of a Pascal program and will start to learn the syntax and structure of the language. We will use the algorithms developed in the previous chapter to introduce some of the elementary statements of Pascal.

We will begin to work with variables in Pascal. You will see that every variable in Pascal is of a certain type, and that the type of every variable must be declared in advance of its use. We will learn about the different statements in Pascal that can be used to implement the concepts introduced in the previous chapter.

4.2 Introduction

The Pascal language was originally designed by Niklaus Wirth. The language has since been standardized by the Institute of Electrical and Electronic Engineers, Inc. (IEEE) Standards Board and the American National Standards Institute (ANSI), as well as the International Standards Organization (ISO) and the British Standards Institution (BSI). There are some minor differences among the languages defined by these organizations but these differences are not in the portion of the language that will concern us. In this book we will consistently refer to the version approved in 1981 by IEEE and 1982 by ANSI (ANSI/IEEE 770 X3.97–1983). The document approved by these two bodies reads something like a legal document, and rather than quote from it, we'll explain in our own words what it says. When we refer to this document, we'll call it the *Pascal Standard*, and when we refer to the language defined by the Pascal Standard, we'll call it *Standard Pascal*. We will, on occasion, say things like "Pascal requires . . . ," or "Pascal does not allow . . . ." Statements like this make it seem like Pascal has a will, which is obviously not the case. Such statements refer to a Pascal compiler and what it requires or will not allow.

4.3   Overview of a Pascal Program

We start the chapter with an overview of a Pascal program. Every Pascal program you see will have the structure shown in figure 4.1.

```
program ⟨programname⟩(⟨filelist⟩) ;
⟨block⟩
•
```

Figure 4.1 The Structure of Every Pascal Program

Before we discuss the structure itself, we need to adopt some conventions regarding the way we type things. Throughout the text, we will type words in `typewriter face` when they must appear in the program just as we type them, and words in ⟨*angular brackets and italics*⟩ when they are symbols that stand for something else that must be put in that place.

Now, consider figure 4.1. It tells us that the word **program** must appear as the first word in every program (except for *white space*, which we'll discuss in a few pages).

After the word **program**, the name of the program, ⟨*programname*⟩, appears. You don't type "**<programname>**." You pick a name of your own choosing and put it there. The name of a program is not used anywhere else in the program but it has to be there. Choose a name that has some meaning; choose a name that makes it clear what the program does. We are going to name our program "**GuessingGame**" rather than "**guessinggame**." The use of the two capital letters in the name makes it easier to read. Standard Pascal doesn't care whether names have capital letters or lowercase letters or a combination of upper and lowercase; you can mix them if you want. We'll elaborate on the rules for choosing names later in the chapter.

After the ⟨*programname*⟩, there is a list of files that the program will use, enclosed in parentheses. A *file* is a collection of data. Files can be saved in permanent memory—as we saw in chapter 2—but it is also possible to treat the data coming from the keyboard and the data going to the screen as files. Pascal does just that.

In figure 4.1 we wrote:

> **program** ⟨*programname*⟩(⟨*filelist*⟩);

Once again, you don't type "**<filelist>**"; you type a list of files.

We will discuss file manipulation in a later chapter, but for now just remember that Pascal treats the input from the user as a file and the output it sends to the screen as a file; so for most of your programs, the ⟨*filelist*⟩ will consist of the two files **input** and **output** enclosed in parentheses.

All this means that the first line of your programs will look something like:

> **program** GuessingGame(input, output);

which is the first line of our guessing game program.

Every Pascal program will have a ⟨*block*⟩ immediately after the first line. This is the main part of the program. We'll see that it is made up of two parts, and that those in turn may be made up of subparts, and so on.

Did you see the period after the ⟨*block*⟩ in figure 4.1? It's easy to miss, but it's necessary. You must always remember to put a period at the end of your Pascal programs.

Now we'll look more closely at the two parts of the ⟨*block*⟩: the ⟨*definition/declaration part*⟩, which does things like list the variables used in the program, and the ⟨*statement part*⟩, which contains the actual statements to be executed.

4.4   The *definition/declaration part*

The ⟨*definition/declaration part*⟩ has several subparts: the ⟨*constant definition part*⟩, the ⟨*type definition part*⟩, the ⟨*variable declaration part*⟩ and the ⟨*procedure/function declaration part*⟩. The names of these various parts make their purpose somewhat clear, and we will discuss all of these in considerable detail as we proceed, but for now, we only want to discuss the ⟨*variable declaration part*⟩.

Data Types

Pascal is a *strongly typed* language. "*Typed*" means that every variable has to be of a particular type and that type must be indicated before the variable can be used. This declaration of data type is accomplished in the ⟨*variable declaration part*⟩ of the program. By "*strongly* typed language" we refer to what values can be assigned to a variable. Before we look at details of the ⟨*variable declaration part*⟩, let's look at the data types supplied in Pascal.

Pascal Simple Supplied Types

The four supplied simple types in Pascal are: `integer`, `real`, `char` and `Boolean`. The types `integer` and `real` are numerical data types. A variable of type `char` may hold a single character. A variable of type `Boolean` may hold either one of the two special values: `true` or `false`.

Numerical Data Types

The types `integer` and `real` are used to hold numeric values and are very similar to the integers and real numbers used in algebra. It might be slightly easier to think of them as "integer" and "decimal."

A variable of type `integer` can hold a value that is essentially the same as a mathematical integer: positive, negative or zero. We say "essentially" since in mathematics there is an infinite number of integers, while on the computer we can only represent a finite number. Indeed, every Pascal implementation has a largest and a smallest integer.

Since different computers may use different methods of storing data, the description of the language makes it legal for different Pascal compilers to have different largest positive integers. There is, however, a supplied constant in Pascal called `maxint`, which will always be equal to the largest positive integer on that compiler. We'll leave it as an exercise for you to write a simple program to display the value of `maxint` on your computer.

A variable of type `real` is used to hold a number that has a decimal, or fractional, part—a part to the right of the decimal point. We don't plan to get into the way the numbers are stored inside the computer. Just remember that `integers` are whole numbers, with no fractional part, and `reals` have fractional parts. It must be noted that any number with a fractional part is a `real` even if that fractional part is zero; that is, the number 3.0 is treated by Pascal as a `real`, not as an `integer`.

As a "strongly" typed language, Pascal is very picky about what gets put into a variable. If you try to put something of the wrong type in a variable, Pascal will usually complain. It doesn't complain when it can convert the value into something of the right type. For example, if you try to put a `real` value into an `integer` variable, Pascal won't let you. You could not put the value 3.0 in an `integer` variable. On the other hand, if you try to put an `integer` value into a `real` variable, Pascal will convert the value to a `real` value by essentially adding a decimal point and a zero on the right end of the integer.

Let's not forget that what we want to discuss here is how to declare variables. It is very important to remember that every variable you use in a program must be declared before it can be used.

Variables are declared in the ⟨*variable declaration part*⟩ of the ⟨*definition/declaration part*⟩ of the ⟨*block*⟩. You do this by typing:

```
var
    ⟨variablelist⟩ : ⟨typename⟩ ;
    ⟨variablelist⟩ : ⟨typename⟩ ;
    ⟨variablelist⟩ : ⟨typename⟩ ;
    ⋮
```

and continue for as many variables as you have. Each ⟨*variablelist*⟩ is a list of variable names—all of the same type—and each ⟨*typename*⟩ is the name of a type, such as `integer`, `real`, etc.

If you look through the algorithm for the guessing game problem, you will see that the following variables are used:

Biggest, Smallest, Guess, Answer and *Hint*.

Each of these names is a legal variable name in Pascal, so we'll just stick with the same names we used in the algorithm. More important is the *type* of each variable. Since `Biggest`, `Smallest` and `Guess` will only be used to hold whole numbers between 1 and 1000, we decide to declare them type `integer`.

So far, the ⟨*variable declaration part*⟩ would look like:

```
var
    Smallest, Biggest, Guess : integer;
```

That leaves `Answer` and `Hint`. These two variables present a small problem. When we wrote the algorithm, we assumed that the user of the program would answer these questions with word answers like, "yes" or "higher." In many languages it is fairly straightforward to implement answers of this form. That is, it is possible to store a word in a variable with a simple type rather than just a character. However, Standard Pascal is not such a language. It is possible to hold a string of characters in Standard Pascal, but it cannot be held in a simple variable. We'll see how to do it in chapter 11.

Since this is our first program, and since we don't want to get bogged down worrying about such details, let's decide to just let the user answer the questions with one letter answers, like Y for "yes" or H for "higher." With this decision made, we can then decide to simply use variables of type `char` to hold the user's answers.

Character Data Type

Recall that a variable can be thought of as a pigeonhole in memory with a name—a location where different values can be stored at different times. A variable of type `char` should be seen as a pigeonhole into which you can put any single character. Suppose, for example, that we declare the variable `Answer` as a variable of type `char`. Then `Answer` can be imagined as a named place in memory:

```
Answer
```

And this variable can hold a single character, like:

```
'Y'
```

Answer

A character need not be a letter. A variable of type char can hold a single digit, '0' through '9', can hold a punctuation symbol, like a left parenthesis: '(', or any number of other things, called *characters*.

Indeed, there is a difference between the character '6' and the number 6. Characters cannot be treated as numbers; you could not expect the computer to multiply something by the character '6', but you could, of course, multiply by the number 6. Normally, numbers are stored in the computer as a base two value while characters are stored according to some coding scheme. The number 6 would be stored in one byte as "0000 0110," while the ASCII representation of the character '6' is "0011 0110."

Boolean Data Type

We don't intend to say much about the type Boolean at this point and will see later where variables of this type can be used. Let's just say that there are only two constants of type Boolean, true and false and a Boolean variable can only contain one of these two values. When we need to store the value of an expression that evaluates to either true or false, we will store the value in a Boolean variable, called a *flag*. We'll say more about flags and show how they're used in chapter 9.

Beginning the Guessing Game Program

We are now ready to write the program heading line and the ⟨*variable declaration part*⟩ for the guessing game program.

```
program GuessingGame(input, output);
var
    Smallest, Biggest, Guess : integer;
    Answer, Hint             : char;
```

4.5 Variable Names and Syntax Diagrams

We'll now make it clear what a valid variable name looks like in Pascal. The rule for building a variable name is the same rule used for building names of other things in our programs that we will see later. Any of these is known in Pascal as an *identifier*. Stated in words, an ⟨*identifier*⟩ consists of a ⟨*letter*⟩

followed by zero or more ⟨*letter*⟩s or ⟨*digit*⟩s. A ⟨*letter*⟩ is one of the usual letters (A–Z and a–z), and a ⟨*digit*⟩ is one of the characters 0–9.

This is a good time to introduce *syntax diagrams*. The *syntax* of a language is the collection of rules that state how the various parts of the language are put together to form larger parts. For example, English syntax indicates how nouns and verbs (and other parts of speech) are used to make sentences, how sentences are used to form paragraphs, etc. It is convenient to use diagrams to explain the syntax of a computer language like Pascal because it is easier to understand—and less ambiguous—than trying to use a bunch of words in sentences.

The syntax diagrams we will use are also called *railroad track syntax diagrams* because you can follow them as if they are railroad tracks. Let's start with the syntax diagram for an ⟨*identifier*⟩ shown in figure 4.2:

identifier:

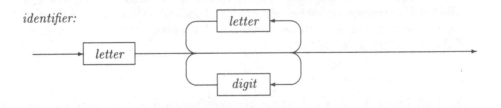

Figure 4.2

Once again, those things that are in ⟨*italics*⟩ are to be replaced with something else. Therefore, we need to define ⟨*letter*⟩ and ⟨*digit*⟩. Look at figures 4.3 and 4.4.

letter:

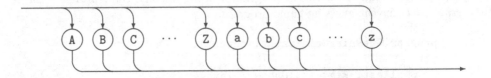

Figure 4.3

Combined, these three syntax diagrams are intended to say the same thing that we said above; an ⟨*identifier*⟩ consists of a letter followed by zero or more letters or digits.

digit:

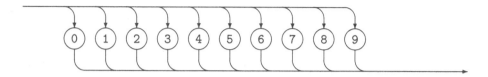

Figure 4.4

Let's look at some examples. The following are valid ⟨*identifier*⟩s:

```
GuessingGame
Answer
Guess
MaximumRateOfChangeDueToAChangeInTime
Distance1
x123
R2D2
```

The following are *not* valid ⟨*identifier*⟩s:

```
Guessing Game   (no space permitted)
3CPIO           (cannot begin with a digit)
Rate-Of-Change  (cannot contain characters other than
                letters and digits)
```

We should mention that many Pascal compilers allow the underscore character "_" as a valid character in an ⟨*identifier*⟩. This would permit names like `Rate_1`. However, Standard Pascal does not allow this character in an ⟨*identifier*⟩ and we will, therefore, not use it in this text.

Additionally, some Pascal compilers do not allow very long ⟨*identifier*⟩s, like `MaximumRateOfChangeDueToAChangeInTime`. Some Pascals will only look at the first 8 letters of such a name, others will look at the first 31 letters. Some compilers will limit names to 31 or fewer characters. We don't consider this a problem since we would not use such a long name in the first place. Such names require too much typing and are easy to mistype. Thoughtful choices will allow you to come up with names that clearly indicate the function of the object being named without resorting to such long names.

Standard Pascal does not notice the *case* of an ⟨*identifier*⟩. That is, you can type them in all uppercase (capital letters), all lowercase or a combination.

```
and        array     begin     case      const     div
do         downto    else      end       file      for
function   goto      if        in        label     mod
nil        not       of        or        packed    procedure
program    record    repeat    set       then      to
type       until     var       while     with
```

Figure 4.5 Pascal Reserved Words

```
abs        arctan    Boolean   char      chr       cos
dispose    eof       eoln      exp       false     get
input      integer   ln        maxint    new       odd
ord        output    pack      page      pred      put
read       readln    real      reset     rewrite   round
sin        sqr       sqrt      succ      true      trunc
unpack     write     writeln
```

Figure 4.6 Pascal (Almost) Reserved Words

In other words, Pascal will consider the following four names as the same ⟨*identifier*⟩:

    `RATE`, `rate`, `Rate`, `RaTe`.

Since we are not going to use the underscore character, and since we will often make up names for ⟨*identifier*⟩s that are a combination of two or more words, we will adopt the convention of using capital letters at the beginning of a name and use capital letters to indicate the beginning of the second or third word in the name. We used this convention earlier for `GuessingGame`. Similarly, we would use the name `RateOfChange` rather than `rateofchange`.

4.6   Reserved Words

We also need to add that there are some words that we cannot use as ⟨*identifier*⟩s. These words are known as *reserved words* and cannot be used by a programmer for an ⟨*identifier*⟩. We won't discuss all of these words at this point. Figure 4.5 gives a list of the reserved words so you will know to avoid using them as names for ⟨*identifier*⟩s.

There are a number of other words that are always used in Pascal the same way but are not reserved. You could redefine them if you wanted to, but if you did, and then tried to use these words with their normal meaning too, your program would do strange things. These words are listed in figure 4.6 and we suggest that you treat them as if they are reserved words.

We capitalize **Boolean** because it is the name of a person, George Boole. Otherwise, when we use a reserved word in a program, we will *not* capitalize it. This should help you distinguish between reserved words and ⟨*identifier*⟩s.

4.7   The Statement Part

We are ready to discuss the ⟨*statement part*⟩ of the program. After the ⟨*definition/declaration part*⟩, every program must contain a ⟨*statement part*⟩. The ⟨*statement part*⟩ consists of the reserved word **begin**, followed by a series of statements—separated by semicolons—and the reserved word **end**.

A railroad track syntax diagram for the ⟨*statement part*⟩ is contained in figure 4.7.

statement part:

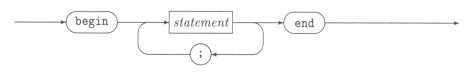

Figure 4.7

Notice that we include two clues as to the nature of the parts of a syntax diagram. Those things in oval shapes are also in a **typewriter font**, so they are to be typed just as they appear. Those things that are in rectangular boxes are in *italics*. They are to be replaced by something. That is, when you see *statement* in a rectangle, you know that you need to put a statement there, not type the word "**statement**." Of course, that means we have to explain what a *statement* is.

Before we do, make sure you see that the statement part of a program will always look like this:

begin
    ⟨*statement*⟩;
    ⟨*statement*⟩;
    ⟨*statement*⟩;

    ⋮

    ⟨*statement*⟩
end

where each ⟨*statement*⟩ is a valid statement in Pascal. It will often turn out that statements require more than one line each.

Notice that there are semicolons *between* the statements in the above example of the ⟨*statement part*⟩. One thing that sometimes gives beginners trouble

is the semicolon. The common misconception is that the semicolon goes at the end of a statement. This is simply *not true!* Semicolons do not go at the end of statements, they go *between* statements. Remember this and it will save you trouble later. Notice that there is no semicolon after the last statement in the above example.

There is never a semicolon between the last statement and the reserved word **end**. Indeed, there is no **end** statement. The **end** marks the end of the ⟨*statement part*⟩, but it is *not* a statement. We'll repeat this admonition several times since it is important and seems to cause students problems. Remember, do not automatically put semicolons on the ends of statements; put semicolons between statements.

Assignment in Pascal

Let's now take a look at a ⟨*statement*⟩. There are several statement forms in Pascal. One statement that appears frequently in Pascal programs is the ⟨*assignment statement*⟩. The purpose of the ⟨*assignment statement*⟩ is to implement the concept of assignment, which, you will recall, involves storing a value in a variable. In our algorithms we said something like:

store ⟨*expression*⟩ in ⟨*variablename*⟩.

In Pascal, we simply say:

⟨*variablename*⟩ := ⟨*expression*⟩

Whenever you want to store a value in a variable, you type the name of the variable, type the special assignment operator ":=," and then type the expression whose value you want stored in the variable.

Formally, we would have the syntax diagram of figure 4.8.

assignment statement:

Figure 4.8

Notice that the assignment operator consists of the symbols ":" and "=" adjacent to one another. You must type both symbols and you must not put a space between them.

Notice also that, unlike in our algorithms, the variable name comes first and the expression follows the := operator. A careless implementation of the algorithmic step:

store First in Second

as:

```
First := Second
```

will introduce a bug that can be hard to find. The correct statement is, of course:

```
Second := First
```

Using the *assignment statement*

Let's now look at a few statements from the algorithm developed in the previous chapter. We cannot do very many since we don't have many Pascal statements to work with yet, but we can handle a couple.

In the algorithm, we wrote:

store 1000 in Biggest
store 1 in Smallest

In Pascal, this would become:

```
Biggest := 1000;
Smallest := 1
```

Notice the semicolon between the two statements. Before we get the program finished there will be other statements following these two, and so later on, there will be a semicolon between the last statement shown here and the next one. For now, we'll leave it off since it doesn't belong at the end of the statement.

Another step in the algorithm looks like:

> *store the number halfway between Smallest and Biggest in Guess*

Before we can implement this step as an assignment statement, we need to know more about expressions. Notice that we have not yet given a syntax diagram for an ⟨*expression*⟩. We won't for now. The syntax diagram for an ⟨*expression*⟩, in its full complexity, is beyond our needs at this point. For now, let's just remember that an ⟨*expression*⟩ is something that has a value.

As we will see, expressions can be of different types and can be used in different ways. Let's look first at *arithmetic* expressions: those that have numerical values and use common arithmetic operations.

Arithmetic Operators

The common operations used in arithmetic are addition, subtraction, multiplication and division. Addition and subtraction are fairly straightforward: for addition we use the "+" symbol, and for subtraction we use the "-." Thus the expression for "the sum of 3 and 4" is written "3 + 4." If we have already stored values in the variables First and Second, the expression "First - Second" represents the difference between these two values. Thus the following assignment statement:

```
Third := First - Second
```

would be legal.

For multiplication we use the "*" symbol because the symbols used in ordinary algebra are not usually found on a keyboard. The expression that represents the product of the values stored in the variables First and Second is "First * Second." A valid assignment statement, using the multiplication operator, would be:

```
Third := First * Second
```

That leaves division. In Pascal—as well as in mathematics—division is more complicated than the other operations due to the distinction between integers and reals. For example, if we divide 10 by 5 we get an integer in mathematics while if we divide 12 by 7 we don't. In fact, if you used a calculator to divide 12 by 7 you would get something like 1.714285714, which is an approximation to the correct answer and certainly not an integer. In Pascal, this kind of division yields a real result and, in Pascal, we use the symbol "/" to represent it.

Thus, another valid assignment statement in Pascal would be:

```
Third := First / Second
```

where `Third` would have to be a variable of type **real**.

The other kind of division is more like the way we used to divide numbers when we were in grade school, before we learned about fractions and decimals—and before we were spoiled by calculators. In those days, when we divided 12 by 7 we got *two* answers, a quotient (1) and a remainder (5). Notice that the quotient and the remainder are both integers. In Pascal, we have two **integer** division operators: `div`, which gives the quotient, and `mod`, which gives the remainder. For more examples, consider:

10 `div` 5 equals 2, while 10 `mod` 5 equals 0;

146 `div` 19 equals 7, while 146 `mod` 19 equals 13.

Thus we could have the two assignment statements:

```
Quotient  := First div Second;
Remainder := First mod Second
```

in a program, where `Quotient` and `Remainder` are **integer** variables.

You might be wondering how useful these last two operators are. You might think they are not used much; however, they are used quite often. You divide integers by integers a lot in the real world, and you often want the integer result of the operation. When you make change for someone, you determine how many quarters, dimes, nickels and pennies are required to add up to a certain amount. The number of quarters equals the amount of change divided by 25. The remainder can be divided by 10 and the quotient will equal the number of dimes. The remainder of this division needs to be broken up into nickels and pennies. The point is, the numbers of quarters, dimes, nickels and pennies are not rational numbers but integers, and a program that determined these numbers would use `div` and `mod`. We seldom use fractions when we discuss ages or weights.

Indeed, we have just such a situation in our current problem. When we refer to the number halfway between 1 and 1000, we mean 500, not 500.5; although the rational number halfway between 1 and 1000 is actually 500.5.

Before we return to the problem, let's review what we have available to us for arithmetic. Consider figure 4.9.

Arithmetic Expressions

It should be clear that we can form arithmetic expressions from other arithmetic expressions by using these operators. An arithmetic expression can be as simple as a constant, like 3 or 67.34, or an arithmetic variable, like `Biggest` or `Guess`, or it can be quite complicated, like `First * (2 * Second - Third)`.

Operator:	Function:	Type of Result:
+	addition	`real` (unless both operands are `integer`)
–	subtraction	`real` (unless both operands are `integer`)
*	multiplication	`real` (unless both operands are `integer`)
/	real division	`real`
`div`	`integer` division giving the quotient	`integer`
`mod`	`integer` division giving the remainder	`integer`

Figure 4.9 Arithmetic Operators in Pascal

How about this expression?

    First * Second + Third

Does that mean add `First` times `Second` to `Third`, or does it mean multiply `First` times the sum of `Second` and `Third`? Are the answers different? Check it out!

Pascal evaluates this expression just like you do in your mathematics class. In such an expression, the multiplication is done first, then the addition. The rules that Pascal uses to decide how to evaluate arithmetic expressions like this are called its *rules of precedence*. Remember, if there aren't any parentheses to tell the computer to do it otherwise, multiplications and divisions will be done before additions and subtractions. You can always put in parentheses to change the order of the operations or to be sure Pascal evaluates the expression in the order you intend. Let's consider a couple of examples. Suppose that `First`, `Second` and `Third` have been declared as integers and given the values 2, 5 and 7, respectively. The expression:

    (First * Second) + Third

and the expression:

    First * Second + Third

would both be evaluated as 17. The expression:

    First * (Second + Third)

would have the value 24.

We should mention that Pascal has other arithmetic capabilities—like taking the square root or the absolute value of a number. These will be introduced as we need them.

Assignment—Continued

Let's go back to the step in our algorithm that got us started on this. In the algorithm, we wrote:

store the number halfway between Smallest and Biggest in Guess.

It should be clear that we want `Guess` to be an `integer`, so we can't just say:

```
Guess := (Smallest + Biggest) / 2
```

because the result of using the division operator "/" is a **real** value. We want the **integer** halfway between `Smallest` and `Biggest`, that is, we want the quotient, and hence we need to use **div** to accomplish the task:

```
Guess := (Smallest + Biggest) div 2
```

4.8 Output in Pascal

Another fundamental concept discussed in the previous chapter—and something we did in the algorithm—is output. We want to be able to have the computer display things on the screen. For now, these things are essentially messages to be read by the user of the program. In the algorithm, we wrote things like:

display "My guess is", Guess, "Is that right?"

We now want to discuss how to accomplish this in Pascal. The statement that does the job is the ⟨*write statement*⟩.

We can display a string of characters like, "`My guess is`," very easily but we have to put them between apostrophes, not between quotation marks as we did in our algorithm. That is, to display the above string, it must be written: `'My guess is'`.

There are two forms for the ⟨*write statement*⟩, which could be considered two separate statements but we'll consider them together. They are:

write(⟨*write expression list*⟩)

and

writeln(⟨*write expression list*⟩)

where ⟨*write expression list*⟩ is just a list of things to be displayed.

Figure 4.10 contains a syntax diagram for the ⟨*write statement*⟩.

write statement:

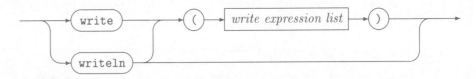

Figure 4.10

To display just the string "**My guess is**," you could code either:

```
write('My guess is')
```

or:

```
writeln('My guess is')
```

The difference between **write** and **writeln** is small but very important. If you use a **write**, the computer will display what you tell it to display on the screen and leave the cursor right there. If you use a **writeln**, the computer will display what you tell it to display but will then position the cursor at the beginning of the *next* line so that the next time it encounters either a **write** or a **writeln**, those things displayed will be on a new line.

Before we continue with the algorithm, let's look at a simple example of this. Suppose you code:

```
write('Hello');
write('world')
```

The computer will display on the monitor screen:

```
Helloworld
```

On the other hand, if you code:

```
writeln('Hello');
writeln('world')
```

the computer will display:

```
Hello
world
```

Alone, `writeln` can be used to display a blank line or to get the cursor off of a line that was written using `write`.

Remember, in Pascal we have to use a single quote (an apostrophe), ', rather than a double quote, ", around what we want displayed. Material surrounded by these single quotes is known in Pascal as a *string constant* and as a *string literal.*

Notice also that the syntax rules of Pascal require us to put the things to be displayed in parentheses.

As an example, let's write some ⟨*write statement*⟩s that could serve as an introduction to the program for the user.

```
writeln('Welcome to the Guessing Game program.  This');
writeln('program will play a number guessing game with you.');
writeln('You get to think of a number and the computer will');
writeln('attempt to guess it.  Think of a number between 1');
writeln('and 1000 (inclusive).')
```

This is just an example, you can change the way the introduction is worded. The point is, you can use ⟨*write statement*⟩s to cause the computer to display any series of messages on the screen that you wish. Notice that you must put each separate line of output in a separate ⟨*write statement*⟩. You cannot put several lines in one ⟨*write statement*⟩. That is, the following ⟨*write statement*⟩ is *not* valid syntax:

```
{  THIS IS NOT VALID SYNTAX  }

writeln('Welcome to the Guessing Game program.  This
        program will play a number guessing game with you.
        You get to think of a number and the computer will
        attempt to guess it.  Think of a number between 1
        and 1000 (inclusive).')
```

You *cannot* put a RETURN character in the middle of a string constant.

Displaying Numbers

Back to the algorithm. Let's look at some more output. We also wanted, as mentioned above, to display a line that contains some words and the current guess. Would the following do what we want?

```
writeln('My guess is Guess.  Is that right?')
```

No, of course not. This would always display the string:

```
My guess is Guess.  Is that right?
```

We don't want the *name* of the variable `Guess` to appear on the screen, we want the contents of the variable to appear on the screen. Let's try again.

To get words in a message to appear on the screen, we put the message in single quotes. To get the contents of a variable to appear, we just put the name of the variable, but not inside quotes. Like:

```
writeln('My guess is', Guess, 'Is that right?')
```

Suppose that the value stored in the variable `Guess` is 500. The above line would cause the computer to display something like:

```
My guess is          500Is that right?
```

That's closer but still needs some work. Each Pascal compiler will display the value of an integer in some fixed number of spaces—usually around 10— unless we tell it to do otherwise. That's why there are so many spaces in front of the 500 in the line shown. We can change that by using a *field-width* indicator.

Field-Width Indicators

A field-width indicator is an `integer` expression that indicates the minimum number of spaces to use to display the value of an `integer`. Since 500 has three digits, it will require three spaces on the monitor to display it. If we change the above line to:

```
writeln('My guess is', Guess:3, 'Is that right?')
```

we get rid of all the extra spaces in front of the 500. It would look like:

```
My guess is500Is that right?
```

which looks even worse, but we're moving in the right direction. Now we failed to tell the computer where we definitely wanted spaces printed. This time consider the statement:

```
writeln('My guess is ', Guess:3, '.  Is that right?')
```

This will cause the computer to display:

```
My guess is 500.  Is that right?
```

which looks pretty good. However, there are still some problems. We used a `writeln`. Should we have? After it finished displaying the line, it would have moved the screen's cursor to the next line and the screen would have looked like:

```
My guess is 500.  Is that right?
```
█

where the ▮ represents the cursor. It would have been better to have the user answer the question on the same line that it's asked, so a **write** would have worked better. Then we would have had to add some more spaces on the end and some sort of "prompt" for the user, yielding:

```
write('My guess is ', Guess:3, '.  Is that right? (Y/N): ')
```

Now the display would look like:

```
My guess is 500.  Is that right?  (Y/N): ▮
```

where again the ▮ character represents the cursor. The cursor would sit there and wait for the user to respond to the question, presumably answering with either a Y or an N.

Caution: some operating systems will "buffer" the output and not print a line until the entire line is ready to print. In such a case, the line containing the question has to be displayed before the user can answer it. This means that, on these systems, you cannot use a **write** as shown here but must use a **writeln** instead.

We can make one more improvement, and then we'll let you take it from there and write it the way you think best.

For our final adjustment, consider what the line in question would look like if the value of **Guess** was 7 instead of 500. The exact same line of code—it's in a loop that we have yet to work on—would cause the line to look like:

```
My guess is   7.  Is that right? (Y/N): ▮
```

Did you notice the extra spaces in front of the 7? Why are they there? Since we used a field-width indicator of 3, it will always use at least three spaces to display the number, even if the number has only one digit. Suppose we change the field-width indicator from 3 to 1, as:

```
write('My guess is ', Guess : 1, '.  Is that right? (Y/N): ')
```

Then when **Guess** contains the value 7, the line displayed would look like:

```
My guess is 7.  Is that right?  (Y/N): ▮
```

But then what would happen when **Guess** contains 500 or 1000? Pascal will always add extra spaces when necessary to display a value correctly. The field-width indicator indicates the *minimum* number of spaces to use. If the number needs more room, the additional room will be provided and the remaining things to be displayed will simply be shifted over to the right.

In summary, use a field-width indicator of 1 when you want an integer value displayed in the midst of a sentence. Pascal will allow just enough space to print the number but not print any extra spaces.

Field-width indicators with values greater than 1 can be used to print tables that contain evenly spaced columns. A variable field-width indicator can be used to do some fancy printing.

Displaying real Numbers

While we're on the subject, let's briefly look at using field-width indicators for real values. Since a real value has two parts—a whole number part and a decimal part—it makes sense for the field-width indicator to have two parts also. However, contrary to what might be guessed at first, the two parts are not used to indicate how many places to display to the left and to the right of the decimal point. Rather, the first part is used to indicate how many places, in total, to use for the number and the second part is used to indicate how many places to display to the right of the decimal point. As an example, suppose the variable First has been declared to be a real variable and has been given a value of 314.15927. The following is a series of examples of how First would be displayed using different field-width indicators:

Pascal statement   Number displayed

```
writeln('First = ', First : 8 : 2)     First = ⊔⊔314.16
writeln('First = ', First : 8 : 3)     First = ⊔314.159
writeln('First = ', First : 8 : 0)     First = ⊔⊔⊔⊔⊔314
writeln('First = ', First : 5 : 1)     First = 314.2
writeln('First = ', First : 3 : 2)     First = 314.16
writeln('First = ', First : 8)         First = 3.14E+02
writeln('First = ', First : 10)        First = 3.1416E+02
writeln('First = ', First)             First = ⊔⊔3.1415927000E+02
```

Several comments are in order. First, we are using the ⊔ symbol to indicate where a space would be displayed.

- In the first example, notice that eight spaces total are used—counting the space used for the decimal point.

- When necessary, the number is rounded off, not truncated. That is, when 314.15927 was displayed with two decimal places, the computer displayed 314.16, not 314.15.

- If not enough space is allocated in the field-width indicator, the compiler will add enough spaces to display the whole number part of the value correctly, along with the indicated number of places in the decimal part.

- If the second indicator is 0, no decimal part—and no decimal point—is displayed.

- If only the first field-width indicator is present, the value is displayed in scientific notation using the indicated number of spaces, rounding where necessary and using at least enough spaces to show one digit on each side of the decimal point. A number expressed in scientific notation consists of a number—with or without a decimal point—followed by the letter "E," followed by an integer. The "E" can be thought of as saying, "times ten to the power of." Thus "3.1416E+02" means "3.1416 times ten to the power of 2," or, "3.1416 times ten squared," or just 314.16.

- If neither field-width indicator is present, the value is displayed in scientific notation.

The exact form of the display caused by the last three examples will vary from compiler to compiler.

Displaying an Apostrophe

One final point of interest and we'll leave output for now. What would happen if you tried to display a message that contains an apostrophe, like the message:

```
I got it, aren't I smart?
```

Since the apostrophe is used to delimit the message, we could not code:

```
writeln('I got it, aren't I smart?')
```

because the second apostrophe would be interpreted as the end of the string constant and the rest of the stuff on the line would confuse the compiler. The trick is to use what's called an *apostrophe image*. An apostrophe image is simply *two* apostrophes typed one immediately after the other. This tells the compiler that you want it to print one apostrophe. Thus the code should be:

```
writeln('I got it, aren''t I smart?')
```

Notice that we typed the apostrophe character twice (''), not the double quote (").

4.9 Input in Pascal

The opposite of output is, of course, input—data moving toward the computer's memory. In the previous chapter we discussed the concept of input and introduced the word *accept* for our algorithmic language to indicate when we wanted the computer to do input from the keyboard. Now we need to learn how to

implement this concept in Pascal. The basic input statement in Pascal (for our purposes) is the ⟨*read statement*⟩.

As with the ⟨*write statement*⟩, the ⟨*read statement*⟩ has two forms, **read** and **readln**. They work differently and both are needed. At this point, however, we only need one form, the **readln**. The best advice we can give a beginner to Pascal is to forget, for the time being, that there is a statement that starts with the word **read**. *Always* use **readln**. We will explain the difference later, and also explain why the **readln** form of the ⟨*read statement*⟩ is the one to use for input from the keyboard.

Figure 4.11 contains a syntax diagram for the ⟨*read statement*⟩.

read statement:

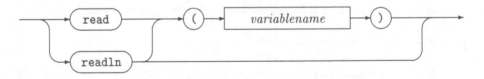

Figure 4.11

In our algorithm, when we wanted the computer to pause and wait for the user to enter something, and to take that something and store it in a variable, we used the construction:

accept ⟨*variablename*⟩

In Pascal, this becomes:

```
readln(⟨variablename⟩)
```

And that's about all there is to it. When the computer comes to this line—as the program is running—it will pause and wait for the user to enter something at the keyboard; after the user presses the RETURN key, the computer will store whatever the user entered in the variable with the name ⟨variablename⟩. Be sure to notice the parentheses around the ⟨variablename⟩.

A couple of things should be said. First, it is possible, if you want, to put more than one variable name in the parentheses. In this case, the user will have to enter that many things and then press RETURN. The things the user enters must be separated from each other by one or more spaces and the user would have to be told that. Second, once again because Pascal is a strongly typed language, if the user enters something that is not of the same type as the corresponding variable, Pascal will not allow the value to be stored in the variable and the program will crash; i.e., the computer will stop running the program and will display some sort of cryptic error message indicating that something happened to cause the program to stop unexpectedly.

The most common situation of this sort is when the variable is of type **integer** and the user types something that cannot be turned into an **integer**. There is little that can be done about this at this point. The best we can do is tell the user to enter an integer and hope. In a later chapter we'll suggest a more clever solution.

Let's look at the algorithm where input is done and implement those steps in Pascal. So that what we do makes sense, we'll include the output steps too, so you can see the entire sequence.

store the number halfway between Smallest and Biggest in Guess
display "My guess is", Guess, "Is that right?"
accept Answer

In Pascal, this becomes:

```
Guess := (Smallest + Biggest) div 2;
write('My guess is ', Guess : 1, '.  Is that right? (Y/N): ');
readln(Answer)
```

where **Guess**, **Smallest**, **Biggest** and **Answer** have already been declared as indicated earlier in this chapter.

The form of the ⟨*read statement*⟩ with the word **readln** all by itself, can be used to get the computer to pause and wait for the user to press the RETURN key.

While we don't have occasion to have the user enter any **real** values in this program, we might mention that the ⟨*read statement*⟩ can be used for **reals** as well as `integer`s and `char`s. The user can type any real number as long as she or he remembers to put a digit on both sides of any decimal points entered. In fact, a real number can be entered in scientific notation, if desired. A user can enter "3e10," which is equivalent to "30000000000," or "3.2E-5," which is the same as "0.000032." The "E" can be in upper or lowercase.

4.10   Selection in Pascal

The next fundamental concept that we need to be able to implement in Pascal is the concept of selection. In our algorithmic language, we are using a construction we call an *if...then...else* for selection. The statement we use in Pascal to implement an *if...then...else* is the ⟨*if statement*⟩ and the fact that it looks very much like the *if...then...else* is no coincidence.

Figure 4.12 contains the syntax diagram for the ⟨*if statement*⟩.

if statement:

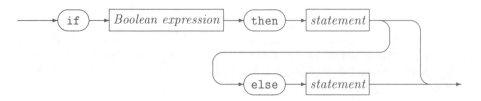

Figure 4.12

Other than the ⟨*Boolean expression*⟩, there is nothing in the syntax that we haven't seen before. A ⟨*Boolean expression*⟩ is just an ⟨*expression*⟩ that has a `Boolean` value, which is a value that is either `true` or `false`. Thus, ⟨*Boolean expression*⟩s are just like those things we called "conditions" in the previous chapter. Whenever we are talking about an algorithm, we'll use the word "condition" and whenever we are talking about a program, we'll use the words "Boolean expression."

Look at the syntax diagram in figure 4.12 and you will note that there is one ⟨*statement*⟩ following the word `then`. It does *not* say ⟨*statement*⟩s! There must be *one and only one* statement after the word `then`.

That does present a problem. If we can only put a single statement after the word `then`, how can we implement an algorithm that requires several steps following the *then*?

For example, consider the following excerpt from the algorithm we're working on:

```
if Answer is "No"
    then
        display "Should I guess higher or lower?"
        accept Hint
        if Hint is "Higher"
            then
                store Guess + 1 in Smallest
            else
                store Guess - 1 in Biggest
```

There are three steps inside the "then part." A step that does some output:

```
display "Should I guess higher or lower?"
```

an input step:

```
accept Hint
```

and another *if...then...else*:

```
if Hint is "Higher"
    then
        store Guess + 1 in Smallest
    else
        store Guess - 1 in Biggest
```

We have to be able to get the computer to do all three of these things if the user says "no." The syntax diagram seems to make that impossible.

compound statement:

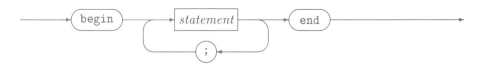

Figure 4.13

The solution to the dilemma lies in another statement form, the ⟨*compound statement*⟩. The ⟨*compound statement*⟩ allows us to group several statements together and get Pascal to treat the group as one statement. The syntax for it is shown in figure 4.13.

If this looks somewhat familiar, it should. It's the same syntax as that for the ⟨*statement part*⟩ of a program. The important thing, however, is to see it as *one* statement. Wherever the syntax of Pascal requires a single statement, we can legally put a ⟨*compound statement*⟩.

In skeleton form, that means that:

```
if ⟨Boolean expression⟩
    then
        begin
            ⟨statement⟩;
            ⟨statement⟩;
                ⋮
            ⟨statement⟩
        end
```

is a perfectly valid ⟨*if statement*⟩. (Remember that the **else** part of the ⟨*if statement*⟩ is optional.)

A second thing that needs to be mentioned is the fact that the ⟨*if statement*⟩ itself is one statement, not two. The **else** part is not a statement. Therefore, since a semicolon is used to *separate* statements, not *terminate* them, you must never put a semicolon directly before the word **else**. The following skeleton is *always* wrong:

```
if ⟨Boolean expression⟩
    then
        ⟨statement⟩;
    else
        ⟨statement⟩
```

Before we can continue with the implementation of the *if...then...else*, we must discuss ⟨*Boolean expression*⟩s. As before, we'll not attempt to give a complete syntax diagram at this point but will give some guidelines for constructing ⟨*Boolean expression*⟩s.

4.11   Relational Operators

The data type **Boolean** and a ⟨*Boolean expression*⟩ are both named after George Boole, the man who was essentially the father of symbolic logic.

Much of the time ⟨*Boolean expression*⟩s are formed with *relational operators*. The ⟨*relational operator*⟩s in Pascal are the simple operators from algebra (slightly rewritten). These operators and their equivalents in English are shown in figure 4.14.

Symbol	English
=	is equal to
<	is less than
>	is greater than
<=	is less than or equal to
>=	is greater than or equal to
<>	is not equal to

Figure 4.14 Pascal Relational Operators

You can put any of these operators between two ⟨*arithmetic expression*⟩s and form a ⟨*Boolean expression*⟩, for example:

    First < Second

which reads, "First is less than Second." This ⟨*Boolean expression*⟩ is **true** if the value currently stored in the variable First is less than the value currently stored in the variable Second, and **false** otherwise.

Similarly, if the value currently stored in the variable Third is 17, the ⟨*Boolean expression*⟩:

    Third >= 17

would be **true**.

The symbol "<>" is used for "not equal to." This symbol is used since it is not possible to type the more usual "≠" on the keyboard. You wouldn't want to think of this as "is less than or greater than," just think of it as "is not equal to."

Remember not to type a space between the two characters in each of the three symbols "<=," ">=" and "<>." Remember also that you must type these symbols in the prescribed order; the compiler will not accept "=<" or "><."

Let's return to the algorithm and see if we're ready to implement the *if...then...else*:

```
if Answer is "No"
    then
        display "Should I guess higher or lower?"
        accept Hint
        if Hint is "Higher"
            then
                store Guess + 1 in Smallest
            else
                store Guess - 1 in Biggest
```

Recall that we decided to have the user enter either Y for "yes" or N for "no." Thus the appropriate ⟨*Boolean expression*⟩ becomes:

```
Answer = 'N'
```

And the ⟨*if statement*⟩ implementing the *if...then* becomes:

```
if Answer = 'N'
  then
    begin
      write('Should I guess higher or lower? (H/L): ');
      readln(Hint);
      if Hint = 'H'
        then
          Smallest := Guess + 1
        else
          Biggest := Guess - 1
    end
```

Look carefully at this and make sure you understand it. First make sure you see that it conforms to the syntax diagram for an ⟨*if statement*⟩. It starts with the word if, followed by a ⟨*Boolean expression*⟩, followed by *one* ⟨*statement*⟩, a ⟨*compound statement*⟩. Notice that this ⟨*if statement*⟩ does not have an `else` part; the `else` part is always optional.

Now look at the ⟨*compound statement*⟩. It contains three ⟨*statement*⟩s: a ⟨*write statement*⟩, a ⟨*read statement*⟩ and another ⟨*if statement*⟩. Observe that this second ⟨*if statement*⟩ satisfies the syntax requirements too. Unlike the first one, however, this ⟨*if statement*⟩ does have an `else` part. Both the ⟨*statement*⟩ following the `then` and the ⟨*statement*⟩ following the `else` are ⟨*assignment statement*⟩s.

Notice also the semicolons. There are semicolons separating the three ⟨*statement*⟩s in the ⟨*compound statement*⟩. And there is no semicolon on the end of either ⟨*assignment statement*⟩. Remember, there must *never* be a semicolon directly in front of an `else`.

Before we go on, we should consider another problem that could occur. If the user obediently types one of the letters Y, N, H or L as instructed to, everything will work fine. However, suppose that the user types "n" rather than "N" when asked the first question. The ⟨*Boolean expression*⟩ as written above would be `false` and the ⟨*compound statement*⟩ would not be executed. Shouldn't we consider "n" to mean the same as "N"? Of course we should. But how do we get the computer to do what we want?

The solution is to get the computer to consider the ⟨*Boolean expression*⟩ to be `true` if `Answer` equals either "N" or "n." To accomplish this, we need to develop more complex ⟨*Boolean expression*⟩s, using *Boolean operators*.

4.12   Boolean Operators

The ⟨*relational operator*⟩s are put between ⟨*arithmetic expression*⟩s to form ⟨*Boolean expression*⟩s. The *Boolean operators* are used in conjunction with ⟨*Boolean expression*⟩s to form complex ⟨*Boolean expression*⟩s. There are three Boolean operators: `and`, `or` and `not`. If we let $\mathcal{P}$ and $\mathcal{Q}$ stand for unspecified ⟨*Boolean expression*⟩s, then

  $\mathcal{P}$ `and` $\mathcal{Q}$,
  $\mathcal{P}$ `or` $\mathcal{Q}$, and
  `not` $\mathcal{P}$

are valid ⟨*Boolean expression*⟩s.

The ⟨*Boolean expression*⟩ $\mathcal{P}$ `and` $\mathcal{Q}$ is `true` only when both $\mathcal{P}$ and $\mathcal{Q}$ are `true`; the ⟨*Boolean expression*⟩ $\mathcal{P}$ `or` $\mathcal{Q}$ is `true` if either $\mathcal{P}$ or $\mathcal{Q}$ is `true` (or both), and the ⟨*Boolean expression*⟩ `not` $\mathcal{P}$ is `true` if $\mathcal{P}$ is `false`.

Using the ⟨*Boolean operator*⟩ `or`, we can form the ⟨*expression*⟩:

    Answer = 'N' or Answer = 'n'

which looks fine but isn't. Earlier we mentioned briefly that Pascal assumes a certain order of precedence in an expression if you don't insert parentheses. The ⟨*arithmetic operator*⟩s, the ⟨*relational operator*⟩s and the ⟨*Boolean operator*⟩s all have their own levels of precedence: multiplications are done before additions, **and**s are done before **or**s, etc. When the Pascal language was designed, the precedence given to the ⟨*relational operator*⟩s was lower than the precedence given to the ⟨*Boolean operator*⟩s. That means that in the expression above, since there are no parentheses to change the default precedence, the **or** is evaluated (or attempted) before either = operator is evaluated. It's as if we had typed:

```
Answer = ('N' or Answer) = 'n'
```

Since 'N' and **Answer** are *not* ⟨*Boolean expression*⟩s, they cannot appear on either side of the **or**, and a syntax error is reported. In such a case, you must include parentheses to force the compiler to alter the normal precedence of the operators. The above ⟨*Boolean expression*⟩ must be typed:

```
(Answer = 'N') or (Answer = 'n').
```

One more caution before we go on. Be careful not to type:

```
if Answer = 'N' or 'n'.
```

That may sound right but it makes no sense at all to the compiler. Even if you add parentheses, it won't be right. What appears on both sides of the **or** must be a ⟨*Boolean expression*⟩.

With all this in mind, we can finish the implementation of the *if...then* from the algorithm:

```
if (Answer = 'N') or (Answer = 'n')
  then
    begin
      write('Should I guess higher or lower? (H/L): ');
      readln(Hint);
      if (Hint = 'H') or (Hint = 'h')
        then
          Smallest := Guess + 1
        else
          Biggest := Guess - 1
    end
```

4.13   Repetition in Pascal

The final construction that we have in our algorithm but have to implement in Pascal is the *loop until*. Once again there is an almost exact counterpart in

Pascal, the ⟨*repeat statement*⟩. This statement is typed almost the same as a *loop until* and it works just as the *loop until* works. The syntax diagram shown in figure 4.15 is a good place to start.

repeat statement:

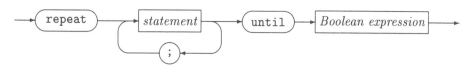

Figure 4.15

In words, this says that a ⟨*repeat statement*⟩ starts with **repeat**, has one or more ⟨*statement*⟩s—separated by semicolons—and then **until** followed by a ⟨*Boolean expression*⟩.

When the computer encounters a ⟨*repeat statement*⟩, it executes all of the ⟨*statement*⟩s between **repeat** and **until** and then evaluates the ⟨*Boolean expression*⟩. If the ⟨*Boolean expression*⟩ is **true**, the loop is exited and control passes to whatever follows. If, on the other hand, the ⟨*Boolean expression*⟩ is **false**, all of the ⟨*statement*⟩s between **repeat** and **until** are executed again. This process repeats until the value of the ⟨*Boolean expression*⟩ is **true**. It is important to notice that the ⟨*statement*⟩s will be executed at least once. Other sorts of loops will be discussed later that may not be executed at all.

Since this is so close to our algorithmic *loop until*, it becomes easy to implement. Let's look at the *loop until* from the algorithm once again:

```
loop
    store the number halfway between Smallest and Biggest in Guess
    display "My guess is", Guess, "Is that right?"
    accept Answer
    if Answer is "No"
        then
            display "Should I guess higher or lower?"
            accept Hint
            if Hint is "Higher"
                then
                    store Guess + 1 in Smallest
                else
                    store Guess − 1 in Biggest
    until Answer is "Yes"
```

Using the pieces we developed earlier, the Pascal for this portion of the program becomes:

```
repeat
  Guess := (Smallest + Biggest) div 2;
  write('My guess is ', Guess : 1, '.  Is that right? (Y/N): ');
  readln(Answer);
  if (Answer = 'N') or (Answer = 'n')
    then
      begin
        write('Should I guess higher or lower? (H/L): ');
        readln(Hint);
        if (Hint = 'H') or (Hint = 'h')
          then
            Smallest := Guess + 1
          else
            Biggest := Guess - 1
      end
until (Answer = 'Y') or (Answer = 'y')
```

It would be a good idea to look at this carefully and make sure you understand each part. Notice that there is no semicolon after the **end** and before the **until**. Notice that we indented the line starting with **until**. Since there is no such thing as an "until statement," no semicolon is needed to separate the ⟨*if statement*⟩ from it.

We should emphasize that the above is *one* ⟨*statement*⟩! If another ⟨*statement*⟩ follows this one later, they will need to be separated by a semicolon.

Avoiding Bugs

There's an expression that carpenters use:

Measure twice, cut once.

A programmer might express the same sentiment as:

Think first, code later.

The above code has a minor problem. Regardless of what the user enters when the program asks if the guess is correct, if **Answer** is neither an 'N' nor an 'n', it will be treated as a "yes" answer. But when it gets to the bottom of the loop, **Answer** will not be a 'Y' or a 'y'. Similarly, when the program asks for a hint, if the user enters H or h, the program will treat that as meaning "higher." Any other response is interpreted as meaning "lower." This could result in an unexpected sequence of events for the user.

One way to prevent this would be to add some sort of loop, making sure that the user enters a valid response before continuing. Since this didn't occur to us when we wrote the algorithm, we could go back and modify the algorithm or just add the necessary steps to the code. In the real world, it is not unusual for such things to occur to us during the coding step. If they are minor details, they are often just added to the code. If they are major, a good programmer will take the time to go back and rewrite the algorithm too. Being able to judge between minor and major is another mark of an experienced programmer.

Obviously, the more we can keep such bugs out of our programs the better they will be. And the sooner we spot them, the easier they will be to keep out. Hence:

Think first, code later.

4.14   White Space

Let's now talk about *white space* and *indentation*. By "white space" we mean the spaces we type at the beginning of each line and the carriage return characters we type on the end of each line. The Pascal compiler does not care about or notice white space. You could, if you wanted to and had a text editor that allowed it, type everything on one line and put no extra spaces at all between things. We cannot illustrate that but we can illustrate what it would look like if we used a nearly constant width for lines and did not indent. The above ⟨*repeat statement*⟩ would then look like:

```
repeat Guess:=(Smallest+Biggest)div 2;write('My guess is ',Guess:1,
'.  Is that right? (Y/N): ');readln(Answer);if(Answer='N')or(Answer
='n')then begin write('Should I guess higher or lower? (H/L): ');
readln(Hint);if(Hint='H')or(Hint='h')then Smallest:=Guess+1 else
Biggest:=Guess-1 end until (Answer='Y')or(Answer='y')
```

This would be handled by the compiler in exactly the same way as the preceding ⟨*repeat statement*⟩. Notice that some spaces are required. We could not have left out the space between **repeat** and **Guess** on the first line; if we had, the compiler would have interpreted **repeatGuess** as an ⟨*identifier*⟩.

Of course, we are not suggesting that you type your programs this way. Since Pascal allows you to include white space in your programs, you should. You should adopt a consistent style that makes your programs easy to read and follow.

Notice that not all of the spaces in the above are white space. Inside the message for the computer to display, we wrote:

```
'.  Is that right? (Y/N): '
```

The extra spaces are there for a purpose; they are intended to be displayed on the screen. If they were removed, what appears on the screen would not look right.

You can break a line at almost any point you wish—as the previous example shows. You can have several statements on one line, and one statement might require several lines. You cannot, however, put a carriage return in the middle of a constant, the middle of a variable name or in the middle of a message like the one shown.

The style we use—and recommend—has succeeding statements start on the same level of indentation. Those statements that are inside others are indented some consistent number of spaces. The question as to how many spaces to use is not easy to answer. If you use too few spaces, the indentation will not be easy to see, while if you use too many, your programs can tend to get "right heavy." You will have to choose the number of spaces depending on the situation. Two spaces is minimal and five is probably too many.

We indent the word **then** and then further indent the statement following it. If that statement is a ⟨*compound statement*⟩, we further indent the statements in the ⟨*compound statement*⟩. Since the word **until** does not begin a new statement, we line it up with the rest of the statements in the ⟨*repeat state-ment*⟩. We always line up the words **begin** and **end**. This method of indentation is not the only way to do it. Some authors indent differently; you should adopt a style you like that makes sense and that makes your programs easy to follow—and then stick with whatever style you adopt.

You should use white space in the midst of a line to make your code easier to read; the line:

```
if (Answer = 'N') or (Answer = 'n')
```

is better than:

```
if(Answer='N')or(Answer='n')
```

although both constitute valid syntax.

Further, a blank line or two between sections of your code will help; especially later when you write larger programs.

Comments

There is another sort of white space that we need to mention. You can—and should—put *comments* in your code that will help someone reading it under-stand what is going on. The compiler will ignore everything placed within curly braces, "{" and "}." The braces and everything between them are considered white space; such white space is called a comment. We'll discuss documentation in more detail in a later chapter.

For now, at the very least, insert some comments that include your name and a brief description of what the program does, something like:

```
program GuessingGame(input, output);

{  Programmer:  Meely Chan                              }

{  This program plays a number guessing game with the user.  }
{  The user gets to think of a number and the computer tries }
{  to guess it.                                         }
```

4.15 The Complete Program

Let's complete this chapter with a complete running program that implements the guessing game algorithm. You may want to type this program in on whatever computer you are using and try it. Let's include yet another copy of the entire algorithm for ease of comparison:

START OF Guessing Game

display an introductory message for the user
store 1 in Smallest
store 1000 in Biggest
loop
   store the number halfway between Smallest and Biggest in Guess
   display "My guess is", Guess, "Is that right?"
   accept Answer
   if Answer is "No"
      then
         display "Should I guess higher or lower?"
         accept Hint
         if Hint is "Higher"
            then
               store Guess + 1 in Smallest
            else
               store Guess - 1 in Biggest
  until Answer is "Yes"
display "I got it, aren't I smart?"
display "Thank you for playing with me."

END OF Guessing Game

The complete program is on the next page.

```
program GuessingGame(input, output);

{ Programmer:  R. K. Harper                                    }

{ This program plays a number guessing game with the user.  }
{ The user gets to think of a number and the computer tries }
{ to guess it.                                                }

var
      Smallest, Biggest, Guess : integer;
      Answer, Hint             : char;

begin
  writeln('Welcome to the Guessing Game program.  This');
  writeln('program will play a number guessing game with you.');
  writeln('You get to think of a number and the computer will');
  writeln('attempt to guess it.  Think of a number between 1');
  writeln('and 1000 (inclusive).  Press RETURN when you''re ready.');
  readln;
  Smallest := 1;
  Biggest := 1000;
  repeat
    Guess := (Smallest + Biggest) div 2;
    write('My guess is ', Guess : 1, '.  Is that right? (Y/N): ');
    readln(Answer);
    if (Answer = 'N') or (Answer = 'n')
      then
        begin
          write('Should I guess higher or lower? (H/L) ');
          readln(Hint);
          if (Hint = 'H') or (Hint = 'h')
            then
              Smallest := Guess + 1
            else
              Biggest := Guess - 1
        end
  until (Answer = 'Y') or (Answer = 'y');
  writeln('I got it, aren''t I smart?');
  writeln('Thank you for playing with me.')
end.
```

4.16 The Coding Step—Once Again

Now we want to use the problem from the "Once Again" section in chapter 3 to give another illustration of the fourth step, the coding step, in the programming process.

Turn the Algorithm into Code

The problem we worked on in chapter 3 was the "21 Matches" game. As you will recall, the problem was to write a program that would let the computer play the game with a user. Here's our algorithm from chapter 3:

```
START OF 21 Matches

display an introduction to the game for the user
store 21 in MatchesLeft
loop
    display "There are", MatchesLeft, "matches left, how many do you pick up?"
    accept UserPicksUp
    if UserPicksUp < 1 or > 4 or more than MatchesLeft
        then
            loop
                display "Sorry, you must choose between 1 and 4 matches"
                display "but not more than", MatchesLeft, "matches."
                accept UserPicksUp
            until 1 ≤ UserPicksUp ≤ 4 and ≤ MatchesLeft
    subtract UserPicksUp from MatchesLeft
    if MatchesLeft > 0
        then
            display "I pick up", 5 − UserPicksUp, "matches."
            subtract 5 − UserPicksUp from MatchesLeft
until MatchesLeft = 0
display "I won, ha ha!"

END OF 21 Matches
```

It is quite straightforward to turn this into a complete Pascal program. Think first about what variables the program needs. Just two `integer` variables: `MatchesLeft` and `UserPicksUp`. The steps in the algorithm correspond closely with statements in Pascal. The code is on the next page.

```
program Matches(input, output);

{  Programmer: Tom Moore                                        }

{  This program plays the game of 21 Matches with a user.      }

var
   MatchesLeft, UserPicksUp : integer;
begin
   writeln('Welcome to the game of 21 Matches.  You and I are');
   writeln('going to see who''s the smartest.  There are 21 matches');
   writeln('on the table.  We will alternate picking up matches');
   writeln('until no matches are left.  Each time we have to pick');
   writeln('up between 1 and 4 matches.  The person who picks up');
   writeln('the last match loses.  I''ll even let you go first.');
   writeln;
   MatchesLeft := 21;
   repeat
     if MatchesLeft > 1
       then
          write('There are ', MatchesLeft : 1, ' matches left, how many ')
       else
          write('There is only 1 match left, how many ');
     write('do you pick up?  ');
     readln(UserPicksUp);
     if (UserPicksUp < 1) or ( UserPicksUp > 4) or
                                  (UserPicksUp > MatchesLeft)
        then
          repeat
            writeln('Sorry, you must choose between 1 and 4 matches');
            writeln('but not more than ', MatchesLeft : 1, ' match(es).');
            write('Try again:  ');
            readln(UserPicksUp)
          until (1 <= UserPicksUp) and (UserPicksUp <= 4)
                             and (UserPicksUp <= MatchesLeft);
     MatchesLeft := MatchesLeft - UserPicksUp;
     if MatchesLeft > 0
       then
          begin
            writeln('I pick up ', 5 - UserPicksUp : 1, ' match(es).');
            MatchesLeft := MatchesLeft - (5 - UserPicksUp)
          end
   until MatchesLeft = 0;
   writeln('I won, ha ha!')
end.
```

You should notice that we made some small changes to the code so that it displayed things in good English. It didn't look right to have the computer say, "There are 1 matches left, how many do you pick up?" so we fixed it slightly. Realize that this is normal; it is often the case that details like this have to be handled when the code is written.

Warning About Missing *compound statements*

Take careful notice of the place where we had to use a ⟨compound statement⟩. Perhaps the biggest single mistake made by beginning Pascal programmers is the failure to turn multiple steps in an algorithm into one ⟨compound statement⟩ in a program. One reason this is so important is because sometimes the resulting code looks right and contains no syntax errors but just doesn't do what it's supposed to do. Consider the last few lines of the above program. If you carelessly left off the **begin** and **end**, and typed instead:

```
        . . .
      if MatchesLeft > 0
        then
          writeln('I pick up ', 5 - UserPicksUp : 1, ' match(es).');
          MatchesLeft := MatchesLeft - (5 - UserPicksUp)
      until MatchesLeft = 0;
    writeln('I won, ha ha!')
  end.
```

The resulting code is free of syntax errors and it looks "right" but it doesn't work! Regardless of what you intended, and regardless of how you indented the program, the compiler will treat this as if you had intended:

```
        . . .
      if MatchesLeft > 0
        then
          writeln('I pick up ', 5 - UserPicksUp : 1, ' match(es).');
      MatchesLeft := MatchesLeft - (5 - UserPicksUp)
      until MatchesLeft = 0;
    writeln('I won, ha ha!')
  end.
```

Think about what happens when the user picks up the last match. When this match is picked up, `MatchesLeft` will equal 0 and the test, `Matches Left > 0` will be false, so the statement:

```
      writeln('I pick up ', 5 - UserPicksUp : 1, ' match(es).')
```

will not be executed.

However, the statement:

```
MatchesLeft := MatchesLeft - (5 - UserPicksUp)
```

will be executed. Thus, `MatchesLeft` will get changed to −4. The loop will never end, since `MatchesLeft` will never equal 0, and, regardless of what the user enters next, it will never be both bigger than 0 and smaller than −4; the program will get stuck in an infinite loop.

The moral to this story is: be very careful to always turn more than one step into a single ⟨*compound statement*⟩ whenever you construct the statement that follows the word `then` or the word `else`.

4.17   Summary and Review

- In this chapter we began looking at the syntax of Pascal. We used the problems and algorithms from the previous chapter as examples of a program to implement. We started by looking at the syntax of a program as a whole. We introduced the concept of a ⟨*block*⟩ and the two parts it consists of: the ⟨*definition/declaration part*⟩ and the ⟨*statement part*⟩. We mentioned the several subparts of the ⟨*definition/declaration part*⟩but only discussed the ⟨*variable declaration part*⟩. Because we had not yet mentioned syntax diagrams when we first discussed them, we did not draw the syntax diagrams for a ⟨*block*⟩, the ⟨*definition/declaration part*⟩, the ⟨*variable declaration part*⟩ or the ⟨*statement part*⟩. A complete collection of Pascal syntax diagrams can be found in appendix A.

- We introduced the concepts of data types and variables. We learned that Pascal is a *strongly typed* language, which means that each variable must have its type declared before it can be used and only things of the right data type can be stored in the variable.

- We learned that Pascal has four simple supplied data types: `real`, `integer`, `char` and `Boolean`. The types `real` and `integer` are numeric types; `char` is used to hold characters; and `Boolean` variables can be either `true` or `false`.

- We worked on the ⟨*statement part*⟩ of a program and learned that every Pascal program must have a ⟨*statement part*⟩, which consists of a collection of statements surrounded by the reserved words `begin` and `end`.

- We started working with syntax diagrams in order to explain the rules of syntax for Pascal.

- In order to implement the algorithm, we learned how to implement each of the fundamental ideas introduced in chapter 3. In particular, we learned about the following statements:

The ⟨*assignment statement*⟩ is used to implement the concept of assignment.

The ⟨*write statement*⟩ is used for output.

The ⟨*read statement*⟩ is used for input.

The ⟨*if statement*⟩ is used for selection.

The ⟨*repeat statement*⟩ is one of three Pascal statements used for looping.

- We discussed white space and indentation, and introduced the notion of inserting comments in a Pascal program to improve its readability and make it easier for others to understand.

- We included a complete Pascal program that serves as an implementation of the guessing game algorithm from chapter 3.

- We implemented the algorithm for the "21 Matches" game from chapter 3.

- We saw how dangerous it can be if a programmer forgets to include a ⟨*compound statement*⟩ when the **then** part of an ⟨*if statement*⟩ is supposed to contain several statements.

4.18   New Terms Introduced

ANSI The American National Standards Institute.

apostrophe image Two apostrophes; used to force Pascal to display one apostrophe.

assignment statement The Pascal statement used to implement the concept of assignment.

block The ⟨*definition/declaration part*⟩ and the ⟨*statement part*⟩.

Boolean A supplied type in Pascal representing a truth value, i.e., either **true** or **false**.

Boolean expression An expression that has a value of either **true** or **false**.

Boolean operators The logical operators: **and**, **or** and **not**.

char A supplied type in Pascal that represents a single character.

comments Information written into a Pascal program that serves as documentation but is treated by the compiler as white space.

compound statement The Pascal statement used where one statement is required by the syntax but more than one statement is desired by the programmer.

data types Every variable in a Pascal program must be of a certain data type. The supplied types in Pascal are `real`, `integer`, `Boolean` and `char`.

definition/declaration part The part of a ⟨*block*⟩ where things are defined and declared.

div The Pascal operator for integer division that yields the quotient.

field-width indicator An `integer` expression (or expressions) used to set the minimum number of spaces to use to display a value.

file A collection of data; often stored in a computer's permanent memory. In Pascal, the source of data entering the program and the destination for data being output by the program.

identifier A valid Pascal name for something.

IEEE The Institute of Electrical and Electronic Engineers, Inc.

if statement The Pascal statement used for the concept of selection.

integer A supplied type in Pascal representing a number much like an integer in mathematics.

maxint The largest `integer` in Pascal; can vary from compiler to compiler.

mod The Pascal operator for integer division that yields the remainder.

Pascal Standard The document that defines Standard Pascal.

precedence Rules in Pascal that indicate which operator to apply first.

read statement The Pascal statement used for input.

real A supplied type in Pascal representing a number much like a decimal in mathematics.

repeat statement The Pascal statement used for the concept of repetition.

reserved word A Pascal word that cannot be used by a programmer as an identifier.

scientific notation A method of expressing a `real` value by using a value times a power of ten.

Standard Pascal The Pascal language as defined by ANSI and IEEE.

statement Each ⟨*statement*⟩ in a Pascal program becomes one instruction to the computer. Statements often contain other statements.

statement part The part of a ⟨*block*⟩ where the statements are placed.

strongly typed Every variable must have its data type declared and only values of that type may be stored in the variable.

syntax diagram A graphical method of defining and explaining the syntax of Pascal.

variable declaration part The part of the ⟨*definition/declaration part*⟩ where variables are declared.

white space That portion of a Pascal program ignored by the compiler; includes extra spaces, tab characters and comments.

write statement The Pascal statement used for output.

4.19   Exercises

1. Define the term *skizmo* by the following syntax diagram:

skizmo:

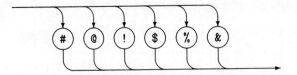

Draw a syntax diagram for a *twiddle*, which consists of one *letter*, then any number of *digits*, followed optionally by a *skizmo* at the end.

Which of the following would be syntactically legal *twiddles*?

    (a) c3456

    (b) Z0$

    (c) 5%

    (d) P!

    (e) abc123#!

    (f) W0123456789%

2. Consider the following syntax diagram for a *whizbang*, where *skizmo* is defined as in the previous problem:

whizbang:

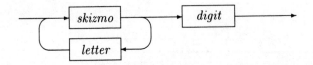

Which of the following would be syntactically legal *whizbangs*?

    (a) $5

    (b) #a5

    (c) a#5

    (d) %P8

    (e) @1B%9

    (f) &N#M@6

3. Determine which of the following are valid Pascal identifiers:

   (a) Pascal

   (b) ProgramName

   (c) Hourly Wage

   (d) x

   (e) Begin

   (f) 123go

   (g) Over30

   (h) Supercalifragilisticexpialidotious

4. It was mentioned in the text that some compilers only look at the first eight characters of an ⟨*identifier*⟩. This would mean, for example, that AvailableSpace and AvailableTime would be treated as the same ⟨*identifier*⟩ by this compiler. Write a simple program that would test this feature for your compiler. What kind of error will your program generate— syntax, run-time or logic—if the compiler used only looks at the first eight characters of an ⟨*identifier*⟩?

5. Assume that each variable in the program segments below is of type integer. What will be the output of each segment?

   (a)
   ```
   First := 4;
   Last  := 18;
   First := First + Last;
   writeln('First is ', First:1);
   writeln('Last is ', Last:1)
   ```

   (b)
   ```
   Num := 1;
   Num := 5;
   Num := Num * Num;
   writeln('The number is ', Num:1)
   ```

   (c)
   ```
   This     := 25;
   That     := 13;
   TheOther := This mod That;
   TheOther := TheOther div 2;
   writeln('The result is ',TheOther:1)
   ```

6. Write a simple program to determine the value of maxint used by your compiler.

7. Implement the following algorithm in a complete Pascal program:

START OF Compute Sum

display a message asking for the first integer
accept First
display a message asking for the second integer
accept Second
display "The sum of", First, "and", Second, "is", First + Second

END OF Compute Sum

Be sure to use field-width indicators and spaces where appropriate to make the output look nice.

8. Implement the algorithm of exercise 2, chapter 3, in a complete Pascal program.

9. Type in the guessing game program and run it. If you made the modifications to the algorithms suggested in the exercises in chapter 3, make the same modifications to the code.

10. In exercise 7, chapter 3, we redefined the "21 Matches" game to make it more fair for the user and more fun to play. Implement the algorithm you wrote there. Run the program and play against the computer. Are there other ways that you can make the game more interesting? How about changing the rules so that the player picking up the last match wins instead of loses?

11. Consider the following poorly formatted Pascal code. Rewrite the code using white space to make it more readable.

```
program Bigger(input, output); var Num1, Num2 : integer; begin
write('Enter an integer: '); readln(Num1); write(
'Enter another integer: '); readln(Num2); if Num1 > Num2 then
writeln(Num1:1,' is bigger than ',Num2:1) else if Num1 < Num2
then writeln(Num2:1,' is bigger than ',Num1:1) else writeln(
Num1:1,' and ',Num2:1,' are equal') end.
```

How many statements are there in the ⟨*statement part*⟩ of the program?

12. Write a program that will prompt the user to enter an integer and indicate to the user whether it was even or odd. The program will continue asking for numbers until the user enters a zero. (You should use div or mod to determine whether an integer is even or odd.) Write an algorithm first,

then write a complete Pascal program. Your program should have "nice looking" output. It should display the number entered by the user and a complete English sentence indicating whether the number entered was even or odd.

13. Write a program that will determine what combination of coins a cashier should give to a customer to add up to a given amount (under \$1). For example, if the amount is 84 cents, the output would be:

```
Quarters: 3
Dimes:    0
Nickels:  1
Pennies:  4
```

Solve the problem using div and mod, write an algorithm, and write the code in Pascal.

Chapter 5

Modular Programming

> The great king Alexander happened along
> Diogenes the cynic one day as Diogenes was drawing in the
> sand. Alexander said, "Ask of me any boon that you will."
> Diogenes replied, "Stand a little out of my sun."
> — Plutarch

5.1 Overview of the Chapter

This chapter begins our discussion of modular programming; i.e., programming with modules. We will discuss the nature of modular programming and the way that modules communicate with each other via parameters. We will introduce the words that will be used in our algorithmic language for modular programming, and we introduce a new kind of loop, the *loop while*.

5.2 Introduction

The terms *modular programming* and *top-down programming* refer to a proven effective method of problem solving. Rather than trying to solve the problem as a whole by writing instructions at the computer's lowest level, the idea is to see the problem as a set of smaller problems and break each of these into a set of yet smaller problems. This process continues until the current problem can be solved with whatever basic instructions the language in question provides. The solution to one of the smaller problems is called a *module* or *subroutine*.

Modular programming is one of the fundamental concepts of programming. From this point on, we will use this method to solve our problems.

Some computer languages are better than others at supporting modular programming. Pascal is one of the best languages for modular programming; in fact, Pascal was specifically designed for modular programming and that's why we use it in this book.

115

Let's think back on the problem we solved in the previous chapter. We could have used a top-down approach there—but didn't, simply because we didn't want to try to introduce too many concepts all at one time. A modular solution to the guessing game problem could have been stated:

1. display an introduction for the user,
2. let the user think of a number,
3. let the computer try to guess the user's number until it guesses it right, and
4. display the appropriate summary.

We could then have worked on each of these subproblems separately and then put them all together as the solution to the main problem.

We'll not take the time to go back and rewrite the previous algorithm and program. Instead, let's look at a new problem. We will state the problem, discuss the refinement of the problem definition, solve the problem with a top-down approach, and develop a collection of algorithms for the modules.

5.3   Define the Problem

This is our first statement of the problem:

Write a program that displays a fraction as a mixed number.

This is not the most exciting problem in the world but it will serve as an example of the things we are discussing. The idea is to have the program take a fraction like 8/3 and display it as a mixed number, namely:

2 & 2/3.

The fraction will have to come from somewhere; the easiest way to produce a fraction is to let the user enter it. Thus, our problem can be restated:

Write a program that allows a user to enter a (possibly improper) fraction and displays it as a mixed number.

Another possibility arises. Suppose the user enters 15/6. Surely we will want the program to display the result in lowest terms; i.e., we will want the program to reduce the fraction and display:

2 & 1/2.

With this in mind, the statement of the problem becomes:

Write a program that allows a user to enter a fraction (as an improper fraction, if desired), reduces the fraction to lowest terms, and displays it as a mixed number.

This completes step 1. We can proceed to solving the problem.

5.4 Solve the Problem

The major point of this chapter is that problems can be solved by breaking them up into modules. Let's look at our problem from a top-down perspective. What we want to do is to get some information from the user, process that information and display the result. More specifically, we want to let the user enter a fraction, have the program reduce the fraction to lowest terms and display the result as a mixed number.

At some point we remember that this is an interactive program and thus should contain an introduction, to tell the user what the program is going to do, and some sort of conclusion, to indicate that the program is finished. Then, our solution becomes:

> First, have the computer display an introduction for the user to read, then let the user enter a fraction, next get the computer to reduce the fraction to lowest terms, then make the computer display the fraction as a mixed number, and finally, display a conclusion.

That's it! We have found a top-level solution to the problem. Of course, we aren't done yet. We still have to look at the solution at a lower level, but we are surely on our way.

We are ready to look at the solution from a top-down viewpoint. We can take our top-level solution and break it into smaller pieces, each of which becomes a subproblem. Each of the subproblems can be worked on independently of the rest. If we look at the solution above, we can identify several subproblems:

- the subproblem of displaying the introduction for the user,

- the subproblem of getting a fraction from the user,

- the subproblem of reducing a fraction to lowest terms,

- the subproblem of displaying a given fraction in lowest terms as a mixed number, and

- the subproblem of displaying a conclusion.

We can concentrate on each of these smaller problems and solve them independently, without being forced to think about the problem as a whole all the time. It should be stressed that *independent* subproblems are important. If you fail to make the subproblems and their solutions independent of one another, you still have to think about the entire problem all the time instead of being able to concentrate on each subproblem. From now on we will think of the solution to a subproblem as a *module*. Rather than continue to refer to the subproblems, we will start referring to the modules that solve them.

It is also important that you write your modules in such a way that other modules have no need of knowing *how* one module gets its job done. The other modules should only have to know *what* the job is that the module does. This is called *procedural abstraction*.

Communication Between Modules

While we say that modules should be independent of each other, we do not mean that there is no communication between them. It is necessary that they be able to send information back and forth. In this sense, modules are not completely independent. It is normal for modules to work on and share data. That is the next topic for discussion.

As one subroutine is doing its job, it can become necessary for another subroutine to get involved. Module A doing its job, for example, might include having modules B, C and D do something. When one module invokes another, we say that the first module is *calling* the second. We will use the word *call* several times in this and subsequent chapters. It simply refers to this invocation of modules.

A Typical Company

To illustrate some of these points, consider a typical company with executives, secretaries, clerks, various departments, and so forth. If the company is big enough, each department might even have sections or sub-departments. Each of these departments and sub-departments is like a smaller company with its own specific purpose; the departments usually function independently. It is rare for someone to work in two different departments, and, for example, shipping clerks don't have to keep track of what purchasing agents are doing.

However, there is clearly a need for the departments to be able to communicate with each other. In a company this is usually done via such things as phones, memos and requisitions. We might imagine someone in one department saying, "Call shipping and ask them when this order was sent out."

Procedures vs. Functions

We should also introduce the words *procedure* and *function*. Procedures and functions are special kinds of modules. As we will see later in this chapter, some modules perform some sort of task, while others calculate and return a value. Modules that perform a task are called *procedures*, while modules that return values are called *functions*.

Parameters

In our algorithms, where each module has its own specific purpose, we say that one module may call another, and, in so doing, pass along or request information in the form of *parameters*.

We use the word *parameter* to indicate a piece of data that is sent from one module to another. Indeed, all of our modules will be called by other modules, so let's say that:

> A parameter is a data item that is passed between modules. Sometimes the data item is sent from one module to another, sometimes the data item is sent both ways and sometimes the data item is just sent back from the module being called.

We can, perhaps, make this clear by use of our current example. Consider the module that displays a fraction. In order for this module to do its job, the fraction will have to be sent to it. That is, the parameter being sent to the module displaying the fraction is the fraction itself.

In the case of the module that gets the fraction from the user, the parameter—the fraction—is being sent *back* from the module to the main program.

Finally, the fraction will have to be sent both *to* and *from* the module that does the job of reducing the fraction.

Since the data exist in both the calling routine and the called routine, we often need to be able to distinguish between the parameter in the calling routine and the corresponding parameter in the called routine. We will refer to the parameters in the *calling* routine as *actual parameters*, and the parameters in the *called* routine as *formal parameters*.

Parameter Passing

In order to accomplish these three ways of passing data between routines— (1) to a routine, (2) to and from a routine, and (3) just from a routine— it is necessary to distinguish between two methods of passing parameters. Sometimes we send the actual parameters themselves and sometimes we send copies of the actual parameters.

A Typical Company—Revisited

Using the example of a large company we discussed earlier, consider the following situation:

Suppose that the head of the accounting department discovers an error on her ledger. She might give the ledger to one of her accountants and ask him to recalculate the numbers (while she, say, goes to lunch). When she gets the ledger back from her assistant, she would expect the numbers on the ledger to be different.

On the other hand, suppose that she wants her assistant to recalculate the numbers, but that she wants to check his work before it's actually entered into the ledger. In this case she might give her assistant a photocopy of the ledger sheet and have him do his work on the copy, while keeping the original in her office.

Pass by Value and Pass by Reference

As we will see, often copies of data will do, while sometimes the actual data themselves must be sent. In the jargon of computer science, when copies of the actual parameters are being sent, the parameters are said to be *passed by value*. When the actual parameters themselves are being sent, the parameters are said to be *passed by reference*. You will also see these referred to as a *call by value* and a *call by reference*, respectively.

When a parameter is *passed by value*, the compiler will prepare a special place in memory for the parameter. The actual parameter—the parameter in the calling routine—will be evaluated and the value placed in this special location. The subroutine uses (and, perhaps, changes) the value in this temporary location. When the subroutine is exited, this memory location is returned to the storehouse of available memory and its contents are lost. Meanwhile, the value of the actual parameter has not changed.

On the other hand, if the parameter is passed by reference, the value of the parameter is not placed in a temporary location. Instead, the location in memory of the actual parameter—its address—is sent to the subroutine. Thus, a *reference* to the actual parameter is being sent; hence the term *pass by reference*. There are other schemes for passing parameters that are used in other languages, but these two schemes seem to be the ones that the majority of computer languages are using today.

Solving the Fraction Problem with Modules

It becomes very important to think about the parameters being used and to make a careful decision as to whether the parameters should be passed by value or passed by reference. Let's go back to our current problem and think about the parameters some more.

The "solution" to the problem stated above will become the main program. The modules—subroutines—that are being called are:

1. A module that displays an introduction for the user

2. A module that gets a fraction from the user

3. A module that reduces a fraction

4. A module that displays a reduced fraction

5. A module that displays a conclusion

The Module Names and Parameters

The first module requires no parameters and consists only of a collection of steps that display an introduction. Let's call the module *Introduce*.

Let's call the second module *GetFraction*. If *GetFraction* is going to get a fraction from the user and send it back to the main program, the main program must have a place to put the fraction. When *GetFraction* is called, the location of the fraction in memory will be sent to the module and the module will fill in the data with whatever the user enters. It should be clear that it will not do to send a copy of the fraction to this module. We will have to send the *address* of the fraction so that the data at this address can be filled with the data entered by the user. In other words, this parameter will have to be *passed by reference*.

Let's call the third module *Reduce*. *Reduce* will take the fraction's numerator and denominator, reduce them to lowest terms and send the fraction back. Since it needs to come back changed, it will not suffice to send a copy of the fraction; once again, the fraction will have to be passed by reference.

Let's call the fourth module *DisplayFraction*. Since this module is not going to change the fraction—just display it—the fraction sent to *DisplayFraction* could be a copy of the actual fraction and therefore will be *passed by value*.

The last module is much like the first; it does nothing but print messages on the screen for the user and it requires no parameters. We'll call it *Conclude*.

It is time to make things more formal and to start developing ways of handling these ideas in our algorithmic language.

The Module *Introduce*

Since *Introduce* requires no parameters, we can simply write it as a separate algorithm. Rather than try to write the entire introduction while we are working on the algorithm, we may just want to indicate that an introduction will be displayed. The actual introduction can be written when we get to the coding step. Thus, for *Introduce*, we can just write:

```
START OF Introduce

display an introduction to the program for the user

END OF Introduce
```

The Module *GetFraction*

Turning to *GetFraction*, we have to develop some way of indicating what the parameters are and whether they are passed by value or by reference. The only parameter for *GetFraction* is the user's fraction. The job of *GetFraction* is to allow the user to supply values for the numerator and denominator of the fraction. As we indicated above, it will make no sense to send a copy of the fraction to this subroutine; it only makes sense to send the location of the fraction itself. Therefore, it needs to be passed by reference.

As far as our algorithms are concerned, let's agree on the following conventions: when we develop an algorithm for a subroutine, we will indicate the names of the parameters (if any) in parentheses after the name of the module, and will indicate on the next lines whether they are passed by value or passed by reference. Thus we will start the algorithm for *GetFraction* by:

```
START OF GetFraction(Fraction)
Passed by value: none
Passed by reference: Fraction
    :
END OF GetFraction
```

We may as well go ahead and complete this algorithm since we know what we want to have done. It amounts to prompting the user for the numerator and denominator, and allowing the user to type in his or her choices. There is one detail that has to be considered, though: since we are talking about fractions, we must be sure that we end up with a valid fraction; the denominator must not be equal to zero. With this in mind, our algorithm could look like:

```
START OF GetFraction(Fraction)
Passed by value: none
Passed by reference: Fraction

display "Enter the numerator of the fraction."
accept Numerator
display "Enter the denominator of the fraction."
accept Denominator
if Denominator equals zero
    then
        loop
            display "You must enter a non-zero integer. Try again."
            accept Denominator
            until Denominator is not equal to zero

END OF GetFraction
```

The Module *Reduce*

Now let's turn to the routine *Reduce*. How do we reduce a fraction? Simple; just divide the numerator and denominator by the largest positive integer that divides evenly into both the numerator and denominator. In mathematics, this integer is called the greatest common divisor, abbreviated "gcd." To reduce a fraction, divide the numerator and denominator by their gcd. That sounds simple, but we do have to be careful.

In the first place, we don't know how to find the gcd. That's okay, we can put that off till later. That's the beauty of modular programming; we don't have to worry about how to find the gcd of two integers *now*. That will become another module that we can work on after we finish this one.

It is necessary, though, to be a bit cautious about how the gcd might be defined. Different mathematical definitions exist for gcd and we don't want to get off track and worry a lot about mathematics. Let's assume that we can find the gcd of any two positive integers, and negative and zero integers *cannot* be sent to the gcd module. This means that inside *Reduce* we will have to make certain that the values we send to a gcd module are positive. That won't present a problem as long as we are careful. It is not necessary to use gcd to reduce a fraction whose numerator is zero.

It should be noticed that *Reduce* has several cases to work with. Sometimes the numerator might be zero, sometimes the fraction might have a negative numerator or a negative denominator, or both. We have to make some decisions about what the result of *Reduce* should be in each of these cases.

Suppose, for example, that the numerator is zero and the denominator is 13. How should we reduce 0/13? It doesn't matter what the denominator is if the numerator is zero; the value of the fraction is zero. Since the fraction is then an integer, and since integers are fractions with a denominator equal to 1, a good answer to this question would be to simply change the denominator to 1 any time the numerator equals zero.

How about −6/8? Clearly, it should be reduced to −3/4, but where should the minus sign be put? We don't have a special place to put the sign. Either the numerator has to be negative, or the denominator has to be negative. It's easier to work with negative fractions if the minus sign is in the numerator, so let's decide that any time the resulting fraction is negative, we'll put the minus sign in the numerator and keep the denominator positive.

How about the parameters to *Reduce*? What do we send? The fraction, of course. Should it be passed by value or by reference?

We indicated earlier how the fraction should be sent, but here we'll introduce a simple test that will always tell us whether a parameter is to be passed by value or by reference. The test consists of asking two questions about each parameter:

1. Is the value of the parameter going to change inside the subroutine?

If the answer to the first question is "no," then you don't even have to ask the second question—just pass the parameter by value. If the answer to the first question is "yes," then ask the second question:

2. Should the changed value be sent back to the calling routine?

If the answer to this question is "no," then pass the parameter by value. If the answer is "yes," pass it by reference. In other words, pass the parameter by value if the answer to either question is "no," and pass it by reference only if the answers to both questions are "yes."

Let's use our test on the parameter to *Reduce*. Ask the first question: Is the value of the fraction going to change inside *Reduce*? The answer, in general, is "yes." That's the whole point, to change the numerator and denominator so that the fraction is reduced. So ask the second question: Do we want the changed value sent back to the calling routine? Again, "yes"—that's what *Reduce* is supposed to do: change the fraction and send it back changed. Therefore, we need to pass the fraction by reference.

One more point should be made before we write the algorithm. We have indicated that the procedure *Reduce* will not work if the denominator of the fraction sent to it equals zero. It is important to make note of such conditions, both in our algorithms and in our code, since if we later use the algorithm, we cannot afford to forget the assumptions about the parameters. We call such conditions *preconditions*, and will always indicate what the preconditions are, if any, when we write an algorithm.

Similarly, most of our procedures will have *postconditions* as well as preconditions. A postcondition is a condition that the algorithm is to guarantee. For *Reduce*, the postconditions are: (1) that the fraction is reduced to lowest terms, (2) if the fraction is negative, the sign has been put in the numerator, and (3) if the fraction equals zero, the denominator is set to 1.

It is the responsibility of the programmer to write the routine in such as way that whenever the preconditions are satisfied, the postconditions are guaranteed. We aren't going to get into it at this point, but this is the essence of what is required to prove that an algorithm is correct. The programmer has to be able to *prove* a statement that says, "if these preconditions hold, then these postconditions will follow." When you get into proving the correctness of algorithms, you get close to the field of logic and mathematics.

Notice below how we indicate the preconditions and postconditions in the algorithm.

Here is an algorithm for *Reduce*:

```
START OF Reduce(Fraction)
Passed by value: none
Passed by reference: Fraction
Precondition(s): Denominator ≠ 0
Postconditions(s): The fraction is reduced and Denominator > 0

if Numerator = 0
   then
       store 1 in Denominator
   else
       determine whether the fraction is positive or negative
       store |Numerator| in Numerator
       store |Denominator| in Denominator
       find the gcd of Numerator and Denominator
       divide Numerator by the gcd
       divide Denominator by the gcd
       if the fraction is negative
          then
              multiply Numerator by -1

END OF Reduce
```

That completes the algorithm for *Reduce*. Notice that we are using $|x|$ for the absolute value of x.

Functions and the Module GCD

Before we work on *DisplayFraction*, let's look at the module GCD. We need a module that calculates the greatest common divisor of two positive integers.

There's something different about GCD. The other modules we have worked on have each had some sort of task that they accomplish. A module for a gcd will sure enough accomplish a task, but in addition it will send back a particular value. Modules that return single values are different from modules that perform tasks. Modules that return single values are called *functions*. We need to discuss functions before we write GCD.

Functions

The difference between functions and procedures is very important. Before we go on, let's review what we said earlier for emphasis:

- A *procedure* is a subroutine that performs a task.

- A *function* is a subroutine that returns a single value.

It will be your responsibility as a programmer to look at a situation that calls for a subroutine and decide whether that subroutine should be written as a procedure or as a function. Sometimes it's a close call; sometimes you can write it either way.

The way to decide is to ask yourself, "Does this subroutine return a value?" Or, better, "Is it the main job of this subroutine to return a single value?" If the answer is "yes," then the subroutine should probably be written as a function and not as a procedure.

You will notice that when we choose a name for a subroutine we choose a name that indicates the type of subroutine we are writing. When we name a procedure, the name we choose will be a verb, or will sound like it does something. The names we choose for functions will be nouns, because functions are treated as values. This will greatly help the readability of our algorithms and programs.

We need to introduce some notation for an algorithm for a function. Before introducing the notation we'll use, we need to discuss *side effects*. As with procedures, data often need to be sent to functions. Functions have parameters and we will allow for passing parameters to a function. However, it is a bad idea to pass data by reference to a function. Passing a parameter to a function by reference results in what's called a *side effect*. Side effects should be avoided. When a function is called, the calling routine uses the value returned by the function, but if the function has a side effect, something besides this value gets changed. It is usually the case that this extra change is hard to see by looking just at the calling routine, and as a result, the side effect can be very hard to trace. If you are looking for a bug in a program or trying to follow the flow of the program, you cannot look just at the returned value. You also have to keep track of the side effect, which can be very hard to do.

While there are exceptions to this rule, for now it's best to remember:

Don't pass parameters by reference to a function!

Since a function always has a value, in an algorithm for a function, we will always use the word *return* to indicate what value is supposed to be returned by the function. It should always be obvious from the context of the subroutine—and from the name of the subroutine, if we are careful in our choice of a name—whether a subroutine is a function or a procedure. In case of doubt, the presence (or absence) of the word *return* will always make it clear.

GCD

Let's work on the module GCD. The gcd of two positive integers is the largest positive integer that divides evenly into both of the numbers. For example, the gcd of 20 and 28 is 4 since 4 divides evenly into both 20 and 28 and since no larger number divides both of them.

What is the gcd of 132 and 342? Work on it; what do you get? You should be able to determine the answer. It's 6. How did you get 6? Just by examination? Trial and error? Neither of these methods is useful to us. We need an algorithm that will determine the gcd of two integers.

It is likely that someone new to computer programming would try to solve this problem by factoring the two numbers and then searching for common factors, such as:

$$132 = 2 \times 2 \times 3 \times 11$$
$$342 = 2 \times 3 \times 3 \times 19$$

The gcd is 2×3 because those are the factors common to both integers.

It turns out that this is not an efficient way to have the computer find the gcd, despite the fact that you were taught to do it that way in grade school. A much better way (at least for our purposes) was discovered by Euclid centuries ago, called the Euclidean algorithm. We won't attempt to prove that it works—that can be left for your math class—we'll just use it.

To start, you divide the larger number by the smaller and look at the remainder. If the remainder is zero, then the smaller number is the gcd. If not, then divide the remainder into the smaller number and examine the new remainder. If this remainder is zero, the previous remainder is the gcd. If not, then divide the newer remainder into the previous remainder and find yet another remainder; continue until a zero remainder is found. The last non-zero remainder is the gcd. Let's try this on a couple of examples before we try to write it as an algorithm.

The remainder of 28 divided by 20 is 8. That's not zero so divide 20 by 8. The remainder is 4, which is not zero. Divide 8 by 4 and the remainder is zero, so the last non-zero remainder, 4, is the gcd. Sure enough, the gcd of 28 and 20 is 4.

This is going to be easier to see if we make up a list of values, like:

$$
\begin{array}{ccc}
28 & 20 & 8 \\
20 & 8 & 4 \\
8 & 4 & 0
\end{array}
$$

As soon as we get a zero, the number just above the zero is the gcd.

Try it with 342 and 132:

First	Second	Remainder	
342	132	78	(78 is the remainder of $342 \div 132$)
132	78	54	(54 is the remainder of $132 \div 78$)
78	54	24	(24 is the remainder of $78 \div 54$)
54	24	6	(6 is the remainder of $54 \div 24$)
24	6	0	(0 is the remainder of $24 \div 6$)

Sure enough, the last non-zero remainder is 6, and, as we saw, the gcd of 342 and 132 is 6.

One more time; what is the gcd of 6230 and 1652? Try it yourself using the Euclidean algorithm before you read on.

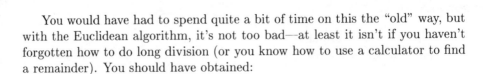

You would have had to spend quite a bit of time on this the "old" way, but with the Euclidean algorithm, it's not too bad—at least it isn't if you haven't forgotten how to do long division (or you know how to use a calculator to find a remainder). You should have obtained:

First	Second	Remainder	
6230	1652	1274	($6230 \div 1652$ has a remainder of 1274)
1652	1274	378	($1652 \div 1274$ has a remainder of 378)
1274	378	140	($1274 \div 378$ has a remainder of 140)
378	140	98	($378 \div 140$ has a remainder of 98)
140	98	42	($140 \div 98$ has a remainder of 42)
98	42	14	($98 \div 42$ has a remainder of 14)
42	14	0	($42 \div 14$ has a remainder of 0)

The gcd of 6230 and 1652 is 14.

Now, how do we turn this into an algorithm? The lists help; notice that we labeled the first column *First*, the second column *Second* and the third *Remainder*. It should be clear that we can use variables to represent the numbers in each column. Let's simply call the variables *First*, *Second* and *Remainder*. We see that *First* and *Second* keep changing until *Remainder* becomes 0. The old value of *Second* becomes the new value of *First*, the old value of *Remainder* becomes the new value of *Second*, and *Remainder* is recalculated.

The *loop while*

Obviously this is a loop. But, it is a different kind of loop than the *loop until* we introduced in chapter 3. The *loop until* has the property that the steps in the body of the loop are executed, a test is made, and the steps are executed again if the test if *false*. This means that the steps in the body of the loop are always executed at least once before the test is made.

That seems reasonable enough at first glance but we have to be more careful than that in our current situation. We have to realize that sometimes we don't want to execute the steps in the body of the loop at all. Consider, for example what would happen if the values of *First* and *Second* were 12 and 4, respectively. Then, if we assume the steps in the loop are executed at least once, the remainder of *First* divided by *Second* (namely 0) would be calculated and stored in *Remainder*; the value of *Second* would be stored in *First*, the remainder of the new *First* divided by the new *Second* would be calculated and stored in *Remainder* and then if that value is non-zero, we do it all again. But, since 12 is evenly divisible by 4, the first remainder equals zero and we do not want to move the value of *Second* to *First* even once. In fact, if we did execute the steps we just described, we would attempt to divide 4 by zero, and the program would crash.

What we need is another kind of loop; a loop such that the body of the loop *might* not get executed at all. Such a loop is called a *loop while*. Figure 5.1 contains a flowchart for a *loop while*.

Compare this flowchart with the one in chapter 3 for a *loop until*. Notice that here the test is at the top of the loop. With a *loop while*, unlike the *loop until*, we test first and then decide whether or not to go through the loop. Also, notice that we go through the steps in the body of the loop if the condition tests *true*! With the *loop until*, we stay in the loop *until* the test is *true*; with the *loop while*, we stay in the loop *while* the test is *true*.

Before we return to writing *GCD*, we should mention that the loop used earlier in the algorithm for *GetFraction* is actually a *loop while* and we would have used a *loop while* if we had introduced the concept by that time. You should modify the algorithm presented there to use a *loop while*.

GCD Continued

Now, using the *loop while*, we can write the *GCD* function.

```
store the remainder of First ÷ Second in Remainder
loop while Remainder is not zero
    store Second in First
    store Remainder in Second
    store the remainder of First ÷ Second in Remainder
return the last non-zero value of Remainder
```

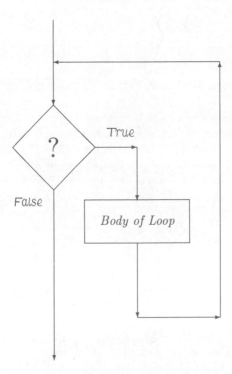

Figure 5.1 Flowchart for a *loop while*

But wait—how can we return the last non-zero value of *Remainder*? That value has been overwritten by the 0—or we would still be in the loop. That looks like a problem; maybe we will have to save the old *Remainder* in another variable. Think about this and see if you can find a solution before you read on.

Look at the lists on page 128. The last non-zero value of *Remainder* is now stored in *Second*. We can simply return the value stored in *Second*. After adding that, the function looks like:

```
store the remainder of First ÷ Second in Remainder
loop while Remainder is not zero
    store Second in First
    store Remainder in Second
    store the remainder of First ÷ Second in Remainder
return the value stored in Second
```

It's a good idea to take a moment and think about what we have. Is it going to work in all cases? We shouldn't just go on to something else without checking our algorithm. One good way to check an algorithm is to send it some numbers and make sure it works. We tried 28 and 20, we tried 342 and 132, and we tried 6230 and 1652.

Are there other numbers that should be tried? You should always test special cases. We didn't try something that will cause the loop to be skipped. Try 100 and 25. What is the gcd of 100 and 25? It's 25, right? If we send 100 and 25 to GCD, the first *Remainder* that is calculated equals 0, and so, the loop is skipped entirely, and the value returned is the value stored in *Second*, namely, 25. So everything looks fine so far.

What would happen if we sent it 25 for *First* and 100 for *Second*? As we said earlier, we start by dividing the *larger* number by the smaller. If we want to do just what the algorithm says, we had better check to make sure that *First* is not smaller than *Second*; if so, swap them around. That's an easy fix, just add an *if ... then* at the beginning that will swap the two values when necessary.

What happens if we send a zero or negative value for *First* or *Second*? That's not quite as easy to fix. In fact, we probably don't want to "fix" the algorithm to handle zero or negative values at all. It's better to have the routine that calls this function watch out for this situation. Recall that when we wrote *Reduce*, we agreed to be careful not to send zero or negative values to GCD. Indeed, we must not forget that we are assuming *First* and *Second* are always positive. This requirement is another example of what we call *preconditions*. As we did for *Reduce*, we list any preconditions in the algorithm itself.

Recall also that we said we will normally pass parameters by value to a function. Since the normal situation is to pass the parameters by value, we won't need to indicate how the parameters are being passed except in the rare case when we pass a parameter by reference.

With all this decided, we can finish the algorithm for GCD:

START OF GCD(First, Second)
Preconditions: First and Second are both positive integers

if First < Second
    then
        swap First and Second
store the remainder of First ÷ Second in Remainder
loop while Remainder is not zero
    store Second in First
    store Remainder in Second
    store the remainder of First ÷ Second in Remainder
return the value stored in Second

END OF GCD

Now that we have written GCD we will always have to be careful not to send it values that could cause it to crash. Whenever we call GCD we will check to make sure that we do not send it negative or zero values, just as we did in Reduce. This check will be put inside the calling routine. It's possible to put the check inside GCD for these cases but it's better and more efficient to do the checking on a higher level. This style of programming requires more discipline on the part of the programmer but it makes for better programs.

More On Loops

Before we go on, we should say a few more words about loops in general. It can be easily proved that we don't need both a loop until and a loop while. In fact, any algorithm you write using a loop while can be written using an if ... then and a loop until. Conversely, anything you can do with a loop until can be done with a loop while, an if ... then, and, maybe, an assignment. Some computer languages don't include both kinds of loops—some languages don't have either kind—but both kinds can usually be constructed using what the language provides. Pascal does have both kinds of loop implemented. We will use the loop while where it seems more natural and the loop until otherwise. We would use both even if Pascal did not implement them both. A programmer needs to be able to implement the algorithm in whatever language is chosen, but shouldn't worry about it until the coding step, which is step 4 of the FIVE + STEPS. When writing the algorithm, use whatever constructions make the intention clear.

The Module *DisplayFraction*

The next routine is *DisplayFraction*. First, the parameters: what has to be sent to *DisplayFraction*? Just the fraction. Should it be passed by value or passed by reference?

Rather than trying to remember what was said earlier about the parameters, let's use our test. Is the value of the fraction going to change inside the routine *DisplayFraction*? No, it is not; all the routine does is display something, it doesn't change anything. Conclusion: pass the fraction by value.

Next, are there any preconditions? Yes; we have already reduced the fraction and can take advantage of that in the routine that displays it.

Thus, the first lines of the routine *DisplayFraction* become:

```
START OF DisplayFraction(Fraction)
Passed by value: Fraction
Passed by reference: none
Preconditions: The fraction has been reduced to lowest terms
               and Denominator > 0

    :

END OF DisplayFraction
```

We will leave the completion of this algorithm as an exercise, but want to give some hints before we end the chapter.

To attack this problem, you should probably start by looking at several fractions and thinking about how you would display each one. Consider some examples: how would you display each of the following fractions?

$$2/3 \qquad 17/3 \qquad 0/1 \qquad -19/33 \qquad 25/1$$

$$12/12 \qquad 45/-8 \qquad 0/-13 \qquad -35/-7$$

But wait, that's not right. The last four examples cannot happen! Since we know the fraction has been reduced to lowest terms, we can't have a case where the fraction is not reduced or where the denominator is negative. With this in mind, consider different cases and see what you do to display the mixed number. Then put those cases where you do the same thing together. A little thought up front will make the algorithm easier.

You will need to make some sort of decision about how to display a number like $-20/3$. Should it be displayed:

```
-6 & 2/3
```

or should it be displayed:

```
-(6 & 2/3) ?
```

Which do you think looks better? Make a decision and implement it.

A good rule of thumb in working with situations where there are several cases is to take care of the easiest cases first and leave the hard cases for later. If you do this, the hard cases are often not so hard after all.

The Module *Conclude*

The final module that has to be written is the module that displays the conclusion for the user. This module may be nothing more than a single step displaying a message that says, "Thank you for using this program." What you want it to say depends a lot on the personality that you decide to give the computer. You could put the conclusion in the main program but it is a good idea to make it a module. This makes the entire main module a series of calls to subroutines, and the resulting program looks cleaner. We'll leave the *Conclude* module for you to write.

Invoking a Subroutine

We have seen that there are two kinds of subroutines: procedures and functions. We need to make some decisions about how each kind of routine can be invoked, or "called," by another routine.

In the case of a procedure, since a procedure performs a task, we'll simply agree to use the word *call* when we want to invoke a procedure. That is, when we want to invoke the procedure *Introduce*, we'll simply write:

```
call Introduce
```

as a step in our algorithm. If the procedure uses parameters, we'll indicate the actual parameters in parentheses. For example, this is how we would call *DisplayFraction*:

```
call DisplayFraction(Fraction)
```

This will work fine for procedures, how about functions? In the first place, we would *not* want to use the word *call* to indicate the invocation of a function. A function returns a single value and we have decided to use nouns as names of functions. It really would not make sense to say *call GCD*, for example, since *GCD* is a number. Instead, we'll just invoke a function by referring to it by name and treating it as a value. We only have one function in this chapter, *GCD*, so we can only list one example; we'll see more examples in chapter 7. The algorithm on the next page is a version of *Reduce* that calls *GCD*.

```
START OF Reduce(Fraction)
Passed by value: none
Passed by reference: Fraction
Precondition(s): Denominator ≠ 0
Postconditions(s): The fraction is reduced and Denominator > 0

if Numerator = 0
    then
        store 1 in Denominator
    else
        determine whether the fraction is positive or negative
        store |Numerator| in Numerator
        store |Denominator| in Denominator
        divide Numerator by GCD(Numerator, Denominator)
        divide Denominator by GCD(Numerator, Denominator)
        if the fraction is negative
            then
                multiply Numerator by -1

END OF Reduce
```

Notice that we are calling GCD by just using its name as a value.

5.5 The Main Program

Before we conclude this chapter we should make it clear that these modules we have written will be *called* from some higher-level module. This higher-level module—at least in this case—can be thought of as the main program. The algorithm for the main program, then, will look something like:

```
START OF Fraction

call Introduce
call GetFraction(Fraction)
call Reduce(Fraction)
call DisplayFraction(Fraction)
call Conclude

END OF Fraction
```

It is often the case that the main program is simply a series of subroutine calls reflecting the top-level solution to the problem.

5.6   Collected Algorithms

The following is a collection of the various algorithms developed in this chapter,
all in one place for easy reference:

START OF Fraction

call Introduce
call GetFraction(Fraction)
call Reduce(Fraction)
call DisplayFraction(Fraction)
call Conclude

END OF Fraction

START OF Introduce

display an introduction to the program for the user

END OF Introduce

START OF GetFraction(Fraction)
Passed by value: none
Passed by reference: Fraction

display "Enter the numerator of the fraction."
accept Numerator
display "Enter the denominator of the fraction."
accept Denominator
if Denominator equals zero
    then
        loop
            display "You must enter a non-zero integer. Try again."
            accept Denominator
            until Denominator is not equal to zero

END OF GetFraction

START OF Reduce(*Fraction*)
Passed by value: none
Passed by reference: Fraction
Precondition(s): Denominator ≠ 0
Postconditions(s): The fraction is reduced and Denominator > 0

if Numerator = 0
   then
      store 1 in Denominator
   else
      determine whether the fraction is positive or negative
      store |Numerator| in Numerator
      store |Denominator| in Denominator
      divide Numerator by GCD(Numerator, Denominator)
      divide Denominator by GCD(Numerator, Denominator)
      if the fraction is negative
         then
            multiply Numerator by -1

END OF Reduce

START OF GCD(*First, Second*)
Preconditions: First and Second are both positive integers

if First < *Second*
   then
      swap First and Second
store the remainder of First ÷ *Second in Remainder*
loop while Remainder is not zero
   store Second in First
   store Remainder in Second
   store the remainder of First ÷ *Second in Remainder*
 return the value stored in Second

END OF GCD

```
START OF DisplayFraction(Fraction)
Passed by value: Fraction
Passed by reference: none
Preconditions: The fraction has been reduced to lowest terms
               and Denominator > 0
   ⋮
END OF DisplayFraction



START OF Conclude
   ⋮
END OF Conclude
```

5.7   The Top-Down Method—Once Again

In this section we'll apply the top-down method to a different problem. We'll define the problem, solve the problem, and write an algorithm for the solution. We will again use modules to make our job easier.

Define the Problem

Let's imagine that two people are playing a game of Ping-Pong. The game is played to a score of 21, but a player must win by a margin of two. One player serves the first five points, the other player serves the next five, and so on. If the score is tied at 20, then the players alternate serving every point for the remainder of the game.

We are to write a program to help us keep score for a game of Ping-Pong. At the beginning of the game, the program should ask the user to enter the name of the player who is to serve first. After that, the program should display the score of the game and who is to serve next, and ask the user to enter the winner of the point. The program should continue until one of the players wins. When this happens, the program is to display the name of the winner and the final score of the game.

Solve the Problem

As usual, we start with a simplified, overall view of the solution. This is to be an interactive program, so it should display an introduction for the user, simulate the game of Ping-Pong, and display the winner and a conclusion. We can get a bit more specific and remember that we want the program to ask the user who is to serve first; this should be done at the start of the game. For simplicity, we'll call the players A and B. Here is the top-level solution to the problem:

> First, display an introduction for the user. Then ask the user who is to serve first. Simulate the game of Ping-Pong, and display the winner and a conclusion for the user.

Write an Algorithm for the Solution

It's easy to see how this top-level solution can be broken down into subproblems; you're probably already thinking of their names:

Introduce
GetFirstServer
PlayGame
DisplayWinner
Conclude

are the ones we'll use. Since *Introduce* and *Conclude* simply display information for the user, we can leave them for the coding step. This means that we have three modules to consider: *GetFirstServer*, *PlayGame* and *DisplayWinner*.

The job of the first module, *GetFirstServer*, is to ask the user to enter the name of the player who will serve first and pass this information back to the main program. This can be accomplished with one parameter, *FirstServer*, to be passed by reference.

The third module, *DisplayWinner*, will need to know which player won the game and the final score of the game. We can pass three parameters—*GameWinner*, *WinnerScore* and *LoserScore*—by value, since they need not be changed or passed back by the module.

The remaining module, *PlayGame*, is the main module of the program. It will need to know who should serve first, and it will have to pass back to the main program the winner of the game and the score, so that this information can, in turn, be passed to *DisplayWinner*. There will be four parameters to this routine: *FirstServer*, to be passed by value, and *GameWinner*, *WinnerScore* and *LoserScore*, to be passed by reference.

So far, we have thought about *what* each module is supposed to do, rather than *how* (which is considered at the next level). We can now be more specific about the main program.

START OF PingPong

call Introduce
call GetFirstServer(FirstServer)
call PlayGame(FirstServer, GameWinner, WinnerScore, LoserScore)
call DisplayWinner(GameWinner, WinnerScore, LoserScore)
call Conclude

END OF PingPong

Now we can concentrate on the three major modules of the program, applying the same top-down approach we used for the program itself. Since *PlayGame* seems like the most complicated of the modules, we'll leave that for last.

The Module *GetFirstServer*

This module will ask the user to type in the name of the player that will serve first, and will accept the response. Since there are only two responses that make sense for our program, we should have this module check to be sure that the response is valid. If it's not, the module should display an error message and ask the user again. In other words, the module should return to the main program a *valid* response from the user.

You might be thinking that *GetFirstServer* should be written as a function rather than as a procedure, since it returns a single value. In fact, the module could very well be written as a function. Recall that the difference between a procedure and a function is that a procedure is a routine that performs a task, whereas a function returns a single value.

In this case we have decided that our module does more than simply return a value. We have specified that it is also to check the response for validity and display messages for the user. We tend to think of this as performing a task. It's a question of style; if you see it the other way, you should write it that way. Remember, though, that if it is written as a function it should have a noun-like name.

The module itself can be written using a *loop while*:

```
START OF GetFirstServer(FirstServer)
Passed by value: none
Passed by reference: FirstServer

display "Please enter the player to serve first (A or B):"
accept FirstServer
loop while FirstServer is neither an 'A' nor a 'B'
    display "Please enter an A or a B:"
    accept FirstServer

END OF GetFirstServer
```

The Module *DisplayWinner*

This module simply displays the winner of the game and the score:

```
START OF DisplayWinner(GameWinner,
                WinnerScore, LoserScore)
Passed by value: GameWinner, WinnerScore, LoserScore
Passed by reference: none

display "Player", GameWinner, "won by a score of "
display WinnerScore, "to" LoserScore

END OF DisplayWinner
```

At coding time we'll have to be careful with our punctuation, but we don't have to worry about that now.

The Module *PlayGame*

In keeping with our top-down approach, we should think about this module from a simplified, general perspective. We know that we have to keep track of the score, and we have to keep track of who is serving. We also have to be able to decide whether one of the players has won the game. The module will have to use some sort of loop, during which the score and the player serving are displayed and the user is asked which player won the point. Since we are certain that the body of the loop will be executed at least once, this should be a *loop until*.

The first draft of the algorithm might look like this:

initialize the variables that keep track of
*   the score and who is serving*
loop
*   display the score and who is serving*
*   accept the winner of the point*
*   add 1 to the winner's score*
*   if the game is not over*
*   then*
*   switch servers*
*   until one of the players has won*
store the proper scores in WinnerScore and LoserScore

The first part of the algorithm could be written as follows:

START OF PlayGame(FirstServer, GameWinner,
*   WinnerScore, LoserScore)*
Passed by value: FirstServer
Passed by reference: GameWinner, WinnerScore, LoserScore

store 0 in AScore and in BScore
store FirstServer in Server
loop
*   display "The score is:"*
*   display "Player A:", AScore, "Player B:", "BScore"*
*   display "Player", Server, "to serve."*
*   display "Who won the point? (A or B):"*
*   accept PointWinner*
*   if PointWinner is 'A'*
*   then*
*   add 1 to AScore*
*   else*
*   add 1 to BScore*
*   ⋮*

At this point our algorithm has to decide whether one of the players has won the game. This decision is based on *AScore* and *BScore*, so we could imagine a function, that receives *AScore* and *BScore* as parameters, and returns an 'A' if player A has won, a 'B' if B has won, or a space otherwise. Let's call this function *Winner*.

The algorithm could then continue:

⋮

```
    store Winner(AScore, BScore) in GameWinner
    if GameWinner is ' '
        then
            switch servers if it's time to do so
    until GameWinner is either 'A' or 'B'
if GameWinner is 'A'
    then
        store AScore in WinnerScore
        store BScore in LoserScore
    else
        store BScore in WinnerScore
        store AScore in LoserScore

END OF PlayGame
```

What remains is for us to write the function *Winner* and to be more specific about the statement *switch servers if it's time to do so*. This latter problem can also be solved by a function *NextServer*, that accepts the score of the game and the current server as parameters and returns the name of the player who should serve next.

Leaving the details of these two functions for later, we now have the entire algorithm for *PlayGame*:

```
START OF PlayGame(FirstServer, GameWinner,
                    WinnerScore, LoserScore)
Passed by value: FirstServer
Passed by reference: GameWinner, WinnerScore, LoserScore

store 0 in AScore and in BScore
store FirstServer in Server
loop
    display "The score is:"
    display "Player A:", AScore, "Player B:", "BScore"
    display "Player", Server, "to serve."
    display "Who won the point (A or B):"
    accept PointWinner
    if PointWinner is 'A'
        then
            add 1 to AScore
        else
            add 1 to BScore
    store Winner(AScore, BScore) in GameWinner
    if GameWinner is ' '
        then
            store NextServer(AScore, BScore, Server) in Server
    until GameWinner is either 'A' or 'B'
if GameWinner is 'A'
    then
        store AScore in WinnerScore
        store BScore in LoserScore
    else
        store BScore in WinnerScore
        store AScore in LoserScore

END OF PlayGame
```

The Function *Winner*

This function receives as its parameters the scores of the two players. If there is not yet a winner, the function returns a space, and if there is, it returns the appropriate letter. Remember that a player wins by having 21 points and having at least two points more than the other player.

Here's how we turn this description into an algorithm:

```
START OF Winner(AScore, BScore)

if AScore ≥ 21 and AScore − BScore ≥ 2
    then
        return 'A'
    else
        if BScore ≥ 21 and BScore − AScore ≥ 2
            then
                return 'B'
            else
                return ' '

END OF Winner
```

The Function NextServer

We pass this function the scores of the players and the current server. Recall that the serve changes every fifth point until the game is over or tied at 20. Once the score is tied at 20, the serve changes every point. We can use mod to decide whether the number of points played so far is divisible by five. Here's how the algorithm would look:

```
START OF NextServer(AScore, BScore, CurrentServer)

if (AScore + BScore) mod 5 is zero
            or AScore and BScore are both ≥ 20
    then
        if CurrentServer = 'A'
            then
                return 'B'
            else
                return 'A'
    else
        return CurrentServer

END OF NextServer
```

Avoiding Bugs

We have left a loophole in the *PlayGame* algorithm. What if, in response to the *accept PointWinner* statement, the user types in Z? The way the algorithm is written, anything but an **A** will be treated as a B. We were careful in the *GetFirstServer* algorithm to make sure that the user types in either an **A** or a B. We should do the same in the *PlayGame* algorithm.

In fact, since the same logic would be used in both places, you might want to write a routine that could be called by both modules, say *GetValidPlayer*, which accepts the input and does the error checking. We'll leave this as an exercise.

5.8   Summary and Review

- Real programs are broken up into modules. Modular programming provides for efficient design and program maintenance. It is not possible to maintain today's large programs unless they have been carefully designed in a modular manner. Modular programming is the same as top-down programming.

- Modules communicate with each other via parameters. A parameter is an item of data sent from one module to another and often from the second module back to the first.

- Parameters can be passed by value or by reference. If a parameter is passed by value, a copy of the value of the actual parameter is sent to the module being called. This can protect the actual parameter from accidentally being changed in the subroutine. If a parameter is passed by reference, the address of the actual parameter is sent rather that the value of the parameter. In this case, the value of the actual parameter can be changed inside the subroutine.

- We refer to the parameters in the calling routine as *actual parameters* and the parameters in the called routine as *formal parameters*.

- We discussed two kinds of module: procedures and functions. A procedure *performs a task* and a function *returns a value*. When you invent a name for a procedure, use a verb. When you invent a name for a function, use a noun.

- We indicated that a procedure will be invoked in our algorithms by using the word *call* followed by the name of the procedure with the actual parameter(s) in parentheses (if any). On the other hand, a function will be invoked by just using the name of the function (and its parameters, if any) and treating the reference as a value.

- The *loop while* was introduced as a second kind of loop. Like the *loop until*, the *loop while* continues to execute a series of steps over and over.

Unlike the *loop until*, however, the test for the *loop while* is at the top of the loop, which means that the steps in the loop may not get executed at all. Also unlike the *loop until*, the steps in the loop are executed over and over while the condition tests *true*. With the *loop until*, when the condition tests *true*, the loop is exited.

- We started to discuss testing. It is not enough to write an algorithm and think it's correct. One needs to test the algorithm. A good programmer makes decisions about the data to use for testing and then traces the algorithm with these data. More testing is done after the coding step. We'll have more to say about testing in chapters 6 and 8.

- We mentioned "proof of correctness." Many programs cannot be tested and, indeed, for some complex algorithms and programs, no amount of testing can ever prove them correct. In more advanced courses you will learn how to prove that an algorithm is correct.

5.9   New Terms Introduced

actual parameter The parameter in the calling routine.

call To invoke a procedure or function.

Euclidean algorithm An ancient algorithm used to determine the gcd of two integers.

formal parameter The parameter in the called routine.

function A subroutine that returns a single value.

gcd The greatest common divisor of two integers.

invoke To call a procedure or function.

modular programming The programming method where a problem is solved by breaking it down into successively smaller problems.

module Another term for a subroutine.

loop while A repetition structure where a condition is tested prior to entry into the loop and the loop continues while the condition is true.

parameter An item of data passed between modules.

pass by reference Passing the actual parameter itself.

pass by value Passing a copy of the actual parameter.

postcondition A condition that a routine guarantees to be satisfied upon its completion.

precondition A condition that a routine assumes it satisfied before it begins.

procedural abstraction The style of programming where each procedure performs a particular task and other routines know only what that task is and not how it is performed.

procedure A subroutine that performs a task.

side effect Changing the value of an actual parameter inside a function. Not a good idea.

subroutine A routine other than the main program that is called by other routines and can itself call other subroutines.

top-down programming Another term for modular programming.

5.10 Exercises

1. Modify the *GetFraction* algorithm to use a *loop while* instead of a *loop until*.

2. It was mentioned in the text that the two kinds of loops we introduced are not strictly necessary. Anything you can do with a *loop while* can be done using a *loop until* and, possibly, an *if...then*. The reverse is also true: anything you can do using a *loop until* can be done with a *loop while* and, possibly, an assignment. Rewrite the following *loop until* using a *loop while*:

loop
    display "Please enter a non-zero integer."
    accept Number
    if Number = 0
        then
            display "Try again."
until Number is non-zero

3. We inserted an *if...then* at the beginning of the algorithm for *GCD* to swap *First* and *Second* if *First* was less than *Second*. Carefully trace the algorithm *without* that step, for various values of *First* and *Second* where *First* is less than *Second*. Why is this step necessary? What happens if that step is left out?

4. Complete the algorithm for *DisplayFraction*.

5. Modify the algorithm for the main program in this chapter so that after displaying the fraction, the program asks the user if he wants to enter another fraction, and continues until he indicates otherwise.

6. Write the algorithm for the procedure *GetValidPlayer* (see page 146), which could be called by both *GetFirstServer* and *PlayGame* to accept a letter entered by the user and do the appropriate error checking. Modify both *GetFirstServer* and *PlayGame* so that they call this procedure.

7. Consider a simple automatic teller machine which handles only cash withdrawals. When you step up, it greets you with an introductory message, and you insert your bank card into the slot. The machine reads your account number from the card and asks you to key in your code number.

   If you don't key in the proper number within three tries, the machine gives the card back. If you enter the proper code, the machine asks for the amount of your withdrawal. Assume that the machine can read your bank balance from some file. It compares your request with your balance and either gives you the money or a message indicating that you have insufficient funds. It then returns your card and the transaction is complete.

Using a top-down approach, write a complete algorithm to simulate an automatic teller machine.

For exercises 8–10, write an algorithm for the given module.

8. A function called *PerimeterOfRectangle*, which returns the perimeter of a rectangle given the length and width as passed parameters.

9. A subroutine called *TestTriangle*. Three values, which represent the sides of a triangle, are passed to the routine. The routine decides whether such a triangle exists, and returns a **Boolean** value to that effect. If the triangle exists, the routine passes back the perimeter of the triangle. Otherwise, it passes back a zero. Should the routine be designed as a procedure or as a function?

10. A procedure called *GetData*. One value, either "rectangle," "square" or "triangle," is passed to the procedure. Depending on which of these is passed, the procedure requests the user to type in the length and width, the side, or the three sides. The procedure passes this data back to the calling module in three variables. For a square and a rectangle, the "extra" variables should contain zeroes.

11. Write an algorithm, using the modules from exercises 8–10, that offers the user a choice of shapes—rectangle, square or triangle—and calculates the perimeter of the shape selected. Use the module *PerimeterOfRectangle* for the square. The algorithm calls *GetData* and the appropriate module and displays the result. It then asks the user whether or not to continue, continuing until the user says "no."

For exercises 12–17, write an algorithm for the given module. In each case be careful to identify the parameters; for *DisplayDate*, indicate whether the parameters are passed by value or by reference, and clearly state what the preconditions are, if any.

The modules involve calendar calculations, and so it should be mentioned that the Gregorian calendar in use today was adopted by most countries in 1582. According to the Gregorian calendar, a year is a leap year, i.e., has 29 days in February, if that year is divisible by 4 but not by 100, except that years divisible by 400 *are* leap years.

12. A Boolean-valued function called *LeapYear*, which is passed a certain year and returns *true* if that year is a leap year and *false* otherwise.

13. A function called *DaysInMonth*, which returns the number of days in a given month when passed the month and year. The month is passed as an integer between 1 and 12, and the year is passed as an integer greater than or equal to 1582 (e.g., 1987). If the month or year passed is invalid, a zero should be returned. This function can call the function *LeapYear*. The year should not be earlier than 1582.

14. A Boolean-valued function called *ValidDate*, which is passed three numbers representing a month, day and year combination. *ValidDate* should return *true* if the date is valid and *false* otherwise. This function can call *DaysInMonth*.

15. A function called *DayOfYear*, which accepts three integers representing a month, day and year combination, and returns the number of days in the given year up to (and including) the given month and day. For example, February 5, 1987 would be day 36. If the date is invalid, the routine should return a zero. Use the modules defined in exercises 12–14.

16. A function called *DayOfWeek*, which returns an integer between 0 and 6, representing the day of the week (Saturday through Friday, respectively), on which a given day of the year falls. The day of the year and the year are to be passed to the function. This function should call the modules from exercises 12–15, as necessary.

17. A procedure called *DisplayDate* that displays a date, along with the day of the week, on the screen in English. The procedure should accept three parameters representing the month, day and year. The procedure should assume the date sent to it is a valid date. For example, if the procedure is sent the values 1, 1 and 1989, it should display:

    ```
    Sunday, January 1, 1989
    ```

    This procedure should call the functions defined in exercises 12–16.

18. Write an algorithm for a *program* that allows the user to enter a date in the form of three integers representing the month, day and year, and prints the date and the day of the week on the screen, in English. For example, when the integers 7, 4 and 1776 are entered by the user, the program should print:

    ```
    Thursday, July 4, 1776
    ```

    If the date entered is invalid, the program should say so. The program should allow the user to continue entering dates until he decides to quit.

Chapter 6

Modular Programming in Pascal

> Adding manpower to a late
> software project makes it later.
> — Frederick Brooks

6.1 Overview of the Chapter

This chapter will implement the techniques learned in chapter 5. We will learn how to write procedures and functions in Pascal. In particular, we will implement the algorithms developed in the previous chapter that allow a user to enter a fraction and see it displayed in reduced form as a mixed number. We will discuss the ⟨*procedure/function declaration part*⟩ of a Pascal program, and will develop a complete program that implements the solution to the problem of getting and displaying a fraction.

6.2 Introduction

As mentioned earlier, Pascal is an ideal language for modular programming. The concepts of procedure and function introduced in the previous chapter have exact counterparts in Pascal. Let's repeat what we said regarding the difference between procedures and functions:

- A *procedure* is a subroutine that performs a task.

- A *function* is a subroutine that returns a single value.

We can include both kinds of subroutine in Pascal. When we write either a procedure or a function, we put it in a special part of the program, called the ⟨*procedure/function declaration part*⟩. This part is one of the subparts of the ⟨*definition/declaration part*⟩, which is, in turn, one of the two parts of a ⟨*block*⟩. (The other part of the ⟨*block*⟩ is the ⟨*statement part*⟩.) The only other part of

153

the ⟨*definition/declaration part*⟩ that we have discussed so far is the ⟨*variable declaration part*⟩.

The ⟨*procedure/function declaration part*⟩ consists of declarations of procedures and functions in either order. As we will see, the order isn't arbitrary, but it is not the case that procedures must come before functions or vice versa.

Procedure Declaration

Let's look first at a ⟨*procedure declaration*⟩. The syntax diagram is in figure 6.1.

In English, a ⟨*procedure declaration*⟩ starts with the word **procedure**, followed by a name for the procedure, optionally followed by a ⟨*formal parameter declaration*⟩ enclosed in parentheses, followed by a semicolon, followed by a ⟨*block*⟩, followed by a semicolon.

You will make a big step forward in your efforts to understand Pascal when you realize that this is the same structure as a program itself. Each procedure declaration contains within itself a ⟨*block*⟩. Each ⟨*block*⟩ consists of two parts, one of which is the ⟨*definition/declaration part*⟩. In this part you can declare additional procedures. This block structure is what gives Pascal its ability to implement modular programming.

When we first introduced the notion of a program in chapter 4, we did not include a syntax diagram for a program. We include one here, and you can compare the syntax diagram in figure 6.2 with the one in figure 6.1. A program starts with the word **program**; a procedure starts with the word **procedure**. The program ends with a period; a procedure ends with a semicolon. A program communicates with the outside world via files, and the first line contains a list of

procedure declaration:

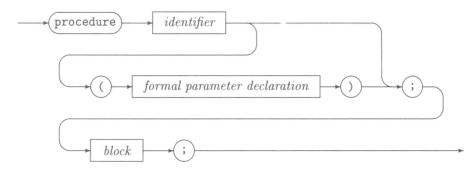

Figure 6.1

program:

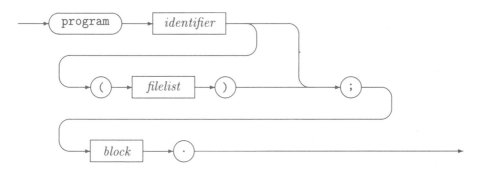

Figure 6.2

these files in parentheses; a procedure communicates with its outside world via parameters and the first line contains a list of these parameters in parentheses.

The optional ⟨*formal parameter declaration*⟩ is where the parameters for the procedure are defined.

We turn now to the process of implementing the algorithms from the last chapter in Pascal.

6.3 Implementation of the Algorithm

Sometimes procedures—like the one that displays an introduction for the user—don't have any parameters, which is why the ⟨*formal parameter declaration*⟩ is optional. Since it's so simple, let's start with the procedure that displays the introduction.

The Procedure for Introduce

Our algorithm isn't very complicated:

START OF Introduce

display an introduction to the program for the user

END OF Introduce

It can be written in Pascal very easily: according to the syntax diagram, we first need the word procedure, then a name for the procedure. Let's choose Introduce for the name. The first line of the ⟨*procedure declaration*⟩ then becomes:

```
procedure Introduce;
```

The semicolon is required. Now we need a ⟨*block*⟩. In the ⟨*block*⟩ we need two parts: a ⟨*definition/declaration part*⟩ and a ⟨*statement part*⟩. In the ⟨*definition/declaration part*⟩ we declare variables, procedures and functions. But in this procedure we don't have any variables or procedures or functions; thus, the ⟨*definition/declaration part*⟩ is not needed. We do, of course, need a ⟨*statement part*⟩. The ⟨*statement part*⟩ consists of the ⟨*write statement*⟩s that display the introduction.

The entire procedure looks something like:

```
procedure Introduce;

{  This procedure simply displays an introduction.  }

begin
    writeln('This program will allow you to enter a fraction and');
    writeln('will reduce the fraction you enter and display it as');
    writeln('a mixed number.');
    writeln('You should enter the fraction as two integers.')
end;
```

You should rewrite the introduction and have the program say what you want to say in your own words; this is just an example. The important point is: this is what a ⟨*procedure declaration*⟩ looks like.

Procedure Invocation

Before we go on to procedures with parameters, we should say something about how a procedure is called. In Pascal, the invocation of a procedure is a ⟨statement⟩. Whenever you want to call a procedure, you simply use the name of the procedure as a new ⟨statement⟩. For example, the ⟨statement⟩ that actually calls the procedure Introduce will be just the single word Introduce. Let's look at that as an example. Leaving out the several procedures, etc., that we have yet to write, the final program will contain the following lines:

```
program Fraction(input, output);
      . . .
   procedure Introduce;

   {  This procedure simply displays an introduction.  }

   begin
     writeln('This program will allow you to enter a fraction and');
     writeln('will reduce the fraction you enter and display it as');
     writeln('a mixed number.');
     writeln('You should enter the fraction as two integers.')
   end;
        . . .
begin   {  Statement part of the main program  }
   Introduce;
        . . .
end.
```

When the program is run, the first statement executed is the first statement in the ⟨statement part⟩ of the main program. That statement invokes the procedure Introduce. Control is transferred, temporarily, to the procedure, and the statements inside Introduce are executed. Once Introduce is finished, control is transferred back to the main program and the rest of the statements there are executed.

We now move on to writing the remaining statements and procedures.

The Procedure for DisplayFraction

Things get a bit more complicated now. The above procedure didn't have any parameters. That is relatively rare; normally procedures use parameters to send data to and from one another. We now discuss procedures that use parameters.

We choose to discuss the procedure for DisplayFraction first because its parameters are simpler than some of the others. Recall that we didn't write the complete algorithm in chapter 5; we left it for you to complete.

Your completed algorithm should look something like:

START OF DisplayFraction(Fraction)
Passed by value: Fraction
Passed by reference: none
Preconditions: The fraction has been reduced to lowest terms
                and Denominator > 0

if Denominator = 1
    then
        display Numerator
    else
        if |Numerator| < Denominator
            then
                display Numerator, "/", Denominator
            else
                store the quotient of |Numerator| ÷ Denominator in Quo
                store the remainder of |Numerator| ÷ Denominator in Rem
                if the fraction is positive
                    then
                        display Quo, "&", Rem, "/", Denominator
                    else
                        display "-(", Quo, "&", Rem, "/", Denominator, ")"

END OF DisplayFraction

Notice that we have taken full advantage of the precondition that the fraction has been reduced.

Abstract Data Types

In order to implement the algorithm, we must decide how to handle a fraction in Pascal. While we were working on the algorithm, we thought of a fraction as a whole, as an object. We did not worry there about the details of how the fraction would actually be stored in memory. A data type that is handled in this manner is an *abstract data type*. We treated a fraction as an abstract data type without worrying about how it would be handled in Pascal. Now that we are ready to implement the algorithm, we have to decide how to turn this abstract data type into something that Pascal can deal with.

As we saw in chapter 4, in Pascal we can work with `integers`, `reals`, `characters` and `Boolean` valued variables. This is true of most computer languages; most languages allow the programmer to manipulate integers, real numbers and characters. So, how can we implement a fraction? A fraction (or, better, a *rational number*) in mathematics is just the ratio of two integers, and that's all we really need; whenever we want to refer to a single fraction, we need only refer to its numerator and denominator. Consequently, whenever we need to manipulate a fraction, we only need to manipulate its numerator and denominator. Further, when we need to send a fraction from one routine to another, we'll actually have to send two things: the numerator and denominator of the fraction.

Variable and Parameter Names

In the main program `Fraction`, we will have variables called `Numerator` and `Denominator` that will represent the fraction. The values of these variables will first be set in the routine `GetFraction`, then be changed by `Reduce`, and finally be displayed via our procedure `DisplayFraction`.

These variables will be declared in the main program's ⟨*definition/declaration part*⟩, and are not the same as the parameters within `DisplayFraction`. Pascal allows us to use the same identifiers (i.e., names) in `DisplayFraction` as used in the main program, but to avoid confusion, in `DisplayFraction` we'll call the parameters `Num` and `Denom`. As you have guessed, they are declared in the first line of the ⟨*procedure declaration*⟩, in the part called the ⟨*formal parameter declaration*⟩.

We use the word "formal" because of the way we refer to the parameters. The parameters in the *calling* routine are known as the *actual* parameters and the parameters in the *called* routine are known as the *formal* parameters.

Using our program as an example, when the main program calls `Display-Fraction`, it refers to the parameters `Numerator` and `Denominator`. These are the *actual parameters*. Within the procedure `DisplayFraction`, however, these parameters are `Num` and `Denom`. These are the *formal parameters*. If the parameters are passed by value—as they are in this case—the formal parameters (`Num` and `Denom`) refer to *copies* of the actual parameters (`Numerator` and `Denominator`). When the parameters are passed by reference, the formal parameters refer to the *very same* location in memory as do the actual parameters.

With all this in mind, we are ready to write the first line of `DisplayFraction`:

```
procedure DisplayFraction(Num, Denom : integer);
```

As you can see, the ⟨*formal parameter declaration*⟩ consists of the names of the parameters and their types. Figure 6.3 contains the syntax diagram for the ⟨*formal parameter declaration*⟩.

We'll explain the optional `var` later in the chapter. The rest of the ⟨*formal parameter declaration*⟩ should look familiar; it's quite similar to the variable declarations we discussed in chapter 4. Indeed, a formal parameter is treated very much like a variable. It is a named place in memory with a particular type and it can hold different values at different times.

Let's look at that first line. The word `procedure` has to be there to tell the compiler that we are declaring a procedure. The word `DisplayFraction` is the name of the procedure we are declaring. `Num` and `Denom` are the formal parameters and are of type `integer`.

formal parameter declaration:

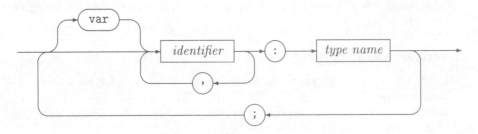

Figure 6.3

The main program has variables `Numerator` and `Denominator` that are of type `integer`; let's see what the program will look like, leaving out the procedure `Introduce` for the moment:

```
program Fraction(input, output);

{  Programmer:  Margaret Uy                                          }

{  This program allows a user to enter a fraction as two integers,   }
{  reduces the fraction and then displays it as a mixed number.      }

var
    Numerator, Denominator : integer;
        . . .

    procedure DisplayFraction(Num, Denom : integer);
        . . .

begin   {  Statement part of the main program  }
    Introduce;
        . . .
    DisplayFraction(Numerator, Denominator);
        . . .
end.
```

Remember that the statements in the main program are executed first. The program will come to the statement:

```
DisplayFraction(Numerator, Denominator)
```

which is the line that calls the procedure `DisplayFraction`. In this line we see the actual parameters: `Numerator` and `Denominator`. Their values are sent to the procedure. The procedure has two formal parameters: Num and Denom. Since the parameters are being passed by value, a copy of what is stored in Numerator is sent to Num and a copy of what is stored in Denominator is sent to Denom. After these values are filled in, the procedure is executed. Since the parameters are being passed by value, when the procedure is finished and control returns to the main program, whatever was stored in Numerator and Denominator will still be there, even if the values stored in Num and Denom are changed.

As you can see, the compiler must be able to tell which actual parameter goes with which formal parameter. The rules are straightforward:

- The number of actual parameters must exactly equal the number of formal parameters.

- The parameters will be passed in the order they appear. The first actual parameter will be sent to the first formal parameter, the second to the second, etc.

- The type of each actual parameter must be assignment compatible with the type of the corresponding formal parameter.

The term *assignment compatible* in the last rule means, for instance, that you can send an integer to a real— just as you can assign an integer to a real— but only if the parameter is being passed by value. Other than this, the types of the actual parameter and the formal parameter must be exactly the same.

The programmer is, of course, responsible for making sure that the actual and formal parameters used in a program follow these rules.

The above three rules can be remembered better as one rule:

- The actual parameters and formal parameters must agree in *number*, *order* and *type*.

Let's finish writing DisplayFraction. Looking at the algorithm, we see that we need to be able to take the absolute value of the numerator and denominator. That's no problem; Pascal supplies several functions that we can use, and one of these is a function that yields the absolute value of its argument. It's called abs. To use abs, you simply type the word abs and the thing you want the absolute value of enclosed in parentheses. We'll say more about other supplied functions in a few pages. For now, look at the program on page 162 and see how we use abs.

Notice that in the algorithm for *DisplayFraction* we use two variables, *Quo* and *Rem*, to hold the quotient and remainder of the numerator divided by the denominator. We'll surely want to use similar variables in the Pascal program but where should these variables be declared?

Since these two variables are used only inside the procedure, they should be declared inside the procedure. Remember, what follows the first line of a procedure declaration is a ⟨*block*⟩. One of the two things that goes in a ⟨*block*⟩

is a ⟨*definition/declaration part*⟩ and in this ⟨*definition/declaration part*⟩ goes
a ⟨*variable declaration part*⟩. Variables declared inside a procedure like this
are called *local variables*. The variables `Quo` and `Rem` are local variables. The
beginning of the procedure will look like:

```
procedure DisplayFraction(Num, Denom : integer);
var
    Quo, Rem : integer;
```

If this procedure needed any other local variables or required any additional
procedures or functions, they would be declared here. Since it doesn't, we can
proceed with the ⟨*statement part*⟩ of `DisplayFraction`. Looking back at the
algorithm, we see that it starts with an *if...then...else*. This is implemented
with an ⟨*if statement*⟩. Inside the *if...then...else* there are more *if...then...elses*.
Leaving out the details, the procedure, including its ⟨*statement part*⟩, will be:

```
procedure DisplayFraction(Num, Denom : integer);

{  Precondition:  The fraction has been reduced and Denom > 0.   }
{  This procedure displays a fraction as a mixed number.         }

var
    Quo, Rem : integer;

begin
  if Denom = 1
    then
      writeln(Num : 1)
    else
      if abs(Num) < Denom
        then
          writeln(Num : 1, '/', Denom : 1)
        else
          begin
            Quo := abs(Num) div Denom;
            Rem := abs(Num) mod Denom;
            if Num > Denom
              then
                writeln(Quo : 1, ' & ', Rem : 1, '/', Denom : 1)
              else
                writeln('-(', Quo : 1, ' & ', Rem : 1, '/', Denom : 1, ')')
          end
end;
```

Let's put all the pieces we have finished together.

```
program Fraction(input, output);

{ Programmer:  Pepe Martinez                                }

{ This program allows a user to enter a fraction as two integers, }
{ reduces the fraction and then displays it as a mixed number.    }

var
    Numerator, Denominator : integer;

    procedure Introduce;

    { This procedure simply displays an introduction.  }

    begin
        writeln('This program will allow you to enter a fraction and');
        writeln('will reduce the fraction you enter and display it as');
        writeln('a mixed number.');
        writeln('You should enter the fraction as two integers.')
    end;
        . . .



    procedure DisplayFraction(Num, Denom : integer);

    { Precondition:  The fraction has been reduced and Denom > 0.  }

    { This procedure displays a fraction as a mixed number.        }

    var
        Quo, Rem : integer;
```

```
  begin
    if Denom = 1
      then
        writeln(Num : 1)
      else
        if abs(Num) < Denom
          then
            writeln(Num : 1, '/', Denom : 1)
          else
            begin
              Quo := abs(Num) div Denom;
              Rem := abs(Num) mod Denom;
              if Num > Denom
                then
                  writeln(Quo : 1, ' & ', Rem : 1, '/', Denom : 1)
                else
                  writeln('-(', Quo : 1, ' & ', Rem : 1, '/', Denom : 1, ')')
            end
  end;
          . . .


begin    { Statement part of the main program }
  Introduce;
       . . .
  DisplayFraction(Numerator, Denominator);
       . . .
end.
```

The two statements in the ⟨*statement part*⟩ of the main program call the two procedures `Introduce` and `DisplayFraction`. In the line that calls `Display-Fraction`, the actual parameters are `Numerator` and `Denominator`. In the procedure `DisplayFraction` itself, the formal parameters are `Num` and `Denom`. When `DisplayFraction` is called, copies of `Numerator` and `Denominator` are sent to `Num` and `Denom`. When the procedure is exited, these copies are discarded and any changes made to them are lost.

Supplied Functions

Before we go on to the implementation of *GetFraction*, let's take a short detour and look at some of the functions other than `abs` that are supplied in Pascal. In mathematics, the word "argument" stands for whatever is sent to a function. We have been using the word "parameter" for this. In the future, we'll feel free to use either word when referring to a function. Figure 6.4 lists the Pascal supplied functions, the type of their arguments and their returned values.

Name	Argument Type	Returned Type	Description
`sqr(x)`	`real` or `integer`	same as argument	x squared
`sqrt(x)`	`real` or `integer`	`real`	square root of x
`abs(x)`	`real` or `integer`	same as argument	absolute value of x
`trunc(x)`	`real`	`integer`	truncate x
`round(x)`	`real`	`integer`	round off x
`odd(x)`	`integer`	`Boolean`	is x odd?
`sin(x)`	`real`	`real`	the sine of x
`cos(x)`	`real`	`real`	the cosine of x
`arctan(x)`	`real`	`real`	the arctangent of x
`exp(x)`	`real`	`real`	e to the x power
`ln(x)`	`real`	`real`	log of x to the base e

Figure 6.4 Supplied Functions in Pascal

The first six of these functions are worthy of some discussion:

- The function **sqr** returns the *square* of its argument, not the square root. Be careful to note this since the same name is used for the square root function in other languages. As a matter of interest, **sqr** is seldom used since the argument can always just be multiplied by itself.

- The function **sqrt**, on the other hand, is valuable; without it, you would have trouble finding the square root of a number. Notice that the argument can be either **real** or **integer** but the returned type is always **real**.

- The function **abs** returns the absolute value of its argument. If the argument is **real**, the returned value is **real**. If the argument is **integer**, the returned value is **integer**. We've already used **abs**.

- The two functions, **trunc** and **round**, are used to convert a **real** value into an **integer**. The first simply truncates the decimal part, the other rounds the **real** value to the nearest **integer**. Since it is a syntax error to assign a **real** value to an **integer** variable, these two functions are necessary whenever you need to change a **real** into an **integer**.

- The sixth function, **odd**, is odd; it's not clear why Wirth decided to include such a function. It returns **true** if the **integer** sent to it is odd, and returns **false** otherwise. One could easily use **mod** to accomplish the same thing accomplished by **odd**.

The last five functions will interest you if you have had courses in trigonometry and/or calculus. We won't have occasion to use them in this text. Remember that to use one of these functions you simply use its name and supply the appropriate argument enclosed in parentheses. In Pascal, the invocation of a function is an *expression*; so be sure you use the function where an expression is expected by the compiler. For example, on the right side of an assignment statement such as:

```
x := 3 * sqrt(y)
```

or in a Boolean expression, such as:

```
if x < 3 * sqrt(y)
   then ...
```

or in a ⟨*write statement*⟩, such as:

```
write(3 * sqrt(y) : 8 : 2)
```

In particular, you *cannot* treat a function invocation as a statement—as you can with a procedure invocation—and you *cannot* put a function invocation on the *left* side of an assignment statement.

The Procedure for `GetFraction`

Let's turn now to the procedure that gets a fraction from the user. Our algorithm is:

```
START OF GetFraction(Fraction)
Passed by value: none
Passed by reference: Fraction

display "Enter the numerator of the fraction."
accept Numerator
display "Enter the denominator of the fraction."
accept Denominator
if Denominator equals zero
   then
      loop
          display "You must enter a non-zero integer. Try again."
          accept Denominator
          until Denominator is not equal to zero

END OF GetFraction
```

Clearly the Pascal parameters are going to be the numerator and the denominator of the fraction, and as the algorithm indicates, they are going to be passed by reference. The question is, how do we tell Pascal that the parameters are to be passed by reference? The answer lies in var which we encountered earlier when we were looking at the syntax diagram for the *(formal parameter declaration)*. The var is included whenever the programmer wants the parameters passed by reference, and is left out otherwise. In this case, we want the parameters passed by reference—so that the values entered by the user will be sent back to the calling routine.

Let's choose some names before we go any further. What should we call the procedure? GetFraction is okay. How about the formal parameters? As before, let's agree to call them Num and Denom rather than Numerator and Denominator—remember, we don't want to confuse the formal parameters with the actual parameters in the main program.

With this decided, we can write the first line of the procedure:

```
procedure GetFraction(var Num, Denom : integer);
```

This looks almost exactly the same as the first line for DisplayFraction, but the little var makes a world of difference. This time the numerator and denominator will be passed by reference instead of by value.

When the actual parameter is passed by reference, Pascal calls the formal parameter a *variable parameter*. When the actual parameter is passed by value, Pascal calls the formal parameter a *value parameter*. Thus, in this procedure, Num and Denom are *variable* parameters.

Completing the procedure is easy. There are no local variables and this routine doesn't depend on any lower-level routines. So, the procedure amounts to nothing more than a few statements that implement the algorithm:

```
procedure GetFraction(var Num, Denom : integer);

{  This procedure allows the user to enter two integers for the  }
{  numerator and denominator of a fraction.  The denominator     }
{  cannot equal zero.                                            }

begin
   write('Enter the numerator of the fraction: ');
   readln(Num);
   write('Enter the denominator of the fraction: ');
   readln(Denom);
   if Denom = 0
      then
         repeat
            write('You must enter a non-zero integer.  Try again: ');
            readln(Denom)
            until Denom <> 0
end;
```

Memory used by the main program

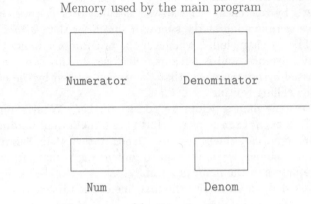

Numerator   Denominator

Num   Denom

Memory used by DisplayFraction

Figure 6.5 Memory Utilization with Value Parameters

It would be a good idea to review the concept of a ⟨*statement*⟩ about now. How many statements are there in this procedure? You should be able to count five "outer-level" statements; the last of which is an ⟨*if statement*⟩. There is an "inner-level" statement after the word **then**; this statement is a ⟨*repeat statement*⟩. Inside the body of the ⟨*repeat statement*⟩ there are two more statements, a ⟨*write statement*⟩ and a ⟨*read statement*⟩. Pay special attention to where the semicolons are put—and where they are *not* put.

Invoking GetFraction

Now how about the statement in the main program that invokes this procedure? It looks just the same as the line that invokes the DisplayFraction procedure:

        GetFraction(Numerator, Denominator)

but it doesn't work the same. Since we are passing the parameters by reference rather than by value, the *addresses* of the actual parameters are sent to GetFraction, not *copies* of their values. When the user enters values into Num and Denom, the values are really being put into Numerator and Denominator.

A couple of pictures that illustrate the two situations might help. With DisplayFraction, memory would look something like that shown in figure 6.5. With GetFraction, memory would look like that shown in figure 6.6.

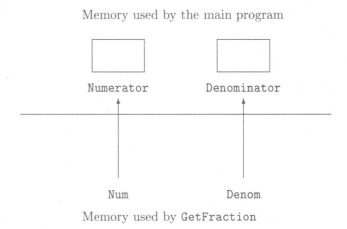

Figure 6.6 Memory Utilization with Variable Parameters

The Procedure for Reduce

Now we can do **Reduce**. Here's the algorithm from the previous chapter:

START OF Reduce(Fraction)
Passed by value: none
Passed by reference: Fraction
Precondition(s): Denominator ≠ 0
Postcondition(s): The fraction is reduced and Denominator > 0

if Numerator = 0
    then
       store 1 in Denominator
    else
       determine whether the fraction is positive or negative
       store |Numerator| in Numerator
       store |Denominator| in Denominator
       divide Numerator by GCD(Numerator, Denominator)
       divide Denominator by GCD(Numerator, Denominator)
       if the fraction is negative
          then
             multiply Numerator by −1

END OF Reduce

As before, we'll send the fraction by sending its numerator and denominator and we'll call the parameters `Num` and `Denom`. Let's call the procedure `Reduce`. As with the other procedures, the first line is easy:

```
procedure Reduce(var Num, Denom : integer);
```

Why did we make `Num` and `Denom` variable parameters? Be sure you understand the reason before going any further.

Before we jump into writing the rest of this procedure, we'll have to think about it a bit more. The first part of the *if...then* is easy to implement: just put a 1 in `Denom` if `Num` equals zero.

The *else* part requires more thought. In the first place, how can we determine whether the fraction is positive or negative? Well, if the numerator and denominator are both positive or both negative, then the resulting fraction is positive. Otherwise, the resulting fraction is negative.

But, notice that the computer has to "remember" whether the fraction is positive or negative. How can we have the computer remember which way it is? Be careful; in the next two steps we are going to change both of them to positive values. One way to handle this is to use a local variable; put a "+" in it if the fraction is positive and put a "−" in it if the fraction is negative. Such a variable would have to be of type `char`. But then later we would have to look at this variable and decide what to do with the fraction. It's easier to use an `integer` local variable and just put either +1 or −1 in it. Later we can just multiply the numerator by this number and make the result either positive or negative. Let's call this variable `Sign`. With this in mind, we can write the procedure in Pascal. It's on the next page.

```
procedure Reduce(var Num, Denom : integer);

{ Precondition:  Denom <> 0   }

{ Postcondition: This procedure reduces a fraction to lowest terms.   }
{ If the fraction is negative, the minus sign is put in the numerator. }

var
  Sign : integer;

begin
  if Num = 0
    then
      Denom := 1
    else
      begin
        if ((Num > 0) and (Denom > 0)) or ((Num < 0) and (Denom < 0))
          then
            Sign := 1
          else
            Sign := -1;
        Num := abs(Num);
        Denom := abs(Denom);
        Num := Num div GCD(Num, Denom);
        Denom := Denom div GCD(Num, Denom);
        Num := Sign * Num
      end
end;
```

Everything looks okay and this routine would run, but it *doesn't work*. It contains a subtle bug that would cause it to return invalid values for Num and Denom. We'll have to fix that bug in a minute. First, how about those two lines that refer to GCD? What's GCD? Of course we expect this to be the value of the greatest common divisor of Num and Denom. There is no such function in Pascal as GCD. That's okay, we'll write one. But, if we write a function for GCD, we have to *call* it. We have not yet discussed how to call a function in Pascal; much less how to write one. That we'll have to do.

It turns out that the way we called GCD in the procedure above is exactly right. We call the functions we write in the same way we call the supplied functions in Pascal—like abs—and just as we did in the algorithm. The invocation of a function in Pascal is an *expression*. Earlier we indicated that we weren't able to give the full syntax diagram for an ⟨*expression*⟩, and we still aren't ready to. However, remember that an ⟨*expression*⟩ is something that has a value. A function returns a single value; thus, it's no surprise that the invocation of a function is an ⟨*expression*⟩.

We're about to discuss functions in Pascal; before we do, though, let's get rid of that bug in the above procedure. But, before we can fix the bug, we have to find it.

One way to find it is to trace the program. Send the procedure values for Num and Denom and see what happens. Let's suppose that we are trying to reduce the fraction 20/28. Num is 20 and Denom is 28. What should the result be? The greatest common divisor of 20 and 28 is 4, 20 divided by 4 is 5, and 28 divided by 4 is 7. The answer should be 5/7.

Let's trace the procedure as written. We start with Num = 20 and Denom = 28. The first ⟨*if statement*⟩ checks to see if Num equals zero, which it doesn't, so the statement following the word else is executed. This ⟨*compound statement*⟩ starts by checking to see if Num and Denom are both positive or both negative— which they are—so Sign is set to 1. Now Num is set to abs(20), which is still 20, and Denom is set to abs(28), which is still 28. No problem yet.

Now Num is divided by GCD(Num, Denom) and the result stored in Num. This results in Num becoming 5. So far, so good. Next Denom is divided by GCD(Num, Denom) and the result stored in Denom. What happens? Do you see it? What is GCD(Num, Denom)? Since we just changed Num to 5, the gcd in this step is *not* the same as it was in the previous step. The GCD(Num, Denom) is now 1. Denom stays 28; it is not changed to 7 as expected. The "reduced" fraction would turn out to be 5/28, not 5/7.

The computer executes the steps sequentially, not in parallel. Sometimes we think in parallel and we have to be very careful not to expect the computer to work that way—at least not in Pascal. (Some languages do allow steps to be executed in parallel but we're not going to get into that here.)

So, how do we fix the bug? Since the bug is in the algorithm, we should fix that first. The solution is to get the greatest common divisor and divide both *Numerator* and *Denominator* by the same number. Another variable will do the job. Let's call it *Common*. We store the value of GCD(*Numerator, Denominator*) in *Common* and then divide both *Numerator* and *Denominator* by *Common*. The algorithm would then be:

```
START OF Reduce(Fraction)
Passed by value: none
Passed by reference: Fraction
Precondition(s): Denominator ≠ 0
Postcondition(s): The fraction is reduced and Denominator > 0

if Numerator = 0
    then
        store 1 in Denominator
    else
        determine whether the fraction is positive or negative
        store |Numerator| in Numerator
        store |Denominator| in Denominator
        store GCD(Numerator, Denominator) in Common
        divide Numerator by Common
        divide Denominator by Common
        if the fraction is negative
            then
                multiply Numerator by −1

END OF Reduce
```

When we implement this, we have to remember to declare **Common** in the ⟨*variable declaration part*⟩.

The entire procedure in Pascal then becomes:

```
procedure Reduce(var Num, Denom : integer);

{  Precondition:  Denom <> 0    }

{  Postcondition: This procedure reduces a fraction to lowest terms.    }
{  If the fraction is negative, the minus sign is put in the numerator. }

var
  Sign, Common : integer;

begin
  if Num = 0
    then
      Denom := 1
    else
      begin
        if ((Num > 0) and (Denom > 0)) or ((Num < 0) and (Denom < 0))
          then
            Sign := 1
          else
            Sign := -1;
        Num := abs(Num);
        Denom := abs(Denom);
        Common := GCD(Num, Denom);
        Num := Num div Common;
        Denom := Denom div Common;
        Num := Sign * Num
      end
end;
```

Bugs like this one can be hard to find. There was no error in the syntax so the Pascal compiler didn't help us. The bug was in the algorithm. Such an error is called a *logic error*. A logic error occurs when we have told the computer to do something perfectly legal, but something that we really don't want it to do. The computer will do it, of course, since it has no way of knowing that it's giving us the wrong answer.

Notice that we had to change both the algorithm and the code. Logic errors often are due to errors in the algorithm and a good programmer must always be willing to go back to the third step of the programming process when an error in an algorithm is discovered. Avoid the habit of just patching up the code; if the problem is in the algorithm, fix the algorithm and then fix the code.

6.4   Functions

Let's now turn to functions. We need to write the function GCD and we need to learn how to declare functions in general in Pascal.

We start with a ⟨*function declaration*⟩. The declaration of a function is not much different from the declaration of a procedure. Figure 6.7 contains the syntax diagram for a ⟨*function declaration*⟩.

function declaration:

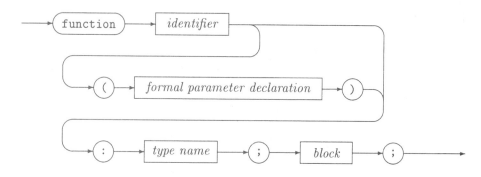

Figure 6.7

There are two differences between this and the declaration for a procedure. First, it starts with the word function; second, after the ⟨*formal parameter declaration*⟩ part, there is a colon, followed by the name of the type returned by the function. Each function returns a single value of a particular type. The type is indicated by the ⟨*typename*⟩.

Additionally, the value to be returned by the function has to be assigned somehow. In Pascal this is done with an ⟨*assignment statement*⟩. At least once within the ⟨*statement part*⟩ of the ⟨*block*⟩ there has to be an ⟨*assignment statement*⟩ that assigns a value to the name of the function. We'll make this clear with an example.

Suppose we need a simple function that determines the larger of two integer values, First and Second. Let's call the function Max. A ⟨*function declaration*⟩ that does the job is on the next page.

```
function Max(First, Second : integer) : integer;

{ This function returns the larger of First and Second  }

begin
   if First > Second
      then
         Max := First
      else
         Max := Second
end;
```

The returned type of the function is **integer**. There are two places where **Max** is assigned a value; which assignment statement is executed depends on whether **First** is greater than **Second** or not.

The function we need, however, is not **Max** but **GCD**. Let's write **GCD**. The algorithm we developed for *GCD* was:

START OF GCD(First, Second)
Preconditions: First and Second are both positive integers

if First < Second then swap First and Second
store the remainder of First ÷ Second in Remainder
loop while Remainder is not zero
   store Second in First
   store Remainder in Second
   store the remainder of First ÷ Second in Remainder
return the value stored in Second

END OF GCD

6.5   The *while statement*

We see that before we can implement this algorithm, we need to implement the *loop while*. It is no accident that this *loop while* has a counterpart in Pascal, the ⟨*while statement*⟩. Figure 6.8 contains the syntax diagram for the ⟨*while statement*⟩.

Recall that a ⟨*Boolean expression*⟩ is an expression that evaluates to either **true** or **false**. The ⟨*while statement*⟩ accomplishes just what we intend with a *loop while*. As long as the ⟨*Boolean expression*⟩ evaluates to **true**, the ⟨*statement*⟩ following the **do** is executed. As soon as the ⟨*Boolean expression*⟩ evaluates to **false**, control passes to whatever follows. Further, it is important to note that the test of the ⟨*Boolean expression*⟩ is done *before* the ⟨*statement*⟩

while statement:

Figure 6.8

is executed; that is, the test is at the top of the loop. Just as we specified in our algorithmic *loop while*, if the test turns out to be **false** the very first time, the ⟨*statement*⟩ inside the ⟨*while statement*⟩ is never executed at all.

There is one difference between the *loop while* and the ⟨*while statement*⟩ that you have to watch out for. Notice that in the algorithm above we put three assignment steps inside the *loop while* with the intention that these three things be done every time. The syntax of the ⟨*while statement*⟩ requires that a *single* statement be put after the word **do**. How can we turn three steps in the algorithm into one ⟨*statement*⟩? Easy: make them into a ⟨*compound statement*⟩ as follows:

```
while Remainder <> 0 do
   begin
      First := Second;
      Second := Remainder;
      Remainder := First mod Second
   end
```

6.6   GCD Continued

Now we can put the above ⟨*compound statement*⟩ and the rest of the function
GCD together:

```
function GCD(First, Second : integer) : integer;
var
    Remainder : integer;

{ Precondition:  First and Second are both positive.  }

{ This function calculates the greatest common divisor of the two   }
{ positive integers First and Second using the Euclidean algorithm. }

begin
    Remainder := First mod Second;
    while Remainder <> 0 do
        begin
            First := Second;
            Second := Remainder;
            Remainder := First mod Second
        end;
    GCD := Second
end;
```

Did we forget to include the step that swaps `First` and `Second` if necessary?
No, we didn't forget. If you think this is a problem, look at exercise 3 at the
end of chapter 5.

6.7   Placement of Procedures and Functions

Figure 6.9 contains the syntax diagram for the ⟨*procedure/function declaration
part*⟩. Notice that the procedure and function declaractions can be included in
either order.

We'll have to say more about this notion in chapter 8 but for now it will
suffice to say that if one module calls another, the one being called must be
placed before the module that's doing the calling. In our current program, the
statement part of the main program contains all the calls to the other routines
except for the call of GCD from Reduce. Therefore, the only thing we have to
do in this program is to make sure that the declaration for GCD comes before
the declaration for Reduce. A skeleton for the entire program would show the
procedure and function declarations in the following order:

procedure/function declaration part:

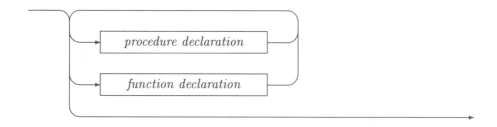

Figure 6.9

```
program Fraction(input, output);

var
    Numerator, Denominator : integer;

    procedure Introduce;
        . . .
    procedure GetFraction(var Num, Denom : integer);
        . . .
    function GCD(First, Second : integer) : integer;
        . . .
    procedure Reduce(var Num, Denom : integer);
        . . .
    procedure DisplayFraction(Num, Denom : integer);
        . . .
    procedure Conclude;
        . . .
begin   { Statement part of the main program  }
    Introduce;
    GetFraction(Numerator, Denominator);
    Reduce(Numerator, Denominator);
    DisplayFraction(Numerator, Denominator);
    Conclude
end.
```

Some rearrangement of this order would be possible, but GCD *must* come before Reduce.

6.8   Documentation

You will have noticed that we put comments at the beginning of each module. Remember the "+" step of the programming process: *Document continuously.* We believe that a well thought-out program, with well-chosen variable names and a consistent style of indentation, doesn't need a lot of documentation, but it does need some.

What we recommend is a set of comments at the beginning of each module that explains *what* the module does, and what the pre- and postconditions are. We do not recommend that you try to explain *how* the module works at this point, just what it does. A reader of your program—and that includes you too—should be able to read the comments at the beginning of the module and understand what job it performs without worrying about how that job is accomplished. If you find it hard to describe in a sentence or two what the module is doing, then you likely have tried to make it do too much. Every module should have one task to perform and you should be able to describe what that task is in a few words. Also, if you find yourself using lots of words, ask yourself if you're explaining *what* the module does or *how* it does it.

In the middle of the module you should include comments that explain *how* the job is getting done. When you have a particularly subtle section, explain *why* that code is there and *how* it works by including some comments.

Sometimes it is helpful to include a comment at the end of a long compound statement to remind the reader how that compound statement started. That is, if you have a long compound statement that, perhaps, extends from one page to another, you might want to include a comment at the end of the compound statement indicating what has just ended. Something like the following can help.

```
while Number < 100 do
   begin
      . . .
   end  { of while Number < 100 }
```

However, don't "over comment." Don't include comments in the middle of the module that explain *what* it is doing. Too many comments can make it harder to read, not easier.

Consider the following example of how *not* to use comments borrowed from GCD:

```
while Remainder <> 0 do

{  Perform the following steps while Remainder <> 0  }

  begin
    First := Second;            { assign the value of Second to First  }
    Second := Remainder;    { assign the value of Remainder to Second  }
    Remainder := First mod Second  { store the remainder in Remainder  }
  end;

{  End of while Remainder <> 0  }

GCD := Second     {  store Second in GCD  }
```

Compare this with GCD on page 178. Surely you will agree that these comments don't help—they don't explain why the statements are there or how the algorithm works—and they make the code harder to read, as well.

Once again, if the algorithm and code have been carefully written, a consistent reasonable style of indentation has been followed, variable names have been chosen carefully and the program has been broken down into single purpose modules, then you will not need to include a lot of comments.

Syntax Considerations Regarding Comments

While we're on the subject, we should say a little more about the syntax of a comment. A few years ago many keyboards did not have a key with the symbols "{" and "}," and so Pascal allows you to substitute "(*" for a "{" and "*)" for a "}." Some programmers use "(* ... *)" for comments, but we prefer the braces. You, of course, can use whichever you prefer. Be careful, however, not to start a comment with "{" and end it with "*)." Even though the Pascal Standard says this is legal, many compilers won't accept it.

You should also be careful not to "nest" comments. If you try to temporarily remove a portion of code by putting comment symbols around the code, and if the portion of code you are trying to remove already contains comments, the first "{" will start the comment, the next "{" will be considered as part of the comment, the first "}" will end the comment and the second "}" will be unmatched and cause a syntax error.

Finally, make sure there is a "}" for every "{." One very easy way to write a lot of code that always compiles, never has any syntax errors, but never does anything, is to put it all in an unintended comment.

6.9   Code for Fraction

The following is a complete program that implements the *Fraction* algorithms.
(Notice that we replaced the ⟨*repeat statement*⟩ in GetFraction with a ⟨*while
statement*⟩).)

```pascal
program Fraction(input, output);

{ Programmer:  Danny Chen                                              }

{ This program allows a user to enter a fraction as two integers,  }
{ reduces the fraction and then displays it as a mixed number.     }

var
    Numerator, Denominator : integer;

procedure Introduce;

{ This procedure simply displays an introduction.  }

begin
    writeln('This program will allow you to enter a fraction and');
    writeln('will reduce the fraction you enter and display it as');
    writeln('a mixed number.');
    writeln('You should enter the fraction as two integers.')
end;

procedure GetFraction(var Num, Denom : integer);

{ This procedure allows the user to enter two integers for the  }
{ numerator and denominator of a fraction.  The denominator      }
{ cannot equal zero.                                             }

begin
    write('Enter the numerator of the fraction: ');
    readln(Num);
    write('Enter the denominator of the fraction: ');
    readln(Denom);
    while Denom = 0 do
        begin
            write('You must enter a non-zero integer.  Try again: ');
            readln(Denom)
        end
end;
```

```
function GCD(First, Second : integer) : integer;

{ Precondition:  First and Second are both positive.  }
{ This function calculates the greatest common divisor of the two  }
{ positive integers First and Second using the Euclidean algorithm. }

var
   Remainder : integer;
begin
   Remainder := First mod Second;
   while Remainder <> 0 do
     begin
       First := Second;
       Second := Remainder;
       Remainder := First mod Second
     end;
   GCD := Second
end;


procedure Reduce(var Num, Denom : integer);

{ Precondition:  Denom <> 0   }
{ Postcondition: This procedure reduces a fraction to lowest terms.   }
{ If the fraction is negative, the minus sign is put in the numerator. }

var
   Sign, Common : integer;
begin
  if Num = 0
    then
      Denom := 1
    else
      begin
        if ((Num > 0) and (Denom > 0)) or ((Num < 0) and (Denom < 0))
          then
            Sign := 1
          else
            Sign := -1;
        Num := abs(Num);
        Denom := abs(Denom);
        Common := GCD(Num, Denom);
        Num := Num div Common;
        Denom := Denom div Common;
        Num := Sign * Num
      end
end;
```

```
procedure DisplayFraction(Num, Denom : integer);

{  Precondition:  The fraction has been reduced and Denom > 0.  }
{  This procedure displays a fraction as a mixed number.        }

var
   Quo, Rem : integer;
begin
  if Denom = 1
    then
      writeln(Num : 1)
    else
      if abs(Num) < Denom
        then
          writeln(Num : 1, '/', Denom : 1)
        else
         begin
           Quo := abs(Num) div Denom;
           Rem := abs(Num) mod Denom;
           if Num > Denom
             then
               writeln(Quo : 1, ' & ', Rem : 1, '/', Denom : 1)
             else
               writeln('-(', Quo : 1, ' & ', Rem : 1, '/', Denom : 1, ')'
         end
end;


procedure Conclude;
begin
   writeln('That concludes the program.  I hope you enjoyed it.')
end;

begin   { Statement part of the main program  }
  Introduce;
  GetFraction(Numerator, Denominator);
  Reduce(Numerator, Denominator);
  DisplayFraction(Numerator, Denominator);
  Conclude
end.
```

6.10 Implementation—Once Again

In this section we'll develop an implementation of the Ping-Pong algorithms from chapter 5. The goal is to write the code for a program that keeps track of the score in a Ping-Pong game. We will take the algorithms one by one in the order they were written in chapter 5, and turn them into code.

The Main Program

We start with the algorithm for the main program:

```
START OF PingPong

call Introduce
call GetFirstServer(FirstServer)
call PlayGame(FirstServer, GameWinner, WinnerScore, LoserScore)
call DisplayWinner(GameWinner, WinnerScore, LoserScore)
call Conclude

END OF PingPong
```

It's clear from looking at the algorithm that we'll need to declare variables `FirstServer` and `GameWinner` of type `char`, and `WinnerScore` and `LoserScore` of type `integer`. We'll also have to declare the procedures `Introduce`, `GetFirstServer`, `PlayGame`, `DisplayWinner` and `Conclude`. We'll write them next. Here's what the program will look like, excluding these procedures.

```
program PingPong(input, output);

{ Programmer:  Adam Philipp                                    }
{ This program keeps score for a game of Ping-Pong.  The user  }
{ indicates the winner of each point, and the program displays the }
{ score.                                                       }

var
   FirstServer, GameWinner : char;
   WinnerScore, LoserScore : integer;
 . . .
begin
   Introduce;
   GetFirstServer(FirstServer);
   PlayGame(FirstServer, GameWinner, WinnerScore, LoserScore);
   DisplayWinner(GameWinner, WinnerScore, LoserScore);
   Conclude
end.
```

The GetFirstServer Procedure

This procedure asks the user to enter the player who is to serve first. It does some error checking to ensure that the user types in an A or a B. Here is the algorithm from chapter 5:

```
START OF GetFirstServer(FirstServer)
Passed by value: none
Passed by reference: FirstServer

display "Please enter the player to serve first (A or B):"
accept FirstServer
loop while FirstServer is neither an 'A' nor a 'B'
    display "Please enter an A or a B:"
    accept FirstServer

END OF GetFirstServer
```

The code follows the algorithm very closely. Beginning programmers sometimes have trouble translating the condition *FirstServer is neither an 'A' nor a 'B'* into the proper Boolean expression. Note how this is done below.

```pascal
procedure GetFirstServer(var FirstServer : char);

{  This procedure gets the first server from the user.  }

begin
    write('Please enter the player to serve first (A or B): ');
    readln(FirstServer);
    while (FirstServer <> 'A') and (FirstServer <> 'B') do
        begin
            write('Please enter an A or a B: ');
            readln(FirstServer)
        end
end;
```

The `DisplayWinner` Procedure

This module simply displays the winner of the game and the score. Here is the algorithm from chapter 5:

START OF DisplayWinner(GameWinner, WinnerScore, LoserScore)
Passed by value: GameWinner, WinnerScore, LoserScore
Passed by reference: none

display "Player", GameWinner, "won by a score of "
display WinnerScore, "to" LoserScore

END OF DisplayWinner

As we mentioned in chapter 5, we'll have to be careful with punctuation when we turn this algorithm into code. Other than that, it's quite simple:

```
procedure DisplayWinner(GameWinner : char;
          WinnerScore, LoserScore : integer);

{  This procedure displays a message indicating which player won.  }

begin
   write('Player ', GameWinner, ' wins by a score of ');
   writeln(WinnerScore : 1, ' to ', LoserScore : 1, '.');
   writeln
end;
```

Notice that we have broken the long *display* step into two statements, for readability.

The `PlayGame` Procedure

As we mentioned before, this procedure is the heart of the whole program. We took some time to develop the algorithm, again using the top-down method. At the end of chapter 5 we mentioned that there should be some additional error checking in the algorithm. The algorithm, with the error checking added, is on the next page.

START OF PlayGame(FirstServer, GameWinner, WinnerScore, LoserScore)
Passed by value: FirstServer
Passed by reference: GameWinner, WinnerScore, LoserScore

store 0 in AScore and in BScore
store FirstServer in Server
loop
    display "The score is:"
    display "Player A:", AScore, "Player B:", "BScore"
    display "Player", Server, "to serve."
    display "Who won the point? (Enter A or B):"
    accept PointWinner
    loop while PointWinner is neither 'A' nor 'B'
        display "Please enter an A or a B:"
        accept PointWinner
    if PointWinner is 'A'
        then
            add 1 to AScore
        else
            add 1 to BScore
    store Winner(AScore, BScore) in GameWinner
    if GameWinner is ' '
        then
            store NextServer(AScore, BScore, Server) in Server
    until GameWinner is either 'A' or 'B'
if GameWinner is 'A'
    then
        store AScore in WinnerScore
        store BScore in LoserScore
    else
        store BScore in WinnerScore
        store AScore in LoserScore

END OF PlayGame

The code starts on the next page. Notice that the functions **Winner** and
NextServer are called by this routine. They will occur before the definition of
PlayGame in the final program.

```
procedure PlayGame(FirstServer : char;
                   var GameWinner : char;
   var WinnerScore, LoserScore : integer);

{ This procedure plays one game of Ping-Pong and returns }
{ the winner and the scores for the winner and the loser. }

var
   AScore, BScore      : integer;
   Server, PointWinner : char;


begin
   AScore := 0;
   BScore := 0;
   Server := FirstServer;
   repeat
      writeln('The score is:');
      writeln;
      writeln('Player A: ', AScore : 3, '  Player B: ', BScore : 3);
      writeln;
      writeln('Player ', Server, ' serves.');
      write('Who won the point? (Enter A or B): ');
      readln(PointWinner);
      while (PointWinner <> 'A') and (PointWinner <> 'B') do
         begin
            write('Please enter an A or a B: ');
            readln(PointWinner)
         end;
      if PointWinner = 'A'
         then
            AScore := AScore + 1
         else
            BScore := BScore + 1;
      GameWinner := Winner(AScore, BScore);
      if GameWinner = ' '
         then
            Server := NextServer(AScore, BScore, Server)
   until (GameWinner = 'A') or (GameWinner = 'B');
```

```
    if GameWinner = 'A'
        then
            begin
                WinnerScore := AScore;
                LoserScore := BScore
            end
        else
            begin
                WinnerScore := BScore;
                LoserScore := AScore
            end
end;
```

The Function Winner

This function determines whether or not one of the players has won the game, and if so, which one. The function is to return a char corresponding to the winning player if there is one, and a space if neither has yet won. Here's the algorithm again:

START OF *Winner*(AScore, BScore)

if AScore $\geq$ 21 and AScore $-$ BScore $\geq$ 2
    then
        return 'A'
    else
        if BScore $\geq$ 21 and BScore $-$ AScore $\geq$ 2
            then
                return 'B'
            else
                return ' '

END OF *Winner*

And here's the code:

```
function Winner(AScore, BScore : integer) : char;

{  This function returns the winner of the game, if there is one,  }
{  and returns a space if there isn't.                             }

begin
   if (AScore >= 21) and (AScore - BScore >= 2)
      then
         Winner := 'A'
      else
         if (BScore >= 21) and (BScore - AScore >= 2)
            then
               Winner := 'B'
            else
               Winner := ' '
end;
```

The Function NextServer

This function determines which player is to serve next, based on the score and who is currently serving. In the main part of the game, the serve changes every five points, but after both players reach 20, the serve changes every point until the end of the game. Here is the algorithm:

START OF NextServer(AScore, BScore, CurrentServer)

if (AScore + BScore) mod 5 is zero
*   or AScore and BScore are both $\geq$ 20*
*   then*
*   if CurrentServer = 'A'*
*   then*
*   return 'B'*
*   else*
*   return 'A'*
*   else*
*   return CurrentServer*

END OF NextServer

The only tricky part in writing the code occurs in the Boolean expression that corresponds to (AScore + BScore) *mod* 5 *is zero or* AScore *and* BScore *are both* $\geq$ 20. Note carefully how parentheses are used. There are two Boolean expressions joined by an **or**. They are: (AScore + BScore) mod 5 = 0 and (AScore >= 20) and (BScore >= 20).

Parentheses are needed in the first Boolean expression so that the **mod** operator acts on the sum of AScore and BScore, rather than just BScore. The second Boolean expression is formed by joining two Boolean expressions with the **and** operator. Parentheses are needed there because of the high precedence of **and**. In fact, since **and** has a higher precedence than **or**, a second set of parentheses is not needed surrounding the second Boolean expression.

```
function NextServer(AScore, BScore : integer;
                       CurrentServer : char) : char;


{  This function switches the current server every fifth game,  }
{  or every game after the score is tied at 20 all.             }


begin
   if ((AScore + BScore) mod 5 = 0) or (AScore >= 20) and (BScore >= 20)
      then
         if CurrentServer = 'A'
            then
               NextServer := 'B'
            else
               NextServer := 'A'
      else
         NextServer := CurrentServer
end;
```

The Full Program

The code for the PingPong program is listed on the next four pages. We have included short versions of Introduce and Conclude; you're advised to elaborate on these to make the program more personable.

```
program PingPong(input, output);

{  Programmer:  William Rollins                                  }

{  This program keeps score for a game of Ping-Pong.  The user    }
{  indicates the winner of each point, and the program displays the }
{  score.                                                         }

var
   FirstServer, GameWinner : char;
   WinnerScore, LoserScore : integer;

   procedure Introduce;

   {  This procedure simply displays an introduction.  }

   begin
      writeln('This program keeps score for a Ping-Pong game between');
      writeln('player A and player B.  The first player to score 21');
      writeln('points and lead the other player by at least 2 points');
      writeln('wins.');
      writeln;
      writeln('Players alternate serves every 5 games.  If the score');
      writeln('is tied at 20, then players alternate serves every');
      writeln('point thereafter.  Flip a coin to see which player');
      writeln('serves first.');
      writeln
   end;

   procedure GetFirstServer(var FirstServer : char);

   {  This procedure gets the first server from the user.  }

   begin
      writeln('Please enter the player to serve first (A or B): ');
      readln(FirstServer);
      while (FirstServer <> 'A') and (FirstServer <> 'B') do
         begin
            write('Please enter an A or a B: ');
            readln(FirstServer)
         end
   end;
```

```
function Winner(AScore, BScore : integer) : char;

{  This function returns the winner of the game, if there is one,  }
{  and returns a space if there isn't.                             }

begin
    if (AScore >= 21) and (AScore - BScore >= 2)
        then
            Winner := 'A'
        else
            if (BScore >= 21) and (BScore - AScore >= 2)
                then
                    Winner := 'B'
                else
                    Winner := ' '
end;

function NextServer(AScore, BScore : integer;
                    CurrentServer : char) : char;

{  This function switches the current server every fifth game,  }
{  or every game after the score is tied at 20 all.             }

begin
    if ((AScore + BScore) mod 5 = 0) or (AScore >= 20) and (BScore >= 20)
        then
            if CurrentServer = 'A'
                then
                    NextServer := 'B'
                else
                    NextServer := 'A'
        else
            NextServer := CurrentServer
end;
```

```
procedure PlayGame(FirstServer : char;
                var GameWinner : char;
   var WinnerScore, LoserScore : integer);

{  This procedure plays one game of Ping-Pong and returns  }
{  the winner and the scores for the winner and the loser. }

var
   AScore, BScore      : integer;
   Server, PointWinner : char;

begin
   AScore := 0;
   BScore := 0;
   Server := FirstServer;
   repeat
      writeln('The score is:');
      writeln;
      writeln('Player A: ', AScore : 3, '  Player B: ', BScore : 3);
      writeln;
      writeln('Player ', Server, ' serves.');
      write('Who won the point? (Enter A or B): ');
      readln(PointWinner);
      while (PointWinner <> 'A') and (PointWinner <> 'B') do
         begin
            write('Please enter an A or a B: ');
            readln(PointWinner)
         end;
      if PointWinner = 'A'
         then
            AScore := AScore + 1
         else
            BScore := BScore + 1;
      GameWinner := Winner(AScore, BScore);
      if GameWinner = ' '
         then
            Server := NextServer(AScore, BScore, Server)
   until (GameWinner = 'A') or (GameWinner = 'B');
```

```
        if GameWinner = 'A'
           then
              begin
                 WinnerScore := AScore;
                 LoserScore := BScore
              end
           else
              begin
                 WinnerScore := BScore;
                 LoserScore := AScore
              end
   end;



   procedure DisplayWinner(GameWinner : char;
              WinnerScore, LoserScore : integer);

   {  This procedure displays a message indicating which player won.  }

   begin
      write('Player ', GameWinner, ' wins by a score of ');
      writeln(WinnerScore : 1, ' to ', LoserScore : 1, '.');
      writeln
   end;

   procedure Conclude;

   begin
      writeln('That concludes the program.  Thanks for playing!')
   end;

begin   { Main Program }
   Introduce;
   GetFirstServer(FirstServer);
   PlayGame(FirstServer, GameWinner, WinnerScore, LoserScore);
   DisplayWinner(GameWinner, WinnerScore, LoserScore);
   Conclude
end.
```

6.11   Summary and Review

This chapter concerned itself with modular programming in Pascal.

- We discussed writing and calling procedures and functions in Pascal.

- We learned how to pass parameters in Pascal.

- When parameters are passed by value, Pascal refers to them as *value parameters*, while parameters passed by reference are *variable parameters*.

- The invocation of a procedure in Pascal becomes a new ⟨*statement*⟩, and the invocation of a function becomes an ⟨*expression*⟩.

- In Pascal, the actual parameters and formal parameters must agree in *number*, *order* and *type*.

- We implemented the algorithms from chapter 5 concerning entering and displaying a fraction.

- We introduced a new Pascal statement, the ⟨*while statement*⟩. The ⟨*while statement*⟩ is an exact counterpart of the *loop while* introduced in chapter 5. Note that the loop we used in the procedure `GetFraction` is actually a *loop while*, and we should implement it that way, now that we know about the ⟨*while statement*⟩.

- We discussed documentation and the use of comments in a Pascal program.

6.12   New Terms Introduced

abstract data type An algorithmic data type considered without regard as to how it may be implemented in a computer language.

argument Another term used for the actual parameter sent to a function.

assignment compatible A situation where the value of an expression can be stored in a variable of possibly a different type, such as storing an `integer` value in a `real` variable or passing an `integer` by value to a `real` formal parameter.

formal parameter declaration The place in a procedure or function declaration where the formal parameters are declared.

function declaration The part of a program where a function is declared.

local variable A variable declared in a procedure or function. The variable does not exist in the world outside that procedure or function and, hence, is *local* to the routine.

procedure declaration The part of a program where a procedure is declared.

supplied functions Those functions that always exist in Standard Pascal.

value parameter A parameter passed by value.

variable parameter A parameter passed by reference; accomplished by including the word `var` in the formal parameter declaration.

while statement The Pascal statement used to implement a *loop while.*

6.13 Exercises

1. Make the following modifications to the program given on pages 182–184:

   (a) Rewrite the `Introduce` and `Conclude` procedures so that they cause the computer to "speak" to the user in a more conversational way.

   (b) Use the Standard Pascal supplied procedure `page(output)` to clear the screen before the program introduces itself. If the compiler you are using does not support `page`, find out how you can clear the screen on your system.

   (c) Modify the main program so that after displaying the fraction, the program asks the user if he or she wants to enter another fraction, and continues until the user indicates otherwise. Modify the algorithm first, then make the changes to the code.

2. Write an algorithm and the code for a subroutine that is passed an integer access code and passes back a Boolean value that is `true` if the user types the correct code within three tries and `false` otherwise. Should this routine be written as a function or as a procedure?

3. There is a Boolean operator called XOR (for *exclusive-or*), which is not implemented in Pascal. This operator acts on two arguments and is `true` only if exactly one of the two arguments is `true`. Write the algorithm and the code for a function to implement XOR.

4. Write a complete Pascal program based on the algorithms from exercises 8–11, chapter 5. The program will calculate the perimeters of various geometric shapes.

5. Write a complete Pascal program based on the algorithms from exercises 12–18, chapter 5. The program will allow the user to enter a date in numeric format and see it displayed in English, including the day of the week.

Chapter 7

Modular Programming—Continued

> Computers do what you tell them to do,
> not necessarily what you want them to do.
> — Pui Hin Wong

7.1   Overview of the Chapter

In this chapter we will continue to discuss modular programming, and extend the problem discussed in chapter 5 concerning fractions. We will see that when modules have been written independently and with each one having its own specific task, they can be used in later applications. The concept of multi-way selection will be introduced.

7.2   Introduction

In chapter 5 we defined a problem concerning a fraction. We solved it and developed an algorithm for the solution. The resulting program wasn't very fancy; it simply allowed the user to enter a fraction and then displayed it as a mixed number. Now we want to extend the problem to do some arithmetic on fractions. We will be able to use many of the modules developed before, which shows the value of using independent modules, each of which has a particular task to perform.

7.3   Define the Problem

Let's start with the definition of our new problem.

> Write a program that allows a user to enter two fractions and an arithmetic operator: "+," "−," "*" or "/." The computer should

then perform the indicated operation on the two fractions and display the result as a mixed number. The operator "*" means multiplication and "/" means division. The computer should display the original fractions (possibly as improper fractions) and display the resulting fraction as a reduced mixed number. The user should be able to continue entering fractions and operators until he decides to exit the program.

For example, if the user were to enter 1/3 and 4/5 as the two fractions, and "+" as the operator, the program should have the computer display:

```
The sum of 1/3 and 4/5 is 1 & 2/15.
```

Then, if the user chose to do it again and entered 17/3 and −3/7 as the two fractions and entered "/" as the operator, the program should have the computer display:

```
The quotient of 17/3 divided by -3/7 is -(13 & 2/9).
```

Since this program is a bit more interesting than the one in the previous chapter, the user may want to try it again and again using different fractions and different operators; that's why we decided to let the user enter fractions over and over until deciding to quit.

This problem is being presented in a well-defined manner, unlike other problems we have presented. Thus, we are not going to have to spend any time going through the refinement of the definition of the problem. Remember, though, that real world problems will not usually be this well defined and you will have to spend that time. We now move on to the solution and the development of the algorithm.

7.4   Solve the Problem

As we did in chapter 5, we solve the problem in a modular fashion. We break the problem into smaller and smaller steps until we get to a bottom level. What has to be done? The computer has to let the user enter two fractions and an operator, the computer has to perform the indicated operation on these fractions, and then display the result. After displaying the result, the program has to ask the user if he wants to enter another pair of fractions, and should follow whichever course of action the user indicates. Of course, an introduction and a conclusion must be displayed on the screen.

Here's what we have as a high-level algorithm:

```
call Introduce
loop
    call GetData
    call PerformOperation
    call DisplayResult
    until the user wants to quit
call Conclude
```

That's a solution on a high level. Let's look at the lower-level modules.

Get the Data From the User

One lower-level module is the module that gets the data from the user. This module itself can be broken down into three yet lower steps: get the first fraction, get the second fraction and get the operator. Notice that the module we developed in chapter 5—*GetFraction*—can be used for the first two steps.

Perform the Operation

How about the step that performs the operation? It can be accomplished by simply looking at the operator and deciding whether to add, subtract, multiply or divide the fractions. It should seem natural by now to use modules that do the actual arithmetic.

Display the Result

The step that displays the result is also straightforward and can use the module from chapter 5 that displayed a fraction as a mixed number.

We are quietly slipping from the "Solve the Problem" step into the "Develop the Algorithm" step, which is a normal state of affairs. Let's write the algorithms more formally.

7.5 Develop an Algorithm

Get the Data From the User

Starting with the step that gets the fractions and the operator from the user, what are the parameters? Clearly, they are the two fractions and the operator.

If we agree to call these *Fraction1*, *Fraction2* and *Operator*, and agree to call the module *GetData*, the algorithm would look like:

```
START OF GetData(Fraction1, Fraction2, Operator)
Passed by value: none
Passed by reference: Fraction1, Fraction2, Operator
Postcondition: Two valid fractions and a valid operator are obtained

display "Enter the first fraction:"
call GetFraction(Fraction1)
display "Enter the second fraction:"
call GetFraction(Fraction2)
call GetOperator(Operator)

END OF GetData
```

This looks simple enough. Since we have already written an algorithm for *GetFraction*, there's nothing more to do there. It will be easy to write an algorithm for *GetOperator* and we'll leave that as an exercise.

Can you explain why the parameters are being passed by reference?

Perform the Operation

Let's look now at the subroutine *PerformOperation*. We know what this routine is supposed to do: take the two fractions, perform the indicated operation on them and send back the result.

Before we get into the algorithm, we should first think about the parameters to *PerformOperation*. There are four parameters: the two fractions, the resulting fraction and the operator.

Let's call these four parameters *Fraction1*, *Fraction2*, *Fraction* and *Operator*.

Should these parameters be passed by value or by reference? Be careful not to assume they all need to be sent the same way. Recall the two questions from chapter 5 that help decide how to pass a parameter:

1. Is the value of the parameter going to change inside the subroutine?

2. Should the changed value be sent back to the calling routine?

Let's apply the test to the four parameters of *PerformOperation*. To be able to answer these questions, it will help to look at an example. Suppose the main program has the following values:

Fraction1 = 24/45,
Fraction2 = 15/50 and
Operator = "+."

In other words, the user wants the computer to add 24/45 and 15/50 together, reduce the result and display it as a mixed number. Add these fractions together yourself by hand and see what you get.

Don't go on reading until you add the two fractions together. If you actually do it by hand and think about what you're doing, it will be a lot easier to figure out how to get the computer to do it.

It will be the job of *PerformOperation* to add 24/45 and 15/50 together and produce the result. The result must be sent back from *PerformOperation* to the main program. That tells us that the result must be passed by reference; the value of *Fraction* is going to change inside the routine and we want the changed value sent back.

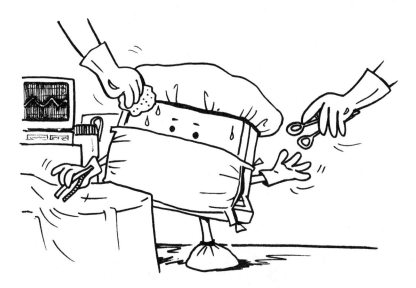

How about the original fractions? Are they going to change inside the routine? In particular, will the value of *Fraction1* change inside *PerformOperation*? When you added 24/45 and 15/50 together and got 5/6, did the first fraction change? (You did add them together, didn't you?)

Many people would reduce 24/45 to 8/15 and 15/50 to 3/10 before adding them, so it looks like the fractions do change. But just because people are taught to reduce fractions before adding them doesn't mean computers have to. One might argue that the computer can work with big numbers just as easily as it can work with small numbers so there's no need to reduce. That argument is valid, except that it is possible that the numbers the computer is working with can get bigger than `maxint`.

Consider another example. Suppose we have the following values:

Fraction1 = 2400/4500,
Fraction2 = 1500/5000 and
Operator = "+."

The result is 5/6 again, right? If the fractions are reduced to 8/15 and 3/10 as before, the computer will get the same answer. However, if we fail to tell the computer to reduce the fractions first, it might very well multiply two of these numbers together and exceed `maxint`.

Try the problem by hand without a calculator and without reducing or finding a lowest common denominator.

Did any of the numbers you worked with get bigger than 32,767? If so, then some computers will have a problem since many microcomputers use 32,767 for `maxint`. While we cannot expect the computer to be able to add *every* possible pair of fractions, we can increase the number of fractions it can handle by reducing the fractions before attempting to perform the indicated operation.

We got onto this tack by trying to answer the question, "Is the value of *Fraction1* going to change inside *PerformOperation*?" The answer seems to be "yes," or at least "maybe." So, we need to ask the second question: "Do we want the changed value of *Fraction1* sent back to the calling routine?"

The answer to this question is "no." There is no reason to send the reduced fractions back to the main program routine. In fact, the statement of the problem indicates that the user's original fractions should be displayed just as they were entered—not reduced—so we had better not send them back reduced.

The answer to the second question is "no," so *Fraction1* should be passed by value. The same argument applies to *Fraction2*.

How about the operator? There is no reason to change the operator inside *PerformOperation*, so it too should be passed by value.

With this taken care of, we can go on to writing the algorithm for *Perform-Operation*. What do we want it to accomplish? It should first reduce the two fractions and then look at the operator and decide whether to add, subtract, multiply or divide the fractions.

That amounts to a top-down solution to the problem facing *PerformOper-ation*. That is, we have reduced the job of performing the desired operation to one of four simpler jobs, adding them, subtracting them, multiplying them or dividing them. The solution to each of these four simpler jobs becomes another subroutine called by *PerformOperation*.

Formalizing this in an algorithm, using the conventions we introduced earlier, we have:

START OF PerformOperation(Fraction1, Fraction2, Operator, Fraction)
Passed by value: Fraction1, Fraction2 and Operator
Passed by reference: Fraction
Preconditions: Denom1 and Denom2 are non-zero;
                    if Operator = '/,' Num2 is non-zero

call Reduce(Fraction1)
call Reduce(Fraction2)
if Operator = '+'
    then
        call Add(Fraction1, Fraction2, Fraction)
    else
        if Operator = '−'
            then
                call Subtract(Fraction1, Fraction2, Fraction)
            else
                if Operator = '*'
                    then
                        call Multiply(Fraction1, Fraction2, Fraction)
                    else
                        call Divide(Fraction1, Fraction2, Fraction)
call Reduce(Fraction)

END OF PerformOperation

We'll discuss the algorithms for *Add*, etc., below. Before we do, however, we want to discuss a new concept, that of *multi-way selection* (also called *multi-way branching*).

7.6   Multi-way Selection

In the algorithm above we use several *if...then...else* steps to decide which routine to call. We indent each *if...then...else* according to the scheme presented in chapter 3, and you will have noticed that the algorithm marched off to the right of the page. If we had more cases to check, we would end up so far to the right that we would not be able to fit what we were writing on the page.

Some programmers prefer to use a different style of indentation when they have more than three or four *if...then...elses* nested this way. There are a number of different ways to indent and, of course, you can use our way of doing it or choose one of these other methods.

Here's an example of a method that is quite popular:

if Operator = '+' then
        call Add(Fraction1, Fraction2, Fraction)
    else if Operator = '−' then
        call Subtract(Fraction1, Fraction2, Fraction)
    else if Operator = '*' then
        call Multiply(Fraction1, Fraction2, Fraction)
    else
        call Divide(Fraction1, Fraction2, Fraction)

Actually, this series of *if...then...elses* is being used to accomplish multi-way selection. It is obvious that multi-way selection can always be implemented with a series of *if...then...elses*, but there are other ways to do it.

The *when* Step

For example, we can invent a *when* step for our algorithms, if we choose to. The idea is to look at the *Operator* and decide which subroutine to call. In English you might say, "when the operator is a '+,' call the addition subroutine; when it's a '−,' call the subtraction subroutine; when it's an '*,' ...." The "it" in the sentence is, of course, the operator; you don't have to keep repeating the word "operator" if you don't want to.

In an algorithm we could say:

when Operator is
    '+',   call Add(Fraction1, Fraction2, Fraction)
    '−',   call Subtract(Fraction1, Fraction2, Fraction)
    '*',   call Multiply(Fraction1, Fraction2, Fraction)
    '/',   call Divide(Fraction1, Fraction2, Fraction)

This captures the same meaning as the series of *if...then...elses* and is a lot easier to understand.

From now on we'll use such a *when* structure when it makes our multi-way branch easy to follow. There will be times that a series of *if...then...elses* will be better.

7.7   Develop an Algorithm—Continued

Subroutines of *PerformOperation*

Now let's look at the subroutines called by *PerformOperation*: *Add, Subtract, Multiply* and *Divide*.

Add

First, the parameters. What needs to be sent to *Add*? We essentially made that decision already. In the call of *Add* above, we sent *Fraction1, Fraction2,* and *Fraction*. (Why didn't we send the operator?)

So that we won't get confused about which routine we're talking about, let's call these three parameters *Fract1, Fract2,* and *Fract* while we're inside *Add*. That is, *Fraction1* is the actual parameter and *Fract1* is the formal parameter.

Once again it is necessary to decide whether the parameters are passed by value or by reference. Ask yourself the two questions about the three parameters before you go any further. Be sure you know which method should be used for each parameter. You can check your answers against the algorithm below but be sure you think about it first.

In order to write *Add*, we need to think back to elementary school. How did people add fractions before calculators came along? For the sake of an example, consider the following simple addition problem:

$$\frac{5}{6} + \frac{3}{8}$$

To add these two fractions, we first find the least common denominator, (namely the least common multiple of 6 and 8), called the *lcm*. The lcm of

6 and 8 is 24. Then we multiply the numerator and denominator of the first fraction by some amount that will make the denominator equal to 24. Then we multiply the numerator and denominator of the second fraction by some amount that will make the denominator of the second fraction equal to 24. What are those amounts? The first is just the lcm divided by 6, i.e., 24 ÷ 6; the second is just the lcm divided by 8 (24 ÷ 8).

$$\frac{5 \times \frac{24}{6}}{6 \times \frac{24}{6}} + \frac{3 \times \frac{24}{8}}{8 \times \frac{24}{8}}$$

which equals:

$$\frac{5 \times 4}{24} + \frac{3 \times 3}{24}$$

Then the sum of the two fractions is found by adding together the two numerators and putting that sum over the lcm:

$$\frac{20 + 9}{24} = \frac{29}{24}$$

This is only one example, but it describes a step-by-step process that gets the job done no matter what the values are. And, of course, that's just what an algorithm is: a description of a step-by-step process that accomplishes some task. In other words, we should be able to to rewrite those steps in our algorithmic language.

Before we can write it, however, there are a couple of details to handle. In the description above, we indicated that we need to find the lcm of the two denominators. Two questions arise: first, how do we find the lcm? And second, where do we put it when we find it?

The answer to the first question is easy: "Don't worry about that now." We'll just assume that the lcm can be found and worry about how to find it when we get *Add* finished. At the risk of repeating it too often, we'll say it again—that's the whole idea of modular programming. Break the job into modules and worry about them one at a time.

The answer to the second question is also easy. Since the denominator of the resulting fraction is always equal to the lcm of the two denominators, just put the lcm there.

Thus, we have the following algorithm for *Add*. Since we have three fractions to deal with, we'll call them *Fraction1*, *Fraction2* and *Fraction*. We'll call the numerator and denominator of the first fraction *Numerator1* and *Denominator1*, etc.

```
START OF Add(Fraction1, Fraction2, Fraction)
Passed by value: Fraction1, Fraction2
Passed by reference: Fraction
Preconditions: The fractions Fraction1 and Fraction2 have been reduced

store the lcm of Denominator1 and Denominator2 in Denominator
store Numerator1 * (Denominator/Denominator1) in Numerator1
store Numerator2 * (Denominator/Denominator2) in Numerator2
store Numerator1 + Numerator2 in Numerator

END OF Add
```

And that's it; it's not nearly as hard as it looked.

Subtract

It would now be easy to write a similar routine for subtracting the second fraction from the first. It would look exactly like the algorithm we just finished except the last step would have a minus sign instead of a plus sign. Rather than write another module, however, we can save some time and effort by realizing that subtraction is really just addition of the additive inverse. That is, in order to subtract *Fraction2* from *Fraction1*, it suffices to add *Fraction1* to the negative of *Fraction2*. Since we already have a routine that does the addition, we don't really have to write another for subtraction.

But then, how do we get it to add the negative? The answer to this is found by realizing that we can change the *actual* parameters—the parameters in the routine *PerformOperation*.

Earlier we wrote:

```
when Operator is
    '+',    call Add(Fraction1, Fraction2, Fraction)
    '−',    call Subtract(Fraction1, Fraction2, Fraction)
    '*',    call Multiply(Fraction1, Fraction2, Fraction)
    '/',    call Divide(Fraction1, Fraction2, Fraction)
```

Consider what would happen if we changed the third line to:

```
    '−',    call Add(Fraction1, −Fraction2, Fraction)
```

Rather than send *Fraction2* to *Subtract*, we send −*Fraction2* to *Add*. Writing this as a mathematical expression might help:

$$\frac{Numerator1}{Denominator1} - \frac{Numerator2}{Denominator2} = \frac{Numerator1}{Denominator1} + \frac{-Numerator2}{Denominator2}$$

This looks great, but is it legal? How is *Fraction2* being passed to *Add*? By value! What happens when a parameter is passed by value? A *copy* of the actual parameter is sent to the subroutine. If *Fraction2* equals 6/7, −*Fraction2* equals −6/7, and −6/7 is sent to *Add*.

It is very important to notice that this cannot be done if the parameter is passed by reference, since what is sent in that case is the *address* of the actual parameter, not a copy of its value. A variable has an address; other values, such as results of evaluations of expressions, do not.

To summarize,

- when the actual parameter is being passed by value, it can be any *expression* of the proper type;

- when the actual parameter is being passed by reference, it can only be a *variable*.

Since this is important, we can say it again in a slightly different way, using some Pascal-like language:

- If the formal parameter is a *value* parameter, the actual parameter can be any *expression* of the same type as the formal parameter.

- If the formal parameter is a *variable* parameter, the actual parameter must be a *variable* of the same type as the formal parameter.

Multiply and *Divide*

We'll leave these for you to write. Notice that—as with subtraction—a separate routine for division is not needed. Once you have a routine that multiplies two fractions, that routine can also be used to divide two fractions. Division is just multiplication by the reciprocal.

If we think about division for a moment, we realize that there is a potential problem. We were careful in *GetFraction* to guarantee that we didn't allow the user to enter a fraction with a zero denominator. We did this because we wanted to make sure the remainder of the program only worked with valid fractions. The subsequent routines, *Reduce* for example, depend on the fraction not having a zero denominator. While we have used *GetFraction* in *GetData*, and thus are sure that each fraction the user enters is a valid fraction, if the user enters a "/," indicating division, and the second fraction entered happens to have a zero for the *numerator*, the fraction resulting from the division will have a zero denominator. When this fraction is sent to *Reduce*, the program will crash.

We have to prevent this from happening. The first question is, where do we put whatever steps are necessary? Clearly we could watch out for this case inside

Multiply and take some action, like have the user enter another pair of fractions. But then the module that is supposed to just multiply the two fractions would contain some input/output steps. This is contrary to the philosophy of modular programming. We should not write modules that perform two jobs. Each module should perform one and only one task. Besides, if we put some I/O inside *Multiply* then it would only be usable in an interactive environment. It is much better to have a module that we can trust to multiply two fractions together and do nothing but that.

Where should we watch out for the possibility of having a second fraction with a zero numerator and a "/" operator? The answer should be obvious by now; inside *GetData*, of course. The job of *GetData* is to get two fractions and an operator from the user. A postcondition of this routine should be that when the operation indicated by the operator is applied to the two fractions, a valid fraction results. To guarantee the postcondition, we need to go back and modify *GetData*.

Notice that we should not change *GetFraction*; it works fine. *GetData* should still get two fractions and an operator, but the routine should not exit until the postcondition is satisfied. We'll leave fixing *GetData* as an exercise.

Before we continue, since there seems to be a tendency for beginning programmers to put such patches in their code, let's say it once again. Don't get in the habit of putting patches in your algorithms or code to fix a problem that is caused by another routine. It is often tempting to "fix" routines in this way but this temptation should be resisted.

The Least Common Denominator

We're almost done. The only thing left in *PerformOperation* is a routine that will yield the least common denominator. As we mentioned before, this is the least common multiple, the lcm. The lcm of two positive integers is the smallest positive integer that both of the given integers divide into exactly.

If you know the gcd of two integers, you can find the lcm by simply multiplying the two numbers together and then dividing by the gcd. For example, the gcd of 20 and 28 is 4. Multiply 20 times 28 and divide by 4. You get 140, and that's the lcm of 20 and 28. Since we already have a way of finding the gcd, this is particularly easy. We're not going to take the time to prove that this procedure is mathematically correct but you should take the time to try it on some more pairs of integers if you're not convinced.

What kind of a routine is the one that yields the lcm? Whereas the earlier routines in this chapter are procedures—they each perform some task—this routine is a function, it returns a single value.

An algorithm for a function that calculates the least common multiple would then look something like:

START OF LCM(First, Second)
Preconditions: First and Second are both positive integers

$$\text{return } \frac{First*Second}{GCD(First, Second)}$$

END OF LCM

We wrote this algorithm for a general purpose function that could be used by any program that needs the lcm of two numbers, not just our program. Since we do plan to use it in our program, we have to make sure that the calling routine guarantees the precondition that the parameters are positive integers. Are we guaranteeing the precondition? Which routine calls *LCM*? *Add*, right? What are the actual parameters being passed to *LCM*? The two denominators of the fractions. Are they guaranteed to be positive? Yes; since we sent the two fractions to *Reduce* before we called *Add*, and since *Reduce* always returns fractions with positive denominators, the precondition is always satisfied.

Notice that writing routines with preconditions makes the routine itself simpler because all the special cases don't have to be watched for, but that doesn't mean that you don't have to watch out for the preconditions. They are guaranteed by a higher-level routine and, as a programmer, you still have to insure that the preconditions are satisfied in the higher-level routines. In this program, the preconditions of all the subsequent routines are actually guaranteed by the postconditions of *GetData*.

DisplayResult, Introduce and Conclude

The algorithms for *DisplayResult*, *Introduce* and *Conclude* will be left as exercises.

When you write *DisplayResult*, remember that the user's fractions are to be displayed as they were entered—i.e., not reduced. And remember that we already have a routine, *DisplayFraction*, that will display a reduced fraction nicely. You should use that routine when you write *DisplayResult*, but don't use it on the user's fractions since they're not reduced.

Make some decisions about how you want to write *Introduce* and *Conclude*. These two routines are easy to write but they are important! This is where you give the computer much of its personality. Don't get lazy and write sloppy introductions and conclusions. If the program is to be easy for a stranger to use, the introduction must be well thought-out and carefully written. This is a major part of what is meant by "user friendliness." Be sure to use complete sentences; be sure to spell things correctly. When most people use a program that displays poor English or misspelled words, they have a tendency to think the computer is dumb; actually the programmer is the one to blame, not the computer.

7.8 The Main Routine

The main routine is straightforward; it's just a series of calls to lower-level routines enclosed in a loop. It might look something like:

```
START OF RationalArithmetic

call Introduce
loop
    call GetData(Fraction1, Fraction2, Operator)
    call PerformOperation(Fraction1, Fraction2, Operator, Fraction)
    call DisplayResult(Fraction1, Fraction2, Operator, Fraction)
    until the user wants to quit
call Conclude

END OF RationalArithmetic
```

By now you have had some experience asking the user whether or not she or he wants to quit; you shouldn't have any problem implementing the loop. Since this sort of thing becomes fairly automatic, we'll leave the details for step 4: coding the algorithm, to be done in the next chapter.

7.9 Problem Extension—Once Again

In this section we will extend the problem discussed in the "Once Again" section in chapters 5 and 6 for keeping score in Ping-Pong. In so doing, we'll provide another example of the usefulness of modular programming.

Define the Problem

Again, we imagine two people playing Ping-Pong. This time we want to use the computer to keep score for an entire match, which consists (for our purposes) of the best two out of three games.

The program should ask the user who is to serve first in the match. The computer should then display **Begin game 1:**, and the first game is played in the same manner as the program in chapter 6. The computer should then display the number of games won by each player up to this point, and then display **Begin game 2:**. The player to serve first in the second game is the player who received serve in the first game; the program should handle this automatically. For the third game, if it's necessary, the player who served to start the match should serve. At the end of the match, the computer should display the winner of the match and the score in games.

Solve the Problem

The top-level solution for this problem is very similar to the one from chapter 5, except that instead of simulating a "game" of Ping-Pong, we are to simulate a "match."

> First, display an introduction for the user. Ask the user who is to serve first. Simulate a Ping-Pong match, and display the winner and a conclusion for the user.

We will be more specific about "simulating a Ping-Pong match" a bit later.

Develop an Algorithm for the Solution

Here is the corresponding top-level algorithm:

```
Introduce
GetFirstServer
PlayMatch
DisplayWinner
Conclude
```

Notice that we will be able to use many of the modules we have already written; this comes as no surprise. Let's look at the parameters to be passed to these routines, and then look more specifically at the algorithm for *PlayMatch*.

Introduce and *Conclude*, of course, can be left for the coding step. *GetFirstServer* can be used exactly as it is from the previous program. The *PlayMatch* module will need to know who is to serve first, and will have to pass the winner of the match and the number of games won by each player back to the main program, so that they can be passed to and displayed by *DisplayWinner*. *DisplayWinner* can also be used just as it is. In fact, it can be used to display the winner of each game and of the match itself. To make the program friendlier, we can include a *display* step before the call to *DisplayWinner* in the main algorithm. Here is the algorithm with the appropriate parameters:

```
START OF PingPongMatch

call Introduce
call GetFirstServer(FirstServer)
call PlayMatch(FirstServer, MatchWinner, WinnerGames, LoserGames)
display "The result of the match:"
call DisplayWinner(MatchWinner, WinnerGames, LoserGames)
call Conclude

END OF PingPongMatch
```

The Module *PlayMatch*

Just as *PlayGame* was the heart of the previous program, *PlayMatch* is the heart of this one. Think in general terms about what we want this module to do. We'll have to keep track of who is serving, so that we can alternate first servers from one game to the next. We'll have to keep track of the number of games won by each player.

The main part of the module will be a *loop until*, since we're sure that the players will play at least one game. Each time through the loop (except for the first), the module should display the number of games won so far by each player. After each game, the module should display the winner of that game and the score, and decide whether the match has been won.

Here's a first draft of the algorithm for *PlayMatch*:

```
initialize the variables that keep track of
                the number of games won by each player
loop
    if it's not the first game
        then
            display the number of games won by each player
    call PlayGame
    display the result of the game
    add 1 to the number of games won by the winner
    if the match is not over
        then
            switch FirstServer
    until one of the players has won the match
store the proper values in WinnerGames and LoserGames
```

We can use *AGamesWon* and *BGamesWon* to store the number of games won by each player. They have to be initialized to zero. The match is over when either of the players has won 2 games, so we can *loop until AGamesWon = 2 or BGamesWon = 2*.

We could have another module, say *DisplayStatus*, which displays the number of games won so far by each player (provided at least one game has been played), and indicates which game is about to begin (unless the match is over). This module would only have to know the number of games won by each player.

As we mentioned before, *DisplayWinner* can be used to display the winner of the game as well as the match. We might want to make the program a little nicer by displaying a message before calling *DisplayWinner*.

So far we have the following algorithm:

START OF PlayMatch(FirstServer, MatchWinner, WinnerGames, LoserGames)
Passed by value: FirstServer
Passed by reference: MatchWinner, WinnerGames, LoserGames

store zero in AGamesWon and in BGames Won
loop
    call DisplayStatus(AGamesWon, BGamesWon)
    call PlayGame(FirstServer, GameWinner, WinnerScore, LoserScore)
    display "The result of the game: "
    call DisplayWinner(GameWinner, WinnerScore, LoserScore)
    ⋮

Now we have to add 1 to the number of games won by the winner. There are two equivalent ways to phrase this; it could be an if...then...else step:

if GameWinner is 'A'
    then
        add 1 to AGamesWon
    else
        add 1 to BGamesWon

or a when step:

when GameWinner is
    'A', add 1 to AGamesWon
    'B', add 1 to BGamesWon

In this case we prefer the when step because it's a bit more concise and because it's more informative. If you were to read the if...then...else without knowing about the rest of the algorithm, you might not know that the only values that are possible for GameWinner are 'A' and 'B'; the when version spells this out clearly. You can decide for yourself which version suits you better.

The last thing we have to do in the body of the loop is be specific about switch FirstServer. Again, this could be written either as an if...then...else or a when; we'll do the latter:

when FirstServer is
    'A', store 'B' in FirstServer
    'B', store 'A' in FirstServer

Finally, after the loop is completed, the algorithm has to store the appropriate values in the variables that are passed by reference:

if AGamesWon is 2
    then
        store 'A' in MatchWinner
        store AGamesWon in WinnerGames
        store BGamesWon in LoserGames
    else
        store 'B' in MatchWinner
        store BGamesWon in WinnerGames
        store AGamesWon in LoserGames

Putting all these pieces together, the algorithm would look like the following:

START OF PlayMatch(FirstServer, MatchWinner, WinnerGames, LoserGames)
Passed by value: FirstServer
Passed by reference: MatchWinner, WinnerGames, LoserGames

store zero in AGamesWon and in BGames Won
loop
    call DisplayStatus(AGamesWon, BGamesWon)
    call PlayGame(FirstServer, GameWinner, WinnerScore, LoserScore)
    display "The result of the game: "
    call DisplayWinner(GameWinner, WinnerScore, LoserScore)
    when GameWinner is
        'A', add 1 to AGamesWon
        'B', add 1 to BGamesWon
    if AGamesWon < 2 and BGamesWon < 2
        then
            when FirstServer is
                'A', store 'B' in FirstServer
                'B', store 'A' in FirstServer
    until AGamesWon = 2 or BGamesWon = 2
if AGamesWon is 2
    then
        store 'A' in MatchWinner
        store AGamesWon in WinnerGames
        store BGamesWon in LoserGames
    else
        store 'B' in MatchWinner
        store BGamesWon in WinnerGames
        store AGamesWon in LoserGames

END OF PlayMatch

DisplayStatus

This is the last module to be written. Its job is to display the number of games won so far by each player (after the first game has been played), and unless the match is over, indicate which game is to begin. To make it clear what's going on, we'll use a variable called *TotalGames*, which will hold the total of *AGamesWon* and *BGamesWon*.

```
START OF DisplayStatus(AGamesWon, BGamesWon)
Passed by value: AGamesWon, BGamesWon
Passed by reference: none

store AGamesWon + BGamesWon in TotalGames
if TotalGames > 0
    then
        display "Games won:"
        display "Player A: ", AGamesWon, "Player B: ", BGamesWon
if TotalGames < 3
    then
        display "Begin game ", TotalGames + 1

END OF DisplayStatus
```

The algorithms from this section will be implemented in the "Once Again" section of chapter 8. You should be sure to trace through each one now to make sure there are no logic errors.

7.10   Summary and Review

- In this chapter we worked more with modules and realized the value of writing independent modules, each having a particular task to perform. Had the modules in chapter 5 not been written in an independent manner, we could not have used them in this chapter as we did. In particular, when we wrote the *DisplayFraction* module in chapter 5, if we had let it display some extra words, like "This is the fraction you entered," then we could not have used that module in this program.

- We introduced the concept of *multi-way selection*. We introduced a new step in our algorithmic language, a *when* step, to handle a multi-way branch.

- We saw that we could use the *Add* module to do subtraction by sending the negative of the second fraction. In doing this we learned two important things about parameters:

> When the actual parameter is being passed by value, it can be any *expression* of the proper type.

When the actual parameter is being passed by reference, it can only be a *variable*.

Since this was so important, we repeated it in Pascal-like terms:

If the formal parameter is a *value* parameter, the actual parameter can be any *expression* of the same type as the formal parameter.

If the formal parameter is a *variable* parameter, the actual parameter must be a *variable* of the same type as the formal parameter.

- We wrote the algorithm for a new mathematical function, LCM. This function calculates the least common multiple of two positive integers.

7.11   New Terms Introduced

lcm The least common multiple of two integers. (Also called the least common denominator when referring to the denominators of fractions.)

multi-way selection A selection or branch point where one of several possible paths is to be taken by the program.

user friendly A program that is written in a way that makes it easy to understand and use.

when step A step in an algorithm that uses multi-way selection.

7.12   Exercises

1. Write the algorithm for *GetOperator*, which uses one parameter, called *Operator*. Should this parameter be passed by value or by reference?

2. Modify the *GetData* algorithm given in the chapter so that it never passes back a zero in the numerator of the second fraction and a '/' in *Operator*. Think carefully about how you want to handle the error checking.

3. Write the algorithm for *Multiply*. Change the *PerformOperation* algorithm so that it uses the *Multiply* module to perform a division.

4. Write the algorithm for *DisplayResult*. Depending on the operation, the output should read as follows:

   ```
   Addition:        The sum of ... and ... is ...
   Subtraction:     The difference between ... and ... is ...
   Multiplication:  The product of ... and ... is ...
   Division:        The quotient of ... divided by ... is ...
   ```

5. Write the algorithms for *Introduce* and *Conclude*. Even though these algorithms will simply be a series of *displays*, it is important for you to think about how to give the program a friendly "look and feel."

6. Write the algorithm for the following simple checkbook program. First, you enter the beginning balance for the month. Then you are presented with a menu of three choices:

   (a) Make a deposit

   (b) Write a check

   (c) End of month

   You then enter the monthly transactions in order. If at any time the balance of the account falls below zero, a $12 charge is made against the account, and no more checks can be written until a deposit is made that brings the balance back into the black. At the end of the month, the following statistics are displayed:

   - The beginning balance
   - The total number of deposits made, and the total amount deposited
   - The total number of checks written, and the total amount of the checks
   - The total amount of fees for insufficient funds
   - The ending balance for the month

7. The game of craps is played with a pair of dice. On the first roll, if the dice total 7 or 11, the player wins, but if they total 2, 3 or 12, the player loses. If the first roll results in any other number, that number becomes the "point." The player then continues to roll until rolling either a 7, in which case he loses, or his "point," in which case he wins. Write the algorithm for a program that simulates one player's turn at the crap table. The program will display an introductory message for the user. It should then display the result of the rolls, pausing each time for the user to read the display. The program should end when the user either wins or loses, and the appropriate message should then be displayed. Use the top-down method to write the algorithm for the program and any appropriate subprograms.

Exercises 8–13 expand on the algorithms developed in exercises 12–18 of chapter 5. Assume that you have available the following modules:

> *LeapYear*
> *DaysInMonth*
> *ValidDate*
> *DayOfYear*
> *DayOfWeek*
> *DisplayDate*

from those exercises. Write an algorithm for each of the modules described in exercises 8–13. You should decide whether each module should be written as a procedure or as a function. Be sure to indicate what the parameters are for each module, and, in the case of a procedure, which are passed by value and which by reference. State carefully the preconditions, if any.

8. *DaysInYear*, which returns either 365 or 366 depending on whether the given year is a leap year. The routine should expect a valid year.

9. *FindMonthAndDay*, which is passed the day of the year and the year, and returns the corresponding month and day as integers. The routine should assume that the date it is sent is valid.

10. *DaysAfter*, which returns a number indicating how many days one date is after another. The given dates should be passed in a "day of the year, year" format. The routine should expect that both of the given dates are valid. If the first date passed is earlier than the second date, this routine should return a positive integer. That is, if the four parameters are 366, 1988, 6 and 1989, the function should return 6—January 6th, 1989 is 6 days after December 31, 1988. On the other hand, if the first date passed occurs *later* than the second date, a negative number should result. The values 6, 1989, 3 and 1989, should result in the value -3 being returned.

You should say to yourself "January 3, 1989 is -3 days after January 6, 1989." To avoid possible maxint problems, you may have to limit the number of years separating the two dates. This should be done outside of *DaysAfter*.

11. *FindOtherDate*: you pass this routine a date in "day of the year, year" format, and a positive or negative integer representing a certain number of days after the given date. The routine passes back the day of the year and year of the corresponding date. The routine should assume that the given date is valid.

12. *DisplayCalendar*, which is passed a month and year (as integers) and displays a calendar for that month and year similar to the one below. You should assume the month and year represent a valid date.

```
                   March   1781

         Sun  Mon  Tue  Wed  Thu  Fri  Sat

                              1    2    3
          4    5    6    7    8    9   10
         11   12   13   14   15   16   17
         18   19   20   21   22   23   24
         25   26   27   28   29   30   31
```

13. A complete program that offers the user a menu of choices:

    (a) Find the number of days between two given dates.

    (b) Find the date which is a certain number of days away from a given date.

    (c) Display the calendar for a given month and year.

    (d) End the program.

    Each of the first three choices should call a module, which in turn prompts the user for any input, allows the user to view the results and returns to the menu. The user should always enter dates in month-day-year format. For the second option, the date should be spelled out in English using the *DisplayDate* module. The last choice should display the concluding message of the program.

Chapter 8

Pascal—Implementation and Testing

> In a way, finding mistakes in a program is not unlike
> using a pitchfork to look for someone in a haystack.
> By shoving the fork into the haystack, we will know
> without a doubt when we have found someone!
> However, we can never be completely
> sure that the haystack is empty.
> — G. Michael Schneider

8.1 Overview of the Chapter

In this chapter we'll introduce program testing and debugging; in particular,
bottom-up testing. We will discuss the additional elements of Pascal needed
to implement the concepts introduced in chapter 7. We'll add the ⟨*case statement*⟩ and the ⟨*empty statement*⟩ to our repertoire of Pascal statements. We'll
discuss *scope* and *activation*, and *global variables*.

8.2 Introduction

In chapter 1 we introduced the FIVE + STEPS of programming. We have
discussed steps 1 through 4, but have only briefly mentioned step 5: testing
and debugging. A critical part of the programming process is the testing and
debugging of programs. Debugging refers to the process of removing errors that
are found in a program. As mentioned previously, we identify three types of
errors: syntax errors, run-time errors and logic errors. Syntax errors are found
for you by the compiler. Run-time errors are discovered when the program
crashes. Logic errors, on the other hand, are hard to find.

A program containing logic errors but free of syntax and run-time errors will
run merrily along without complaint. Unless you test the program carefully,

the logic errors can remain undetected, sometimes for a long time. The best way to prevent logic errors from corrupting your programs is not to allow them in the programs in the first place. That's one of the main reasons we have spent so much effort on writing an algorithm before writing the code, and why we emphasize the problem definition and problem-solving steps of the process. However, regardless of how carefully steps 1–4 are done, logic errors do get into our programs. One of the things we'll discuss in this chapter is how to locate logic errors through a process of "bottom-up" testing. We'll illustrate this procedure using the problem introduced in the previous chapter as an example.

Modular programs involve several modules, all of which have to be placed in the correct position in the code relative to one another. We'll indicate what sort of placements are valid and what sort of guidelines you should follow when deciding where to put the modules.

We'll also discuss the Pascal ⟨*case statement*⟩ and the ⟨*empty statement*⟩. The ⟨*case statement*⟩ is a new statement that allows us to do a limited sort of "n-way" branch. The ⟨*empty statement*⟩ is a strange statement—one that only a mathematician would love—which permits a bit of laziness on the part of a programmer.

8.3   Program Testing

The algorithm presented in the previous chapter was well thought-out and a programmer might just proceed to implement its various parts in Pascal. Instead, let's think first about the complexity of the program that we have designed. The outermost routine—the main program—calls several other routines. In particular, the main routine calls the procedure `PerformOperation`. This routine calls the procedure **Reduce** and then one of the two procedures **Add** or **Multiply**. **Add** calls the function **LCM**, and **LCM** calls **GCD**. What if one of these routines has a bug in it? How hard will it be to find the bug? Imagine that the complexity of this example is many times greater—as it will be in real-world programs. If we just dive right into writing procedure after function after procedure, and have them call each other in a complex series of calls, and if one or more of the routines contains a bug, the bug(s) can be very hard to detect, much less track down.

The first three steps of the FIVE + STEPS of the programming process are there to keep bugs from getting into a program in the first place. The better these steps are done, the fewer bugs the program will contain. However, regardless of how carefully the algorithm is designed, bugs can and do get into programs. The fifth step, testing and debugging, is there to enable a programmer to find the bugs and get rid of them.

Also, real-world programs are normally written by more than one person. It is not uncommon for several groups—teams—of programmers to be working on one program, each team responsible for a particular part of the whole program. In such a situation, each team must know exactly what incoming data to expect—as parameters—and exactly what data or action to produce. If a bug exists in one of several modules that have been written by different teams and is not detected until the modules are combined, it can be even more difficult to trace down; each team will be convinced that the code written by another team contains the error.

One solution to these problems lies in testing. We talked earlier about the top-down approach. We now want to demonstrate bottom-up testing.

Algorithms are often written in a top-down manner but code is often written from the bottom up. The lowest-level modules are written *and tested* first and then the next lowest, then the next, etc., until the highest-level routines are finally completed.

With this in mind, since the Pascal functions **GCD** and **LCM** are at the lowest level, let's write them and routines that test them. Since **LCM** calls **GCD**, we'll do **GCD** first.

Testing **GCD** and **LCM**

Most of the time our test routines will be the same. All we want to do is allow the user to type in the values for the parameters to be passed to the routine, call the routine and display the result.

We want to be able to test a variety of input, so we can put a loop in the algorithm:

START OF TestRoutine

loop
    Let the user enter appropriate values for the routine to be tested
    Call the routine with these values
    Display the values returned from the routine
    until the user decides to quit

END OF TestRoutine

So, let's write a program that tests GCD.

Chapter 6 contains a Pascal function for GCD:

```
function GCD(First, Second : integer) : integer;
var
  Remainder : integer;

{ Precondition: First and Second are both positive. }

{ This function calculates the greatest common divisor of the two   }
{ positive integers First and Second using the Euclidean algorithm. }

begin
   Remainder := First mod Second;
   while Remainder <> 0 do
     begin
       First := Second;
       Second := Remainder;
       Remainder := First mod Second
     end;
   GCD := Second
end;
```

A Pascal program that tests GCD might look something like the one on the next page.

```
program TestGCD(input, output);

{  Programmer: Keith Ching               }

{  This program tests the GCD function.  }

var
   Num1, Num2 : integer;
   Answer     : char;

   function GCD(First, Second : integer) : integer;
      . . .
begin   { Main program }
   writeln('This program tests the GCD function.');
   repeat
      write('Enter two positive integers with a space between them: ');
      readln(Num1, Num2);
      writeln('The GCD of ', Num1 : 1, ' and ', Num2 : 1, ' is ',
                  GCD(Num1, Num2) : 1);
      write('Try GCD again? (Y/N): ');
      readln(Answer)
   until (Answer = 'N') or (Answer = 'n')
end.
```

It isn't necessary to put checks on the data in the testing routine to make sure they are valid. We simply remember not to test the routine with data that violate the preconditions. If you compile and run this program, your screen will show:

```
This program tests the GCD function.
Enter two positive integers with a space between them: 20 28
The GCD of 20 and 28 is 4
Try GCD again? (Y/N): y
Enter two positive integers with a space between them: 124 123
The GCD of 124 and 123 is 1
Try GCD again? (Y/N): y
Enter two positive integers with a space between them: 132 342
The GCD of 132 and 342 is 6
Try GCD again? (Y/N): n
```

Everything looks okay so far. You shouldn't quit there though. You should try some values that will potentially cause some trouble; a pair of numbers where one number divides into the other exactly and perhaps some values close to maxint, for example. Let's run it again and try some "hard" numbers:

```
This program tests the GCD function.
Enter two positive integers with a space between them: 100 25
The GCD of 100 and 25 is 25
Try GCD again? (Y/N): y
Enter two positive integers with a space between them: 91 91
The GCD of 91 and 91 is 91
Try GCD again? (Y/N): y
Enter two positive integers with a space between them: 6230 1652
The GCD of 6230 and 1652 is 14
Try GCD again? (Y/N): y
Enter two positive integers with a space between them: 2000 3000
The GCD of 2000 and 3000 is 1000
Try GCD again? (Y/N): y
Enter two positive integers with a space between them: 32000 11648
The GCD of 32000 and 11648 is 128
Try GCD again? (Y/N): n
```

Again, everything looks okay; we can conclude that GCD works fine. Now let's write the routine that tests the LCM function. First, we need the LCM function itself. Looking back at the discussion in chapter 7, this seems straightforward:

```
function LCM(First, Second : integer) : integer;

{ Precondition: First and Second are both positive. }

{ This function calculates the least common multiple of the }
{ two positive integers First and Second.                   }

begin
  LCM := First * Second div GCD(First, Second)
end;
```

We can just add this to our testing routine for GCD and make a few changes in the main program:

```
program TestLCM(input, output);

{  Programmer: Sandy Ritter                   }

{  This program tests the LCM function.   }

var
   Num1, Num2 : integer;
   Answer     : char;

   function GCD(First, Second : integer) : integer;
      . . .
   function LCM(First, Second : integer) : integer;
      . . .
begin  { Main program }
   writeln('This program tests the LCM function.');
   repeat
      write('Enter two positive integers with a space between them: ');
      readln(Num1, Num2);
      writeln('The LCM of ', Num1 : 1, ' and ', Num2 : 1, ' is ',
                  LCM(Num1, Num2) : 1);
      write('Try LCM again? (Y/N): ');
      readln(Answer)
   until (Answer = 'N') or (Answer = 'n')
end.
```

Compile this program and run it, trying the values you used for GCD.

Did you find any errors?

On many systems, you may encounter a run-time error when the values sent to the routine are too large. Others might experience results that are simply wrong, such as:

```
Enter two positive integers with a space between them: 2000 3000
The LCM of 2000 and 3000 is -29
```

Where is the error? Since we tested the GCD routine, we know not to look there. The problem has to be in LCM. Let's look at LCM and see if we can find the problem. The function only has one line:

```
LCM := First * Second div GCD(First, Second)
```

So we can be pretty sure that the problem is in this line. If we send LCM the values 20 and 28, it works fine. Even when we send it 150 and 200, there's no problem. Let's see what it does if we let `First` equal 2000 and `Second` equal 3000.

We haven't said a great deal about the precedence of the arithmetic operators but we have mentioned that multiplication and division have the same level of precedence. When two operators have the same precedence, they are evaluated from left to right. Thus, in the line above, the multiplication will be done first and then the division. So, `First` is multiplied times `Second` and the product divided by the value returned by GCD when sent `First` and `Second`. Thus, 2000 times 3000 is divided by 1000. Doing the operations in that order yields 6,000,000 divided by 1000; which is 6000.

So where's the problem? Do you see it? Think about it before you go on to the next paragraph.

Pascal can only work with `integer`s up to the value of `maxint`. On most microcomputers, the value of `maxint` is 32,767. When the computer attempts to multiply 2000 by 3000, it simply cannot hold the answer, even temporarily. Some systems give a run-time error such as, "arithmetic overflow," while others simply give incorrect results. In a nutshell, we must *never* tell the computer to perform calculations with integers that would result in mathematical values greater than `maxint`.

Now that the error has been located, what can we do about it? Don't just throw up your hands and assume that nothing can be done. In this case there is a very simple "fix." We can simply tell the computer to divide before it multiplies. Change the line above to:

```
LCM := First * (Second div GCD(First, Second))
```

And now it will divide `Second` by the GCD *before* it multiplies. Thus 3000 will be divided by 1000, yielding 3, which will be multiplied times 2000, yielding 6000, as expected.

We cannot always fix logic errors so simply, but in this case it was easy. After making this change, we can run the program once again and get the following:

```
Enter two positive integers with a space between them: 3000 4000
The LCM of 3000 and 4000 is 12000
Try LCM again? (Y/N): y
Enter two positive integers with a space between them: 2000 3000
The LCM of 2000 and 3000 is 6000
Try LCM again? (Y/N): y
Enter two positive integers with a space between them: 190 169
The LCM of 190 and 169 is 32110
Try LCM again? (Y/N): y
```

```
Enter two positive integers with a space between them: 193 169
The LCM of 193 and 169 is 32617
Try LCM again? (Y/N): y
Enter two positive integers with a space between them: 194 169
The LCM of 194 and 169 is
```

At this point different systems will again cause different results. If maxint on your system is greater than 32,767, the program would have run with no problem on these data. On the other hand, if maxint = 32,767 on your system, the last two values would cause a problem; either an incorrect value or a run-time error. We have fixed the problems of the previous test but we also see that the routine does not always run or give the correct answer. In fact, there is no easy fix possible here. Since the mathematical lcm in the last example is greater than maxint (on the system we are using), there is no way that the value of LCM can be held in an integer variable. Should it be necessary to work with values greater than maxint, we would have to find another solution—such as using reals instead of integers for the numbers. We'll not continue any further with this problem. We'll conclude that we have written a function that returns the correct value for the least common multiple whenever that value is less than or equal to maxint.

Testing Reduce

Now that we are confident that GCD and LCM do their jobs correctly, we can move up one level and test Reduce.

Here's the code for Reduce from chapter 6:

```
procedure Reduce(var Num, Denom : integer);

{ Precondition:  Denom <> 0   }

{ Postcondition: This procedure reduces a fraction to lowest terms.    }
{ If the fraction is negative, the minus sign is put in the numerator. }

var
    Sign, Common : integer;
```

```
begin
  if Num = 0
    then
      Denom := 1
    else
      begin
        if ((Num > 0) and (Denom > 0)) or ((Num < 0) and (Denom < 0))
          then
            Sign := 1
          else
            Sign := -1;
        Num := abs(Num);
        Denom := abs(Denom);
        Common := GCD(Num, Denom);
        Num := Num div Common;
        Denom := Denom div Common;
        Num := Sign * Num
      end
end;
```

Leaving out the ⟨*definition/declaration part*⟩, the following ⟨*statement part*⟩ would be a reasonable choice for a program that tested the routine Reduce.

```
begin
  repeat
    writeln('Enter two integers for the numerator and denominator');
    write('of a fraction (separated by a space): ');
    readln(Numerator, Denominator);
    Reduce(Numerator, Denominator);
    write('After calling Reduce, the numerator is ', Numerator : 1);
    writeln(' and the denominator is ', Denominator : 1);
    write('Do it again? (Y/N): ');
    readln(Answer)
  until (Answer = 'N') or (Answer = 'n')
end.
```

Testing and Documentation

Before we run the program, we should spend some time thinking about test data. We have to make sure we test as many combinations as possible. We surely want to test a situation where the fraction can be reduced, like 34/68. We would also want to try a fraction that cannot be reduced, like 71/29. We would want to try a fraction with a negative denominator, a fraction with both numerator and denominator negative, a fraction with the numerator and denominator equal, a fraction with a zero numerator, etc.

Part of the process of documenting your program is choosing test data. You have to make careful choices and you have to keep records of what test data you chose. Later, if a bug is reported, you can check your records and see whether or not the test should have revealed the bug.

A run of this program with some of these test data would look like:

```
Enter two integers for the numerator and denominator
of a fraction (separated by a space): 34 68
After calling Reduce, the numerator is 1 and the denominator is 2
Do it again? (Y/N): y
Enter two integers for the numerator and denominator
of a fraction (separated by a space): 71 29
After calling Reduce, the numerator is 71 and the denominator is 29
Do it again? (Y/N): y
Enter two integers for the numerator and denominator
of a fraction (separated by a space): 189 -513
After calling Reduce, the numerator is -7 and the denominator is 19
Do it again? (Y/N): y
Enter two integers for the numerator and denominator
of a fraction (separated by a space): 100 100
After calling Reduce, the numerator is 1 and the denominator is 1
Do it again? (Y/N): y
Enter two integers for the numerator and denominator
of a fraction (separated by a space): -6000 -3
After calling Reduce, the numerator is 2000 and the denominator is 1
Do it again? (Y/N): y
Enter two integers for the numerator and denominator
of a fraction (separated by a space): 0 4
After calling Reduce, the numerator is 0 and the denominator is 1
Do it again? (Y/N): y
Enter two integers for the numerator and denominator
of a fraction (separated by a space): 0 -191
After calling Reduce, the numerator is 0 and the denominator is 1
Do it again? (Y/N): n
```

It seems that Reduce works fine. We are now confident that GCD, LCM and Reduce all work as expected and are ready to go on to yet a higher level. Before we do go on, however, we should repeat something we said in the previous chapters: no amount of testing can prove that a program works. Indeed, some programs cannot be tested. How do you test software for a space flight that will visit Halley's comet? While testing is very important to the process, to *prove* that a program is correct is a much more complex process. Essentially, what is required is a proof that whenever the preconditions of a procedure are met, the postconditions are guaranteed. Such proofs become much like the proofs encountered in mathematics and the ability to construct such proofs is an ability that a computing science professional must develop. Since this is a beginning course in programming, we won't take the subject any further.

Testing Add and Multiply

The algorithm for *Add* was developed in chapter 7. It will be easy to implement in Pascal. The procedure would look like:

```
procedure Add(N1, D1, N2, D2 : integer; var N, D : integer);

{  This procedure adds together the two fractions represented  }
{  by N1/D1 and N2/D2.  The result is returned via N/D.        }

begin
  D := LCM(D1, D2);
  N1 := N1 * (D div D1);
  N2 := N2 * (D div D2);
  N := N1 + N2
end;
```

Look back at the discussion about this routine in chapter 7 if you are unclear about it; in particular, be sure you see why some of the parameters are value parameters and some are variable parameters. Notice too that, as in chapter 6, we are implementing the abstract data type of *fraction* as a pair of **integers**.

Whenever an algorithm refers to a fraction as a single entity, we manipulate the numerator and denominator of the fraction.

This procedure calls the function LCM. Where should LCM appear in the code? It would be valid syntax for LCM to be placed in the ⟨*definition/declaration part*⟩ of Add, but, since LCM is rather a general purpose mathematical function that could conceivably be called from routines besides Add, we'll put it on the outermost level, above Add. This is an important point; we'll come back to it below when we discuss scope and activation.

The Pascal procedure for **Multiply** is even easier than the one for **Add**. You should write it.

We'll leave it for you to write a program that tests **Add** and **Multiply**. Your routine should have a few lines that allow you to enter two fractions and then allow you to call either **Add** or **Multiply**. You will have to include those procedures and functions that **Add** and **Multiply** call, as well as those that they call in turn. In particular, that means you will need LCM and GCD.

Documentation

You should plan a strategy that will insure as complete a test as possible. When we tested `Reduce`, we selected pairs of integers that covered as many combinations as we could think of. You should do the same with your test data for `Add` and `Multiply`. Spend some time thinking about what combinations of integers you should try. Clearly, when you test `Add`, you will want to try fractions that will need to use a lowest common denominator. You will also want to try many combinations: positive numerators and negative denominators, negative numerators and positive denominators, all positive, all negative, some zeros in numerators, etc. The data you choose should be documented also. Recall the FIVE + STEPS of programming. The + is "document continuously." In step 5 of the process, while you are testing the program, you must document which combinations of numbers you have tested. Then, if you later encounter a bug, you will be able to check your documentation to see how the bug slipped by undetected.

Your test program needed `GCD` and `LCM` in addition to `Add` and `Multiply`. By now you should see why we call this process "bottom-up" testing. As we write the lower-level routines and test them, we can confidently include them when we test the higher-level routines.

Testing `GetData` and `DisplayResult`

Now let's write `GetData` and `DisplayResult`. The procedure `GetData` calls the two routines `GetFraction` and `GetOperator` so they should be written and tested first, and then incorporated into `GetData`. `GetFraction` was written in chapter 6; here it is again:

```
procedure GetFraction(var Num, Denom : integer);

{ This procedure allows the user to enter two integers for the }
{ numerator and denominator of a fraction.  The denominator    }
{ cannot equal zero.                                           }

begin
   write('Enter the numerator of the fraction: ');
   readln(Num);
   write('Enter the denominator of the fraction: ');
   readln(Denom);
   while Denom = 0 do
      begin
         write('You must enter a non-zero integer.  Try again: ');
         readln(Denom)
      end
end;
```

A simple test program that calls `GetFraction` would look something like:

```
program TestGetFract(input, output);

{  Programmer: Orlando Rarangol                          }

{  This program tests the GetFraction procedure.  }

var
  Numerator, Denominator : integer;
  Answer                 : char;

  procedure GetFraction(var Num, Denom : integer);
    . . .


begin    { Main Program }
  writeln('This program tests GetFraction');
  repeat
    GetFraction(Numerator, Denominator);
    writeln('The numerator is ', Numerator : 1);
    writeln('and the denominator is ', Denominator : 1);
    write('Try another fraction? (Y/N): ');
    readln(Answer)
    until (Answer = 'N') or (Answer = 'n')
end.
```

You might want to leave off the `var` in the first line of `GetFraction`, compile and run it, and see what happens.

A similar test program should be written for `GetOperator`. Once these routines are tested, they and `Reduce` can be combined to test `DisplayResult`. We leave the details as exercises.

8.4   The *case statement*

The remaining routine to be implemented is the routine for *PerformOperation*. Before we get into this one, we need to discuss a new Pascal statement.

In the previous chapter we introduced the concept of multi-way selection and an algorithmic "n-way branch," the *when* step. There is a Pascal statement that comes pretty close to the *when* step we used in chapter 7. This statement is the ⟨*case statement*⟩. We begin by looking at the syntax diagram (see figure 8.1).

Following the word **case**, there must be an ⟨*expression*⟩. Then there are one or more ⟨*statement*⟩s, each preceded by a colon and a list of ⟨*constant*⟩s.

case statement:

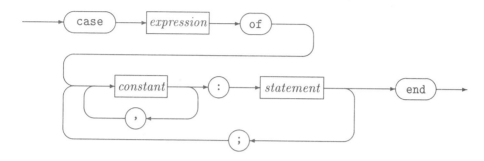

Figure 8.1

The type of each ⟨*constant*⟩ must match the type of the ⟨*expression*⟩ and no ⟨*constant*⟩ may appear more than once. The end of the ⟨*case statement*⟩ is marked with an **end**. (This is an instance where a program will have an **end** but not have a matching **begin**.)

When the ⟨*case statement*⟩ is encountered, the ⟨*expression*⟩ is evaluated and a ⟨*constant*⟩ with the same value is found. The ⟨*statement*⟩ following that ⟨*constant*⟩ is executed; this ⟨*statement*⟩ may, of course, be a ⟨*compound statement*⟩ or any other kind of ⟨*statement*⟩.

Indeed, this is very similar to the *when* we introduced. If you say "when" to yourself whenever you see the word **case**, say "is" whenever you see the word **of**, and say "do" whenever you see the ":," the meaning of a ⟨*case statement*⟩ will be easier to follow.

In order to see the ⟨*case statement*⟩ in action, let's implement the *when* step we wrote in the previous chapter in the routine for *PerformOperation*. The step (after modifying it to eliminate the routines for subtraction and division) looks like:

```
when Operator is
    '+',    call Add(Fraction1, Fraction2, Fraction)
    '−',    call Add(Fraction1, −Fraction2, Fraction)
    '*',    call Multiply(Fraction1, Fraction2, Fraction)
    '/',    call Multiply(Fraction1, 1/Fraction2, Fraction)
```

In Pascal, using a ⟨*case statement*⟩ and using numerators and denominators, this will look like:

```
case Operator of
  '+' : Add(Num1, Denom1, Num2, Denom2, Num, Denom);
  '-' : Add(Num1, Denom1, -Num2, Denom2, Num, Denom);
  '*' : Multiply(Num1, Denom1, Num2, Denom2, Num, Denom);
  '/' : Multiply(Num1, Denom1, Denom2, Num2, Num, Denom)
  end
```

Notice how we "inverted the denominator" when we implemented the division. With the exception of the additional number of parameters, this looks very much like the algorithm, which is no coincidence. A "multi-way branch" like this is a useful tool. All structured languages include a way of implementing it.

Limitations of the *case statement*

The ⟨*case statement*⟩ in *Standard* Pascal does not have an "otherwise" case. That is, there is no way of saying, "if the value of the expression doesn't match any of the ⟨*constant*⟩s, do this." The programmer is responsible for making sure that exactly one of the ⟨*constant*⟩s in the ⟨*case statement*⟩ equals the value of the expression. If it happens that there is no ⟨*constant*⟩ equaling the value of the expression, an error results. Different compilers handle the error in different ways—the Standard does not specify how the error is to be handled—and so an unpredictable result can occur. A careful programmer will make sure that the value of the expression matches one of the ⟨*constant*⟩s, possibly by putting the ⟨*case statement*⟩ in an ⟨*if statement*⟩ (see exercise 4 at the end of this chapter). Many Pascal compilers include some sort of "otherwise" case; since these extensions are not Standard Pascal, we'll not discuss them here.

A second limitation is that there is no provision for a range of values in the ⟨*constant*⟩ list. It would be nice to be able to say something like, "in the case that the value of the expression is between 5 and 50, do this; in the case that the value is between 51 and 100, do this . . . ." Without typing all of the integers between 5 and 50, and all of the integers between 51 and 100, etc., the ⟨*case statement*⟩ cannot be used this way. Of course, you can always implement this notion with a series of ⟨*if statement*⟩s.

8.5   The Semicolon, Revisited

Look at the ⟨*case statement*⟩ above and notice that there was no semicolon after the **end**. In a complete program there might well be another statement following this one, in which case this statement and the next one would be separated by a semicolon. On the other hand, however, if no statement followed this one, no semicolon would be needed. That's why we didn't put a semicolon after the **end**.

Now look at the next to the last line:

```
'/' : Multiply(Num1, Denom1, Denom2, Num2, Num, Denom)
```

There is no semicolon on the end of this line. Should there be? No. Since semi-colons are used to separate statements in Pascal, and since there is no statement following this one, no semicolon is needed on the end. This is consistent with how we have been writing ⟨*compound statement*⟩s in earlier examples. We have never put a semicolon just before an **end**.

The *empty statement*

However, you may have, for one reason or another, put a semicolon directly before an **end** or seen some code with a semicolon directly before an **end** and not gotten a syntax error message from the compiler. You may have wondered why that's not a syntax error.

It turns out that programmers often have to add statements or delete statements, sometimes just before an **end**. If they always had to go to the previous line and either add or delete a semicolon, they might have found that frustrating. With this in mind, Wirth invented a special statement that allows a semicolon directly before an **end**. This statement is the ⟨*empty statement*⟩. Figure 8.2 contains the syntax diagram for the ⟨*empty statement*⟩.

empty statement:

Figure 8.2

What this says is the ⟨*empty statement*⟩ consists of absolutely nothing, not a space, not a RETURN, nothing! Moreover, that's just what the ⟨*empty statement*⟩ tells the computer to do: nothing! Strange; a statement that you cannot see that tells the computer to do nothing. It would be easy to conclude that such a statement has little or no effect on what we do, but that is not the case.

With the invention of the ⟨*empty statement*⟩, the following ⟨*compound statement*⟩ conforms to the syntax rules of Pascal:

```
while Denom = 0 do
  begin
    write('The denominator cannot be zero, enter another: ');
    readln(Denom);
  end
```

This ⟨*compound statement*⟩ is legal; it contains not two but *three* statements: a ⟨*write statement*⟩, a ⟨*read statement*⟩ and an ⟨*empty statement*⟩.

The ⟨*empty statement*⟩ also allows you to put a semicolon just before the word `until`, i.e., just after the last statement in a series of statements in the body of a ⟨*repeat statement*⟩. What you are really doing is adding an ⟨*empty statement*⟩ to the series.

But now some programmers might get into the habit of always putting semicolons just in front of the word `end`. To allow them to always do that, the syntax for the ⟨*case statement*⟩ has to have a little patch added on the end to allow a semicolon just before the word `end`. The full syntax diagram for the ⟨*case statement*⟩ is contained in appendix A.

Problems with the *empty statement*

This little bit of freedom might make some programmers happier, but it can cause other problems. With freedom comes responsibility. Many people who don't really understand the rules think they can put semicolons on the ends of all statements, and that's just not true! Consider the following example borrowed from chapter 4:

```
if (Hint = 'H') or (Hint = 'h')
  then
    Smallest := Guess + 1;
  else
    Biggest := Guess - 1
```

Is that semicolon okay? No! If you put a semicolon there, you are essentially putting an extra statement there, an ⟨*empty statement*⟩. But then there are two statements between the word **then** and the word **else**. You *cannot* have two statements between **then** and **else**. The syntax rules of Pascal require exactly one statement there.

At least the compiler would catch that one and you could figure out what was wrong. Things can get worse. Consider this awful example, borrowed from the GCD function and modified:

```
while Remainder <> 0 do;
  begin;
    First := Second;
    Second := Remainder;
    Remainder := First mod Second;
  end;
```

A programmer that types something like this has gotten into the terrible habit of putting a semicolon on the end of every line. While you might think this is a silly example, the point is, it is *perfectly valid syntax*! The ⟨*compound statement*⟩ is valid; it just contains *five* statements instead of three—two ⟨*empty statement*⟩s and three ⟨*assignment statement*⟩s. However, notice the semicolon after the **do**. That's legal too. Now the body of the ⟨*while statement*⟩ is the statement between the word **do** and the semicolon—an ⟨*empty statement*⟩. When values of **First** and **Second** result in a non-zero value for **Remainder**, the ⟨*empty statement*⟩—a statement that does nothing—will be executed forever.

Some Pascal programmers deliberately place semicolons at the end of the last statement in a compound statement, just before the **end**. Then if they have to add another statement to the compound statement later, they don't have to add the semicolon on the end of the previous line. While this practice has some merit if you do a lot of changing of your code, we don't follow it. Today's editors make it fairly easy to insert the semicolon when needed and we feel it's more important to think carefully about how the semicolon was designed to be used, i.e., as a statement *separator*. Other than possibly placing a semicolon at the end of the last statement in a compound statement, don't get into the habit of automatically putting semicolons on the ends of statements. Sometimes they cause no problems, sometimes they cause problems resulting in syntax errors that the compiler will catch, but sometimes they change the meanings of your code in unexpected and dangerous ways.

8.6   The *Dangling Else* **Problem**

While the "dangling else problem" hasn't come up yet in the text, it might have in something you have written. This seems like as good a place to mention it as any. Consider the following code:

```
if condition
    then
            if condition
                then
                    statement
        else
            statement
```

Does the **else** match the first **then** or the second? Either way, the syntax is valid, there are the proper number of statements in the proper places. It could be interpreted as:

```
if condition
    then
            if condition
                then
                    statement
                else
                    statement
```

or as:

```
if condition
    then
            if condition
                then
                    statement
        else
            statement
```

We have used indentation to indicate which **then** is paired with the **else**. Since Pascal pays no attention to indentation and since the compiler cannot guess which of the two is meant, there has to be a special rule to decide how the compiler will treat it. That rule specifies that in cases like this where the syntax can be interpreted either way, the **else** will always be paired with the closest **then**, yielding the first meaning.

Suppose, on the other hand, you wanted the second meaning. How can you force the compiler to give you that meaning?

There are two simple ways. The first makes another use of the ⟨*empty statement*⟩. Consider:

```
if condition
    then
            if condition
                then
                    statement
                else
    else
        statement
```

The first `else` is followed by an ⟨*empty statement*⟩. Thus, the second `else` can only be paired with the first `then`; there is no other possible interpretation. Since this results in code that looks like something was forgotten, we prefer a second method. Consider:

```
if condition
    then
        begin
            if condition
                then
                    statement
        end
    else
        statement
```

The ⟨*compound statement*⟩ surrounds the inner ⟨*if statement*⟩ and the `else` can only be paired with the first `then`; once again avoiding the dangling else.

Be careful that you don't inadvertently include dangling elses—use ⟨*compound statement*⟩s when in doubt.

8.7 PerformOperation

We wrote part of `PerformOperation` in the section above on the ⟨*case statement*⟩. We should finish it, however, by adding the procedure declaration line and the calls to `Reduce`. The complete procedure would look like:

```
procedure PerformOperation(Num1, Denom1, Num2, Denom2 : integer;
                                              Op : char;
                                var Num, Denom : integer);

{ This procedure performs the indicated operation on the two  }
{ fractions Num1/Denom1 and Num2/Denom2 producing Num/Denom.  }
```

```
      procedure Reduce
         .  .  .
      procedure Add
         .  .  .
      procedure Multiply
         .  .  .

begin
  Reduce(Num1, Denom1);
  Reduce(Num2, Denom2);
  case Op of
    '+' : Add(Num1, Denom1, Num2, Denom2, Num, Denom);
    '-' : Add(Num1, Denom1, -Num2, Denom2, Num, Denom);
    '*' : Multiply(Num1, Denom1, Num2, Denom2, Num, Denom);
    '/' : Multiply(Num1, Denom1, Denom2, Num2, Num, Denom)
    end;
  Reduce(Num, Denom)
end;
```

At this point it's not necessary to write a special routine to test **Perform-Operation**. If all of the other modules have been tested correctly, any bugs that show up must be in **PerformOperation**. The main program itself can serve as its test routine. As you recall, the algorithm for the main program was straightforward:

START OF RationalArithmetic:

call Introduce
loop
    call GetData(Fraction1, Fraction2, Operator)
    call PerformOperation(Fraction1, Fraction2, Operator, Fraction)
    call DisplayResult(Fraction1, Fraction2, Operator, Fraction)
    until the user wants to quit
call Conclude

END OF RationalArithmetic

The Pascal program is very similar. Assuming that all the routines except **PerformOperation** have been fully tested, the ⟨*variable declaration part*⟩ and the ⟨*statement part*⟩ of the program would look something like those on the next page.

```
program RationalArithmetic(input, output);

{ Programmer: Jimmy Cheng                            }

{ This program performs basic arithmetic operations on }
{ fractions and displays the result as a mixed number. }

var
  Numerator1, Denominator1,
  Numerator2, Denominator2,
  Numerator, Denominator   : integer;
  Operator, Answer         : char;
      . . .


begin  {  Main Program  }
  Introduce;
  repeat
    GetData(Numerator1, Denominator1, Numerator2, Denominator2, Operator);
    PerformOperation(Numerator1, Denominator1, Numerator2, Denominator2,
                     Operator, Numerator, Denominator);
    DisplayResult(Numerator1, Denominator1, Numerator2, Denominator2,
                     Operator, Numerator, Denominator);
    write('Do you want to do it again? (Y/N): ');
    readln(Answer)
    until (Answer = 'N') or (Answer = 'n');
  Conclude
end.
```

8.8 Scope and Activation

Before you can type the rest of this program in, you will need to think about the placement of the procedures and functions. The block structure of Pascal allows procedures and functions to be placed inside other procedures and functions. The positioning has to be done carefully. Let's talk about that for a bit.

It is possible to get deeply into the Pascal Standard while trying to explain *blocks*, *scope* and *activation*, but we'll try not to do that. Rather, we'll try to explain the concepts without going overboard.

We have already seen the idea of a ⟨*block*⟩. The *scope* of an identifier is, essentially, that portion of the code where the identifier can be referred to without causing a syntax error. If a variable is declared, for example, in the variable declaration part of any block, then that variable can be referred to in the statement part of the same block.

Global Variables

However, if the routine in question has other routines declared within the ⟨*procedure/function declaration part*⟩ of that block, then, unless the name of the variable is redeclared in these routines, it can also be referred to in the statement parts of the inner blocks. A silly example can make this clear:

```pascal
program Silly(output);
var
  Num : integer;

  procedure Funny;
  begin
    Num := 777
  end;

begin
  Num := 1;
  writeln('The number is ', Num : 1);
  Funny;
  writeln('The number is ', Num : 1)
end.
```

The reference to Num within the statement part of procedure Funny is syntactically valid. Looking at just the statements in the main program, one would not see anything that changes the value of Num after it is assigned the value 1; yet, when the second writeln prints the value of Num, it would print 777, not 1. Look at the procedure Funny—Num is not declared anywhere in Funny; it's declared as a local variable in Silly. A variable that is declared outside of a particular block, as in this example, is called a *global variable*.

Let's look at a more useful example. Although many Pascal compilers supply a random-number generating function, there is no such function in Standard Pascal. It is often helpful to have a routine that generates a random number; programs that simulate real-world events often need such a function. We don't plan to go into the details, but here is a function that would return a pseudorandom real number between 0 and 1:

```pascal
function Random : real;
begin
  Seed := (Seed * 40 + 3641) mod 729;
  Random := Seed / 729
end;
```

Every time Random is called, it will return a real value between 0 and 1, and will return 729 different reals before it starts to repeat. (A different choice of the values 729, 40 and 3641 will cause different numbers to be returned before it starts to repeat, but these values do need to be chosen with care.)

As we said, we don't want to get into random number generation. The point we want to make concerns `Seed` in the above routine. Notice that `Seed` is neither declared as a parameter nor as a local variable in `Random`. Therefore, it must be a global variable. In order for this function to work, an outside routine—probably the main program itself—would have to declare an `integer` variable `Seed` and give it some initial value between 0 and 728. The starting value could be entered by a user (and the program should change whatever value the user enters to that value `mod` 729). `Seed` is used and changed by the function but it is not passed to the function. In this way, `Random` can be used by any other function or procedure at any level, without having to pass `Seed` to every routine that uses `Random`.

We think of using variables this way as passing them "under the table." Because it is possible to use variables this way, and because it is then possible to change the value of a variable in a subroutine and never see the change happen in the outer routine, the use of global variables is not recommended in general. In fact, there is a simple rule that governs the use of global variables; see figure 8.3.

DON'T

Figure 8.3 Golden Rule for Using Global Variables

As with most rules, there are exceptions that an expert programmer will need to know. The global variable `Seed` used in our `Random` function is one of these exceptions. There is a tendency to make every variable global so that you don't have to bother passing it from routine to routine. This tendency should be vigorously resisted. At this point in your development, you should forget that there are exceptions and just follow the golden rule. If a module needs a particular item of data, don't get that item to the module via a global variable, pass it to the module as a parameter.

Activation

Let's not spend any more time on variables. We do, however, have to concern ourselves with procedures and functions. The place in a program where a routine—procedure or function—is invoked is referred to as the *activation-point* of the routine. We need to know where in one routine it is legal to activate another routine.

If you check the syntax diagram for a ⟨*procedure declaration*⟩, you will see that the declaration of a procedure contains a ⟨*block*⟩. A ⟨*block*⟩ can contain other ⟨*procedure declaration*⟩s and ⟨*function declaration*⟩s. The programmer needs to decide where each subroutine should be placed. First, the programmer

needs to know what sort of placements are legal. Look at the skeleton in figure 8.4—where we have left off the variable declarations, function return types, etc., in each block.

The indentation is intended to make the nesting clear. The normal state of affairs is for one routine to call other routines that are declared earlier in the same block on the same level, or earlier in another block on a higher level.

It might be easier to see the block structure of the program in figure 8.4 if we draw boxes around each module. Figure 8.5 is the same program but with the boxes.

Consider either figure 8.4 or 8.5 and the following. If you look closely at the figure and each of the examples, you'll get a better feeling for which calls are valid and which are not.

- There could be statements in the statement part of procedure C which call procedure B.

- Statements in function F could call procedure B or C.

- Procedure A could call procedure B or function F.

- Procedure A could *not* call procedure C—C is hidden from calls from anywhere other than from function F.

- Function G could call procedure A, since A is above G and on the same level, and could call procedure D, since D is inside G.

- Function G could not call B, F or C.

- Procedure D could call procedure A.

- Procedure D could not call B, F or C.

- Procedure E could call procedure A or function G.

- Procedure E could not call B, C, D or F.

- The main program could call procedure A, function G or procedure E.

- In all cases, no procedure or function can call another procedure or function that is declared later in the code; procedure C could not call function G, for example.

Other valid calls are possible. A procedure or function can call itself—this is known as *recursion*; there is an entire chapter on recursion later in the book.

Further, it would be possible for procedure C to call function F. Such a call could also constitute a form of recursion but is very unusual; neither author of this book can remember ever using a call of this sort.

All of this is designed to aid the *modularity* of your programs. Any routine should be a module and should be as self-contained as possible. Imagine that each module is a separate package that, when finished, can be put aside on a shelf somewhere. If the module is needed later, it can be removed from the shelf and inserted into the program. Due to the block structure of Pascal, a package might well contain other smaller packages that are concealed from the outside world. When the large package is removed from the shelf, the smaller internal packages are automatically brought along with it.

Remember what we said earlier about procedural abstraction: no module should ever need to know *how* another module does its job, it should only know *what* that job is. The only communication between modules should be via the parameters.

```
program Main;
   procedure A;
      procedure B;
      begin  { statement part of B }
         ⋮
      end;
      function F;
         procedure C;
         begin  { statement part of C }
            ⋮
         end;
      begin  { statement part of F }
         ⋮
      end;
   begin  { statement part of A }
      ⋮
   end;
   function G;
      procedure D;
      begin  { statement part of D }
         ⋮
      end;
   begin  { statement part of G }
      ⋮
   end;
   procedure E;
   begin  { statement part of E }
      ⋮
   end;
begin  { statement part of Main }
   ⋮
end.
```

Figure 8.4 Skeleton of Nested Procedures and Functions

```
program Main;
   procedure A;
      procedure B;
      begin  { statement part of B }
         ⋮
      end;
      function F;
         procedure C;
         begin  { statement part of C }
            ⋮
         end;
      begin  { statement part of F }
         ⋮
      end;
   begin  { statement part of A }
      ⋮
   end;
   function G;
      procedure D;
      begin  { statement part of D }
         ⋮
      end;
   begin  { statement part of G }
      ⋮
   end;
   procedure E;
   begin  { statement part of E }
      ⋮
   end;
begin  { statement part of Main }
   ⋮
end.
```

Figure 8.5 Nested Procedures and Functions in Boxes

8.9   RationalArithmetic, Completed

Now that we have an idea of what sort of calls are valid, we need to decide what sort of calls we are making in our current program and where to locate the various routines.

Earlier we put `Add` and `Multiply` inside `PerformOperation`. We also indicated that we would *not* put GCD nor LCM inside `Add`. Since `PerformOperation` calls `Add` and `Multiply`, they must be declared either inside `PerformOperation` or above `PerformOperation`. Either placement is legal syntax. One way to decide which is better—and to see why we put them where we did—is to ask yourself, "Will this subroutine be called by any other routines?" If the answer to this question is "yes," the subroutine should probably be put outside the routine being written; otherwise, it probably belongs inside. With this in mind, let's look at the routines we have.

Let's start with `GetData`; it calls `GetFraction` and `GetOperator`. Do other routines call `GetFraction` or `GetOperator`? No; so make `GetFraction` and `GetOperator` part of `GetData`. Do these routines call other routines? No; so we're done with `GetData`.

Now, `PerformOperation`. What routines does it call? Just `Add`, `Multiply` and `Reduce`. Should they be inside `PerformOperation`? Surely `Add` and `Multiply` should. They are part of the process of performing the operation. How about `Reduce`? One could argue either way. You could argue that reducing a fraction is a process that might be done any time, not just while performing an arithmetic operation on a pair of fractions. Or, you could argue that the way the program is written, the only time any reducing is done is while the program is inside `PerformOperation`. Both arguments make sense. Pascal will allow you to do it either way you see it.

Now how about LCM and GCD? GCD is called by `Reduce` and by LCM so it cannot be put inside either one. As we mentioned above, LCM is only called from `Add` and could be put inside `Add` but it seems to make better sense to put it on the outermost level of the program, since the mathematical functions GCD and LCM are general purpose functions and not particular to working with fractions.

Finally, only `DisplayResult` calls `DisplayFraction`, so `DisplayFraction` should be inside `DisplayResult`.

All of this suggests the following skeleton to the program (look carefully at the indentation):

```
program RationalArithmetic
  procedure Introduce
  function GCD
  function LCM
  procedure Reduce
  procedure GetData
    procedure GetFraction
    procedure GetOperator
  procedure PerformOperation
    procedure Add
    procedure Multiply
  procedure DisplayResult
    procedure DisplayFraction
  procedure Conclude
```

We leave it as an exercise to finish the program, type it in and run it. Try different combinations of fractions and operators until you're convinced it does what it's supposed to do.

8.10 Response Verification

We have written the statement part of the main program in a simple way because that's all that was needed in this case. In particular, we trust the user of the program to type either 'Y' or 'N' in response to the question:

```
Do you want to do it again?  (Y/N):
```

Because it is an important skill, let's assume that it is necessary that we make sure that the user types either 'Y' or 'N' (or 'y' or 'n') in response to the prompt. It isn't that critical in this program, of course, but is critical in other situations. How can we make sure that the user has typed the right thing?

An easy solution is obtained by using a *loop while*. Algorithmically, it would look something like:

prompt the user for a response
accept an answer from the user
loop while the answer is invalid
    display "That's an invalid answer, try again."
    accept an answer from the user

Supposing that a valid answer is 'Y' or 'N', as above, another version might look like:

prompt the user for a yes-no response
accept an answer from the user
loop while the answer is neither "yes" nor "no"
    display "That's an invalid answer, try again."
    accept an answer from the user

How would this be coded in Pascal? Consider:

```
write('Please answer Y for yes or N for no: ');
readln(Answer);
while (Answer <> 'Y') or (Answer <> 'N') do
  begin
    write('You must answer Y for yes or N for no: ');
    readln(Answer)
  end
```

Many students implement the test this way and wonder why their program gets stuck. Think about this before you read on. Try to understand why this constitutes an infinite loop.

The ⟨*Boolean expression*⟩ is always true, regardless of what the user types. It is true that **Answer** is either not equal to 'Y' or not equal to 'N' whatever is stored in **Answer**. The problem is with the word **or**. The correct word is **and**. The answer is invalid only if **Answer** is not equal to 'Y' *and* not equal to 'N'. The ⟨*while statement*⟩ must be:

```
write('Please answer Y for yes or N for no: ');
readln(Answer);
while (Answer <> 'Y') and (Answer <> 'N') do
  begin
    write('You must answer Y for yes or N for no: ');
    readln(Answer)
  end
```

Now it will work better, but it still won't quite be satisfactory. If the user types 'y', the program will complain that the answer was invalid. Surely you would want 'y' to mean "yes."

In order to permit the user to enter the response in either upper or lowercase, the ⟨*Boolean expression*⟩ and the ⟨*while statement*⟩ should be:

```
while (Answer <> 'Y') and (Answer <> 'y') and
      (Answer <> 'N') and (Answer <> 'n') do
  begin
    write('You must answer Y for yes or N for no: ');
    readln(Answer)
  end
```

This will do the job, but it is a bit ungainly. There is a better way, using sets.

Sets in Pascal

The Pascal language allows quite a bit of manipulation of sets; you can do unions, intersections, set inclusion and set membership. You can even work with variables that are sets. We won't do all that now, though; we'll just do some set membership. In our current situation, deciding whether or not the user entered a valid response, we would say the response was valid if it was in the set containing 'Y', 'y', 'N' and 'n'. Or, symbolically:

$$\text{Answer} \in \{ \text{'Y'}, \text{'y'}, \text{'N'}, \text{'n'} \}$$

This can be done in Pascal, although we cannot type the "∈" symbol, and the braces—"{" and "}"—have meaning already. The Pascal equivalent to the above is:

```
Answer in ['Y', 'y', 'N', 'n']
```

This ⟨*Boolean expression*⟩ will be true whenever the user's response is valid. What we want is the opposite, and we can get that by just adding the word not. Thus, an easier way to code:

```
while (Answer <> 'Y') and (Answer <> 'y') and
      (Answer <> 'N') and (Answer <> 'n') do
  begin
    write('You must answer Y for yes or N for no: ');
    readln(Answer)
  end
```

is to code:

```
while not (Answer in ['Y', 'y', 'N', 'n']) do
  begin
    write('You must answer Y for yes or N for no: ');
    readln(Answer)
  end
```

instead. Notice the parentheses; they are necessary because of the high precedence of **not**. Also notice that:

```
while Answer not in ['Y', 'y', 'N', 'n'] do      { bugged! }
  . . .
```

may sound okay in English, but it's not valid Pascal. Do you see why? Remember that if $\mathcal{P}$ is a ⟨*Boolean expression*⟩ then so is **not** $\mathcal{P}$, but you cannot sneak the **not** into the middle of $\mathcal{P}$.

Sets are also very useful in insuring that the value of the expression in a ⟨*case statement*⟩ matches one of the constants in the constant lists. An ⟨*if statement*⟩ that checks to see if the value of the expression is in a particular set can contain the ⟨*case statement*⟩. This notion will be expanded in the exercises.

Pascal allows us to refer to a range of values in certain instances. These are called *subrange* types. We'll have more to say about subranges later, but since it is similar to what we are doing here, let's mention that the mathematical expression:

$$Answer \in \{1, \dots, 100\}$$

can be coded in Pascal as:

```
Answer in [1 .. 100]
```

Be sure to notice that Pascal requires *two* dots, not three, and no commas.

8.11   Testing vs. Proof of Correctness

We've mentioned several times that you can't *prove* the correctness of a program just by testing it. Proving that an algorithm works is often very difficult, and sometimes impossible. This doesn't mean that we don't have to worry about correctness; on the contrary, many very complicated programs closely affect our lives. Programs that make important decisions about human lives must be as correct as possible; whenever possible, their correctness must be proved. Unfortunately, real programs are so complex that complete verification of their correctness cannot always be accomplished. Consider, for example, the computer system used by the U. S. Department of Defense to detect incoming missiles. This program cannot be tested in a real situation, while at the same time, it cannot be proved correct because it's so complicated.

8.12   Memory Map

The **Rational Arithmetic** solution includes several levels of routines. The main routine calls **PerformOperation**, which calls **Reduce**, which in turn calls **GCD**. Let's take a look at an idealized picture of memory during these calls.

Figure 8.6 Memory After **GetFraction**

Consider figure 8.6. Suppose that the user has entered 24/45 for the first fraction, 15/50 for the second fraction, and + for the operator.

Now suppose **PerformOperation** has just been called.

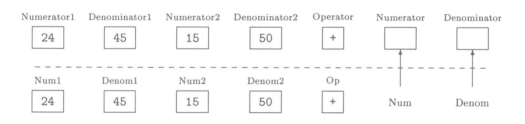

Figure 8.7 Memory at Start of **PerformOperation**

Figure 8.7 shows what memory looks like just as **PerformOperation** gets started. Num1, Denom1, Num2, Denom2 and Op are copies of the actual parameters Numerator1, Denominator1, Numerator2, Denominator2 and Operator. Num and Denom refer back to the actual parameters Numerator and Denominator, since Numerator and Denominator were passed by reference. We'll use arrows to connect the formal parameters to their corresponding actual parameters whenever they are passed by reference.

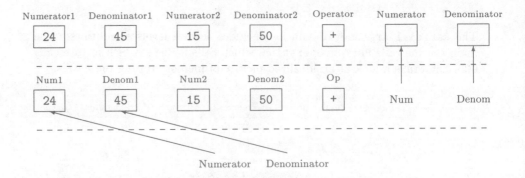

Figure 8.8 Memory at First Call of **Reduce**

When **Reduce** is called the first time, memory would look like figure 8.8. **Num1** and **Denom1** are passed by reference to **Reduce**.

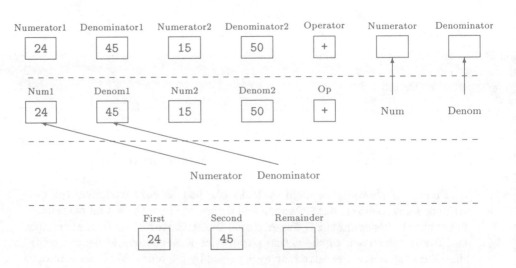

Figure 8.9 Memory at Start of First Call of GCD

When **Reduce** calls the function GCD, sending it **Numerator** and **Denominator**, memory would look like figure 8.9.

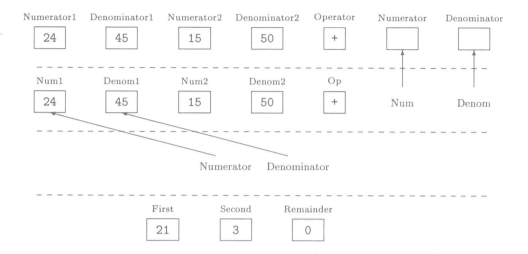

Figure 8.10 Memory at Conclusion of First Call of GCD

Look at figure 8.10 and consider the values in **First** and **Second** when GCD is finished. In the process of finding the gcd of 24 and 45 with the Euclidean algorithm, GCD would change **First** and **Second** as shown and return the number 3. Notice how important it is that **Numerator** and **Denominator** are *not* passed to GCD by reference!

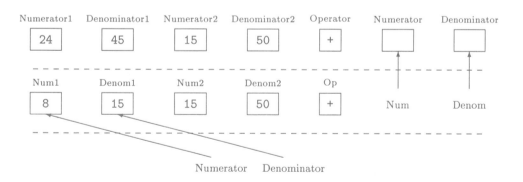

Figure 8.11 Memory After First Call of **Reduce**

After **Reduce** divides **Numerator** and **Denominator** by 3, memory would look like figure 8.11.

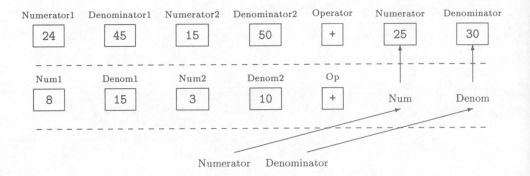

Figure 8.12 Memory After Adding the Two Fractions

Later, after `Reduce` is called and passed 15/50, and after `Add` is called to add the two reduced fractions together, `Reduce` is again called and passed `Num` and `Denom`, which are the results of adding the two fractions. See figure 8.12.

When `Reduce` is called the last time, the parameters are `Num` and `Denom`, so `Numerator` and `Denominator` refer back to `Num` and `Denom`, which in turn refer back to the main routine's `Numerator` and `Denominator`.

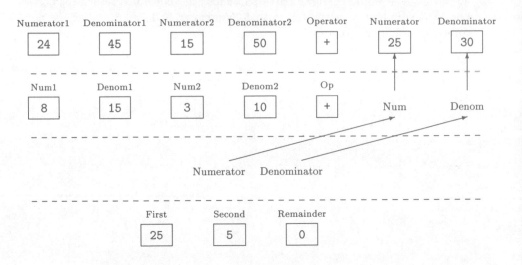

Figure 8.13 Memory at Conclusion of Last Call of `GCD`

Consider figure 8.13. `Reduce` calls `GCD`. `GCD` changes `First` and `Second`, determines the gcd of 25 and 30, and returns the gcd, 5, to `Reduce`. Inside `Reduce`, `Numerator` and `Denominator` are divided by 5 and the final result, 5/6, is determined. This time the values in the main routine get changed.

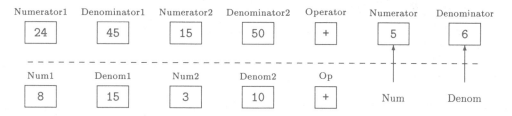

Figure 8.14 Memory at Conclusion of `PerformOperation`

Just before `PerformOperation` is exited, memory will look like figure 8.14.

A couple of things are worth emphasizing. Notice that the original fractions entered by the user were never changed. Copies of these two fractions got reduced but not the originals. The numerator and denominator of the result, on the other hand, did get reduced, because when we passed them to `PerformOperation`, we did not send copies.

Also, notice that we used the same names for the formal parameters in `Reduce` that we used for two of the variables in the main routine. That causes no problem whatsoever. In fact, we could have used `Numerator1` for the first numerator throughout without causing any problems. We decided to use different names to keep ourselves from getting confused. The compiler would not have become confused. That's another of the benefits of modular programming; the names of the local variables used in each module exist only in that module. Since data are passed to and from modules via the parameters, no confusion is created.

Look over the previous nine figures and accompanying text until you get a good understanding of the way parameters are passed and why it is so important to pass them carefully. Once again, don't go on reading until you really understand the difference between passing a parameter by value and passing it by reference.

8.13   Implementation and Testing—Once Again

As another example of implementation and testing, we'll write the code for the program from the "Once Again" section of chapter 7, that keeps score for a Ping-Pong match. We will be able to use some of the Pascal modules that were written in chapter 6 just as they are, although we'll take another look at them in the light of the new techniques learned in this chapter.

The Main Program

Let's first look at the main program. Consider the algorithm from chapter 7:

```
START OF PingPongMatch

call Introduce
call GetFirstServer(FirstServer)
call PlayMatch(FirstServer, MatchWinner, WinnerGames, LoserGames)
display "The result of the match:"
call DisplayWinner(MatchWinner, WinnerGames, LoserGames)
call Conclude

END OF PingPongMatch
```

This suggests the following for the main program, except for the declarations of the procedures and functions:

```pascal
program PingPongMatch(input, output);

{ Programmer:  Cliff Yuen                                            }

{ This program simulates a Ping-Pong match between Player A and      }
{ Player B.  The match is two out of three games to 21.   The       }
{ program keeps track of the score and who is to serve.  Flip a     }
{ coin to see who serves the first game.                            }

var
   FirstServer, MatchWinner : char;
   WinnerGames, LoserGames  : integer;


   . . .



begin
   Introduce;
   GetFirstServer(FirstServer);
   PlayMatch(FirstServer, MatchWinner, WinnerGames, LoserGames);
   write('The result of the match:  ');
   DisplayWinner(MatchWinner, WinnerGames, LoserGames);
   Conclude
end.
```

The Existing Modules

The `Introduce` and `Conclude` modules will again be messages for the user. These will be slightly modified from the corresponding modules in chapter 6. The modules `GetFirstServer` and `DisplayWinner` have already been written, and we could use them as is. In fact, we'll do so with `DisplayWinner`, but let's take another look at `GetFirstServer`:

```
procedure GetFirstServer(var FirstServer : char);

{  This procedure gets the first server from the user.  }

begin
   write('Please enter the player to serve first (A or B): ');
   readln(FirstServer);
   while (FirstServer <> 'A') and (FirstServer <> 'B') do
      begin
         write('Please enter an A or a B: ');
         readln(FirstServer)
      end
end;
```

In writing the module like this we are insisting that the user enter capital letters. As we've seen in this chapter, it's easy to make the program a little friendlier by allowing lowercase letters as input. We do this with sets:

```
procedure GetFirstServer(var FirstServer : char);

{  This procedure gets the first server from the user.  }

begin
   write('Please enter the player to serve first (A or B): ');
   readln(FirstServer);
   while not (FirstServer in ['A', 'B', 'a', 'b']) do
      begin
         write('Please enter an A or a B: ');
         readln(FirstServer)
      end
end;
```

Although this allows the user to type in lowercase letters, it would be better for the rest of the program if this module returned an uppercase letter. This can be done with an ⟨*if statement*⟩. See how we do it on the next page.

```
procedure GetFirstServer(var FirstServer : char);

{ This procedure gets the first server from the user.  }

begin
   write('Please enter the player to serve first (A or B): ');
   readln(FirstServer);
   while not (FirstServer in ['A', 'B', 'a', 'b']) do
      begin
         write('Please enter an A or a B: ');
         readln(FirstServer)
      end;
   if FirstServer = 'a'
      then
         FirstServer := 'A'
      else
         if FirstServer = 'b'
            then
               FirstServer := 'B'
end;
```

You should write a test program for this procedure and run it. You should type in 'A', 'a', 'B' and 'b' and be sure that it passes back the proper char value. Any other entry should trigger the error message.

The PlayMatch Procedure

Here's another look at the algorithm from chapter 7:

START OF PlayMatch(FirstServer, MatchWinner, WinnerGames, LoserGames)
Passed by value: FirstServer
Passed by reference: MatchWinner, WinnerGames, LoserGames

store zero in AGamesWon and in BGames Won
store a space in MatchWinner
loop
    call DisplayStatus(AGamesWon, BGamesWon)
    call PlayGame(FirstServer, GameWinner, WinnerScore, LoserScore)
    display "The result of the game: "
    call DisplayWinner(GameWinner, WinnerScore, LoserScore)
    when GameWinner is
        'A', add 1 to AGamesWon
        'B', add 1 to BGamesWon
    if AGamesWon < 2 and BGamesWon < 2
       then
            when FirstServer is
                'A', store 'B' in FirstServer
                'B', store 'A' in FirstServer
    until AGamesWon = 2 or BGamesWon = 2
if AGamesWon is 2
   then
      store 'A' in MatchWinner
      store AGamesWon in WinnerGames
      store BGamesWon in LoserGames
   else
      store 'B' in MatchWinner
      store BGamesWon in WinnerGames
      store AGamesWon in LoserGames

END OF PlayMatch

The implementation in Pascal follows the algorithm closely. Note the *when* steps, which are implemented as ⟨*case statement*⟩s:

```
procedure PlayMatch(FirstServer : char;
                var MatchWinner : char;
      var WinnerGames, LoserGames : integer);

{ This procedure simulates a Ping-Pong match, consisting of two  }
{ out of three games.  It passes back the winner and the score.  }

var
    GameWinner                : char;
    WinnerScore, LoserScore,
    AGamesWon, BGamesWon      : integer;


begin
    AGamesWon := 0;
    BGamesWon := 0;
    repeat
        DisplayStatus(AGamesWon, BGamesWon);
        PlayGame(FirstServer, GameWinner, WinnerScore, LoserScore);
        write('The result of the game:  ');
        DisplayWinner(GameWinner, WinnerScore, LoserScore);
        case GameWinner of
            'A' : AGamesWon := AGamesWon + 1;
            'B' : BGamesWon := BGamesWon + 1
            end;
        if (AGamesWon < 2) and (BGamesWon < 2)
            then
                case FirstServer of
                    'A' : FirstServer := 'B';
                    'B' : FirstServer := 'A'
                    end
    until (AGamesWon = 2) or (BGamesWon = 2);
```

```
      if AGamesWon = 2
         then
            begin
               MatchWinner := 'A';
               WinnerGames := AGamesWon;
               LoserGames  := BGamesWon
            end
         else
            begin
               MatchWinner := 'B';
               WinnerGames := BGamesWon;
               LoserGames  := AGamesWon
            end
   end;
```

This module calls three others: `DisplayStatus`, `PlayGame` and `Display-Winner`. The first one, `DisplayStatus`, hasn't been coded yet, but the other two have. We'll code `DisplayStatus` and then take another look at `PlayGame`.

The `DisplayStatus` Procedure

Here is the algorithm from chapter 7:

START OF DisplayStatus(AGamesWon, BGamesWon)
Passed by value: AGamesWon, BGamesWon
Passed by reference: none

store AGamesWon + BGamesWon in TotalGames
if TotalGames > 0
   then
      display "Games won:"
      display "Player A: ", AGamesWon, "Player B: ", BGamesWon
if TotalGames < 3
   then
      display "Begin game ", TotalGames + 1

END OF DisplayStatus

and the corresponding code:

```
procedure DisplayStatus(AGamesWon, BGamesWon : integer);

{  This procedure displays the number of games won by each  }
{  player, after the first game.  If there are more games    }
{  to be played, it indicates which game is next.            }

var
   TotalGames : integer;


begin
   TotalGames := AGamesWon + BGamesWon;
   if TotalGames > 0
      then
         begin
            writeln('Games won: ');
            write('Player A: ', AGamesWon : 3);
            writeln('   Player B: ', BGamesWon : 3);
            writeln
         end;
   if TotalGames < 3
      then
         begin
            writeln('Begin game ', TotalGames + 1 : 1, ':');
            writeln
         end
end;
```

We have added `writeln`s to make blank lines appear on the screen between messages.

Another Look at PlayGame

Here's the code for the PlayGame procedure from chapter 6:

```
procedure PlayGame(FirstServer : char;
                   var GameWinner : char;
        var WinnerScore, LoserScore : integer);

{ This procedure simulates a game of Ping-Pong, played to 21  }
{ points by a margin of 2.  It passes back the winner of the  }
{ game and the score.                                         }

var
    AScore, BScore       : integer;
    Server, PointWinner : char;


begin
    AScore := 0;
    BScore := 0;
    Server := FirstServer;
    repeat
        writeln('The score is:');
        writeln;
        writeln('Player A: ', AScore : 3, '  Player B: ', BScore : 3);
        writeln;
        writeln('Player ', Server, ' serves.');
        write('Who won the point? (Enter A or B): ');
        readln(PointWinner);
        while (PointWinner <> 'A') and (PointWinner <> 'B') do
            begin
                write('Please enter an A or a B: ');
                readln(PointWinner)
            end;
        if PointWinner = 'A'
            then
                AScore := AScore + 1
            else
                BScore := BScore + 1;
        GameWinner := Winner(AScore, BScore);
        if GameWinner = ' '
            then
                Server := NextServer(AScore, BScore, Server)
    until (GameWinner = 'A') or (GameWinner = 'B');
```

```
if GameWinner = 'A'
    then
        begin
            WinnerScore := AScore;
            LoserScore := BScore
        end
    else
        begin
            WinnerScore := BScore;
            LoserScore := AScore
        end
end;
```

Again, we have insisted that the user type in a capital letter, which isn't as friendly as it could be. We can use sets to allow either upper or lowercase. We will use a ⟨case statement⟩ right after that to add 1 to AScore or BScore. This could still be done using an ⟨if statement⟩, but we feel that the ⟨case statement⟩ is more informative here. We'll also rewrite the last ⟨if statement⟩ as a ⟨case statement⟩. Here's the revised statement part for PlayGame:

```
begin
    AScore := 0;
    BScore := 0;
    Server := FirstServer;
    repeat
        writeln('The score is:');
        writeln;
        writeln('Player A: ', AScore : 3, '    Player B: ', BScore : 3);
        writeln;
        write('Player ', Server, ' serves.');
        write('  Who won the point? (Enter A or B): ');
        readln(PointWinner);
        while not (PointWinner in ['A', 'B', 'a', 'b']) do
            begin
                write('Please enter an A or a B: ');
                readln(PointWinner)
            end;
        writeln;
```

```
        case PointWinner of
           'A', 'a' : AScore := AScore + 1;
           'B', 'b' : BScore := BScore + 1
           end;
        GameWinner := Winner(AScore, BScore);
        if GameWinner = ' '
           then
              Server := NextServer(AScore, BScore, Server)
        until (GameWinner = 'A') or (GameWinner = 'B');
     case GameWinner of
        'A' : begin
                 WinnerScore := AScore;
                 LoserScore := BScore
              end;
        'B' : begin
                 WinnerScore := BScore;
                 LoserScore := AScore
              end
        end
end;
```

This procedure calls two functions, `Winner` and `NextServer`, both of which can be used as is from the previous program.

The Structure of the Program

All that remains is to assemble the parts of the program together. As far as the main procedures are concerned, the statements in the main program block suggest the following structure:

```
program PingPongMatch
   procedure Introduce
   procedure GetFirstServer
   procedure PlayMatch
   procedure DisplayWinner
   procedure Conclude
```

Of these procedures, only `PlayMatch` calls anything else. Look at the code for `PlayMatch`; you can see that it calls `DisplayStatus`, `PlayGame` and `DisplayWinner`. The first two of these aren't called by anything else; it makes sense for them to be declared within `PlayMatch`.

`DisplayWinner`, on the other hand, is also called by the main program. If we declare `DisplayWinner` inside `PlayMatch`, the main program could not call it—it would only be callable from inside `PlayMatch`. Hence, we must put the declaration for `DisplayWinner` outside of and before `PlayMatch`. This analysis suggests the following structure:

```
program PingPongMatch
   procedure Introduce
   procedure GetFirstServer
   procedure DisplayWinner
   procedure PlayMatch
      procedure DisplayStatus
      procedure PlayGame
   procedure Conclude
```

There are two more modules in the program: the functions `Winner` and `NextServer`. In the program in chapter 6, these functions were declared prior to `PlayGame`. Now that we've discussed scope and activation, you might think it makes more sense to declare them within `PlayGame`. We would agree with that, so that gives us the following structure:

```
program PingPongMatch
   procedure Introduce
   procedure GetFirstServer
   procedure DisplayWinner
   procedure PlayMatch
      procedure DisplayStatus
      procedure PlayGame
         function Winner
         function NextServer
   procedure Conclude
```

We'll leave it to you to assemble the pieces of the program which we have presented in this section. You'll need to write an `Introduce` section and a `Conclude` section to complete the program. Most of the modules are from another program, so we assume that they have been adequately tested. Those modules that are new to this program should be tested first before being inserted into the program.

8.14   Summary and Review

- This chapter implemented the rational arithmetic program from chapter 7.

- In this chapter we spent considerable time on program testing and debugging. Programs and algorithms are normally designed from the top down but the code is written and tested from the bottom up. We indicated that no amount of testing will ever *prove* that a given real program is correct. That kind of proof requires mathematical techniques that are beyond the scope of this textbook. Even those techniques are inadequate for very large programs.

- We discussed the dangling else problem, the problem where an **else** can validly be paired with more than one **then**. We indicated that the rule followed by Pascal is simply that the **else** is always paired with the nearest **then** that results in valid syntax.

- We discussed the appropriate and necessary placement of procedure and function declarations. We gave some rules regarding where routines that are called by other routines should be placed.

- We discussed *scope* and *activation*. These terms refer to the region where an identifier is recognized and from where a routine can be called. We defined *global variable* and mentioned the golden rule for using global variables: DON'T.

- We introduced two new Pascal statements: the ⟨*case statement*⟩ and the ⟨*empty statement*⟩. The ⟨*case statement*⟩ is used to implement "multi-way selection." The ⟨*empty statement*⟩ is used to allow programmers to put semicolons on the ends of some statements.

- We introduced the way that Pascal handles sets, and showed how sets can be used to simplify input verification routines.

- We looked deeper into the way parameters are passed between modules and we looked at an idealized picture of memory as the data are passed around.

8.15   New Terms Introduced

activation-point That place in a program where it is legal to invoke a procedure or function.

bottom-up testing A testing procedure where the lowest-level modules are written and tested first, then the next lowest is tested, continuing until the entire program is completed.

case statement A Pascal statement that allows a limited implementation of multi-way selection.

dangling else An **else** that can be paired with more than one **then**.

empty statement A Pascal statement that consists of absolutely nothing and performs no action. Can be used to allow semicolons where otherwise a syntax error would result.

global variable A variable declared in a higher-level routine and used in an inner routine.

Golden Rule For Using Global Variables DON'T.

proof of correctness A mathematical verification of an algorithm or program's correctness. Often very hard or impossible for complex situations.

random numbers Generation of pseudo-random numbers by a program.

scope That portion of a Pascal program where a variable, procedure or function exists and may be used.

sets in Pascal Pascal's ability to work with sets allows for simpler Boolean expressions.

8.16 Exercises

1. How would you expect the procedure `GetFraction` to behave if you were to leave off the `var` in the parameter declaration? Try it using your testing routine.

2. Write and test the modules for `Add` and `Multiply`. Design and document a set of test data to use to make sure that `Add` and `Multiply` are working correctly.

3. Finish writing the modules for `RationalArithmetic`, testing as you go. The remaining modules are: `Introduce`, `GetOperator`, `DisplayResult` and `Conclude`. Compile and test the complete program.

4. If the module `GetOperator` is correctly written, it would not accept a character other than `'+'`, `'-'`, `'*'` or `'/'`. The module `PerformOperation` depends on this, since only these characters appear as constants in the ⟨*case statement*⟩. Using sets and an ⟨*if statement*⟩, write a version of `PerformOperation` that would not yield an error if an invalid operator were passed. Let the routine return zeros in `Num` and `Denom` in this case.

5. Assemble the pieces from the `PingPongMatch` program, first testing the new modules. Compile and run the complete program.

6. Using the bottom-up method of coding and testing, write a complete checkbook program, based on the algorithm from exercise 6 in chapter 7.

7. Write a program to implement the game of craps from exercise 7 of chapter 7. Your version of Pascal may have a built-in random number generator, but, as indicated on page 248, Standard Pascal doesn't have one. The function given there can be used to generate real numbers between 0 and 1, which will appear to be random. `Seed` is an arbitrary integer that the user enters at the start of the program to start the sequence. The sequence will be the same whenever the same seed is entered. To generate integers from 1 to 6, multiply the real number generated by the function by 6, truncate the result and add 1.

8. Using the bottom-up method, write and test a complete Pascal program based on the calendar algorithms from exercises 8–13 in chapter 7.

Chapter 9

Arrays, Searching and Sorting

Sorting is an ideal subject to demonstrate
a great diversity of algorithms,
all having the same purpose,
many of them being optimal in some sense, and
most of them having advantages over others.
— Niklaus Wirth

9.1 Overview of the Chapter

In this chapter we will introduce the concepts of searching and sorting using
arrays. An array is an example of a more complex data type than the simple
data types we've used so far; it contains not just one value but an ordered list
of values of a particular type. We'll develop algorithms for searching arrays for
specific values, and sorting arrays into a particular sequence.

9.2 Introduction

Searching and sorting are done so often in computing applications that many
techniques to accomplish them have been developed over the years. As a beginning student in computing science, it's important for you to be familiar with
some of the more common ones.

An *array* is a list of values considered as a unit and stored in one variable.
We can refer to any particular value by the name of the list and the position of
the value in the list; we call this position a subscript.

The values stored in arrays usually are of simple data types like `reals`,
`integers`, `Booleans` or `chars`. We can, however, construct arrays of values
that are themselves arrays—arrays of arrays! These are called multi-dimensional arrays, and we'll study them in later chapters. For now, we'll only use
one-dimensional arrays.

9.3   Arrays

Let's look at a picture of an array—or, at least, what we can pretend an array looks like—in memory. Figure 9.1 shows a simple array that has eighteen *slots* (or *cells* or *elements*).

Figure 9.1 An Array with Eighteen Elements

The array is called A, and the eighteen slots are A_1, A_2, A_3, ..., A_{18}. Of course we could have used eighteen different variables, but using an array allows us to refer to the elements of the array by subscript number, so that we can deal with them much more efficiently.

Notice that we use subscripts in the true sense of the word; the subscript is written lower than the variable name. When you read A_5, you should say "A sub 5." If you are handwriting your algorithms, you may find it easy to use subscripts this way, but if you're typing them you may find it awkward. In that case you could type A(5) instead of A_5, but you must then be careful not to confuse it with a function or procedure A being passed the parameter 5. Another sensible choice would be to use A[5], since the square brackets will remind you that you are not calling a function or procedure. In this chapter, we'll use the subscripts.

Of course, arrays will not always have eighteen slots; we can have arrays of just about any size we want. The algorithms we will develop will work for arrays of any size at all.

For much of what we do in this chapter, we'll assume we're working with an array whose elements are real numbers. When we consider arrays holding other data types, even more complicated ones, it will be easy to see how to adapt our algorithms to handle these arrays.

9.4   Elementary Array Manipulations

To get us started using arrays, let's assume that we have an array filled with N numbers. Suppose we want to know the sum of the numbers in the array, the average of the array values and the maximum and minimum values stored in the array. Suppose the array is called A and that the N numbers have already been stored in the array. (Since it's usually more of an implementation question, we'll discuss how to get some numbers into an array in the next chapter.)

To find the sum of the numbers in the array, we need only to initialize a variable, say *Sum*, to zero and then use a loop to go through the array and add each array value to *Sum*:

```
store 0 in Sum
store 1 in i
loop while i ≤ N
    add Aᵢ to Sum
    add 1 to i
```

Once we have found *Sum*, the average value can quickly be determined by simply dividing *Sum* by N:

```
store Sum / N in Average
```

To determine the maximum value stored in an array, we can start by storing the first value in the array in a variable, say *Max*, and then looking at each of the remaining values adjusting *Max* whenever a larger value is found. Here are the steps that will do the job:

```
store A₁ in Max
store 2 in i
loop while i ≤ N
    if Aᵢ > Max
        then
            store Aᵢ in Max
    add 1 to i
```

There are several modifications to this routine that can be made. For instance, you might want to know not only what the largest value is, but where it is.

Also, we have not written these examples as complete modules. We'll leave these modifications and the completion of the modules for the exercises.

9.5   Searching

Another thing that is often done in working with computers and the data stored by computers is *searching*. With the vast amount of data that can be stored in a computerized database, it is increasingly important to be able to find items of data frequently and quickly. A great deal of what takes place in computer science is the study of storing and retrieving data. In this section we will only be able to introduce two of the most basic techniques used to search for data. There are many other techniques used both to store and to search for data. Our goal here is just to get started. In the real world, the data that is stored in a database usually consists of much more than simple numerical data, but since we have to start somewhere, we'll start by just searching for numbers.

Let's assume we have an array filled with N real numbers. What we want to do is to search through the array and decide whether or not a particular real number, called the *Key*, is somewhere in the array.

Linear Search

The most obvious search technique—and the one that is as good as any if the elements are in no particular order—is a simple linear search. Start by looking at the first element, then the second, and so on, until you either find the *Key* or come to the end of the list.

Suppose that the array is called A, and it contains N numbers. Let's write an algorithm for a linear search. Our routine would have to know what array is being searched, the number of elements in the array, and the *Key* value being searched for. These would be passed by value. The routine would determine whether or not the *Key* is in the array and if so, where it is.

To determine whether or not the search was successful, we'll use a Boolean valued parameter, *Found*. The routine will set *Found* to true if the number is found, and false otherwise. We'll also use an integer valued parameter, *Place*, that we'll set to the location of the *Key* in the array if it's found. These two parameters will be passed by reference to the search routine, so that the results can be sent back to the calling routine.

The method is probably obvious: look at the first element in the array. If it equals the *Key*, store 1 in *Place*, true in *Found*, and quit looking. Otherwise, look at the second element and compare it to the *Key*. Continue until you either find the *Key* or come to the end of the array. If you get to the end of the array and haven't found the *Key*, set *Found* to false.

Rather than set *Found* to false at the end of the search if we don't find the *Key*, we can start *Found* off at false, set it to true only if the *Key* is found, and use it to decide whether or not to continue searching. We then also start *Place* off at 1 and add 1 to it every time through the loop. That scheme yields the following algorithm.

> START OF LinearSearch(A, N, Key, Found, Place)
> Passed by value: A (an array of N elements), N, Key
> Passed by reference: Found, Place
> Postconditions: If the Key is in the array, Found is set to true and
>   Place set to the location. Otherwise, Found is false.

```
store false in Found
store 1 in Place
loop while not Found and Place ≤ N
    if A_Place = Key
        then
            store true in Found
        else
            add 1 to Place

END OF LinearSearch
```

Notice that the Boolean variable *Found* is used to terminate the loop if an element in the array equal to the *Key* is located. A variable used this way is called a *flag*, because we think of it either as raised—to indicate that some condition has been met—or down—to indicate that the condition has not been met. This is like a flag on a rural mailbox used to indicate to the mail carrier whether or not the mailbox contains outgoing mail.

Take the time to trace through the algorithm at this point. You should notice that if the *Key* is found in some element of the array, then the subscript of that element is returned in the variable *Place*. Furthermore, once the *Key* has been found, we don't want to continue the search; that's why we include the "*not Found*" condition in the *loop while*.

You might notice that although we said initially that the array was filled with real numbers, nothing in the algorithm relies on the type of data stored in the array.

You might wonder why we used a *loop while* instead of a *loop until*. Although it's quite unlikely, we used the *loop while* so that the algorithm will still work if the array is empty, i.e., if *N* happens to equal zero.

Binary Search

A linear search is such a slow method of searching that it should only be used on very short lists. Suppose you have an array containing 1000 items. If the element being searched for is present, it will require an average of 500 "looks" into the array to find it. If the element is not present, the routine will examine all 1000 elements before it learns that the element is not there.

If lists containing more than a couple of dozen elements are to be searched, it's better to keep the list in some order and use a binary search, like the one we used in the guessing game algorithm and program in chapters 3 and 4.

The advantage of the binary search is easy to see. Again imagine that the list contains 1000 elements but this time let's suppose they are arranged in ascending order. We start by examining the element in position 500. If the element there is larger than the *Key*, all of the elements from 500 through 1000 can be eliminated from the search. If the element there is smaller, the elements in the list from 1 through 500 can be eliminated. In just one look into the array, we can reduce the size of the list being searched from 1000 to 500. If you continue with this example, you'll see that if the element being searched for is in the array, it can be located in eleven looks or less. If it's not there, only eleven looks will be necessary to determine that it's missing. This is a tremendous improvement over an average of 500 looks and a maximum of 1000 required by a linear search.

Let's write a general algorithm for a binary search. Once again, suppose that the array is called *A*, and that it contains *N* elements, but this time assume the elements are arranged in ascending order. As before, we'll send two parameters, *Found* and *Place* to be used by the calling routine to determine whether or not the search was successful, and, if so, where the *Key* is located; they will be passed by reference. The algorithm is on the next page.

START OF BinarySearch(A, N, Key, Found, Place)
Passed by value: A (an array of N elements), N, Key
Passed by reference: Found, Place
Precondition: The array A is arranged in ascending order
Postconditions: If the Key is in the array, Found is set to true and
*   Place set to the location. Otherwise, Found is false.*

store 0 in Left
store N+1 in Right
store false in Found
loop while Left+1 < Right and not Found
*   store the value halfway between Left & Right in Middle*
* if A_{Middle} = Key*
*   then*
*   store true in Found*
*   store Middle in Place*
*   else*
*   if Key > A_{Middle}*
*   then*
*   store Middle in Left*
*   else*
*   store Middle in Right*

END OF BinarySearch

As before, the variable *Place* tells where in the array the *Key* was found, and the variable *Found* is set appropriately.

You probably noticed that we didn't really need the local variable *Middle*, that we could have just used *Place* instead. That's right. We chose to include *Middle* just to make the algorithm a bit easier to follow. If you want to do away with *Middle* and use *Place* instead, we wouldn't object.

Binary Search Variations

There is a subtle difference between this algorithm and the one we used in the guessing game. Let's discuss the algorithm a bit.

Here we start by setting the variable *Left* to 0 and *Right* to $N + 1$. In this way, *Left* and *Right* always point *just outside* the range of numbers remaining to be searched. As the binary search proceeds, *Left* and *Right* come together until *Left* is next to *Right*; that is, until $Left + 1 = Right$. After each examination of A_{Middle}, if the *Key* was not found, we store *Middle* in either *Left* or *Right*, depending on whether A_{Middle} is smaller or larger than the *Key*.

Before, we set *Left* to 1 and *Right* to *N* at the start, and at each pass we either set *Left* to $Middle + 1$ or *Right* to $Middle - 1$. In this case, we would have to "loop while $Left \leq Right$ and not Found." You should fill a small array with numbers and trace the algorithm through each way. You should see what happens when the starting points of *Left* and *Right* are not set carefully.

The two variations both get the job done and you can use either one but you cannot mix them. If you start off with *Left* and *Right* pointing *inside* the array, make sure that you keep them pointing at numbers that have not been eliminated. If you start them off outside the array, keep them outside the array.

In each case be sure you see what the condition is that ends the loop. One method loops while *Left* + 1 is less than *Right* and the other loops while *Left* is less than or equal to *Right*. You cannot mix the two methods!

Efficiency of the Searching Algorithms

If you increase the size of the array being searched, the average number of looks required by the linear search increases at the same rate. However, the number of looks required by the binary search goes up much more slowly. Indeed, if you double the number of numbers in the array, the number of looks required in a binary search only increases by one. That is, you can completely search a sorted array containing 1000 elements with eleven looks, and it will only take twelve looks to search a sorted array with 2000 elements. The more numbers the array contains, the greater the difference between the linear search and the binary search.

9.6   Sorting

In computer science, the term *sorting* is used to mean something more like *rearranging*. When we say we want to sort a list of things, we don't mean that we want to separate them into groups or categories, like sorting laundry. We really mean that we want to rearrange the list in some particular order. The term *sort* might not be the best one to use, but we won't attempt to invent a better one here.

For the sake of the examples in this chapter, let's assume we want things arranged in ascending order; the algorithms can later be modified to sort things in descending order instead. You can imagine that we're sorting numbers if it makes things easier to understand, but as far as the algorithms go you don't have to worry about exactly what's being sorted.

We have stated the problem to be solved and are now ready to find a solution. There are many different solutions to the sorting problem, and we'll present only a few of the better known ones.

The Bubble Sort

The bubble sort may be the easiest sorting algorithm to understand, but it's usually not the most efficient. We'll discuss it mainly to "get our feet wet" with sorting algorithms.

The bubble sort uses a switching technique. The contents of two adjacent cells in the array are compared, and if they are not in the proper order, they are switched or "swapped." We'll use a module *Swap* that exchanges the contents of two variables. Following our usual top-down approach, the details of this module will be left for later.

The basic idea of the bubble sort is to use this compare-and-swap technique on the first and second elements of the array, then the second and third, the third and fourth, and so on until the next to last and the last elements are compared and, if necessary, swapped.

Does this leave the array in the proper order? It's easy to see that it doesn't; consider an array containing the numbers:

    30 25 13

The first comparison would swap the 30 and the 25, leaving:

    25 30 13

The next (and last) comparison would swap the 30 and the 13, leaving:

    25 13 30

Although the array is not yet in order, we are certain that the largest number is now at the right end of the list.

We have reduced the problem of sorting the original list to that of sorting the first $N - 1$ elements of the list. We can, of course, repeat the process, each time stopping one element short of the last "pass." Eventually, the list will be sorted. Let's look at the algorithm for the first pass.

The first thing we do is to compare the first two elements and swap them if they're not in order:

if $A_1 > A_2$
    then
        call Swap(A_1, A_2)

Next we compare the second and third elements:

if $A_2 > A_3$
    then
        call Swap(A_2, A_3)

This continues until we compare the next to last element with the last:

if $A_{N-1} > A_N$
    then
        call Swap(A_{N-1}, A_N)

If we put all these together, we get:

if $A_1 > A_2$
    then
        call Swap(A_1, A_2)
if $A_2 > A_3$
    then
        call Swap(A_2, A_3)
   ⋮

if $A_{N-1} > A_N$
    then
        call Swap(A_{N-1}, A_N)

It should be clear that this constitutes some kind of loop. We could write the algorithm using a *loop until* or a *loop while*, but we'll take this opportunity to introduce a third kind of loop, which is especially designed for this situation.

The *loop for*

The *loop while* tests a Boolean condition at the top of the loop, and the *loop until* tests a condition at the bottom of the loop. The *loop for* doesn't use a Boolean condition, but instead performs the loop a specific number of times.

A variable, called the *index of the loop*, is set to some initial value. Each time the loop is executed, the index is incremented. This continues until the index exceeds another value. We'll write the *loop for* like this:

loop for i going from ⟨*value1*⟩ *to* ⟨*value2*⟩
    ⟨*step*⟩
    ⟨*step*⟩
    ⋮
    ⟨*step*⟩

The variable i is the index of the loop, and the steps that are indented in the above example constitute the *body of the loop*. The idea is that the body of the loop is to be executed again and again; the first time with i equal to ⟨*value1*⟩, the second time with i equal to ⟨*value1*⟩ + 1, the third time with i equal to ⟨*value1*⟩ + 2, etc. The last time the body of the loop is executed, i will equal ⟨*value2*⟩. The advantage of the *loop for* is that we don't have separate steps to initialize or increment the index.

We have to be a bit more precise about the behavior of the *loop for* in certain situations. First, if ⟨*value1*⟩ equals ⟨*value2*⟩ at the start of the loop, the body of the loop is to be executed just one time. Second, if ⟨*value1*⟩ is greater than ⟨*value2*⟩ at the start of the loop, the body of the loop is to be skipped entirely. (Although most computer languages have a construction similar to this, some assume that the body of the loop is always executed at least once. This is not the case with Pascal and it's not the case with what we will intend in our algorithms.)

We would write the first pass of the bubble sort using a *loop for* as follows:

loop for i going from 1 to N−1
    if $A_i > A_{i+1}$
        then
            call Swap(A_i, A_{i+1})

For the second pass, the index would only have to go from 1 to N − 2:

loop for i going from 1 to N−2
    if $A_i > A_{i+1}$
        then
            call Swap(A_i, A_{i+1})

And for the third pass, the index would stop at N − 3, and so on. The last pass would compare the first two elements of the list.

To make it look like the others, we write that pass:

```
loop for i going from 1 to 1
    if A_i > A_{i+1}
        then
            call Swap(A_i, A_{i+1})
```

Putting this all together, we get:

```
loop for i going from 1 to N−1
    if A_i > A_{i+1}
        then
            call Swap(A_i, A_{i+1})
loop for i going from 1 to N−2
    if A_i > A_{i+1}
        then
            call Swap(A_i, A_{i+1})
loop for i going from 1 to N−3
    if A_i > A_{i+1}
        then
            call Swap(A_i, A_{i+1})
    ⋮
loop for i going from 1 to 1
    if A_i > A_{i+1}
        then
            call Swap(A_i, A_{i+1})
```

You can see that the only thing that changes from one pass to the next is the ending value of each *loop for*, which changes from $N - 1$ to 1. We have yet another loop, this time one whose index goes backward. We'll write it:

```
loop for j going from N−1 down to 1
    loop for i going from 1 to j
        if A_i > A_{i+1}
            then
                call Swap(A_i, A_{i+1})
```

These loops are called *nested loops*. You should construct a small array of about six or seven numbers and trace this algorithm until you understand how these loops work. (If this doesn't convince you of the efficiency of using arrays, try writing an algorithm that sorts six or seven numbers in separate variables!)

Since this completes the algorithm for the bubble sort, we should finish it by putting our normal starting and ending words around it. Before we do, however, we have to clear up any uncertainty concerning the parameters. What are the parameters for the bubble sort? What is being sent to (or back from) the procedure? Clearly the array A has to be sent. The number of elements in the array also has to be known by the algorithm. Are they passed by value or by reference? Since the number of elements in the array won't change during the sorting process, the parameter N should be passed by value. The array, on the other hand, must be passed by reference since it will be changed inside the procedure and sent back changed; that's the whole purpose, after all, of the procedure. Thus there are two parameters, A and N. N is passed by value and A is passed by reference. Since A is an array, we will make that clear in the statement of the algorithm in case a reader has any doubts. Thus our first bubble sort becomes:

```
START OF BubbleSort(A, N)
Passed by value: N
Passed by reference: A (an array of N elements)
Postcondition: The array is in ascending order

loop for j going from N−1 down to 1
    loop for i going from 1 to j
        if A_i > A_{i+1}
            then
                call Swap(A_i, A_{i+1})

END OF BubbleSort
```

An Improved Bubble Sort

Even at its best, the bubble sort is not very efficient. We can, however, make some improvements to the algorithm presented above.

Think of what would happen if we passed to this module an array that was already sorted. What would the algorithm do? It would run just the same way, and take just as long as if the array were not sorted. It would keep on comparing adjacent elements of the array, but it would never swap any of them, since they wouldn't be out of order. In fact, we can use this as a test to see if the routine should continue with the next pass: if a pass finishes with no elements being swapped, the array must be in order.

How do we keep track of whether or not there has been a swap? We use another flag, which is set to true at the beginning of every pass. Let's call this flag *Sorted*. If two elements are found out of order and need to be swapped, we would store false in *Sorted*. Thus, if a pass is completed and *Sorted* is still true, then we don't need to continue sorting.

With this in mind the algorithm becomes:

```
START OF ImprovedBubbleSort(A, N)
Passed by value: N
Passed by reference: A (an array of N elements)
Postcondition: The array is in ascending order


store N−1 in j
loop
    store true in Sorted
    loop for i going from 1 to j
        if A_i > A_{i+1}
            then
                call Swap(A_i, A_{i+1})
                store false in Sorted
    subtract 1 from j
    until Sorted


END OF ImprovedBubbleSort
```

The algorithm still contains two loops, one inside the other, but the outer loop—which was a *loop for*—has been replaced with a *loop until*. This is necessary because we do want to go through the body of the loop at least once—we have to make at least one pass—but do not know ahead of time how many passes will have to be made.

You should trace this algorithm carefully, using an array with six elements or so. Notice especially what happens if at least one swap is made on every pass. In this case *j* actually becomes 0. Does this cause a problem? What happens when the routine tries to "*loop for i going from 1 to 0*"?

An Even Better Bubble Sort

Yes, we can even make another improvement. Let's say that on a given pass the fifth and sixth elements are swapped, but that no other elements are swapped for the rest of that pass. On the next pass, then, there's no need to compare beyond the fifth element, since the array is already in order from that point on. We can just set *j* to 5 and continue the routine.

In general, each pass only needs to go as far as the last exchange of the pass before. A variable, say *LastSwap*, whose value "points to" the location of the last element switched could be used to keep track of where the last swap took place. We'll leave the details of this algorithm for an exercise.

The Insertion Sort

We can easily describe a sorting algorithm that is better than the bubble sort. It is easy to understand if you can picture trying to arrange a shuffled deck of playing cards. Place the shuffled deck of cards face down on the table. Pick up the top two cards and put them in order. Pick up the third card and put it in order with the first two. Pick up the fourth card and put it in order with the first three. Continue picking up cards one at a time until they are all in order.

It should be clear that this is a loop; a loop that works its way through the elements of the array, inserting each one where it belongs in the earlier part of the array. The loop must start with the second element—since you cannot sort just one thing—and continues through the rest of the array. Thus, it becomes a *loop for* that loops from the second through the Nth element.

The cards are easy to manipulate; you can easily slip one card between the two cards that you are already holding. With the array, on the other hand, you will have to slide the elements of the array over as you insert the others in place. Suppose, for example, you have already arranged the first twelve elements; when you come to element number thirteen, you will have to determine where it belongs and slide the others over. One way to do this is to look first at A_{12}. If the value there is greater than A_{13}, then slide it over into position 13. But then, the value we are trying to insert would be lost. To keep that from happening, we can put it in a temporary variable, say *Temp*. The procedure becomes something like:

Put the current element in a temporary variable. Compare this value with the elements in the array to the left of the current element. If the first element to the left is greater than the temporary value, slide it over one slot to the right and keep looking. Continue searching and sliding elements over until you find the place the current element should be inserted. When you find the place the current value belongs, insert it into the array at that point.

The "search and slide" clearly constitutes a loop. What kind of loop is it? It can't be a *loop for* since you don't know where the current value goes yet. So, it's either a *loop while* or a *loop until*. Which is it? Does it matter? How do you decide? What is the basic difference between these two loops? Recall that the *loop while* has the test at the top of the loop, while the *loop until* has the test at the bottom. This means the *loop until* always goes through the body of the loop at least once. Can we use a *loop until*? Can we afford to always "slide" an element over at least once? No! If it turns out that the element to be inserted is already where it belongs, we need not slide the next element over. Thus, we don't want to use a *loop until*, we want a *loop while*.

Enough vague talk about the solution, it's time to be more precise; that is, it's time we wrote the algorithm. An algorithm for this procedure, using the same notation for the array, A, and the number of elements, N, as before, would be:

```
START OF InsertionSort(A, N)
Passed by value: N
Passed by reference: A (an array of N elements)
Postcondition: The array is in ascending order

loop for j going from 2 to N
    store A_j in Temp
    store j−1 in i
    loop while i > 0 and A_i > Temp
        store A_i in A_{i+1}
        subtract 1 from i
    store Temp in A_{i+1}

END OF InsertionSort
```

We start each iteration of the main loop by placing the jth element in a local variable called *Temp*. Then we search for the place to put *Temp* by looking first at the place just before the jth place. If the element there is greater than *Temp*, we slide that element over one slot and subtract 1 from i. This continues until we find an element that is smaller than or equal to *Temp*. When we do, we insert *Temp* into the array just to the right of that point.

Figure 9.2 illustrates an insertion sort in progress. The elements from 1 through 6 have already been sorted. The index j equals 7, and we are searching for the place to insert A_7, which has been temporarily put into *Temp*.

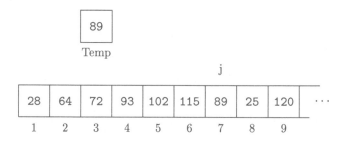

Figure 9.2 Insertion Sort in Progress, j = 7

As you can see, *Temp* belongs in position 4. After the elements from 4 through 6 have been slid over, and *Temp* inserted into A_4, j will become 8, and the big loop will continue. Then the array will look like figure 9.3.

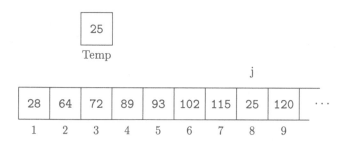

Figure 9.3 Insertion Sort in Progress, j = 8

Rules of Thumb on Loops

The questions we have been asking ourselves concerning which loop to use are important and we can write them down as "rules of thumb":

- If you know where the loop starts and ends, or know how many times you want to go through the loop, use a *loop for*; otherwise use either a *loop while* or a *loop until*.

- If you are trying to decide whether to use a *loop while* or a *loop until* and you know you always want to go through the loop at least one time, use a *loop until*.

- If you are trying to decide whether to use a *loop while* or a *loop until* and you know you might have a situation where the loop should be skipped entirely, use a *loop while*.

The Insertion Sort, Continued

If, while the insertion sort is in progress, it turns out that *Temp* is smaller than all of the numbers in the list from A_1 through A_{j-1}, then we have to move them all over and put *Temp* into A_1. That's the reason the inner *loop while* says:

> *loop while $i > 0$ and $A_i > $ Temp*

It is important to note that if i becomes zero before a value less than or equal to *Temp* is found in the array, we *do not* want to compare A_i to *Temp*; indeed, there is no A_i when i equals zero. In this case, if we implement the algorithm just as it appears, some Pascal compilers will look at both operands of the **and** before deciding whether the expression is true or false. But then the compiler will attempt to see whether A_0 is greater than *Temp*; since A_0 doesn't exist, the program will crash. This is an important issue that can cause major problems if not handled with care. However, since it is not a problem with the meaning of the algorithm, we'll not say any more about it at this point.

Partially for the above reason and for another reason that will become apparent in a few pages, we'll introduce another way to write the algorithm. We can separate the "search" part from the "slide" part. That is, we can have part of the routine find the proper place for *Temp*, and have another part slide things over to make room for it.

The part that finds the proper place would be a Boolean function, say *InsertPlace*, that accepts the array and the current position as parameters and returns the place where the current element should be inserted. This routine would just call *InsertPlace*:

> *store InsertPlace(A, j) in Place*

The part that slides things over would simply be:

> *loop for i going from $j-1$ down to Place*
> *   store A_i in A_{i+1}*

and finally we would

> *store Temp in A_{Place}*

Notice we are storing the value returned by *InsertPlace* in local variable, *Place*, because we need to use it twice and we don't want to call the function twice. Indeed, since we are changing what's stored in A_j in the slide part, we cannot call *InsertPlace* after the slide part.

The entire insertion sort algorithm becomes:

```
START OF InsertionSort2(A, N)
Passed by value: N
Passed by reference: A (an array of N elements)
Postcondition: The array is in ascending order

loop for j going from 2 to N
    store A_j in Temp
    store InsertPlace(A, j) in Place
    loop for i going from j−1 down to Place
        store A_i in A_{i+1}
    store Temp in A_Place

END OF InsertionSort2
```

InsertPlace **with a Linear Search**

We can write *InsertPlace* using a flag and a linear search routine that starts by examining the array at position A_{j-1}. Here's our version of *InsertPlace*:

```
START OF InsertPlace(A, j)
Postcondition: Returns the place where A_j belongs in A_1
                        through A_j

store j−1 in i
store false in Found
loop while not Found and i > 0
    if A_i > A_j
        then
            subtract 1 from i
        else
            store true in Found
return i+1

END OF InsertPlace
```

Note that if *Found* never becomes true, then the loop ends with $i = 0$, and the value returned is 1. We return $i+1$ because we want to insert the current element to the right of the first element we encounter that is smaller than or equal to it. Does *InsertPlace* still work if A_j is larger than all the elements to the left? Check it out! You should also take the time to compare this routine with the linear search routine at the beginning of this chapter.

Insertion Sort with Binary Search

You probably already knew how to improve the insertion sort, even before reading the title of this section. During the search part of *InsertPlace*, the part of the array being searched is already in order, and we know that a binary search is much more efficient than a linear search when this is the case. Since we discussed the binary search earlier, it should be easy to see how we can use it here. The linear search inside *InsertPlace* can be replaced with a binary search. We'll leave this improvement to the insertion sort for an exercise.

You will want to be careful to return the "best" place to do the insertion. If the list doesn't contain duplicates, the "right" place and the best place are the same. However, if the list contains duplicates, there can be several right places to do the insertion, but you don't want the routine to do any unnecessary sliding. Be sure you consider this when you write the binary search version of *InsertPlace*.

The Heap Sort

Our final sorting algorithm is faster than either of the sorting methods we have considered so far, and it uses quite a different approach to the problem. Rather than viewing an array as a linear sequence of numbered cells, we can view an array as a structure known as a *tree*, so called because it looks like an upside-down tree (it really looks more like an upside-down bush but no one calls them "bushes"). It's worth noting that we are not really working with a tree. The array is not being changed in any way at all. We are just thinking of the array as a tree. Real binary trees are data structures discussed in detail in more advanced texts.

Tree Notation

Let's consider some of the terminology we'll use to talk about trees. When we view the array as a tree, we will call the cells *nodes*. In figure 9.4, the nodes of the array are drawn in layers, with one node on the first layer, two on the next, four on the next, and so on until we run out of nodes. We connect the nodes so that each node is connected to one on the level above, which is called its *parent*, and at most two on the level below, which are called its *children*. A tree like this whose nodes have at most two children is called a *binary tree*.

Note that the only node that does not have a parent is the node corresponding to the first cell of the array, A_1. We call this node the *root node*, since it's like the root of the tree. Also note that some nodes have only one child, and some have no children at all. A node with no children is called a *leaf*.

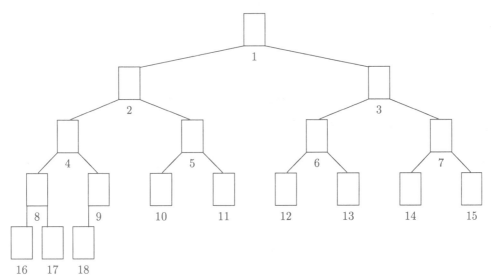

Figure 9.4 An Array Viewed as a Binary Tree

It is easy to find which node is the parent of a given node, and which nodes (if they exist) are its children. The parent of the node A_i is $A_{i \text{ div } 2}$, for $i > 1$. The children of the node A_i are A_{2*i} and A_{2*i+1}, as long as these indices are not bigger than N.

A *subtree* of a tree is the collection of all the nodes starting at a given node and including all the descendants of that node (i.e., its children, its children's children, etc.). The first node in the collection is called the *root node for the subtree*. For example, the subtree with root node 3 in figure 9.4 consists of the nodes numbered 3, 6, 7, 12, 13, 14 and 15.

A Heap

We will call a tree or a subtree a *heap* if every node in the tree (or subtree) contains a value larger than or equal to those of both its children. A subtree that is a leaf is considered a heap by default.

Consider the tree in figure 9.5. The tree is not a heap since node 3 contains a value smaller than that of node 6, its child. However, if we exchange A_3 and A_6, the resulting tree (see figure 9.6) is a heap.

Making a subtree into a heap is the key to the heap sort. If the entire tree is a heap, then the root node contains the largest value in the array. We can exchange the first element with the last element and know that the largest element is in the right place. Doing this will, of course, mess up the heap structure of the entire tree. However, if we simply ignore the last element—it is in the right place, after all—then we can continue to work on the remainder of the array.

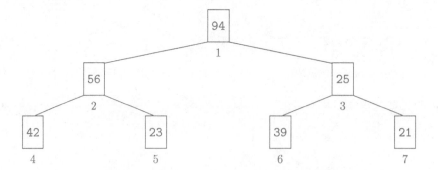

Figure 9.5 A Tree that is Not a Heap

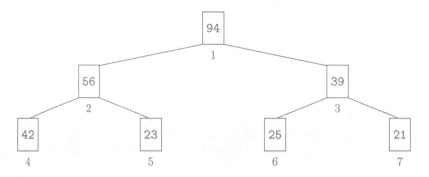

Figure 9.6 A Tree that is a Heap

Let's imagine that we have a module that will "heapify" any subtree, including the whole tree, and that this routine will heapify a tree that consists of array elements from one point in the array through another point. Here's how we could sort the array using such a routine:

Heapify the whole tree.
Exchange the first element with the last.
Heapify the subtree from the first node through the next-to-last.
Exchange the first element with the next-to-last.
Heapify the subtree from the first node through the next-to-next-to-last.
Continue until the entire array is sorted.

This routine gets the largest element in the array into position 1, swaps it with the element in position N and then works on the subtree from 1 through N−1. Continuing to "prune" elements off the tree as they are put in order.

A refined version of the algorithm would look like the one on the next page—assuming we have a procedure *Heapify*(A, i, j), that turns the subtree from i through j into a heap.

Heapify the whole tree
loop for i going from N down to 2
    exchange A_1 and A_i
    call Heapify(A, 1, i−1)

Heapify

Now we need to write the procedure *Heapify*. It turns out that it's easier to heapify a subtree if both children of the root node of that subtree are heaps already. (You might want to read that last sentence again.) We'll see how to heapify that kind of subtree first, then we'll see how that method can be used to heapify a subtree in the general case.

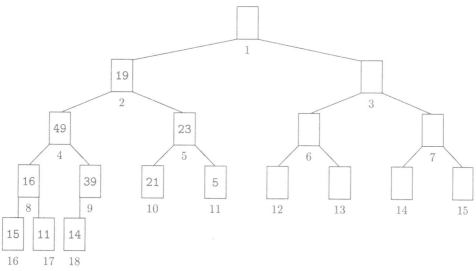

Figure 9.7 The Subtree with Root Node 2 is Not a Heap

Consider the tree in figure 9.7. Suppose we want to heapify the subtree with root node 2. Notice that the subtrees with root nodes 4 and 5 are heaps already. The subtree with root node 2 is not a heap because the 19 is smaller than the contents of one of its children—smaller than both in fact.

To heapify this subtree, start by swapping the root node with the larger of its children—in this case, swap A_2 and A_4. We now consider the subtree with root node 4. If that subtree is a heap, we're finished; if not, we have to heapify it. In this case, it's not a heap because the contents of node 9 (**39**) is larger than the root node (**19**).

We now have the problem of heapifying a smaller subtree, the subtree with root node 4. Swap the root node with the larger of its children—in this case, swap A_4 and A_9. Is that subtree a heap? Yes it is, so we're finished. If it

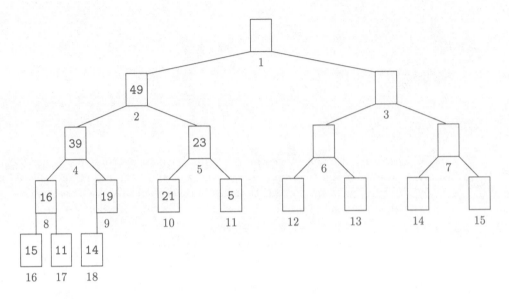

Figure 9.8 The Subtree with Root Node 2 is Now a Heap

weren't, we would just continue on the same way. In this case, the resulting tree looks like the one in figure 9.8.

Now that we see how the process works, we can simplify it a little. You would end up with the same heapified subtree if you performed the following steps:

> *Set aside the contents of the root node.*
> *Trace a path down the tree, passing through the larger of the two children of each node, each time moving that child up to its parent's node.*
> *Continue until you arrive either at a leaf, or at a node both of whose children are less than the contents of the root node.*
> *Finally, put the contents of the original root node into the node where you end up.*

This analysis results in the algorithm on the next page for *Heapify*.

```
START OF Heapify(A, Start, Stop)
Passed by value: Start, Stop
Passed by reference: A, an array with at least Stop elements
Precondition: The subtrees with root nodes 2*Start and 2*Start + 1 are heaps
Postcondition: The subtree with root node Start is a heap

store A_Start in Temp
store 2*Start in k
store false in Done
loop while not Done and k ≤ Stop
    if k < Stop and A_k < A_{k+1}
        then
            add 1 to k
    if Temp < A_k
        then
            store A_k in A_{k div 2}
            store 2*k in k
    else
            store true in Done
store Temp in A_{k div 2}

END OF Heapify
```

You should trace the algorithm with a few examples to be sure how it works.

The Heap Sort, Completed

Now that we can heapify in the special case (where the subtrees of the children of the root node are already heaps), we can turn the entire tree into a heap by starting at the bottom and working our way to the top, heapifying subtrees as we go. In fact, we don't have to start all the way at the bottom, because roughly the last half of the tree consists of nodes with no children, which are heaps by definition. We can start at the last node that has a child. This will be the parent of the last node in the array, i.e., the node N div 2. The following would heapify the entire tree:

```
loop for i going from N div 2 down to 1
    call Heapify(A, i, N)
```

Putting all the pieces together, the following becomes the complete algorithm for the heap sort:

```
START OF HeapSort(A, N)
Passed by value: N
Passed by reference: A
Postcondition: The array is in ascending order

loop for i going from N div 2 down to 1
    call Heapify(A, i, N)
loop for i going from N down to 2
    exchange A₁ and Aᵢ
    call Heapify(A, 1, i−1)

END OF HeapSort
```

$$A_1 \text{ and } A_i$$

```
START OF Heapify(A, Start, Stop)
Passed by value: Start, Stop
Passed by reference: A, an array with at least Stop elements
Precondition: The subtrees with root nodes 2*Start and 2*Start + 1 are heaps
Postcondition: The subtree with root node Start is a heap

store A_Start in Temp
store 2*Start in k
store false in Done
loop while not Done and k ≤ Stop
    if k < Stop and A_k < A_{k+1}
        then
            add 1 to k
    if Temp < A_k
        then
            store A_k in A_{k div 2}
            store 2*k in k
        else
            store true in Done
store Temp in A_{k div 2}

END OF Heapify
```

Notice the first *if...then* in the *loop while*. This step is there to get k pointing at the larger of the two children, but we don't want to examine A_{k+1} if $k \geq Stop$. We again have an *and* that may cause trouble later. (Refer to the discussion on page 296.) If it turns out that $k \geq Stop$, we do not want the computer to evaluate the second half of the *and*—it might be the case that A_{k+1} is not even in the array and attempting to examine it could cause a run-time error. Once again, we will have to be careful to implement the algorithm in a way that will prevent this from occurring. We'll return to this point in the next chapter when we implement the algorithm.

Example of the Heap Sort

Let's work through an example using an array of 18 elements. Suppose the array is arranged initially as shown in figure 9.9.

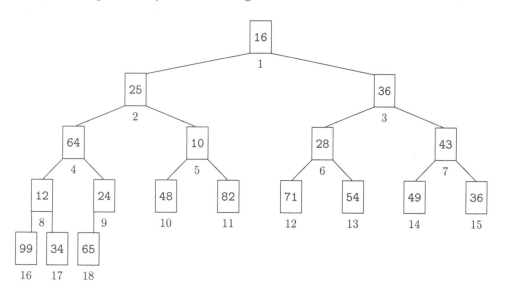

Figure 9.9 The Original Array seen as a Tree

The first loop starts heapifying the array with node 9. Since $A_{18} > A_9$, they are exchanged. Then i moves down to 8 and the subtree with root node 8 is heapified. Since 99 is greater than 12, the 99 is exchanged with the 12. This leaves figure 9.10.

The loop continues with i moving down to 1. After completion of the first loop, the tree looks like figure 9.11. (Make sure you trace each of these steps!)

Notice that the entire tree is now a heap.

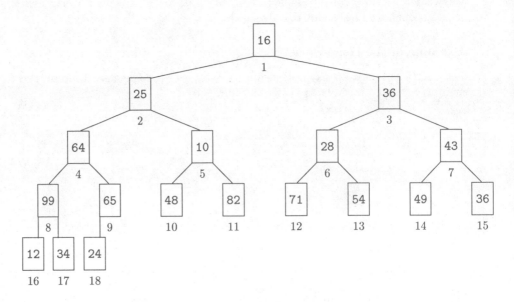

Figure 9.10 The Array in the Middle of the First Loop

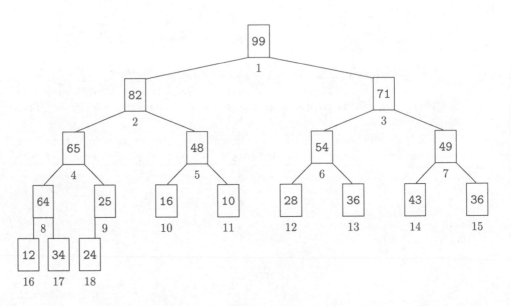

Figure 9.11 The Array After the First Loop: a Heap

The second loop starts by exchanging the contents of node 1 with the contents of node 18, i.e., the **99** in A_1 is exchanged with the **24** in A_{18}. Then the tree from 1 down through 17 is heapified, resulting in the tree in figure 9.12. (Again, trace the steps yourself.)

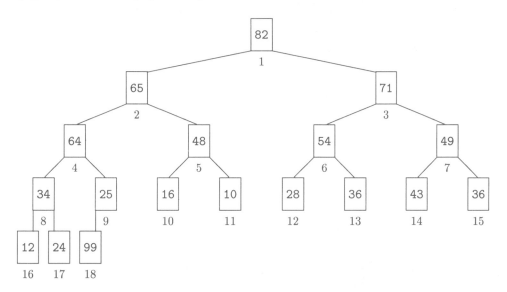

Figure 9.12 The Subtree from 1 through 17 is a Heap

The second iteration of the second loop starts by exchanging the **82** in A_1 with the **24** in A_{17}. Then the tree from 1 down through 16 is heapified.

We'll leave this example at this point and let you complete it. Be sure you do so; don't just take our word for it!

The final tree would look like figure 9.13.

9.7 Efficiency of the Sorting Algorithms

In the preceding discussion of the various sorting algorithms we have often made comments referring to one algorithm being "better" than another. You may have wondered how this is determined. Indeed, after all the work we did on the heap sort, you may find yourself doubting that it was worth all the effort. You may even doubt that it is better than the others. While we are not able to say much about it at this point, we should say that there are ways of measuring the efficiency of algorithms. In essence, one algorithm is considered better than another if it gets the same job done but takes less time or causes the computer to do less work. Things are not that simple, though. The data itself can affect

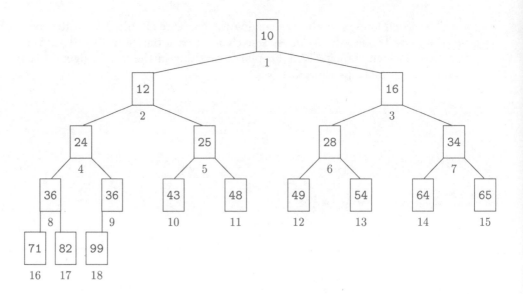

Figure 9.13 The Sorted Array

the efficiency of an algorithm. The bubble sort, for example, works better than the heap sort when the array is very nearly sorted already. The heap sort works much better on arrays with random or very unsorted data.

We will get further into the notion of efficiency of algorithms in a later chapter and will use some of the algorithms discussed in this chapter as examples. In the next chapter we will implement the algorithms discussed in this chapter and will spend a little time discussing the speed of each one.

9.8   Using Arrays—Once Again

We have discussed several of the fundamental tasks performed on and with one-dimensional arrays: finding the largest value of a collection of values, finding the sum and average of a collection of numbers, searching an array for a particular value, and rearranging an array into a particular order. While we wrote several algorithms that sorted an array, we never discussed a method of checking to see whether or not the resulting array was correctly sorted. We were very careful when we wrote the algorithms and we're always careful when we implement an algorithm to make sure that the code corresponds to the algorithm, but in spite of all that care, things can go wrong; the resulting array might not be correctly sorted. For the "Once Again" section of this chapter, let's consider the problem of verifying that an array was sorted correctly.

Define the Problem

The definition of the problem is straightforward: given two arrays, one unsorted and one (allegedly) sorted, write a module that will verify that the second array is a sorted version of the first.

Notice that it is not sufficient to just check to see that the second array is in ascending order. If the sorting algorithm simply put N copies of the first element in the "sorted" array, it would be in ascending order—or at least in nondescending order—but it could not be considered correctly sorted. Thus the problem we want to solve consists of two parts: first, make sure the second array is in ascending order, and second, make sure that every element in the first array is in the second array and, in the case of duplicates, occurs with the same frequency.

Solve the Problem

There are a number of ways we might attack this problem. The first half of the problem is very easy; just make one pass through the second array and check to make sure that no element is smaller than the element that comes before it. The second half is not as obvious. Surely we would want the routine to work as quickly as possible and we need to make sure it handles the situation where some values appear more than once.

Think about it before you go on reading. How would you check to make sure that every element of the first array is in the second array?

Our solution depends on the fact that we know the second array is in ascending order, and hence we can use a binary search to locate a particular value in the array. After checking to see that the second array is in ascending order, we'll start with the first element in the first array and search for it in the second array, using a binary search. If the second array does not have an element with this value, we'll know that the sorting was not done properly. If an element with this value is located, we'll remove it from the second array—because it might appear more than once and we must make sure that every element appears in the second array the same number of times that it appears in the first array. When we remove an element, we'll slide every other element up one place to keep the array in order. If we get all the way to the end of the first array, finding matching values in each case, we'll know that the sorting was done correctly.

We should be ready to write an algorithm for this solution.

Turn the Solution into an Algorithm

The solution described above becomes an algorithm very easily. Here's ours:

```
START OF Sorted(A1, A2, N)

store true in Ok
loop for i going from 1 to N−1
    if A2_i > A2_{i+1}
        then  .
            store false in Ok
store 1 in i
store N in NewN
loop while Ok and i ≤ N
    call BinarySearch(A2, NewN, A1_i, Ok, Place)
    if Ok
        then
            loop for j going from Place to NewN−1
                store A2_{j+1} in A2_j
            subtract 1 from NewN
            add 1 to i
return Ok

END OF Sorted
```

Notice that we wrote this module as a function. With this function we could, in a calling routine, say things like:

```
if not Sorted(A, B, N)
    then

        ⋮
```

and display some appropriate message or take some appropriate action. You should also notice that we were able to use the binary search routine from the chapter without change. We used the Boolean variable *Ok* as a flag to decide when to execute the *loop while* and we used it as one of the actual parameters (passed by reference) to *BinarySearch*.

In the next chapter we'll turn this routine into code and use it to verify that our sorting algorithms are working correctly.

9.9 Summary and Review

- In this chapter we introduced the concept of an array. We think of arrays as being data types that are more complex than the simple types we worked with previously. The advantage of an array is that we can refer to a collection of items with one name and can refer to any item in the collection by varying the subscript. This makes it possible to access many different elements of an array with a simple loop.

- We presented two searching techniques: a linear search and a binary search, and presented algorithms for each technique.

- We discussed several sorting algorithms: three versions of the bubble sort, two versions of the insertion sort, and the heap sort. The bubble sort is easy to understand but is not very efficient. The insertion sort is a bit better, and the insertion sort with a binary search even better than that, if we are sorting things more complicated than integers. The heap sort is a more complicated algorithm but is much more efficient, in general, than either the bubble sort or the insertion sort.

- We introduced a new loop, a *loop for*. The *loop for* is heavily used with arrays. We mentioned an assumption regarding the *loop for* that determines the number of iterations the loop will make in some special cases. As examples, consider the following four loops:

loop for i going from 1 to 1
    ⟨*body of loop*⟩

loop for i going from 20 down to 20
    ⟨*body of loop*⟩

loop for i going from 10 to 9
    ⟨*body of loop*⟩

loop for i going from −8 down to −5
    ⟨*body of loop*⟩

The assumptions we are making require that the bodies of the first two loops be executed exactly once, and that the bodies of the third and fourth loops be skipped entirely.

- We mentioned some rules of thumb regarding which kind of loop to use:

   If you know where the loop starts and ends, or know how many times you want to go through the loop, use a *loop for*; otherwise use either a *loop while* or a *loop until*.

If you are trying to decide whether to use a *loop while* or a *loop until* and you know you always want to go through the loop at least one time, use a *loop until*.

If you are trying to decide whether to use a *loop while* or a *loop until* and you know you might have a situation where the loop should be skipped entirely, use a *loop while*.

- The problem with implementing *and* was encountered twice, once in the insertion sort and again in the heap sort. Briefly, the problem is that in the Boolean expression:

  $\mathcal{P}$ *and* $\mathcal{Q}$

  the entire expression will be false if $\mathcal{P}$ is false, regardless of the value of $\mathcal{Q}$. Sometimes we put such Boolean expressions in our algorithms on the assumption that if the first operand is false, the second operand will not be evaluated. Sometimes we expect both operands to be evaluated. Sometimes it is not important whether the second operand is evaluated or not, but there are times when it is very important that it not be evaluated; consequently, there are times when this can cause a run-time error on a compiler that always evaluates both operands regardless of the truth value of the first operand.

  The same problem occurs with the *or*. The value of:

  $\mathcal{P}$ *or* $\mathcal{Q}$

  is true if $\mathcal{P}$ is true, regardless of the value of $\mathcal{Q}$.

  Since this is not really a problem regarding how to write the algorithm, we've decided to leave further discussion of it for later chapters.

- In the "Once Again" section, we developed an algorithm for a Boolean valued function that will check to see whether or not an array was sorted correctly.

9.10   New Terms Introduced

array A list of values considered as a unit and stored in one variable.

array element One of the values in an array.

binary search A search accomplished on an ordered list by successively throwing away half of the list each time.

binary search tree A tree such that each node has at most two children.

bubble sort A sorting algorithm where the rearranging is accomplished by repeatedly swapping adjacent elements.

child A nonempty node pointed at by another node, called its parent.

efficiency of an algorithm A relative measure of the speed of execution of an algorithm.

flag A Boolean variable.

heap A subtree such that every node contains a value larger than both of its children.

heap sort A sorting algorithm accomplished by making subtrees into heaps.

index of a loop for The variable used to control the number of repetitions in a loop for.

insertion sort A sorting algorithm accomplished by inserting successive values into the sorted portion of the array.

leaf A node with no children.

linear search A search accomplished by looking at each element in an array in succession starting from the first.

loop for A looping structure used when the starting and stopping points are known in advance.

nested loops A situation occurring when one of the steps in the body of a loop is itself a loop.

node The basic component of a tree.

parent The node containing a pointer to a given node, called the child.

root node The only node in a tree that has no parent.

searching The process of attempting to locate a given value in an array.

sorting The process of rearranging an array in either ascending or descending order.

subscript A value that indicates the position of an array element.

subtree The collection of all nodes in a tree starting at a given node and including all of its descendants.

tree A collection of nodes characterized by parent/child relationships.

9.11   Exercises

1. On page 281 we used a *loop while* rather than a *loop until* to determine the sum of the values in an array and the maximum value stored in an array. Why didn't we use a *loop until*? Notice that we could have used a *loop for*, had it been introduced earlier.

2. Suppose you need a module that will accept an array and the number of numbers in the array and determine the sum of the numbers stored in the array. Would you write it as a procedure or as a function? Write an algorithm for the module. You will need to think about what parameters are required. Use a *loop for* rather than a *loop while*.

3. Suppose you need a module that will accept an array and the number of numbers in the array and determine the minimum value of the numbers stored in the array as well as the location of the minimum value. Would you write it as a procedure or as a function? Write an algorithm for the module. You will need to think about what parameters are required. Use a *loop for*.

4. Let A be an array containing ten integers:

   89, 54, 56, 4, 25, 79, 24, 21, 50, 53

   Trace the algorithm for the linear search (page 283) assuming the following calls:

   call LinearSearch(A, 10, 79, Found, Place)

   call LinearSearch(A, 4, 79, Found, Place)

5. Let A consist of the ten integers from the previous exercise, but in ascending order:

   4, 21, 24, 25, 50, 53, 54, 56, 79, 89

   Trace the algorithm for the binary search (page 285) assuming the calls:

   call BinarySearch(A, 10, 56, Found, Place)

   call BinarySearch(A, 10, 36, Found, Place)

6. Rewrite the *BinarySearch* algorithm (page 285) so that it starts with the lines:

store 1 in Left
store N in Right

7. Trace through the bubble sort algorithm using a list of six integers:

   21, 39, 11, 25, 16, 46

   Write down the contents of the array after each pass.

8. Trace the "improved" bubble sort for the same six integers as in exercise 7. Does it require fewer passes?

9. Trace the "improved" bubble sort using a list of four integers:

   89, 31, 26, 12

   Notice that these numbers are in descending order. Note carefully what happens when j becomes zero.

10. Write an algorithm for a procedure *Swap* which exchanges the values stored in two variables. This procedure should be written in such a way that it can be used in any of the sorting programs that need to exchange two elements in an array as well as any future program that might need to exchange the values stored in two variables.

11. Write the algorithm for the "even better" bubble sort. Trace your algorithm using the data from exercise 7.

12. Modify the binary search algorithm so that if there are duplicates of the key in the array, the "place" returned by the routine is the one just after the last such duplicate. If the key is *not* found in the array, the "place" returned should be the location of the first value in the array larger than the key. Notice that the routine written this way would be very useful whenever you wish to insert a new element into the array.

13. Modify the algorithm for the insertion sort so that it uses a binary search technique, as mentioned on page 298.

14. Trace the insertion sort with a binary search for the same six integers as in exercise 1. Does it require fewer assignments and/or comparisons than the bubble sort?

15. Write an algorithm for the following sorting technique, commonly known as a *selection sort*: First, find the largest element in the list (of N elements). Swap this value with the element at the bottom of the list. Next, find the largest element among the first $N-1$ values, and swap it with the $(N-1)^{st}$ element. Continue until the array is sorted.

16. The following algorithm is a variation of a famous sorting algorithm invented by Donald Shell. Trace the algorithm and explain how it works.

```
START OF ShellSort(A, N)
Passed by value: N
Passed by reference: A, an array with N elements

store N div 2 in k
loop while k > 0
    loop for i set to k thru N−1
        store i − k + 1 in j
        store false in Done
        loop while j > 0 and not Done
            if A_j ≤ A_{j+k}
                then
                    store true in Done
                else
                    call Swap(A_j, A_{j+k})
            subtract k from j
    store k div 2 in k

END OF ShellSort
```

Chapter 10

Arrays in Pascal

> I have no idea what the most commonly used
> computer language of the 1990s will be like,
> but suspect it will be called *Fortran*.
> — W. Wesley Peterson

10.1   Overview of the Chapter

This chapter implements, in Pascal, the searching and sorting algorithms from chapter 9. We see how Pascal handles one-dimensional arrays. The ⟨*constant definition part*⟩ and the ⟨*type definition part*⟩ are introduced. We add the Pascal ⟨*for statement*⟩ to our list of Pascal statements in order to implement the *loop for*. We also discuss the problem of equality of two real values and present a solution to the problem. The problem that can occur when implementing an *and* will be discussed. In the "Once Again" section, we'll implement the algorithm that we wrote in chapter 9 that verifies that an array was sorted correctly.

10.2   Introduction

As you have surely realized, it is possible to implement arrays in Pascal; in fact, that's true of most programming languages in wide use today. In this chapter we will see how arrays are implemented in Pascal. We will learn how to define new types, using the ⟨*type definition part*⟩, and see how a type—the variables of which are arrays—can be defined. We will write Pascal routines that implement our searching and sorting algorithms from chapter 9. The *loop for* that we introduced in chapter 9 has a Pascal counterpart, the ⟨*for statement*⟩; we will learn how to use the ⟨*for statement*⟩ and will discuss the restrictions on its use. We'll leave the implementation of the routines that determine the sum of the values stored in an array, the average value of the numbers in an array, and the maximum and minimum values stored in an array for the exercises.

10.3   Arrays

In Pascal, we have seen the simple data types `real`, `integer`, `Boolean` and `char`. An array in Pascal is a supplied type, but not a simple type. It is composed of several components of the same type, and the type of these components has to be described when the array is declared. Specifically, we have to specify the limits on the subscripts of the array and the type of the components of the array. For example, we could declare the variable `A` to be an array containing 18 `real` values as follows:

```
var
    A : array [1 .. 18] of real;
```

Notice the square brackets: "[" and "]."

This declaration could be placed in the ⟨*variable declaration part*⟩ of any ⟨*block*⟩; then `A` would become a local variable in that block.

We also have to see how to refer to elements of the array. In our algorithms we wrote either A_i, $A(i)$ or $A[i]$ to refer to the ith element of the array `A`. Neither of the first two schemes are used in Pascal; obviously we cannot type A_i because we have no way to enter a subscript. The language could have been designed to allow `A(i)`, but it wasn't because parentheses are used to indicate the parameters for a procedure or function. Instead the third method, using square brackets, "[" and "]," was adopted. Thus, in Pascal, to refer to the ith element of the array `A`, you type `A[i]`.

However, things are not quite as simple as we have presented them. As we saw in the previous chapter, we frequently need to pass arrays from one routine to another. If we were to declare `A` as shown here, it would not be possible to pass it to another routine.

The reason for this is found in the syntax for the ⟨*formal parameter declaration*⟩. If you refer to figure 6.3 in chapter 6, you'll notice that following the colon there has to be a *type name*. If we were to declare `A` as we did above, `A` would actually be a variable of an *anonymous* type; that is, a type without a name. Since the type doesn't have a name, we cannot declare a parameter of that type in the formal parameter declaration of a procedure or function, and the array cannot, therefore, be passed as a parameter. It can be declared and worked with in a single block, but not passed. That's not good enough in general; we have to be able to pass an array.

The *type definition part*

The way to accomplish this is to give the type a name rather than let it remain anonymous. This is done in the ⟨*type definition part*⟩ of the ⟨*definition/declaration part*⟩ of the ⟨*block*⟩.

As we mentioned in chapter 4 and saw in more detail in chapter 6, every ⟨*definition/declaration part*⟩ has four subparts: the ⟨*constant definition part*⟩, the

⟨*type definition part*⟩, the ⟨*variable declaration part*⟩ and the ⟨*procedure/function declaration part*⟩. They must appear in that order.

Let's examine the syntax for the ⟨*type definition part*⟩. It's not much different from the ⟨*variable declaration part*⟩ we've already seen; look at the syntax diagram for the ⟨*variable declaration part*⟩ in appendix A and compare it to figure 10.1.

type definition part:

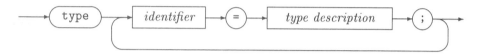

Figure 10.1

The ⟨*type definition part*⟩ starts with the word **type**, then has the name of a new type, an equal sign and a type description. This is repeated for each new type to be defined. Notice that the syntax for the ⟨*variable declaration part*⟩ allows a list of variables and requires a colon, whereas a type definition allows one type per definition and requires an equal sign. If you pay attention to these details, you'll avoid some silly syntax errors.

An Example

Let's use our array of 18 elements as an example; we first need to choose a name for the new type. The obvious choice is "array," but that can't be used since it is a reserved word and has to be used in the description of the type. Other names are possible, but we'll use the word **List**. The description of the type is the same as the description we used earlier, so the ⟨*type definition part*⟩ becomes:

```
type
   List = array [1 .. 18] of real;
```

We are not including a syntax diagram for a ⟨*type description*⟩ simply because the complete syntax is quite complicated and we don't need all the details at this point. The syntax diagram is in appendix A.

Remember that **List** is the name for a *type*, not the name for a variable. The type **List** is like the type **integer** in the sense that we can now declare variables of that type.

Indeed, having declared the type `List`, let's declare the variable `A`:

```
var
    A : List;
```

Now that the type has a name, we can pass an array of type `List` to a procedure or function. For example, the Pascal code for *LinearSearch* would begin:

```
procedure LinearSearch(var A : List; ... );
        . . .
```

The *constant definition part*

It might turn out that you write the program defining the type `List` as above and then later realize that you want to run the same program on a different size array. It would be easy enough to change the definition of `List`, but you would also have to go through your entire program and change every place that refers to the number of elements in the array. Making changes like this is a good way to introduce errors in your code.

There's a better way; we should define the array type to hold the largest number of elements that will ever be needed. Furthermore, although Pascal requires that we define the size of an array with constants, we will want to use *named* constants, so that if it has to be changed, we only have to change it once. That brings us to yet another subpart of the ⟨*definition/declaration part*⟩: the ⟨*constant definition part*⟩.

It is possible to define identifiers as names of constants. A named constant is quite different from a variable, however. A constant cannot be changed; it doesn't vary. It would never be valid to put the name of a constant on the left side of an assignment statement.

Another difference between named constants and variables is that you may use constants in defining the size of an array, and you cannot use a variable that way. We used the constants 1 and 18 above when we defined `List`. We could have used named constants instead. Before we show how that is done, we need to examine the syntax for the ⟨*constant definition part*⟩. Look at figure 10.2.

The ⟨*identifier*⟩ is the name of the constant and the constant on the right side of the equal sign is the value of the constant. The constant has to be of some type—remember, every value in Pascal is of a particular type—and the named constant gets its type from the type of the value on the right.

Pascal programmers often use capital letters in their constant identifiers so that they can easily be distinguished from variable identifiers. We'll follow that style in this book.

constant definition part:

Figure 10.2

For example, we could define a constant called **MAXSIZE** as follows:

```
const
   MAXSIZE = 100;
```

Now **MAXSIZE** is a constant of type **integer** and has the value 100. We can use it in the program anywhere we could use 100. You might be saying, "So why define **MAXSIZE** in the first place? Why not just use 100?" Because we might later realize that **MAXSIZE** should have been 500 instead of 100. By using a named constant, you would only have to change the definition of **MAXSIZE** to 500 and compile the program again. Otherwise you would have to search through the entire program and change every occurrence of 100 to 500. You might miss some and you might accidentally change some 100s to 500 that were supposed to remain 100. Additionally, using **MAXSIZE** makes the program easier to read.

Similarly, if we were going to be doing a lot of work in geometry or trigonometry, we could define the constant **PI** as:

```
const
   PI = 3.14159265;
```

The advantages of this should be clear. Now, whenever we want to use π in our programs, we can just type **PI**. That's easier to type than 3.14159265 and would keep us from typing 3.14195265 by mistake.

Now that we've seen how to define **MAXSIZE** let's see how we will use it. Combining the constant definition, the type definition and the variable declaration we would have:

```
const
   MAXSIZE = 100;
type
   List = array [1 .. MAXSIZE] of real;
var
   A : List;
```

This is not a good example of anything other than the syntax. We'll see better examples when we implement the algorithms from the previous chapter.

Random **Revisited**

In chapter 8 (page 248) we introduced the function `Random`, that generates random numbers. You may have wondered where the numbers 729, 40 and 3641 came from. We still don't intend to explain why those particular numbers were chosen, but if the function had been written as follows you would at least have a clue.

```pascal
function Random : real;

{  This function returns a pseudo-random real number      }
{  between 0 and 1.  Seed is a global integer variable.   }

const
  MULTIPLIER = 40;
  INCREMENT  = 3641;
  MODULUS    = 729;

begin
  Seed := (Seed * MULTIPLIER + INCREMENT) mod MODULUS;
  Random := Seed / MODULUS
end;
```

The point is that another reason to used named constants is as a form of documentation. Aside from making it easier to change MODULUS, should you decide to, using named constants in this instance makes the routine a little more understandable.

10.4   Searching Algorithms in Pascal

Let's use our new knowledge about arrays in Pascal to implement the searching algorithms from the previous chapter.

Linear Search

We start with the simple linear search. We will leave it for the reader to write an entire program that tests the linear search and will content ourselves with just writing the procedure itself. It will depend on having defined some constants and types, so let's assume that we have defined MAXSIZE and List as we did earlier, and as shown again on the next page.

```
const
   MAXSIZE = 100;
type
   List = array [1 .. MAXSIZE] of real;
var
   A : List;
```

Then, consulting the algorithm for the linear search in chapter 9 (page 283), our procedure would be:

```
procedure LinearSearch(A : List;
                       N : integer;
                     Key : real;
             var Found : Boolean;
             var Place : integer);

{  This procedure searches an array of real values for a particular }
{  value, Key.  If Key is in the array, Found is set to true and     }
{  the location is returned in Place.  If Key is not in the array,   }
{  Found is set to false.  A linear search is used.                  }

begin
   Found := false;
   Place := 1;
   while not Found and (Place <= N) do
      if A[Place] = Key
         then
            Found := true
         else
            Place := Place + 1
end;
```

Notice that we passed the array, the number of elements in the array and Key by value, and passed Found and Place by reference.

This looks just right; it looks just like the algorithm and you might be tempted to move along to the binary search algorithm. There is, however, a rather serious problem.

As we've said before, it is the responsibility of the programmer to insure that the algorithm is implemented in a manner that gets the job done correctly. The above procedure would compile and run just fine. You could write a test routine and test it. It's likely the procedure would pass the test in carefully controlled situations. But, it still would not give you the results you would expect.

Equality of real Values

The problem is with how the computer holds real numbers. The computer stores an integer exactly (at least integers between -maxint and maxint), but it cannot hold real numbers exactly. A rational number like 1/3 cannot be represented exactly as a decimal; it would require an infinite number of places to hold 0.3333333.... Other real numbers, like π, don't repeat or terminate. They also require an infinite number of places to be represented as a decimal. Even if we were using a real value that could be expressed with a finite number of decimal places, say a number like 3.13156723412, the computer probably cannot hold that many places. Finally, even some simple real values, like 3.7, cannot be represented exactly in the computer. In the computer numbers are stored in binary (base 2) and numbers like 3.7 become non-terminating numbers when expressed in base 2.

The consequence of all this is that we might have two values stored in the computer that we intend to be the same value but which the computer would consider different.

Try writing and running a program containing the following statements and see what happens:

```
R1 := sqrt(2);
if R1*R1 = 2
   then
      writeln('They are equal.')
   else
      writeln('They are not equal.')
```

In general, suppose *Real1* and *Real2* are both **real** expressions. If we put the following Pascal Boolean expression in an ⟨*if statement*⟩, it will evaluate to true only if the computer's representations of the two real values are exactly the same.

```
if Real1 = Real2
   then
            . . .
```

The two values for *Real1* and *Real2* might have been calculated in slightly different ways and thus might not be represented in the computer exactly the same way, while mathematically they are the same.

One way to solve this problem is to consider two **real** values to be the same if they are *almost* the same, i.e., if they differ by an amount less than the computer's margin of error.

A quick and dirty solution is to define a constant, say EPSILON (mathematicians use the Greek letter epsilon (ϵ) to represent a tiny real number), to be a small real value, maybe like 10^{-9}, and consider *Real1* and *Real2* to be equal if they differ by less than `EPSILON`. That is, include the following constant definition:

```
const
   EPSILON = 10e-9;
```

(we discussed scientific notation in Pascal in chapter 4) and replace the above Boolean expression with:

```
if abs(Real1 - Real2) < EPSILON
    then
        ...
```

This would work if the values of *Real1* and *Real2* had values near 1.0 and if the compiler you were using held real numbers to about ten significant places. Consider, however, what would happen if *Real1* and *Real2* were near 10^{-9} themselves. Then they could be very different from one another and still be considered the same by our "solution." Similarly, if they were larger than 1.0, they would have to be exactly the same in order to be considered equal, taking us right back where we started.

We need a *relative* measure of equality, not such an absolute measure. We need to be able to determine if the two values are the same in all but perhaps their last one or two places. We might want the computer to consider 100000.001 and 99999.999 to be equal, for example. One way to accomplish this is by looking at the magnitudes of the numbers and scaling `EPSILON` by an amount near the magnitudes. We'll scale `EPSILON` by the average of the two values. Since this becomes too complicated to do in a simple Boolean expression, let's write a Boolean-valued function, `Equal`, to do the job:

```
function Equal(Real1, Real2 : real) : Boolean;

{  This function determines whether two real values are close  }
{  enough together to be considered equal.                     }

const
   EPSILON = 10e-9;

begin
   Equal := 2 * abs(Real1 - Real2) <= EPSILON * abs(Real1 + Real2)
end;
```

Notice that instead of dividing on the right side of the inequality by 2, we multiply on the left side. This function will work as long as neither number

equals zero. (Imagine that one of the two values exactly equals zero and see
what happens.)

Scaling numbers near zero is a problem. An easy solution is to just consider
a **real** value to be equal to zero if it's within EPSILON. Thus, the fuction can
be rewritten as:

```
function Equal(Real1, Real2 : real) : Boolean;

{  This function determines whether two real values are close  }
{  enough together to be considered equal.                     }

const
   EPSILON = 10e-9;

begin
   if (Real1 = 0) or (Real2 = 0)
      then
         Equal := abs(Real1 - Real2) <= EPSILON
      else
         Equal := 2 * abs(Real1 - Real2) <= EPSILON * abs(Real1 + Real2)
end;
```

Now we can use this function in our if statement:

```
if Equal(Real1, Real2)
   then
      ...
```

Notice that the function **Equal** assigns the value of a **Boolean** expression to
Equal. We could also have written it as on the next page.

```
function Equal(Real1, Real2 : real) : Boolean;

{  This function determines whether two real values are close  }
{  enough together to be considered equal.                     }

const
   EPSILON = 10e-9;

begin
   if (Real1 = 0) or (Real2 = 0)
      then
         if abs(Real1 - Real2) <= EPSILON
            then
               Equal := true
            else
               Equal := false
      else
         if 2 * abs(Real1 - Real2) <= EPSILON * abs(Real1 + Real2)
            then
               Equal := true
            else
               Equal := false
   end;
```

but the first version works just as well. Since Equal is of type Boolean, it is valid to assign to it the value of a Boolean expression, which is just what we did. The first version seems more elegant; it's simpler and probably more efficient.

You might notice that, as a consequence of our decision of how to handle numbers near zero, both 0.0000000001 and 0.0000000002 are Equal to zero, but they are not Equal to each other. When these two values are sent to the function, the scaling we have done causes Equal to consider them as far apart from each other as it considers 1 and 2.

Linear Search, Completed

We got started on this problem in our discussion of the linear search, so let's
rewrite the linear search procedure using Equal:

```
procedure LinearSearch(A : List;
                       N : integer;
                     Key : real;
                 var Found : Boolean;
                 var Place : integer);

{  This procedure searches an array of real values for a particular }
{  value, Key.  If Key is in the array, Found is set to true and     }
{  the location is returned in Place.  If Key is not in the array,   }
{  Found is set to false.  A linear search is used.                  }

begin
   Found := false;
   Place := 1;
   while not Found and (Place <= N) do
      if Equal(A[Place], Key)
         then
            Found := true
         else
            Place := Place + 1
end;
```

You will notice that the ⟨*if statement*⟩ reads just as well as before.

Binary Search

The algorithm for the binary search is just as easy to code, now that we have
written Equal. The algorithm is on page 285; the code is on the next page.

```
procedure BinarySearch(A : List;
                       N : integer;
                     Key : real;
               var Found : Boolean;
               var Place : integer);
var
   Top, Bottom, Middle : integer;

{ This procedure searches an array of real values for a particular }
{ value, Key.  If Key is in the array, Found is set to true and    }
{ the location is returned in Place.  If Key is not in the array,   }
{ Found is set to false.  A binary search is used.                  }

begin
   Found := false;
   Top := 0;
   Bottom := N + 1;
   while not Found and (Top + 1 < Bottom) do
      begin
         Middle := (Top + Bottom) div 2;
         if Equal(A[Middle], Key)
            then
               begin
                  Found := true;
                  Place := Middle
               end
            else
               if Key > A[Middle]
                  then
                     Top := Middle
                  else
                     Bottom := Middle
      end
end;
```

The "Once Again" section of this chapter contains an implementation of the algorithm from chapter 9 that checks to see whether or not an array was correctly sorted. The algorithm uses a binary search; when you get to this section, you'll notice that we were able to use the above procedure just as it stands.

Improvements to the Binary Search Algorithm

While the binary search algorithm is straightforward and easy to implement, there are some improvements that can be made. Sometimes the binary search is used to insert elements in an array, as we mentioned in chapter 9 when we discussed the insertion sort. In such a case, we have to move elements around in the array and would not want to move more than necessary. If the array contains several elements with the same value, we would like to have the algorithm find the "best" place for the new element. That is, we would like the procedure to locate the place just below any and all elements that equal the Key. We'll leave it as an exercise to rewrite the binary search procedure in this way.

10.5   Implementation of Sorting Algorithms

Let's turn now to implementing the various sorting algorithms we wrote in chapter 9. We will implement the last version of each that we wrote and leave the rest for the reader.

The *for statement*

Before we can do the bubble sort, we have to implement the new loop structure that we introduced in chapter 9—the *loop for*.

It will come as no surprise that Pascal has a statement that does the job, the ⟨*for statement*⟩. Take a look at the syntax diagram in figure 10.3.

for statement:

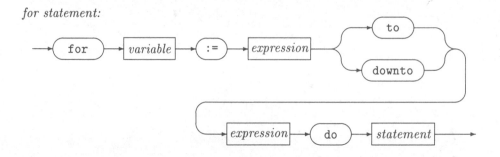

Figure 10.3

The Pascal syntax is not very different from the way we write the algorithms; in the algorithms we write *going from* and in Pascal we must use the assignment operator, :=. In the algorithms we write *to* or *down to*, in Pascal we must type **to** or **downto**. Thus a simple *loop for* like:

```
store 0 in Sum
loop for i going from 1 to N
    store Sum + i in Sum
```

that could be used to find the sum of the integers between 1 and N would be coded in Pascal as:

```
Sum := 0;
for i := 1 to N do
    Sum := Sum + i
```

The ⟨*for statement*⟩ works just as we want it to. It assigns to i the value of the expression following the := symbol, evaluates the second expression, and as long as the value of i is less than or equal to the value of the second expression, the statement following the word do is executed and the value of i is incremented by 1 after each execution of the statement. The variable i is called the *index* of the ⟨*for statement*⟩.

Reread the above paragraph carefully, bearing in mind the assumptions we made concerning the *loop for* in the previous chapter (page 289).

Note that if the value of the second expression is equal to the value of the first expression, the statement following the word do is executed exactly one time. And, if the value of the second expression is less than the value of the first expression, the statement following the word do is skipped entirely. Another way of saying all this is to say that the test of the Boolean expression is done at the top of the loop—as it is with the ⟨*while statement*⟩—rather than at the bottom—as it is with the ⟨*repeat statement*⟩.

Everything is reversed when the word **downto** is used instead of the word **to**. That is, the statement following the word do is executed as long as the value of the index is *greater than or equal to* the value of the second expression, and the index is *decremented* after every iteration instead of incremented.

Be very careful to notice that, as with the ⟨*while statement*⟩, there can only be *one* statement following the word do. If you need to put more than one statement in the loop, you must turn these statements into one statement by making them one ⟨*compound statement*⟩, i.e., by surrounding them with the words **begin** and **end**. By the way, this statement is known as the "*body of the loop*" just as it is with the ⟨*while statement*⟩.

Special Rules for the ⟨*for statement*⟩

1. *The index of a ⟨for statement⟩ must be a local variable.* This means that you cannot use a global variable as the index (since you are a good programmer and aren't going to use global variables anyway, this restriction doesn't apply to you, right?) and you cannot use a parameter, neither a value parameter nor a variable parameter. Actually, this restriction doesn't come into play very often. You wouldn't normally want to use a parameter as the index of a ⟨*for statement*⟩, and unless you forget to declare the index, you would probably never use a global variable as an

index anyway. This rule thus becomes a protection for you rather than a restriction.

2. *The index of a ⟨for statement⟩ must be of an ordinal type.* We haven't yet discussed "ordinal" types so we cannot say much at this point. Suffice it to say that `integer` is an ordinal type and `real` is *not* an ordinal type. Therefore, you may use a variable of type `integer` as the index of a ⟨for statement⟩, and you may not use a variable of type `real` as the index of a ⟨for statement⟩. One easy way to see why this is the case is to recall that real numbers do not have successors, i.e., given any real number, there is no such thing as "the next real number." Since a ⟨for statement⟩ depends on the concept of "next element," the index cannot be of type `real`.

   The types `char` and `Boolean` are, as a matter of interest, *ordinal* types also. One could use variables of these types as indices of ⟨for statement⟩s, if desired. For example, on a system using ASCII, the following ⟨for statement⟩ would print the uppercase letters of the alphabet:

```
for ch := 'A' to 'Z' do
   write(ch : 2)
```

   as long as `ch` is a variable of type `char`.

3. *The index of a ⟨for statement⟩ may not be changed (or "threatened") within the body of the loop.* The word "threatened" means, in particular, that the index of the ⟨for statement⟩ could not be passed by reference to a function or procedure. You would not be likely to want to do this either, so don't worry about it. The word "changed" can cause a problem, however. We should look at this. Suppose you wanted—for some reason—to print the even integers between 1 and 100. Relying on the ⟨for statement⟩ to increment N at the end of each iteration, you might be tempted to code:

```
for N := 1 to 99 do    {  bugged:  will not work!  }
   begin
      N := N + 1;
      write(N : 5)
   end;
writeln
```

That is, thinking that N would start at 1, this loop is supposed to change N to 2, display the value of N, change N to 3 at the end of the loop, change it to 4 at the beginning of the loop, display 4, and continue until N is bigger than 99. People who have begun their programming experiences with BASIC have a tendency to try to write loops this way. It simply *cannot* be done this way in Pascal. You may not change the value of the index within the body of the loop.

That's not to say, however, that the job of displaying the even integers between 1 and 100 cannot be accomplished. Consider:

```
for N := 1 to 50 do
    write(2 * N : 5);
writeln
```

or, if you insist, you could use a ⟨*while statement*⟩:

```
N := 2;
while N <= 100 do
    begin
        write(N : 5);
        N := N + 2
    end;
writeln
```

We leave it for you to decide which is better.

4. *The value of the index is undefined upon completion of the* ⟨*for statement*⟩. This means that you cannot count on the index having any particular value after the loop is done. For example, consider:

```
for N := 1 to 10 do
    writeln(N : 5);
writeln(N : 5)
```

Will this print the integers from 1 through 11? Will it print 10 twice? There's no way to say. According to the Standard, the value of N after the loop is done could be anything; it should be thought of as containing garbage. You should write your code in such a way that you never depend on the value of the index being defined after the loop is finished. (There will be something in N—it can't be empty—but what it is is unpredictable.)

This is particularly dangerous if your code is being moved to another environment. On some compilers the above code can work one way and on others, another way. If you write a ⟨*for statement*⟩ like this, even if you test it thoroughly and make sure it works properly on your system, it may fail on a different system. The answer is to not depend on the value of the index after the completion of the loop. Whenever you depart from Standard Pascal, you reduce the portability of your programs.

The Bubble Sort

With all this behind us, the actual implementation of the bubble sort becomes
rather easy. Refer to the algorithm for the improved bubble sort in chapter 9
(page 292).

```
procedure BubbleSort(var A : List; N : integer);

{ This procedure sorts the array A from 1 through N into ascending }
{ order using a version of the bubble sort algorithm.              }

var
   i, j   : integer;
   Sorted : Boolean;

begin
   j := N - 1;
   repeat
      Sorted := true;
      for i := 1 to j do
         if A[i] > A[i+1]
            then
               begin
                  Swap(A[i], A[i+1]);
                  Sorted := false
               end;
         j := j - 1
      until Sorted
end;
```

This procedure depends on another procedure, Swap, that exchanges the
values stored in two real variables. We left the algorithm for *Swap* as an exercise
in chapter 9 and we'll leave the code as an exercise in this chapter.

Testing the Bubble Sort

While we have been very careful in developing the algorithm and the code for
the bubble sort and are quite certain it is correct, we still have to write a test
program that makes sure it does indeed sort an array of numbers. The test
routine could follow the same logic as the test routines from chapter 8: allow
the user to enter some test data, call the routine being tested and display the
resulting data. If we only sort a small array, it will be easy to check the list
of numbers and make sure that they are in order. However, if we are sorting a
long list of numbers and want to make sure the algorithm worked correctly on
this long list, checking it by hand can be laborious and we might not be able to
tell that all the numbers in the original array are in the sorted array. What we

need is a routine that verifies that the list has been sorted correctly even for a long list. The algorithm for such a routine was discussed in the "Once Again" section of chapter 9 and we'll implement the algorithm in the "Once Again" section of this chapter.

Since the sorting routine sorts an array of numbers, the test routine will have to allow the user to enter several numbers for the array. Sometimes you might want to enter only a very few numbers and other times you might want to enter lots of numbers. The routine should be written in a way that allows the user to decide—at run time—how many numbers to enter. Indeed, you might want to let the computer pick the numbers for the array at random, since you won't want to waste your time typing in numbers.

Entering a List of Numbers

It's important, in any case, to be able to allow the user to enter a list of any length so let's think about some different ways it can be done.

- One way to get the job done is to ask the user how many numbers he or she wants to enter and then use a *loop for* that accepts that many numbers from the user, putting them into the array one at a time. The disadvantage of this method is that the user has to know ahead of time how many numbers are being entered. For a test routine that's not a big deal. In the real world, however, it's a nuisance. Suppose that the user needs to enter a bunch of data that's stored on several sheets of paper. Requiring her or him to first count the number of items would not be very friendly.

- Another way is to accept the first number and then ask the user if she or he has more numbers to enter, continuing until the answer is "no." This gets by the problem in the previous solution but has its own drawback. The user will get very tired of having to respond to the question, "Do you have more numbers to enter?" after entering each number.

- A third way is to use what's commonly known as a *trailer* or *sentinel*. We can assume that there is a special number that is not an item of data to be entered and have the routine simply accept numbers from the user until that special number is entered. Often the number zero is used if it is known in advance that all the data items are positive numbers. This method is better than the two previous ones, but the choice of the trailer is a bit of a problem. You might let the user enter his or her own trailer; that is, first ask the user to enter a number that is known not to be in the list of data, and then accept numbers from the user until that number is seen again.

The second and third of these two methods also have to "count" how many numbers are entered by the user. If you use the third method, make sure you don't count the trailer. We'll leave it as an exercise for you to choose one of

these methods—or devise another that you like better—and implement your choice as well as a main program that calls the input routine and the bubble sort. We'll also leave it as an exercise to develop a "verify" routine that will check to make sure the numbers were sorted properly.

We don't have any more to say about the bubble sort. We spent a great deal of time in chapter 9 on the algorithm and as a result, the coding step was easy. We can't resist saying one more time that that is always the way it will be; if you spend the time on the algorithm, making sure you understand it and have written it correctly, the coding step will be much easier. If you find yourself spending an inordinate amount of time coding your programs, ask yourself if you spent enough time on the algorithm.

And please remember that the bubble sort is not very efficient. In the real world, it should only be used on "small" arrays, with less than 20 elements or so.

The Insertion Sort

Let's start this section by simply implementing the first version of the insertion sort. The algorithm is on page 294. Here's the code:

```
procedure InsertionSort(var A : List; N : integer);

{  This procedure sorts the array A into ascending order by the  }
{  first version of the insertion sort algorithm.                }

var
    i, j : integer;
    Temp : real;

begin
    for j := 2 to N do
        begin
            Temp := A[j];
            i := j - 1;
            while (i > 0) and (A[i] > Temp) do
                begin
                    A[i+1] := A[i];
                    i := i - 1
                end;
            A[i+1] := Temp
        end
end;
```

The and Problem

We simply translated the algorithm into code, and that's what the coding step is, as long as the intent of the algorithm is retained. There is a problem here, however. The problem is with the Boolean expression in the ⟨while statement⟩. Our intent is clear: as long as i is positive, check to see if A[i] is greater than Temp. If both of these conditions are met, execute the compound statement. However, regardless of our intentions for this, what actually happens depends on the compiler we are using. When Wirth designed Pascal, he left it up to the implementor of a particular compiler how a Boolean expression containing and and or should be implemented.

Let's consider only the and for now. There are two choices available:

1. If both operands of the and are true, assign the Boolean expression the value true. Otherwise, assign it the value false.

2. If the first operand of the and is true, assign the Boolean expression the value of the second operand. Otherwise, assign it false.

The primary difference between the two methods is what happens if the first operand is **false**. The first method still evaluates the second expression, while the second method doesn't.

Let's see what this does to the Boolean expression in the ⟨*while statement*⟩. Suppose a compiler uses the first method. If it should happen that the element being inserted belongs in the first position in the array, the value of **i** will become zero. The first operand, (**i > 0**), is false, but because the compiler is using method one, the second operand will be evaluated anyway. That is, the computer will attempt to determine the value of (**A[i] > Temp**). Since **i** equals zero, there is no **A[i]**. On many systems, this will cause a run-time error. Typically you would see an error message that says there was a subscript out of range.

If the compiler uses the second method, the second operand is not evaluated when the first operand evaluates to **false**, and the loop is exited, as desired.

So, what do we do? If we have a compiler that uses the second method, we can write the code as we have and it will work fine. If we have a compiler that uses the first method, we have to fix the code in some way. However, writing code that will work on one system and not another is not good programming style. That is, even if we are working on a system that uses the first method, we should not be satisfied with the above code. Since Pascal is a standardized language, we should always write our code so that it is transportable; so that it doesn't matter which of the two methods a particular compiler uses.

It is unfortunate that Wirth let the language implementor choose between these two methods. It would have been much better if he had decided on one method or the other. But, since he didn't, we should write our programs so that they will work on all compilers. That means we should write our programs assuming that the first method is used, not the second.

Look back at the program. How would you change it so that it will always work? This is not a trivial fix. It is not just a matter of adding an ⟨*if statement*⟩ somewhere. In fact, it's not easy at all. Try it if you aren't convinced.

Some programmers have "fixed" the problem by adding an element on the front end of the array; i.e., by changing the type definition of **List** so that the array starts at **0** instead of **1**.

We have already seen a better fix. By separating the "search" portion of the routine from the "slide" part, we avoid the problem altogether. In fact, one reason for our second version of the insertion sort is that it avoids this problem entirely.

The **or** Problem

It is easy to see that the **or** has a similar problem. Once again, suppose there are two operands to an **or**. If the value of the first operand is **true**, the Boolean expression containing the **or** will be **true** regardless of the value of the second operand. Should the second operand be evaluated? The same two choices exist and there are two methods, as before. If method two is chosen for the **and**, surely one would choose the same method for the **or**. The second method is often known as *short-circuit evaluation*. Short-circuit evaluation can be summarized by simply saying that the evaluation of the expression is terminated as soon as the value of the expression can be determined.

Language Design Considerations

Before going on to an implementation of the second version, we should add that decisions such as the one we've been discussing are very important in the design of a computer language. When a new language is in the process of being designed, the designer has to decide how such things are going to be done. Once they're decided and the language is released, it is not at all easy to make changes. Once people start using the language and a body of code becomes established, changes in the design are very costly.

Thus, even though a majority of people probably wish Pascal could be changed so that Boolean expressions would always be evaluated by short-circuit evaluation, it's too late now to change it.

Incidently, Wirth has since designed another language, *Modula-2*, and this time he did use short-circuit evaluation of Boolean expressions. Further, several other languages, such as LISP and C, are designed to use short-circuit evaluation. The real problem with Pascal is not that it doesn't use this method, but that Wirth did not decide which method to use.

The Insertion Sort, Version 2

The implementation of the second version of the insertion sort is quite simple, especially since we've already handled the difficult part: separating the "search" from the "slide" and avoiding the **and** problem. The algorithm is on page 297. Here is the code for version two of the insertion sort:

```
procedure InsertionSort(var A : List; N : integer);

{ This procedure sorts the array A from 1 through N into ascending }
{ order using a version of the insertion sort algorithm.           }

var
   i, j, Place : integer;
   Temp        : real;
```

```
function InsertPlace(var A : List; j : integer) : integer;

{  This function returns the place to insert A[j] in the array A  }
{  from 1 through j.                                              }

var
    i     : integer;
    Found : Boolean;

begin
    i := j - 1;
    Found := false;
    while not Found and (i > 0) do
        if A[i] > A[j]
            then
                i := i - 1
            else
                Found := true;
    InsertPlace := i + 1
end;



begin
    for j := 2 to N do
        begin
            Temp := A[j];
            Place := InsertPlace(A, j);
            for i := j - 1 downto Place do
                A[i+1] := A[i];
            A[Place] := Temp
        end
end;
```

Passing a Large Array by Reference

You might notice that, contrary to what we've said earlier about the parameters passed to a function, we have passed the array A to InsertPlace by reference—notice the var. Why? The array A is not being changed inside InsertPlace, and until now have we have always passed parameters to a function by value. There is a very good reason for this exception to the rule. If we pass the array by value to InsertPlace, a copy of the entire array will have to be made every time InsertPlace is called. Since the function will be called many times while the insertion sort is working, sending a copy of the entire array over and over will slow the routine down considerably. Sending the address of the array will be much quicker. Since nothing in the array is being changed, we have not introduced a side effect, and that was the purpose of the rule forbidding passing parameters by reference to a function.

Insertion Sort with Binary Search

In the insertion sort above we used a linear search technique inside of `Insert-Place` to find the place to insert `Temp`. Since the array from 1 through `j-1` is already in order, we could have used a binary search to find the place to do the insertion. In a large array, the binary search would make the algorithm much faster. We left the insertion sort with a binary search as an exercise in chapter 9. We'll leave the implementation as an exercise in this chapter.

The Heap Sort

It makes sense to write the heap sort using the same scheme to pass the parameters as we used with the bubble sort and the insertion sort; i.e., the first line of the procedure should look like:

```
procedure HeapSort(var A : List; N : integer);
```

How about `Heapify`? Should it be a separate procedure declared earlier than `HeapSort` or should it be declared inside the ⟨*definition/declaration part*⟩ of HeapSort? In chapter 8 we listed some questions to ask before making such decisions. In particular, we asked whether the routine would ever be called from another routine. In this case it is obvious that `Heapify` would never be called from some routine other than `HeapSort`. Also, we want `HeapSort` to be a self-contained package that could be taken from our "shelf" of sorting routines. This should make it clear that `Heapify` belongs inside `HeapSort`.

What local variables will we need for `Heapify`? Looking at the algorithm on page 304, we see that we need a **real** variable `Temp`, a **Boolean** variable `Found` and an **integer** variable `k`.

The procedure would look like:

```
procedure Heapify(var A : List; Start, Stop : integer);

{ This routine turns the subtree with root node Start into }
{ a heap.  The process extends no further than Stop.        }
{ Both children of Start are heaps to start with.           }

var
   Temp : real;
   Done : Boolean;
   k    : integer;

begin
   Temp := A[Start];
   k := 2 * Start;
   Done := false;
   while not Done and (k <= Stop) do
      begin
         if (k < Stop) and (A[k] < A[k+1])
            then
               k := k + 1;
         if Temp < A[k]
            then
               begin
                  A[k div 2] := A[k];
                  k := 2 * k
               end
            else
               Done := true
      end;
   A[k div 2] := Temp
end;
```

We again found it easy to implement the algorithm; the code looks very much like the algorithm. There is, however, a subtle bug. Can you see it? Look for it before reading on. We will give you a hint: remember what we said in chapter 9 about the way programmers use the word *and*.

The and Problem, Again

Once again, the problem is with the Boolean operator **and** and with the way we intended the *and* to work. Look at the statement above that says:

```
if (k < Stop) and (A[k] < A[k+1])
    then
        k := k + 1;
```

The purpose of this was to get k pointing at the larger of A[k div 2]'s two children, but we do not want to change k to k+1 if the $(k+1)^{st}$ element is beyond Stop. Everything will work just fine as long as Stop < N or N < MAXSIZE. However, if this routine is called when Stop = N = MAXSIZE, and k happens to equal Stop, some systems—depending on the compiler—might evaluate the expression:

```
(k < Stop) and (A[k] < A[k+1])
```

by evaluating *both* sides of the **and**. In such an instance, the system would attempt to look at what was stored in A[MAXSIZE + 1], which would cause a run-time error. While the chance of all this happening at once is slim, that doesn't mean you don't have to worry about it. In fact, since it is unlikely for the error to be noticed while testing, and thus the bug might remain in the program for some time until it pops up after the program is released, it is even more important that we find it and fix it now. Remember, we should write our code assuming the compiler does not use short-circuit evaluation.

The "fix" turns out to be easy this time. We just need to make sure the second half of the **and** is only evaluated if the first half is true. We can do this by simply making it two ⟨*if statement*⟩s:

```
if k < Stop
    then
        if A[k] < A[k+1]
            then
                k := k + 1;
```

The Heap Sort, Completed

Now we can finish HeapSort. It's very straightforward too. The only local variable is an index i. The completed procedure, containing Heapify, starts on the next page.

```
procedure HeapSort(var A : List; N : integer);

{ This procedure sorts the array A from 1 through N into  }
{ ascending order using the heap sort algorithm.          }

var
   i : integer;

   procedure Heapify(var A : List; Start, Stop : integer);

   { This routine turns the subtree with root node Start into }
   { a heap.  The process extends no further than Stop.        }
   { Both children of Start are heaps to start with.           }

   var
      Temp : real;
      Done : Boolean;
      k    : integer;
   begin
      Temp := A[Start];
      k := 2 * Start;
      Done := false;
      while not Done and (k <= Stop) do
         begin
            if k < Stop
               then
                  if A[k] < A[k+1]
                     then
                         k := k + 1;
            if Temp < A[k]
               then
                  begin
                     A[k div 2] := A[k];
                     k := 2 * k
                  end
               else
                  Done := true
         end;
      A[k div 2] := Temp
   end;
```

```
begin  {  HeapSort  }
   for i := N div 2 downto 1 do
      Heapify(A, i, N);
   for i := N downto 2 do
      begin
         Swap(A[1], A[i]);
         Heapify(A, 1, i - 1)
      end
end;
```

10.6   Efficiency of Sorting Algorithms

We will leave it as an exercise for you to write Pascal programs that measure the time these routines take in order to get some idea of how fast they are relative to one another. On one of the computers we use for Pascal, we got the following results after using the bubble sort, the insertion sort, the insertion sort with a binary search, and the heap sort on arrays containing 500 and then 1000 real numbers chosen at random. You might want to try running your sorting routines and timing them with a stopwatch, and compare your results with ours.

```
This program compares sorting algorithms.  You may sort any
number of numbers from 2 to 1000
Enter the number to be sorted - 500

The bubble sort took 14.1 seconds.
The insertion sort took 7.9 seconds.
The binary insertion sort took 2.7 seconds.
The heapsort took 0.9 seconds.

This program compares sorting algorithms.  You may sort any
number of numbers from 2 to 1000
Enter the number to be sorted - 1000

The bubble sort took 57.7 seconds.
The insertion sort took 32.9 seconds.
The binary insertion sort took 10.8 seconds.
The heapsort took 2.0 seconds.
```

Notice that the times for the bubble and insertion sort went up by about a factor of four when the number of numbers to be sorted doubled. Notice how much faster the heap sort is than the others. If you used a stopwatch and timed your routines, your times might be a lot different than ours, but the relative times should be similar. The time your bubble sort took for 1000 numbers should be about four times longer than the time it took for 500 numbers. The time it takes to sort 300 numbers should be about nine times longer than the time it takes to sort 100. In other words, if the number of numbers to be sorted increases by a factor of n, the time it takes to sort them goes up by a factor of n^2. Such a situation is described in computer science by saying that "the bubble sort algorithm is of order n squared." The time required for the heap sort to do its job also increases as the number of numbers being sorted increases, but the rate at which it goes up is much slower.

10.7   Arrays in Pascal—Once Again

In chapter 9 we developed an algorithm for a Boolean-valued function, *Sorted.* This function accepts two arrays and the number of elements in the arrays and determines whether or not the second array is a sorted version of the first. The algorithm is on page 310. A Pascal function that implements the algorithm is easy to write. Look at ours on the next page.

```
function Sorted(A1, A2 : List; N : integer) : Boolean;

{ This function returns true if array A2 is a correctly }
{ sorted version of array A1 and false otherwise.       }

var
  i, j, NewN, Place : integer;
  Ok : Boolean;

begin
  Ok := true;
  for i := 1 to N - 1 do
    if A2[i] > A2[i+1]
      then
        Ok := false;
  i := 1;
  NewN := N;
  while Ok and (i <= N) do
    begin
      BinarySearch(A2, NewN, A1[i], Ok, Place);
      if Ok
        then
          begin
            for j := Place to NewN - 1 do
              A2[j] := A2[j+1];
            NewN := NewN - 1;
            i := i + 1
          end
    end;
  Sorted := Ok
end;
```

By collecting the various pieces of code from this chapter and adding a simple routine that has the computer choose some random numbers for the array, we can put together a complete Pascal program that implements and verifies the correctness of any of the sorting routines.

Leaving out the sorting routine, here's what the program would look like.

```pascal
program SortTest(input, output);

{  Programmer: Doug Fernandez                                  }

{  This program implements and tests a sorting routine.   }

const
   MAXSIZE = 1000;

type
   List = array [1 .. MAXSIZE] of real;

var
   A, B : List;
   N, Seed : integer;

   function Random

      . . .

   procedure GetArray(var A : List; N : integer);

   {  This procedure fills the array with N pseudo-random  }
   {  real values between 0 and 100.                       }

   var
     i : integer;

   begin
     for i := 1 to N do
       A[i] := 100 * Random
   end;

   function Equal

      . . .

   procedure BinarySearch

      . . .
```

```
      procedure ???sort
         . . .   { put the routine to be implemented here.  }

      function Sorted
         . . .

   begin  { Main Program }
      writeln('This program implements and tests the ??? sort routine.');
      write('Enter a value for the random number seed:  ');
      readln(Seed);
      write('How many numbers do you want to sort?  ');
      readln(N);
      while (N < 2) or (MAXSIZE < N) do
         begin
            write('I can''t sort that many numbers, try again:  ');
            readln(N)
         end;
      GetArray(A, N);
      B := A;
      ???Sort(B, N);
      if Sorted(A, B, N)
         then
            writeln('The numbers were sorted correctly.')
         else
            writeln('The numbers were not sorted correctly.')
   end.
```

We should say a few things about this program. First notice that unlike what
we had earlier, we passed the array A by reference to both BinarySearch and
to Sorted. In truth, we decided to do this *after* the code was written on our
computer. When we tried to run it and pass the arrays by value, we got a run-
time error because we were trying to pass too much data. As we said earlier,
even when arrays (especially large arrays) are not being changed in the called
routine, it often is a good idea to pass them by reference, since this will amount
to a savings of time and space. We had to modify our code to get rid of the
run-time error.

In this situation, however, there is a further point to notice. The array B is
passed to Sorted *and changed* inside the routine. We have introduced a side
effect. In fact, the array B is going to be very different when Sorted is finished.
Had we planned to use the sorted array after returning from Sorted, we would
be in trouble. However, since we are only using this program to test the sorting
routines, it doesn't really matter in this program. It might matter in other
applications, though. Be careful.

Notice that we are using Seed for the random number generating function
and we are treating it as a global variable. If we didn't, we would have to pass

it from routine to routine whenever a routine needed to call `Random`. In this case, we have decided that it's better to use a global variable, to keep from having `Seed` complicate matters.

You can now replace the `???Sort` with the name of a real procedure, include that procedure and run this program to test it.

10.8   Summary and Review

- This chapter developed the parts of Pascal necessary to implement the searching and sorting algorithms from chapter 9.

- We learned how to define new data types using the ⟨*type definition part*⟩.

- We learned how to define named constants using the ⟨*constant definition part*⟩. We saw that using named constants can make our programs easier to read and to modify.

- We identified and discussed a situation wherein real values that would be equal mathematically might not be equal in the computer since the computer cannot hold all real values exactly. We wrote a routine in Pascal that would compare two `real` values and consider them equal if they were within a margin of error. The value of `EPSILON` we used was 10^{-9} but on your computer you may have to use a different value depending on how many significant places of accuracy your computer uses for a `real` value.

- We introduced and explained the Pascal ⟨*for statement*⟩, which is an implementation of our algorithmic *loop for*. We stated the several restrictions on the ⟨*for statement*⟩ that are in Pascal.

- We discussed three different ways to allow a user to enter a list of numbers. Each method had its advantages and disadvantages. You should be familiar with them and able to choose an appropriate method when necessary.

- We wrote the code for Pascal routines for the second versions of the bubble sort and the insertion sort and for the heap sort.

- We indicated that often it is more efficient to pass a large array by reference even when it is not being changed.

- We mentioned the problem with implementing an *and*. Some Pascal compilers evaluate both sides of an **and** while the algorithm might have been written on the assumption that only one side should be evaluated in certain cases. We saw that this requires care in implementing the algorithm.

  Similar situations can arise when implementing an *or*. If the left operand of an **or** is true, there is no need to evaluate the right operand but some compilers will evaluate it anyway. One of the most important responsibilities of a programmer is to insure that the *and* and *or* are implemented correctly.

- We briefly mentioned the efficiency of algorithms. This topic is discussed in more detail in advanced texts.

10.9   New Terms Introduced

and problem The problem with different ways of evaluating Boolean expressions involving the **and** operator.

anonymous type A type without a name.

array components Array elements.

constant definition part The part of the ⟨*definition/declaration part*⟩ where constants are defined.

equality of real values An ambiguity caused by the way real numbers are stored in a computer.

for statement The Pascal statement implementing the *loop for.*

index of a for statement A variable that controls the repetitions of a ⟨*for statement*⟩.

named constant An identifier used to hold a value that does not change.

or problem The problem with different ways of evaluating Boolean expressions involving the **or** operator.

order n squared A measure of the efficiency of an algorithm where the execution time increases as the square of the number of elements.

sentinel A special value used to indicate the end of a collection of data.

short-circuit evaluation A method for evaluating Boolean expressions where the evaluation terminates as soon as the final value is known.

trailer A sentinel.

type definition part The part of the ⟨*definition/declaration part*⟩ where new types are defined.

10.10   Exercises

1. Write and run a test program similar to the routine on page 324 that compares the result of multiplying a `real` number by 100 with the same number added to itself 100 times. Does the compiler consider them to be exactly equal? Try your program on `real` numbers both with and without decimal parts. Does it make a difference? Why do we discuss the problem of the equality of `real`s in this chapter rather than in chapter 9?

2. Write the Pascal code for the modified binary search algorithm of exercise 12 of chapter 9.

3. Write the Pascal code for the procedure `Swap` as defined in exercise 10 in chapter 9. Write it so that it exchanges the values of two `real` variables.

4. Write a module that allows a user to fill a given array with `real` values from the keyboard. The user should be allowed to enter as many `real` numbers as desired, up to a preset limit (the maximum size of the array). This module should also keep track of how many numbers the user enters and return this number.

5. Write a module that fills a given array with a given number of random `real` values, using either the random number generator supplied with your version of Pascal or, if your system does not have one, the random number generator from the program in the "Once Again" section of this chapter. The one supplied with your compiler is likely a better generator of pseudo-random numbers. If your system has a function that generates random numbers, rewrite the program in the "Once Again" section to use that function.

6. Write an algorithm and a complete Pascal program using the above two exercises and the algorithms from chapter 9, exercises 2–3. The algorithm should allow a user to fill an array, either by entering the numbers at the keyboard or by having the computer pick them randomly. The algorithm should then find the sum of the numbers and their average value, and the minimum and maximum values and their locations within the array.

7. Write the code for the selection sort based on exercise 15 of chapter 9. Test your code using the routine from the "Once Again" section.

8. Write the code for the insertion sort with a binary search, using the algorithm from exercise 12, chapter 9, and the code from exercise 2 above. Test this routine using the routine from the "Once Again" section.

9. Write the code for the Shell sort from exercise 16 of chapter 9. Test this routine using the routine from the "Once Again" section.

10. Using the modules developed in the exercises above, write a complete program that allows the user to compare various searching and sorting routines. Specifically, the program should allow the user to:

(a) determine the size of the array and either enter the numbers individually or have the computer generate them randomly;

(b) choose one of the sorting routines and sort the array;

(c) perform either a linear or a binary search of the array for a particular value.

For example, the program could present the user with the following main menu:

```
<-------------- Main Menu -------------->

Please select a number and press Return:

                (1) Generate a new array
                (2) Sort array
                (3) Search array
                (4) Quit

        Enter your choice:
```

If the user chooses to do a linear search, either the original array or the sorted array could be searched; however, only the sorted array could be used for the binary search. Your program should be "smart" enough to not try a binary search unless the array has been sorted.

Chapter 11

Records and Strings

'The time has come,' the Walrus said,
'To talk of many things:
Of shoes—and ships—and sealing wax—
Of cabbages—and—kings—
And why the sea is boiling hot—
And whether pigs have wings.'
— Lewis Carroll

11.1   Overview of the Chapter

In this chapter we will discuss the processing of data in the form of strings of characters. We will see how to create and manipulate strings of characters in Pascal, and we will learn about records, a structured type in Pascal that consists of components of mixed types. Records are often useful in implementing abstract data types in Pascal. In this chapter where we will combine our discussion of algorithms and their Pascal implementation.

11.2   Introduction

Up until now we have been dealing with data that is mostly numeric in nature. The only kinds of non-numeric data we have worked with are chars, which represent only one character at a time.

It's safe to say that with the popularization of word processors, a significant amount of the data processed by computers these days is in the form of streams of characters, or text. The algorithms we need to develop to process text depend very heavily on the constructs we are provided with by the programming language. For this reason, our discussion of algorithms and Pascal in this chapter will be closely intertwined. In the case of Standard Pascal, we are provided with only the barest essentials as far as text manipulation is concerned, and so it is up to us to use these as building blocks for more powerful tools.

355

Our goal is to write a basic set of routines to manipulate text data, and to use those routines in somewhat more complicated situations. It should be noted that many implementations of Pascal have built-in functions and procedures to handle text data, but there is no standardization of these features. If you were to write a program using these features in one version, they would most likely fail to work in another version. We'll confine our discussion to Standard Pascal. Let's start by examining the data types, procedures and functions from which we can build.

11.3   Strings

A *string* is a sequence of one or more characters. A *string constant* is a sequence of two or more characters between apostrophes. A single character enclosed in apostrophes is not a string but a `char` constant. We have already been using string constants extensively; for example, the statement

```
writeln('I got it, aren''t I smart?')
```

contains a string constant.

It is easy to define named string constants in Pascal. For example, we can define the following:

```
const
   NAME   = 'Johnny';
   BLANKS = '        ';
```

We could then use the ⟨write statement⟩ to print or display these constants just as in the above example:

```
writeln(Name);
writeln(Blanks)
```

Clearly, though, if we want to be able to do any useful manipulation of strings we have to be able to define string variables.

String Variables

We have seen that we can build an array data type from the simple data types by indicating in a type definition the range of the subscript variable and the type of the components of the array. If we want to handle a string of characters, we might construct an array in the following way:

```
const
   MAXLEN = 10;
type
   String = array [1 .. MAXLEN] of char;
```

We could then declare a variable of type `String`. Note that this would limit the number of characters in a variable of type `String` to 10. If 10 is too small a limit, you can let the constant `MAXLEN` name a higher value, but no matter how large `MAXLEN` is, it still represents a limit on the number of characters a `String` can contain. We would also be wasting memory if we were to define an unnecessarily high length for `String`. Unfortunately, there's no dynamic way to allocate space for an array in Pascal (as there is in other languages), so we will have to be careful when we choose this value.

A note of caution: In Standard Pascal, `String` is *not* a reserved word. There are a number of non-Standard Pascal compilers, however, that have made it a reserved word.

Another, more important, consideration is that if we were to define `String` this way, even simple assignments would be cumbersome. We would have to assign `char` values to the elements of the array one by one, rather than in a single assignment statement. We can avoid this difficulty by using what Pascal calls a *packed array*.

Packed Arrays

Pascal allows its structured types to be *packed*; this means that the processor can store data of that type in a more efficient manner. On large machines that store 32 bits at a time, this can result in a considerable savings of memory; on microcomputers storing 8 bits, it doesn't make much difference. On either kind of machine, however, Pascal supplies certain facilities that can be used with a string type, which is a special case of a `packed array of char`. For a `packed` `array of char` to be a string type, the index of the array must be an `integer` whose range must begin with 1 and must end with an `integer` greater than 1. In particular, ranges such as `[1 .. 1]` and `[0 .. 5]` are not allowed.

To pack a data type, you simply include the word `packed` in the declaration. In the above definition of the `String` type, we could say:

```
type
   String = packed array [1 .. MAXLEN] of char;
```

This gives us additional features that prove very useful:

1. The relational operators (=, >, <, <=, >=, <>) can be used.

2. String variables can be assigned values as a whole.

3. `write` and `writeln` can be used on the string as a whole.

For example, using the constant and type declarations above, we could legally include the following lines in a program:

```
var
   S1, S2, S3 : String;
   ...

   S1 := 'programmer';
   S2 := 'hacker    ';
   if S1 > S2
      then
         S3 := S1
      else
         S3 := S2;
   writeln('Fred is a ', S3)
   ...
```

Notice that the string constant `'hacker    '` had to be padded with four blanks in order to make it a legal `String`, according to the given type definition. You can define string types of various lengths in a program, but two strings, whether they are string variables or string constants, must have the same length to be assignment compatible. Many Pascal compilers relax this requirement.

Although the relation operators are defined for strings, the value of a particular relation depends on the collating sequence of the characters for a given processor. It will always be true that `'Frank' < 'Fred '`, but whether `'Frank' < 'FRANK'` depends on the character set. If ASCII is being used, then the capital letters are smaller than the lowercase letters, and the digits are smaller than all the letters. Pascal always compares two strings from left to right and continues until two components are found that are unequal. Thus `'Frank' < 'Fred '` because the `'a'` is smaller than the `'e'`, and, in ASCII, `'Frank' > 'FRANK'` because the `'r'` is greater than the `'R'`.

Manipulating Strings

Even though it is a special type of array, a string is still an array. We can refer to one of the characters in a string by the string name and the character's position in the string. For example, let's make the following definitions:

```
const
    MAXLEN = 5;
type
    String = packed array [1 .. MAXLEN] of char;
var
    Name : String;
```

If the variable `Name` held the value `'Frank'`, then the statement

```
    Name[5] := ' '
```

would result in the value of `Name` changing to `'Fran '`. Note that `Name[5]` is a variable of type `char`.

This gives us a powerful way of manipulating the characters in a string, but we are limited to treating them one by one. What we'd like is a way of manipulating more than one character at a time.

Substrings

Any part of a string consisting of consecutive characters from it is called a *substring* of the given string. A substring can be as small as a single character or as large as the entire string itself. We can specify a substring by indicating the position within the string where the substring starts, and the number of characters in the substring. We'd like to be able to perform the following operations on strings and substrings:

1. *extract* a substring of a given string by specifying its position and length,

2. *insert* a substring into a given string at a particular position,

3. *delete* a substring from a given string, given its length and position,

4. *concatenate*, or join, two substrings producing a third, and

5. *find* whether a given string is a substring of another string, and if so, its position within that string.

The Actual Length of a String

Although a string type in Pascal is defined as being a certain length, we may intend for a string of that type to be shorter than its defined length. For example, we usually don't consider trailing blanks in a string to be part of the string. We might want the string `'Fran '` to be thought of as having a length of 4, whereas its defined length is 5. On the other hand, sometimes we might want to consider trailing blanks as part of the string.

To give us the most flexibility, we can think of a string as an abstract data type that consists of two parts: the string of characters itself and the string's actual length. For what follows, then, when we refer to a "string" we'll mean one of these abstract data types. When we get to the implementation stage, we'll decide how to represent this abstract data type in Pascal.

11.4   String Handling Algorithms

Let's take a look at how we might implement the string handling routines mentioned above. When we develop such a module, we usually decide at the start whether the module should be written as a procedure or as a function. For the routines we develop here, we will have to keep in mind that a Pascal function can only return a simple (supplied or user-defined) type; that is, it cannot return an array. Any module that returns a string type must be implemented in Pascal as a procedure.

Extract a Substring

Consider a procedure called *Extract*, which will return a substring of a given string. We would pass as parameters the original string, the starting position and length of the substring, and the string in which this substring is to be returned. The first three values can be passed by value and the last by reference.

Let's call these variables *OrigStr*, *Pos*, *Len* and *ResultStr*. It wouldn't make much sense for the module to receive a non-positive number for *Pos* or *Len*, nor would it make sense to try to return a substring that goes beyond the actual or defined length of *OrigStr*. If either of these situations occur, let's agree to return a zero for the length of *ResultStr*, and, of course, let the character part remain undefined. It would also present a problem if the defined length of a string were less than *Len*. We won't check for that in the module, but instead state a precondition.

Our module would then begin with:

START OF Extract(OrigStr, Pos, Len, ResultStr)
Passed by value: OrigStr, Pos, Len
Passed by reference: ResultStr
Precondition: Len is a valid string length.

if Pos < 1 or Len < 1 or Pos + Len − 1 > the length of OrigStr
   then
       store 0 in the length of ResultStr
   else
       . . .

Now that we have the exceptions out of the way, we can proceed with the rule. We want to assign the characters in OrigStr, beginning with Pos, to ResultStr, beginning with 1. That is, we would start with the assignment:

store $OrigStr_{Pos}$ in $ResultStr_1$.

Then we would follow with

store $OrigStr_{Pos+1}$ in $ResultStr_2$

and so on until

store $OrigStr_{Pos+Len-1}$ in $ResultStr_{Len}$.

A *loop for* is called for to accomplish this:

loop for i going from 1 to Len
    Store $OrigStr_{Pos+i-1}$ in $ResultStr_i$.

And finally, we would

store Len in the length of ResultStr.

The final algorithm would be:

START OF Extract(OrigStr, Pos, Len, ResultStr)
Passed by value: OrigStr, Pos, Len
Passed by reference: ResultStr
Precondition: Len is a valid string length.

if Pos < 1 or Len < 1 or Pos + Len − 1 > the length of OrigStr
   then
      store 0 in the length of ResultStr
   else
      loop for i going from 1 to Len
         Store OrigStr$_{Pos+i-1}$ in ResultStr$_i$
      store Len in the length of ResultStr

END OF Extract

Insert a String

Next let's write the algorithm for a procedure that inserts a given string into another. For example, we might have the string

> `'I can come to dinner.        '`

and wish to insert the string `'not'` after the word `can`, to form the string

> `'I cannot come to dinner.     '`

To accomplish this, we would have to pass the original string, the string to be inserted, and the starting position for the insertion. Let's call these parameters *OrigStr*, *InsStr* and *Pos*, respectively. We would want to pass *OrigStr* by reference, since it will be sent back with *InsStr* inserted and its length changed.

As before, we should make sure that the passed values make sense. In this case, the combined lengths of *OrigStr* and *InsStr* should not be greater than the defined length of a string, and *Pos* should point somewhere within *OrigStr*. We should make this more precise.

The insertion is to begin at *Pos*, and continue for the length of *InsStr*, after which the remainder of *OrigStr* continues.

Using the above example, *OrigStr* would be

> `'I can come to dinner.        '`

the length of *OrigStr* would be 21, *InsStr* would be 'not', its length would be 3, and *Pos* would be 6. After the insertion, *OrigStr* would be

```
'I cannot come to dinner.    '
```

and its length would be 24.

If *Pos* is 1, then we want *InsStr* to be inserted at the beginning of *OrigStr*, so that, for example, if *OrigStr* were

```
'Come Back              '
```

and *InsStr* were

```
'Please                 '
```

then *OrigStr* would be returned as

```
'Please Come Back       '
```

Notice that we have to account for spaces on the end of a string with the length of the string. If *Pos* is equal to the length of *OrigStr* (10, in this case, allowing for a space on the end), then *OrigStr* would be returned as

```
'Come BackPlease        '
```

If we want to be able to use the *Insert* routine to return

```
'Come Back Please       '
```

we have to allow *Pos* to vary between 1 and the length of *OrigStr* + 1.

Taking all this into account, our restriction on the passed value of *Pos* is that it be between 1 and one more than the length of *OrigStr*. If it is not, then we should return *OrigStr* unaffected. We will state our restriction on the combined lengths of the strings as a precondition. The algorithm can begin:

```
START OF Insert(OrigStr, InsStr, Pos)
Passed by value: InsStr, Pos
Passed by reference: OrigStr
Precondition: The sum of the lengths of OrigStr and InsStr
                       is not greater than the defined string length.
Postcondition: InsStr is inserted into OrigStr at position Pos.

if Pos is between 1 and one more than the length of OrigStr
   then
       . . .
```

We then continue with the main part of the module. Some of the characters of *OrigStr* may have to be moved to make room for the insertion. If so, this must be done first, and then the characters from *InsStr* assigned to the "vacated" positions. We would want to move each of the characters of *OrigStr* from the one at *Pos* to the last one over as many places as there are characters in *InsStr*. This could be accomplished with this part of the routine:

loop for i going from the length of OrigStr down to Pos
    store $OrigStr_i$ in $OrigStr_{i+\text{the length of InsStr}}$

Note that this loop has to work its way backward through the array.

Once these characters are out of the way, we are free to assign the characters in *InsStr* to the "vacated" places in *OrigStr*:

loop for i going from 1 to the length of InsStr
    store $InsStr_i$ in $OrigStr_{Pos+i-1}$

The last thing we need to do is adjust the length of *OrigStr*. Its length would be the old length plus the length of the inserted string:

add the length of InsStr to that of OrigStr

So the final algorithm would look like this:

START OF Insert(OrigStr, InsStr, Pos)
Passed by value: InsStr, Pos
Passed by reference: OrigStr
Precondition: The sum of the lengths of OrigStr and InsStr
                        is not greater than the defined string length.
Postcondition: InsStr is inserted into OrigStr at position Pos.

if Pos is between 1 and one more than the length of OrigStr
    then
            loop for i going from the length of OrigStr down to Pos
                store $OrigStr_i$ in $OrigStr_{i+\text{the length of InsStr}}$
            loop for i going from 1 to the length of InsStr
                store $InsStr_i$ in $OrigStr_{Pos+i-1}$
            add the length of InsStr to that of OrigStr

END OF Insert

Delete **and** Concatenate

The algorithms for these routines will be left as exercises. For the *Delete* routine, you will have to pass the original string, and the position and length of the substring to be deleted. The resulting string should be returned in the same variable as the original string.

Be sure to deal with the exceptional cases as we have so far; for example, what should happen if you try to delete a substring that is not entirely within the given string?

The *Concatenate* routine will allow you to use the string 'not' and the string 'able' to form the string 'notable'. The routine will require three parameters: the first string, the second string and the new string.

Which one(s) of the three parameters must be passed by reference? What should happen if *Concatenate* tries to build a string which is longer than the defined length of a string?

Finding a Substring

Now let's turn to the routine that determines whether a given substring is contained in a given string. We will have to pass the original string, the string we're looking for, and variables to tell the calling routine whether or not the substring was found and if so, in what position.

We'll use the following variables: *OrigStr*, *SubStr* and *Place*. If the substring is not found, we will return a zero in *Place*; otherwise, it will indicate the position of the first character of the first occurrence of the substring within *OrigStr*. This way, we don't have to pass back a Boolean value to indicate whether or not the substring was found, and in fact we can write the routine as a function since it's only returning one variable, which is a simple type (**integer**). Let's call the function *Position*.

The easiest way to do what we want is to test each substring of *OrigStr* using the *Extract* module, starting from position 1 and continuing until we've found a match or we come to the end of *OrigStr*. Although that would certainly work, it would not be very efficient. It would be faster to step through the characters of *OrigStr* one by one, looking for a match with the first character of *SubStr*. Only when we find a match do we look at the rest of the characters. Since *OrigStr* is an array, we can easily step through the characters of *OrigStr* without having to call *Extract*.

Notice that it's not necessary to step through *all* of the characters of *OrigStr*. You can stop when the end of *SubStr* meets the end of *OrigStr*, or when the beginning of *SubStr* is several characters before the end of *OrigStr*. For example, if the length of *OrigStr* were 20, and the length of *SubStr* were 6, then the last character of *OrigStr* to be checked would be the 15th. In general it would be one more than the difference between the lengths of the two strings. Let's call this number *Last*. We would first initialize *Last*, initialize *Place* to zero and initialize an index i to 1.

Then we would

```
loop while i ≤ Last and Place = 0
    loop while OrigStrᵢ ≠ SubStr₁ and i ≤ Last
        add 1 to i
    if i ≤ Last
        then
            compare the remaining characters of SubStr
            and OrigStr and set Place to i if they match,
            otherwise add 1 to i
return Place
```

Comparing the remaining characters can be done either by calling *Extract* or by looping and comparing them one by one.

We'll leave it as an exercise to complete this algorithm and the corresponding Pascal code. We should remind you about the problem that can occur when implementing an *and*. The above algorithm contains a couple of *ands*. You should be careful when you implement the algorithm; check to see if the algorithm makes any assumptions about the way the *and* is handled. If so, implement the algorithm so that the same assumptions are true for the code.

11.5 String Handling in Pascal

It's time to code our string handling algorithms. We'll do **Extract** and **Insert** and leave the others for you.

We now have to think about how we should implement our abstract data type in Pascal. Our data type consists of a sequence of characters along with a number indicating its actual length. It seems as though the most natural way to proceed would be to have a **packed array of char** for the characters and an **integer** for the actual length. In other words, every time we pass a string as a parameter we actually pass two variables, one a **packed array of char** and one an **integer**. The algorithm variable *OrigStr* will become two Pascal variables: **OrigChars** and **OrigLen**.

Extract **in Pascal**

The Pascal code for the *Extract* algorithm would require such definitions as:

```
const
    MAXLEN = 80;
type
    String = packed array [1 .. MAXLEN] of char;
```

the module would then be coded as follows:

```pascal
procedure Extract(OrigChars : String;
          OrigLen, Pos, Len : integer;
            var ResultChars : String;
              var ResultLen : integer);

{ This procedure extracts a substring of OrigChars of }
{ length Len starting at position Pos.                }

{ Precondition:  Len is less than or equal to MAXLEN.  }

var
   i : integer;

begin
   if (Pos < 1) or (Len < 1) or (Pos + Len - 1 > OrigLen)
      then
         ResultLen := 0
      else
         begin
            for i := 1 to Len do
               ResultChars[i] := OrigChars[Pos + i - 1];
            ResultLen := Len
         end
end;
```

Insert **in Pascal**

Assuming the same constant and type definitions as above, the *Insert* algorithm could be coded like this:

```pascal
procedure Insert(var OrigChars : String;
                   var OrigLen : integer;
                         Pos : integer;
                     InsChars : String;
                       InsLen : integer);

{ This procedure inserts InsChars into OrigChars beginning at Pos. }

{ Precondition:  OrigLen + InsLen is not greater than MAXLEN.      }
```

```
var
   i : integer;

begin
   if Pos in [1 .. OrigLen + 1]
      then
         begin
            for i := OrigLen downto Pos do
               OrigChars[i + InsLen] := OrigChars[i];
            for i := 1 to InsLen do
               OrigChars[Pos + i - 1] := InsChars[i];
            OrigLen := OrigLen + InsLen
         end
end;
```

A Program for the String Routines

As an example of a complete program which uses the string handling routines we have developed in this chapter, we will write a program that allows the user to run any of the routines with strings entered at the keyboard. This program will present the user with a menu like this:

```
(1) Extract a substring
(2) Insert a substring
(3) Delete a substring
(4) Concatenate two strings
(5) Find the position of a substring

(Q)uit
```

Depending on which choice the user makes, the program will ask for the appropriate information, call the corresponding routine and display the result. Here's a top level algorithm for the main program:

```
call Introduce
loop
    display menu of choices
    accept user's choice
    if "quit" hasn't been chosen
        then
            call the chosen routine
    until "quit" is chosen
call Conclude
```

Each of the string routines will prompt the user for the required information, call the module and display the result. For the first four modules, this result will be in the form of a string, but for the `Position` module, the result is a numeric value. We will write a `DisplayString` module that can be called by the first four; this module will simply display a string that is passed to it. It will display the string surrounded by quotation marks, so that leading or trailing blanks that are part of the string can easily be seen.

The code for this routine is easy. We can use the length of the string as a field-width indicator, except when the length is zero, in which case the routine should simply display two pairs of quotation marks with nothing in between. We want the routine to pause for the user, so we add an appropriate prompt and a `readln`:

```
procedure DisplayString(Str : String;
                        Len : integer);


{  This procedure displays the passed string, surrounded by    }
{  quotation marks, and pauses until the user presses Return.   }

begin
   writeln;
   write('The resulting string is: "');
   if Len > 0
      then
         write(Str : Len);
   writeln('"');
   writeln;
   write('Press Return to continue: ');
   readln
end;
```

Each of the modules will also have to accept one or more strings typed in at the keyboard. Many implementations of Pascal allow you to use `readln` with a string type parameter, but this is not a feature of Standard Pascal. According to the Standard, `readln` can only accept parameters of type `integer`, `real` or `char`. You could, of course, use `readln` to enter the string one character at a time, but that would mean that the user would have to press RETURN after every character, and somehow indicate when the last character has been entered.

Reading Strings

The solution to the problem of reading strings from the keyboard involves the **read** form of the ⟨*read statement*⟩. In chapter 4 you were told that the ⟨*read statement*⟩ had two forms, **read** and **readln**, and that it was better to use **readln** to accept input from the keyboard.

The **read** form of the ⟨*read statement*⟩ can be used to read one character at a time from the keyboard without requiring the user to press RETURN every time. We *do*, however, have to know when the user has pressed RETURN so that we know that the last character of the string has been entered.

eoln

Pascal supplies a Boolean function **eoln** (*end of line*) that becomes true when the user presses the RETURN key. Using this function, it is easy to code a routine that will read characters from the keyboard one by one until the RETURN key is pressed, keeping track of how many characters have been entered:

```
procedure ReadString(var Str : String;
                     var Len : integer;
                         Max : integer);

{  This procedure reads a string from the keyboard,  }
{  up to a maximum of Max characters.                }

begin
   Len := 0;
   while (Len < Max) and not eoln do
      begin
         Len := Len + 1;
         read(Str[Len])
      end;
   readln
end;
```

The parameter **Max** is there to ensure that the routine doesn't try to read too many characters. For example, we would never want **Len** to be greater than **MAXLEN**, and in some cases we might want to allow even fewer characters to be read. The **readln** is there so that the computer will correctly process subsequent calls to the ⟨*read statement*⟩. When this procedure is called, the user has the impression that he is simply typing in the string and pressing RETURN. The **eoln** function and the ⟨*read statement*⟩ will be discussed more fully in the next chapter.

The Modules Called by the Main Program

As usual, we will leave the *Introduce* and *Conclude* modules for the coding step and concentrate on the ones called from the main menu loop. Each of these modules gets some input from the user, calls a string routine, and displays the result. The information required for each module is different, but in each case we should make sure that the parameters we pass to the string routine satisfy its preconditions. For example, the precondition for the **Insert** routine is that

the length of the string resulting from the insertion is less than or equal to
MAXLEN.

We will write the algorithms and the code for the modules that call Extract
and Insert, the two routines we have already written. We'll then finish coding
the main program, leaving you to fill in the missing modules.

The RunExtract Module

This module will ask the user for the original string, the starting position of
the substring to be extracted and the length of the substring. It will then call
Extract and DisplayString. Here's the algorithm:

START OF RunExtract

display "Please enter the original string,"
display "not longer than", MAXLEN, "characters"
call ReadString(OStr, OLen, MAXLEN)
display "Please enter the starting position of the substring"
accept Pos
loop while Pos is not between 1 and OLen
    display "Please enter a number between 1 and ", OLen
    accept Pos
display "Please enter the substring length"
accept Len
loop while Len is not between 1 and OLen − Pos + 1
    display "Please enter a number between 1 and ", OLen − Pos + 1
    accept Len
call Extract(OStr, Pos, Len, RStr, RLen)
call DisplayString(RStr, RLen)

END OF RunExtract

You might have noticed that the two error-checking loops are quite similar.
In both cases we want the user to type in an integer within a certain range,
and we display an error message if he doesn't do so. For this module and the
others as well it would be convenient to have a procedure, say ReadInteger,
that does this.

The procedure would follow the logic of the loops in the algorithm, as follows:

```
procedure ReadInteger(var Int : integer;
                      Min, Max : integer);

{ This procedure reads an integer from the keyboard,  }
{ between Min and Max inclusive.                       }

begin
   readln(Int);
   while not (Int in [Min .. Max]) do
      begin
         write('Please enter an integer between ');
         write(Min : 1, ' and ', Max : 1, ': ');
         readln(Int)
      end
end;
```

Now we're ready to code the **RunExtract** module. Normally when we accept input from the keyboard we use the **write** form of the ⟨*write statement*⟩ so that the cursor is displayed after the prompt. In this case, we use a **writeln** so that the cursor is at the left of the screen, giving the user more room to enter the strings. We've also used some **writeln**s to space things out a bit; you might also want to add a statement to clear the screen at the beginning of the routine.

```
procedure RunExtract;

{ This runs the Extract module based on parameters  }
{ entered at the keyboard.                           }

var
   OStr, RStr            : String;
   OLen, Pos, Len, RLen : integer;
```

```
begin
   writeln('*** Extract ***');
   writeln;
   write('Please enter the original string below, not longer than ');
   writeln(MAXLEN : 1, ' characters.');
   writeln;
   ReadString(OStr, OLen, MAXLEN);
   writeln;
   write('Please enter the starting position of the substring: ');
   ReadInteger(Pos, 1, OLen);
   write('Please enter the substring length: ');
   ReadInteger(Len, 1, OLen - Pos + 1);
   Extract(OStr, OLen, Pos, Len, RStr, RLen);
   DisplayString(RStr, RLen)
end;
```

The RunInsert Module

This module will ask the user for the original string, the starting position at which to insert the new string and the new string itself. It doesn't make much sense to allow the original string to have a length of MAXLEN, because then we couldn't insert anything. We'll ask the user to enter an original string whose length OLen is at most MAXLEN − 1. The maximum length for the substring is then MAXLEN − OLen. Remember that we are allowing the insertion to begin just after the end of the original string; that is, at OLen + 1. The code is very similar to that for RunExtract:

```
procedure RunInsert;

{ This runs the Insert module based on parameters    }
{ entered at the keyboard.                            }

var
   OStr, IStr      : String;
   OLen, Pos, ILen : integer;
```

```
begin
  writeln('*** Insert ***');
  writeln;
  write('Please enter the original string below, not longer than ');
  writeln(MAXLEN - 1 : 1, ' characters.');
  writeln;
  ReadString(OStr, OLen, MAXLEN - 1);
  writeln;
  write('Please enter the starting position of the string to insert: '
  ReadInteger(Pos, 1, OLen + 1);
  write('Please enter the string to insert below, not longer than ');
  writeln(MAXLEN - OLen : 1, ' characters.');
  writeln;
  ReadString(IStr, ILen, MAXLEN - OLen);
  writeln;
  Insert(OStr, OLen, Pos, IStr, ILen);
  DisplayString(OStr, OLen)
end;
```

The Main Program

We have written three general-purpose modules that will be called at various places in the program: `ReadString`, `ReadInteger` and `DisplayString`. Even though `Extract` is only called from `RunExtract`, we will declare `Extract` in the main program, since we're thinking of it as a general-purpose module. The same is true for each of the string manipulation modules, so the program will have the structure shown on the next page.

```
program StringRoutines
   procedure Introduce
   procedure ReadString
   procedure ReadInteger
   procedure DisplayString
   procedure Extract
   procedure Insert
   procedure Delete
   procedure Concatenate
   function Position
   procedure RunExtract
   procedure RunInsert
   procedure RunDelete
   procedure RunConcat
   procedure RunPosition
   procedure Conclude
```

We'll present the code for **StringRoutines** below, leaving out the declarations of the submodules. We'll ask you to flesh out the rest of the program in the exercises.

```
program StringRoutines(input, output);

{  Programmer:  Dan Barbato                            }

{  This program allows the user to run various string   }
{  routines on strings entered at the keyboard.         }

const
   MAXLEN = 80;

type
   String = packed array [1..MAXLEN] of char;

var
   Choice : char;

   {  The declarations go here  }
```

```
begin   { Main Program }
  Introduce;
  repeat
    repeat
      writeln('*** String Routines ***');
      writeln;
      writeln('Please select option and press <Return>:');
      writeln;
      writeln;
      writeln('              (1) Extract a substring');
      writeln('              (2) Insert a substring');
      writeln('              (3) Delete a substring');
      writeln('              (4) Concatenate two strings');
      writeln('              (5) Find the position of a substring');
      writeln;
      writeln('              (Q)uit');
      writeln;
      write('    Your choice: ');
      readln(Choice)
    until Choice in ['1'..'5', 'q', 'Q'];
    if Choice in ['1' .. '5']
      then
        case Choice of
          '1'  : RunExtract;
          '2'  : RunInsert;
          '3'  : RunDelete;
          '4'  : RunConcat;
          '5'  : RunPosition
        end { Case }
  until Choice in ['q', 'Q'];
  Conclude
end.
```

Bulletproof Input

In chapter 4 we indicated that if the user was supposed to enter an integer but didn't, the program would crash and there was little we could do about it. Now that we know how to handle strings, we can do better. We can write input routines that are *bulletproof*; i.e., routines that will allow the user to enter anything he wants and not crash. We can write a routine that expects the user to enter an integer but accept the input as a string and look at it before trying to put it into an integer variable.

Such a routine, let's call it GetInt, would call ReadString to get the string and then look at each character in the string, converting the characters one at a time into an integer until either the end of the input is encountered or until a character is encountered that could not be part of an `integer`. Notice that we are not saying the string can only contain digits; it might start off with a '-' if the `integer` is negative—or even a '+' if the `integer` is positive. Normally such a routine would skip leading blanks too. We'll leave it as an exercise to write the algorithm and the code for `GetInt`.

11.6 Records

Recall that when we developed the algorithms for the string manipulation routines, we regarded the string as an abstract data type that consists of two parts—the "character" part and the "length" part. In our Pascal implementation we had to use two separate variables to represent this data type. It would be more in keeping with our notion of a string if Pascal would allow us to store two different types of information in one variable. More generally, it's useful to be able to define a variable with many parts, each of which could be of a different type. In Pascal, this is done via *records*.

A record is a collection of data of various types, logically regarded as a unit. The individual parts of a record are called *fields*. Think of each field in a record as a variable on its own; as such it can be of any type except `file`, which we discuss in the next chapter. The syntax for declaring the field list of a record type is similar to the syntax for variable declarations.

Declaring a record Type

Here is how we could define a string type in Pascal using records:

```
type
   CharArray = packed array [1 .. MAXLEN] of char;
   String = record
         Str : CharArray;
         Len : integer
      end;
```

Notice that after the word **record** is the field list, which is very similar to the ⟨*variable declaration part*⟩ of a ⟨*block*⟩ after the word **var**. The type of the last field in the list doesn't have a semicolon after it; instead, the field list is followed by an **end** and a semicolon.

Once the record type **String** has been declared, you can declare variables of type **String** in the usual way:

```
var
   Original : String;
```

Accessing Fields

To access a particular field in the record, you use a *field designator*, which consists of the name of the record variable, a period and the field name. For example, the **integer** variable corresponding to the length of the string **Original** would be

```
Original.Len
```

The variable of type **CharArray**, which is the actual "character" part of **Original**, would be referenced as

```
Original.Str
```

This variable is a **packed array of char**, and therefore its components are of type **char**. These components can be referenced in the usual way; that is, with the variable name followed by the index in square brackets. For example, the third character of **Original.Str** would be

```
Original.Str[3]
```

Assignment, Input and Output

As usual in Pascal, an assignment can be made between any two variables of the same type. For example, if the variable `ThisArray` were of type `CharArray`, then the assignment

```
Original.Str := ThisArray
```

would be a valid assignment of one `packed array of char` to another. The assignment

```
Original.Len := 10
```

would assign the value 10 to the `integer` variable `Original.Len`. If `Result` were another variable of type `String`, then the assignment

```
Result := Original
```

would be a valid assignment of one `String` to another. It would be equivalent to assigning, in turn, every field of `Result` the value in the corresponding field of `Original`.

It is *not* valid to *compare* variables of type `record` using the relation operators (=, >, <, <=, >=, <>).

You can read into or write from field variables as long as they are of a type that can be read or written. For example:

```
writeln('Original string: ', Original.Str : Original.Len)
```

Notice that `Original.Str` is a `packed array of char`, and `Original.Len` is an `integer`. In this case, `Original.Len` is used as a field-width indicator in the `writeln` statement.

Extract and Insert Revisited

Now that we have the tools to do the job, let's rewrite string handling routines using records. We'll assume the declarations

```
const
   MAXLEN = 80;

type
   CharArray = packed array [1 .. MAXLEN] of char;
   String = record
         Str : CharArray;
         Len : integer
      end;
```

We would code the **Extract** procedure as follows:

```
procedure Extract(Original : String;
                  Pos, Len : integer;
                  var Result : String);

{  This procedure extracts a substring of Original of   }
{  length Len starting at position Pos.                 }

{  Precondition:  Len is less than or equal to MAXLEN.  }

var
   i : integer;

begin
   if (Pos < 1) or (Len < 1) or (Pos + Len - 1 > Original.Len)
      then
         Result.Len := 0
      else
         begin
            for i := 1 to Len do
               Result.Str[i] := Original.Str[Pos + i - 1];
            Result.Len := Len
         end
end;
```

The modified **Insert** procedure would also be close to the earlier version. See the new version on the next page.

```
procedure Insert(var Original : String;
                          Pos : integer;
                     Inserted : String);

{ This procedure inserts Inserted into Original beginning at Pos. }

{ Precondition:  Original.Len + Inserted.Len is not greater than  }
{ MAXLEN.                                                         }

var
  i : integer;

begin
  if Pos in [1 .. Original.Len + 1]
    then
      begin
        for i := Original.Len downto Pos do
          Original.Str[i + Inserted.Len] := Original.Str[i];
        for i := 1 to Inserted.Len do
          Original.Str[Pos + i - 1] := Inserted.Str[i];
        Original.Len := Original.Len + Inserted.Len
      end
end;
```

We'll leave the remaining string routines as exercises.

Other Examples of Records

In general, there can be any number of fields in the field list, and fields of the same type can be grouped together as in a variable declaration; for example:

```
type
  CharArray = packed array [1 .. MAXLEN] of char;
  StudentRec = record
        Name     : CharArray;
        Class    : integer;
        YearGPA,
        CumGPA   : real
      end;
```

The fields in the field list can be of almost any type, including **arrays** and records.

Consider the following example, where the first field of `StudentRec` is another `record`:

```
type
    CharArray = packed array [1 .. MAXLEN] of char;
    String = record
            Str : CharArray;
            Len : integer
        end;
    StudentRec = record
            Name    : String;
            Class   : integer;
            YearGPA,
            CumGPA  : real
        end;
var
    Student : StudentRec;
```

In this case, the variable representing the student's name would be

```
Student.Name.Str
```

and its length would be

```
Student.Name.Len
```

In other words, `Student` is a variable of type `StudentRec`, and `Name` is one of its fields. `Student.Name` is a variable of type `String`, and `Str` and `Len` are its fields. `Student.Name.Str` is a `CharArray` and `Student.Name.Str` is an `integer`.

The *with statement*

It sometimes gets tiresome to keep repeating the record identifier, so for convenience, Pascal supplies a way of specifying the record identifier once for an entire (usually compound) statement. This is done via the ⟨*with statement*⟩. The statement consists of the word `with`, followed by the name of a record-type variable, followed by the word `do`, and finally a single statement (see figure 11.1).

For the duration of the statement following the `do`, which in most cases is a compound statement, the record variable name and the period can be omitted in any reference to one of its fields. For example, these lines:

```
writeln('Student: ', Student.Name.Str : Student.Name.Len);
writeln('Cumulative GPA: ', Student.CumGPA : 5 : 3)
```

with statement:

Figure 11.1

are equivalent to the following ⟨*with statement*⟩:

```
with Student do
   begin
      writeln('Student: ', Name.Str : Name.Len);
      writeln('Cumulative GPA: ', CumGPA : 5 : 3)
   end
```

In this statement, `Name.Str` is short for `Student.Name.Str`, `Name.Len` is short for `Student.Name.Len`, and `CumGPA` is short for `Student.CumGPA`.

When a field of a record is another record, as in this case, it is meaningful (although sometimes confusing) to have nested ⟨*with statement*⟩s. The above example could be written as:

```
with Student do
   with Name do
      begin
         writeln('Student: ', Str : Len);
         writeln('Cumulative GPA: ', CumGPA : 5 : 3)
      end
```

Notice that the reference to `Student.CumGPA` is unambiguous because there is no `CumGPA` field in the record `Student.Name`. The only ambiguity that might arise is when the field names at one level of the ⟨*with statement*⟩ match those at another level. In this case, the inner level takes precedence over the outer level.

Finally, a nested ⟨*with statement*⟩ like the one above can be abbreviated as:

```
with Student, Name do
   begin
      writeln('Student: ', Str : Len);
      writeln('Cumulative GPA: ', CumGPA : 5 : 3)
   end
```

See appendix A for the complete syntax diagram for the ⟨*with statement*⟩.

Arrays of Records

We've seen a situation where it is natural to have a single variable that holds
more than one type of data. You will find many more uses for the `record` type
as you go along. Consider once more the example we used above:

```
type
   CharArray = packed array [1 .. MAXLEN] of char;
   String = record
         Str : CharArray;
         Len : integer
      end;
   StudentRec = record
         Name     : String;
         Class    : integer;
         YearGPA,
         CumGPA  : real
      end;
```

If you were to store this combination of information in a record, you would
probably want to keep track of more than one student at a time. To do this,
you could declare an *array* of records by adding the following type declaration
to the above:

```
StudentArrayType = array [1 .. MAXARRAYLEN] of StudentRec;
```

where `MAXARRAYLEN` is a previously declared constant. You could then declare
a variable of this type:

```
var
   SA : StudentArrayType;
```

The same rules for accessing the fields within a record would apply. For example,
the variable `SA[15]` would be of type `StudentRec`, the variable `SA[15].GPA`
would be **real**, the name of the 15th student would be stored in

```
SA[15].Name.Str
```

and if you should happen to need it, the first letter of the 15th student's name
would be

```
SA[15].Name.Str[1]
```

An array of records is a very useful type. Imagine that you had information
about the students in a school stored in such an array. You could, for example,
print an alphabetic list of the students, or print a list of the students in order
of their class rank. Either of these tasks would require sorting the array. In the

first case, you would sort the array according to the value in the `Name.Str` field. In the second case, you would sort the array according to the `CumGPA` field, but in *descending* order.

Sorting an Array of Records

As an example, consider modifying the heap sort module from Chapter 10 so that it sorts the array by the `CumGPA` field in descending order. We'll present the code below, but you should look at the code from Chapter 10 first and see what modifications you would have to make. Then, compare your modified code to the code that follows.

```
procedure HeapSortRec(var SA : StudentArrayType; N : integer);

{ This procedure sorts SA by the CumGPA field in descending order.  }

var
   i : integer;

   procedure Heapify(var SA : StudentArrayType; Start, Stop : integer);

   { This procedure makes the subtree with root node at Start into  }
   { a heap.                                                        }

   var
      Temp : StudentRec;
      Done : Boolean;
      k    : integer;
```

```
begin
    Temp := SA[Start];
    k := 2 * Start;
    Done := false;
    while not Done and (k <= Stop) do
        begin
            if k < Stop
                then
                    if SA[k].CumGPA > SA[k + 1].CumGPA
                        then
                            k := k + 1;
            if Temp.CumGPA > SA[k].CumGPA
                then
                    begin
                        SA[k div 2] := SA[k];
                        k := 2 * k
                    end
                else
                    Done := true
        end;
    SA[k div 2] := Temp
end;

begin   { HeapSortRec }
    for i := N div 2 downto 1 do
        Heapify(SA, i, N);
    for i := N downto 2 do
        begin
            SwapRec(SA[1], SA[i]);
            Heapify(SA, 1, i - 1)
        end
end;
```

Notice that comparisons are made using the *fields* of the records, and assignments are made using the records as a whole. What changes did we make so that the sort is in descending order? How would `Swap` have to be rewritten so that this routine could use it as `SwapRec`?

11.7   String Manipulation—Once Again

Imagine a program that maintains information about students as in the last few sections. The name field is a record whose fields are `Str` and `Len`. Let's say that the name of the student is stored in last name first order with a comma following the last name; for example, `'St John, Mary'`. This makes it easy to sort the records alphabetically, but when the names are printed it would be nicer to see `Mary St John`.

Our problem is to write a module that will accept a name in last name first order and pass back the name in first name first order. We will develop a module that calls the various string manipulation modules from the chapter, and then take a look at a different way to accomplish the same goal. Let's call the module *FormatName*.

The *FormatName* Algorithm

We are assuming that the string passed to *FormatName* consists of the last name followed by a comma and a space, followed by the first name. If the name is in this format, then the algorithm should first find the position of the comma in the string, then consider all of the characters up to (but not including) the comma as the last name, and all of the characters starting with the second one after the comma to the end of the string as the first name. It should then build the new string by assembling the first name, followed by a space, followed by the last name.

If the name passed to *FormatName* is not formatted correctly, let's agree to pass back the original name unchanged. We will assume that the name is correctly formatted if there is a comma within the name before the last two characters. Here is how the algorithm could use our existing string routines to accomplish this:

```
START OF FormatName(Original, Formatted)
Passed by value: Original
Passed by reference: Formatted

store Position(Original, ",") in Place
if Place is between 1 and Original.Len - 2
    then
        call Extract(Original, 1, Place - 1, Last)
        call Extract(Original, Place + 2,
                        Original.Len - Place - 1, First)
        call Concatenate(First, Last, Formatted)
        call Insert(Formatted, First.Len + 1, " ")
    else
        store Original in Formatted

END OF FormatName
```

In other words, we *Extract First* and *Last*, *Concatenate* them together and *Insert* a space between them.

The Code for `FormatName`

The only difficulty that arises in implementing the *FormatName* algorithm has
to do with finding the position of the comma and inserting a space in the final
string. The problem occurs because the string manipulation modules expect
to be passed parameters of type `String`, whereas a comma and a space are of
type `char`.

To resolve the problem we declare a variable `Temp` of type `String` and assign
to it a length of 1. It can then be used to pass `chars` to a routine that expects
a `String`. Once again we assume the following type definitions:

```
type
   CharArray = packed array [1 .. MAXLEN] of char;
   String = record
         Str : CharArray;
         Len : integer
      end;
```

and we would code the module as follows:

```
procedure FormatName(Original : String;
                   var Formatted : String);

var
   Temp, First, Last : String;
   Place             : integer;

begin
   Temp.Len := 1;
   Temp.Str[1] := ',';
   Place := Position(Original, Temp);
   Extract(Original, 1, Place - 1, Last);
   Extract(Original, Place + 2, Original.Len - Place - 1, First);
   Concatenate(First, Last, Formatted);
   Temp.Str[1] := ' ';
   Insert(Formatted, First.Len + 1, Temp)
end;
```


Name Formatting Another Way

We have described above how we could store a name in last name first order
and display it in first name first order, using the string manipulation modules.
The same goal could be accomplished another way, by constructing the record
that stores the data so that the name formatting is greatly simplified. One
could, for example, use the following structure:

```
StudentRec = record
      Last,
      First   : String;
      Class   : integer;
      YearGPA,
      CumGPA  : real
    end;
```

in which case the first and last names would not have to be extracted at all.

In general, we can accomplish goals in programming in two related ways: by developing algorithms and choosing how to store the data. The same result can often be obtained either with a complex algorithm operating on simple data types, or with simpler algorithms operating on more complex data structures.

11.8   Summary and Review

- In this chapter we learned how to work with text data in Pascal. In particular, we learned about strings of characters.

- We learned how to define strings as **packed array of char**. We developed string manipulation modules to extract substrings, insert substrings, delete substrings, concatenate two strings together and find a substring within another string.

- We learned how to use the **read** form of the ⟨*read statement*⟩ with the Boolean function **eoln** to read strings of characters from the keyboard.

- We introduced the **record** data type, which we can use to store different kinds of data in one variable. We learned how to declare a variable of type **record**, how to access the fields within a particular record, and how to perform assignments, input and output.

- We rewrote some of the string manipulation modules using variables of type **record**.

- We introduced arrays of records, and discussed the notion of sorting an array of records according to one of the fields in the record. As an example, we modified the heap sort module from chapter 10 so that it sorts an array of records.

- We developed the algorithm and the code for a name formatting module using the string manipulation modules from the chapter.

- We saw that we can accomplish programming goals in two related ways: by developing algorithms and by choosing how to store the data. The same result can often be obtained either with a complex algorithm operating on simple data types, or with simpler algorithms operating on more complex data structures. The computer programming process involves working with algorithms and with data structures.

11.9   New Terms Introduced

actual length of a string The number of characters in the string, not the defined size of the array.

bulletproof input The programming technique that ensures the program will not crash regardless of what the user types.

data structure A collection of data organized in a manner allowing ease of use.

eoln function A Boolean-valued function that indicates when the end of an input line has been reached.

field One of the individual parts of a record.

field designator The Pascal syntax used to refer to one field in a record.

packed array A method used by Pascal to allow for some saving of storage space; not always implemented. A string is a `packed array of char`.

record A collection of data of various types treated as a unit.

string In general, an array of characters. In Pascal, a `packed array of char`.

substring A part of another string.

with statement The Pascal statement used to refer to the fields of a record without having to use the name of the record itself.

11.10 Exercises

1. Think of some character strings to test the algorithms for *Extract* (see page 362) and *Insert* (page 364). Trace through each algorithm step by step, using your test data.

2. Write the algorithm for the *Delete* module and the *Concatenate* module. Make sure you handle the exceptional cases, either by stating preconditions or by means of conditional statements in the body of the routine. Finish the algorithm for the *Position* module.

3. Write the code for `Delete`, `Concetenate` and `Position`.

4. Finish the `StringRoutines` program by writing `RunDelete`, `RunConcat` and `RunPosition`. Compile and test the program with some well-chosen data.

5. Write a Pascal procedure for `GetInt` as described on page 376. This routine will accept a string of characters from the user and will return a Boolean value to indicate whether the string represents a valid `integer`. If it does, the procedure should pass back an `integer` with the appropriate value. Recall that a valid `integer` can begin with a digit or a "+" or "–" sign, and it might contain leading blanks.

6. Consider the problem of working with "long integers." Regardless of the size of `maxint`, it can become necessary to work with integers that are larger than `maxint`. One way to get around this problem is to treat a long integer as an array of characters. Then you would have to develop your own routines to do the arithmetic on these "integers." Write a program that would allow a user to enter two long integers, add or multiply them, and display the result. You should break the problem up into subproblems; a routine that adds two long integers and another that multiplies two long integers would be natural choices. When you think about how to multiply two long integers, remember how you did long multiplication in grade school and remember that you can call the routine that adds two integers.

7. Write the algorithm and the code for a module that is passed a string of characters representing a Roman numeral and returns the corresponding integer value. There are seven Roman "digits:"

M	1000
D	500
C	100
L	50
X	10
V	5
I	1

The value of a Roman numeral is calculated by adding the values, except that the values of any digits appearing out of descending order are subtracted. For example:

$$\text{MCMXLVII} = 1000 - 100 + 1,000 - 10 + 50 + 5 + 1 + 1 = 1947$$

You should make a reasonable assumption about the length of the string being passed. Write and run a test program for the module.

8. Rewrite the `Swap` procedure from chapter 10 so that it could be used by the `HeapSortRec` procedure in this chapter. Call the new procedure `SwapRec`.

9. Using the rewritten `HeapSortRec` procedure as a model, choose at least one of the other sort routines from chapter 10 and rewrite it so that it sorts a `StudentArray` in descending order according to the `CumGPA` field.

Chapter 12

Files

> It is customary to consider a file
> as being in one of two *states*:
> either in the state of being constructed (written)
> or of being scanned (read).
> — Niklaus Wirth

12.1   Overview of the Chapter

In this chapter we explore much further the *file* data type, which was introduced early in the book. A file is the only data type that can exist independently of the program's execution. We will learn about text files other than the files `input` and `output`. We will also learn about files whose components are more complex than just characters. We will discuss the `write` and `read` procedures in more detail.

12.2   Introduction

There are many reasons why we would like a data type that exists independently of the program itself. In fact, it is very rare that real-world computer programs don't involve such a data type. For one thing, the data available to a program does not have to be limited to the size of the computer's memory, but can be as large as the secondary storage medium allows. For another, the same set of data can be available to many different programs; often the output of one program becomes the input for another.

12.3   Files

Recall the ⟨*procedure declaration*⟩ from chapter 6. The structure of a procedure is very similar to that of the program itself. A procedure communicates with the outside world via parameters, and this list of parameters follows the name of the procedure in the declaration. In the same way, a Pascal program communicates with the outside world via *files*, and a list of these files follows the name of the program. The files we have been working with so far are the predefined files `input` and `output`. We'll have more to say about these two files as we discuss files in general.

Sequential and Random Files

In Standard Pascal, files are of a kind known as *sequential* files. The best way to imagine a sequential file is to think of the data being stored on a long tape that can be rewound all the way to the beginning and read in the forward direction only. You cannot back up except to go all the way to the beginning, and in order to read the 50th piece of data in the file, you have to first read the previous 49. A random or direct-access file, on the other hand, is more useful in real applications. Using these files, a program can read any piece of data directly, without first having to read through irrelevant parts of the file. Most Pascal compilers allow some form of direct-access files, but since Standard Pascal doesn't implement them, we'll only consider sequential files here.

File Components

In Pascal, a file consists of components of a particular type. The components of a given file must be of the same type, and the components cannot be files themselves or contain files as substructures. You can have files of `real` numbers, `integers`, `arrays`, `sets`, `records` and so on. There is one supplied file type, `text`, which means a file of `chars`. Later in the chapter we will discuss the other kinds of files; for now we'll focus on textfiles.

Textfiles

The files mentioned in the program heading, input and output, are textfiles. In a typical microcomputer environment the file input corresponds to the keyboard, and the file output corresponds to the screen or the printer. These files have certain properties that make them special, but like all textfiles they can be regarded simply as streams of characters grouped into *lines*. Each line is terminated by an *end-of-line character*, and the file itself is terminated by an *end-of-file marker*.

Imagine, for example, running a typical program such as the ones we have written so far. Usually there is an introductory message, followed by the main program, which prompts for input and generates output, and then a concluding message. The two messages and the input prompts can all be regarded as streams of characters (including such characters as spaces and end-of-line characters) that are sent to the output file (i.e., the screen). The actual input typed in at the keyboard is also a stream of characters, usually a sequence of keyboard characters ending with a RETURN to signify the end of the input line.

The read and write Procedures

Up to now, we have used write and writeln to send characters to the screen, and read and readln to accept characters from the keyboard. In doing this we have actually been invoking, in a specific way, procedures supplied by Pascal which can be used more generally to communicate with any kind of file. Since chapter 4 we have called them the ⟨write statement⟩ and the ⟨read statement⟩, but in fact it would be correct to call them the ⟨write procedure⟩ and the ⟨read procedure⟩. In what follows we assume that the files with which we are communicating are output (for the ⟨write procedure⟩) and input (for the ⟨read procedure⟩), and we will see later how to handle other textfiles.

The *write procedure*

We can now be more precise about exactly what the ⟨write procedure⟩ does. Note that it is invoked just as a procedure should be—by a statement consisting of the procedure name and the parameter list in parentheses. The ⟨write procedure⟩ is different, however, in that the number of parameters in the list can vary. The syntax diagram for the ⟨write procedure⟩ is contained in figure 12.1.

write

In the simplest case of using write, there is just one parameter in the list. This parameter can belong to one of the simple types real, integer, char or Boolean, or it can be a string type, as we have seen. Regardless of the type of the parameter, the actual output of the procedure is a sequence of characters. In the case of a real or integer parameter, the value to be output is first converted to its character representation, and then this sequence of characters

write procedure:

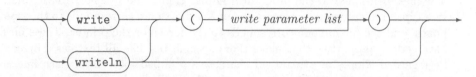

Figure 12.1

is sent out. In the case of a Boolean value, a character representation such as `true` or `TRUE` or perhaps just `T` is output.

If there is more than one parameter in the list, the ⟨*write procedure*⟩ just repeats itself until the last parameter is output. In other words, if the parameter list is $P_1, P_2, \ldots, P_n$, then the call:

```
write(P₁, P₂, ..., Pₙ)
```

is equivalent to the call:

```
begin
   write(P₁);
   write(P₂);
   ⋮
   write(Pₙ)
end
```

We have also seen how field-width indicators can be used with the ⟨*write procedure*⟩; the output is simply padded with blank spaces or truncated to create the appropriate format.

writeln

The simplest case of using `writeln` involves no parameters at all. In this case, the procedure simply outputs an end-of-line character. If there is nothing else on the line, this has the effect of creating a blank line. If other characters have already been sent to the line, this has the effect of ending the line so that subsequent characters will be directed to the next line.

In general, the `writeln` call involves a parameter list. If so, then a call such as:

```
writeln(P₁, P₂, ..., Pₙ)
```

is equivalent to the call:

```
begin
    write(P₁);
    write(P₂);
        ⋮
    write(Pₙ);
    writeln
end
```

The *read procedure*

The ⟨*read procedure*⟩ is also invoked as a procedure should be, and it is also
different from normal procedures in that the number of parameters in the parameter list can vary. Figure 12.2 contains a syntax diagram for the ⟨*read
procedure*⟩.

read procedure:

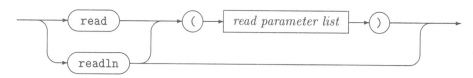

Figure 12.2

We can think of the ⟨*read procedure*⟩ as having parameters passed to it by
reference, whereas the ⟨*write procedure*⟩ has its parameters passed by value.
This is in keeping with the fact that the main purpose of the ⟨*read procedure*⟩
is to assign values to the variables in the parameter list and return them to
the calling routine, whereas the ⟨*write procedure*⟩ simply sends the values out
and doesn't return anything. It only makes sense, then, for the parameters in
a **read** call to be variables, not constants.

Using read

In the simplest case of a call to **read**, there is one variable in the list; this
variable might be **real**, **integer**, or **char** (not **Boolean** or string type!). As
long as the next item to be read is not the end-of-file marker, it is read as
described below. We'll discuss what happens at end-of-file a little later.

Reading chars

If the variable is of type `char`, things are pretty straightforward. The file
being read is, after all, a file of `chars`; the call to `read` simply returns the next
character on the current line. The only special case is when the end-of-line
character is read; this character is read as a space.

Reading integers

If the variable is an `integer`, then it gets a little more complicated. An `integer`
consists of a string of digits, possibly preceded by a plus or minus sign. Figure 12.3 contains the syntax diagram for a signed integer.

Spaces and end-of-line characters are interpreted as separating values on
the input line, so leading spaces and end-of-line characters are ignored by the
⟨*read procedure*⟩. The first character after these leading characters is regarded
as the first character of the integer being read. The system continues to read
characters until it encounters one that's not a digit, and so couldn't be part
of an `integer`. This character will be the first one read by subsequent calls
to the ⟨*read procedure*⟩. When the system has read all the digits (including a
leading + or -) that represent the integer, this string of characters is converted
into that integer and is sent back by the ⟨*read procedure*⟩.

signed integer:

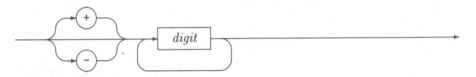

Figure 12.3

Reading reals

Reading `reals` is handled in much the same way as `integers`. Leading blanks
and end-of-lines are ignored, and characters are read in as long as they could
represent a valid `real` value. Remember that a `real` is represented by characters including + and - signs, digits, a decimal point and perhaps an "e" (see
figure 12.4). This string of characters is converted to the corresponding `real`
and sent back by the ⟨*read procedure*⟩.

signed real:

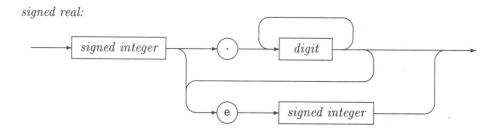

Figure 12.4

Multiple Parameters

The call to **read** may involve more than one parameter on the list. In this case, a call such as:

   read($P_1, P_2, \ldots, P_n$)

is equivalent to the call:

```
begin
   read(P₁);
   read(P₂);
      ⋮
   read(Pₙ)
end
```

Using readln

The simplest case of a call to **readln** involves no parameters at all. In this case, the remainder of the current line is discarded, and the first character on the next line, if it exists, becomes the about-to-be-read character. If there is a parameter list in the call to **readln**, then a call such as:

   readln($P_1, P_2, \ldots, P_n$)

is equivalent to the call:

```
begin
   read(P₁);
   read(P₂);
    ⋮
   read(Pₙ);
   readln
end
```

eof and eoln

As we mentioned earlier, the call to the ⟨*read procedure*⟩ behaves as we have described provided that the next character to be read is not the end-of-file character. If it is, then the call results in an error. How do we know when we're about to read the end-of-file character? Pascal supplies us with a Boolean function, `eof`, that answers this question. The value returned by `eof` is `false` unless the next character to be read is the end-of-file character; in which case it's `true`. This function is similar to the `eoln` function, which tells whether the next character to be read is the end-of-line character.

There is a problem with this scheme, which so far we have ignored. Pascal was originally designed for batch processing environments; that is, environments where the input file is known in its entirety when the program is run. In interactive mode, however, this is not the case. The file `input` (i.e., the keyboard) consists of a stream of characters that is not known in advance. In a sense, this file is *always* at end-of-file, and so it is always an error to read data from the keyboard! Obviously, this won't do, and so every implementation of Pascal that is used interactively must depart from the Standard to get the job done. Needless to say, different implementations have done it differently.

Many implementations simply ignore the end-of-file requirement for the `input` file. In fact, many implementations turn control over to the operating system in response to a `read` call, and the operating system only returns control to the Pascal program when a RETURN is pressed.

That presents an additional problem. The RETURN that the user has to type to get the operating system to return control to the program is part of the input stream and the programmer has to account for it as well as the other characters the user types. As mentioned earlier, Standard Pascal requires the RETURN (the end-of-line character) to be read as a space. Since both `read` and `readln` skip over leading spaces when they are reading into an `integer` or `real` variable, the RETURN causes no problem if the *next* `read` or `readln` encountered is reading into a numerical variable. On the other hand, if the next `read` or `readln` is reading into a `char` variable, that variable will have a space stored in it rather than the actual character typed.

This can get confusing so let's look at a simple example. Consider the following piece of code:

```
write('Do you want to exit? (Y/N): ');
read(Answer);
while not (Answer in ['Y', 'y', 'N', 'n'] do
    begin
        write('Invalid response.  Do you want to exit? (Y/N): ');
        read(Answer)
    end
```

The variable `Answer` is of type `char`. The piece of code is intended to force the user to type either a `y` or an `n` (upper or lowercase). Suppose the user responds to the first prompt with an invalid response, say `X`, and presses RETURN. Since the `'X'` is not in `['Y', 'y', 'N', 'n']`, the loop is entered and the second prompt is displayed. Suppose the user now types a `Y` and presses RETURN. The next character that gets put into `Answer` is not the `'Y'` but the space character that was sitting in the input stream from the previous RETURN. The loop is entered again—despite the user's intention—and the second prompt displayed again. Regardless of what character the user types this time, it and two spaces from the two RETURNs all get placed on the input stream to be read at some point in the future. `Answer` gets the `'Y'` that the user typed *before* the second prompt was displayed. The whole picture gets even more muddied if the user types a string of characters, like `Yes`, before pressing RETURN.

Rather than belaboring the point any further, let's just say that this is why we have usually been using `readln` to accept input from the keyboard. The extra RETURN at the end of what the user types (as well as any other characters the user might have typed) is simply skipped over. If you replace the two `reads` in the above code with `readlns`, all the problems go away.

Note: We should mention that some compilers have implemented other "solutions" to these problems. The best things for you to do are to check the manual carefully and try some small pieces of code to make sure you understand how your compiler handles the ⟨*read procedure*⟩, the end-of-line and the end-of-file situation.

Other Textfiles

So far we have been discussing the supplied files `input` and `output`. We communicate with other textfiles in almost the same way, but there are some differences. Let's examine these.

First of all, to use an external textfile in a program you have to include it in the ⟨*filelist*⟩ following the name of the program. For example, we could use a file called `MyFile` in a program the following way:

```
program FileDemo(input, output, MyFile);
```

The identifier used for the file is declared in the ⟨*variable declaration part*⟩ of the main program as:

```
var
    MyFile : text;
```

Even though `input` and `output` occur in the program parameter list, they are not declared in the ⟨*variable declaration part*⟩.

reset and rewrite

Recall that a textfile is a sequential file, and, like a tape, it can be read or written in the forward direction only, and "rewound" only back to the beginning. There are two supplied procedures that "rewind the tape" and position the file pointer at the beginning of the file. The first is `reset`, which prepares the file to be read from, and the second is `rewrite`, which prepares the file to be written to. To prepare `MyFile` to be read, we would call the `reset` procedure like this:

```
reset(MyFile)
```

Subsequent calls to the ⟨*read procedure*⟩ would begin reading at the beginning of the file.

To prepare `MyFile` to be written to, we would call the `rewrite` procedure like this:

```
rewrite(MyFile)
```

Note that any contents of `MyFile` are lost when such a call is made. Subsequent calls to the ⟨*write procedure*⟩ actually create the file from the beginning. There's no direct way to write information into the middle of a file or add it on to the end. For the `input` and `output` files, the `reset` and `rewrite` calls are unnecessary.

The read and write Procedures with Textfiles

In order to use the `read` and `write` procedures with textfiles other than `input` and `output`, simply include the name of the file as the first parameter in the parameter list. For example:

```
writeln(MyFile, 'Hello')
```

would cause the letters of the word `Hello` and the end-of-line character to be sent to `MyFile`. If there is no filename as the first parameter for a call to the ⟨*write procedure*⟩, the file `output` is assumed. If there is no filename as the first parameter for a call to the ⟨*read procedure*⟩, the file `input` is assumed.

The eof and eoln **Functions**

If the Boolean functions eof and eoln are used with no parameters, they refer to the input file. To use these functions with other textfiles, we simply include the filename as a parameter in the function call. For example, if Ch were a variable of type char, then

```
while not eoln(MyFile) do
   begin
      read(MyFile, Ch);
      write(Ch)
   end
```

would read characters from MyFile into the variable Ch one at a time and display them on the screen, until the end of the current line of MyFile is reached.

Physical Files and Pascal files

One more important point has to be made. A file in Pascal is not the same thing as a physical file on a computer system. You have been dealing with physical files for a while now; for example, the source files you write and the object files generated by the compiler (which is in turn another file) are all physical files, but not files in the Pascal sense. The external files in a Pascal program are in fact stored on the computer system as physical files, but there is no provision in the Pascal Standard as to how to make this connection.

It is the operating system of the computer that creates and manages physical files, so the Pascal program somehow has to tell the operating system what Pascal file corresponds to what physical file. For example, in Turbo Pascal, a non-standard procedure, assign, is used to associate the internal file with the physical file, as in:

```
assign(DataFile, 'B:SAMPLE.DOC');  {  Non-Standard  }
reset(DataFile)
```

where B:SAMPLE.DOC is a file residing on the disk in drive B:.

In other Pascals, the syntax of the reset and rewrite procedures is extended. The usual syntax is something like:

```
reset(DataFile, 'sample')  {  Non-Standard  }
```

where sample is a file to be opened for input.

You will have to find out how this is done on your computer. For reference, we list in appendix B how it's done on some common systems.

12.4   The Spelling Checker

You may have seen a program that checks the spelling of a word processing document. Sometimes this feature is built into the word processor, and sometimes it's a separate program. Most of these programs use sophisticated techniques that allow them to scan a large document and compare the words with those in an even larger dictionary—and do all this very quickly. The document being checked and the dictionary against which it's being checked are both files which are external to the program.

We will write a simplified spelling checker, which isn't as fancy, but will illustrate the advantages and techniques involved in using external files.

Let's refine the statement of the problem. Our spelling checker will have two input files: the document file and the dictionary file. It will create another file containing a list of words from the document which are not found in the dictionary. All of these will be textfiles.

The document file can be any textfile; you can create one easily using your text editor. We will assume that the words in the document are no longer than 15 letters (any combination of upper and lowercase), and that there are no more than 1000 unique words in the document. These numbers should be generous enough for our purposes, but you can adjust them to suit your needs if you like.

The dictionary file will be a textfile especially created before the program is run. It should consist of an alphabetic list of words of 15 characters or less in uppercase only. The dictionary can be as long as you care to make it, but the words in it should consist only of uppercase letters (i.e., no hyphens or apostrophes) and must be sorted in ascending order.

We'll call the file to be created the `NotFound` file. It will be similar in format to the dictionary file but it will contain only those words found in the given document file but not found in the dictionary file.

The Overall Design

Here's how the spelling checker will work: it will read the words in the document one by one, convert the letters to uppercase, and store them in an array sorted alphabetically. If it reads a word that is already stored in the array, it will ignore the word. That way, the array only has to be as big as the number of unique words in the document.

Once this array has been built, the program will begin comparing the words in the array with those in the dictionary, and when it finds a word in the array that is not in the dictionary, the program will write the word into the `NotFound` file.

The introductory part of the program might include prompts for the user to tell the system what the various physical file names are, but we'll leave that part of the program for you to do. The main algorithm for the program should then look something like this:

```
call Introduce
call ReadDocFile
call ProcessWords
call Conclude
```

The Parameters

Let's think about what parameters need to be passed. The `Introduce` module will display an introductory message for the user, but that doesn't require any parameter passing. If you decide to prompt the user for physical filenames, they would have to be passed by reference, since the names will have to be returned to the main program.

The *ReadDocFile* module will build the array of unique words in the document, and so this array will have to be passed by reference. The number of words in this array should also be passed by reference. The document file itself should also be passed to the module, but how should it be passed? The module is not going to change the document file, just read it. At first thought, then, the file should be passed by value, but this would not work in Pascal. You can see why if you give it a little thought.

Whenever something is passed by value, a copy of the actual parameter is made and it is the copy that is sent to the module. Passing a file by value would require the operating system to make a copy of the entire file! This is not practical in general; for this reason, there is a restriction in Pascal that **files** can only be passed by reference.

The *ProcessWords* module would have to be passed the array of unique words and its length, the dictionary file and the **NotFound** file. The files, of course, are passed by reference, but how should the array be passed? Since the array and its length are not changed they can be passed by value, but consider again what this means—the processor must make a copy of the entire array to process within the module. If the array is large, this may take a lot of time and memory space. It may be better to pass the array by reference even though it's not being modified within the module.

Finally, the *Conclude* module displays a concluding message for the user, and doesn't require any parameters. The algorithm would then be:

> START OF *Spelling Checker*
>
> call *Introduce*
> call *ReadDocFile*(*Document*, *WordArray*, *ArrayLength*)
> call *ProcessWords*(*WordArray*, *ArrayLength*, *Dictionary*, *NotFound*)
> call *Conclude*
>
> END OF *Spelling Checker*

The *ReadDocFile* Procedure

This procedure reads the words in the document file and builds the array of unique words. We could do this by building an array of all the words in the document, sorting it using a heap or Shell sort, and then eliminating the duplicates, but this would require the array to be as big as the total number of words in the document. It would be better for our purposes to use a modified insertion sort, which eliminates the duplicates as it goes along. The procedure would read a word, search (using a binary search) the list of words already read, and insert the word in the list *only* if it's not already there.

This whole process would continue until the end of the document file is reached. Since the document file might possibly be empty, we should use a *loop while*:

> loop while not at end of *Document* file
>   *ReadNextWord*
>   *InsertInList*

The *ReadNextWord* module would be passed the document file and the word to be returned, both by reference. We would pass the word to the *InsertInList* module by value, and the array and its current length by reference. Initially, we should set the "current length" of the array to zero.

The algorithm would look like this:

START OF ReadDocFile(Document, WordArray, ArrayLength)
Passed by reference: Document, WordArray, ArrayLength

store 0 in ArrayLength
loop while not at end of Document file
  ReadNextWord(Document, Word)
  InsertInList(Word, WordArray, ArrayLength)

END OF ReadDocFile

ReadNextWord

This module begins reading the next characters in the document file. As long as the characters it reads are letters, it continues to assign the positions in *Word* the corresponding uppercase **char** values. Once it reads a non-letter (which may be on the first try), it fills the remaining positions in *Word* with spaces and returns *Word* to the calling routine.

To convert the characters to uppercase, we'll write a function *Upper* that is passed a letter (in either upper or lowercase) and returns the corresponding uppercase letter. We'll leave the writing of this module until we are at the coding stage, since the method we use is specific to Pascal.

Assuming we have the *Upper* function, the algorithm for *ReadNextWord* is fairly straightforward:

store 1 in i
loop
  read next character in Document into Ch
  if Ch is a letter
    then
      store Upper(Ch) in Word$_i$
      add 1 to i
  until Ch is not a letter
store spaces in the rest of Word

We should, as usual, consider what happens in exceptional cases. For example, if the very first character read in is not a letter, what will the module return? As it is written, it will return a string of spaces. This is all right, as long as the calling routine knows not to insert this string in the list of words it is building.

We could take care of this by adding an *if ... then* to the *ReadDocFile* algorithm:

```
START OF ReadDocFile(Document, WordArray, ArrayLength)
Passed by reference: Document, WordArray, ArrayLength

store 0 in ArrayLength
loop while not at end of Document file
    ReadNextWord(Document, Word)
    if Word is not spaces
        then
                InsertInList(Word, WordArray, ArrayLength)

END OF ReadDocFile
```

Could the array index become larger than the declared length of the array? In this case, that could happen if the word being read from the document is longer than the maximum allowed word length—15 characters in our program. Although we have stated the assumption that the document contains no words longer than 15 characters, it would be easy to modify *ReadNextWord* so that it doesn't cause a run-time error if this should happen. Let's say that if a word longer than 15 characters is encountered, then the first 15 characters will comprise a word, and the characters from 16 on will comprise a second word. That would require only a minor change to the algorithm, so the final algorithm would be:

```
START OF ReadNextWord(Document, Word)
Passed by reference: Document, Word

store 1 in i
loop
    read next character in Document into Ch
    if Ch is a letter
        then
                store Upper(Ch) in Word_i
                add 1 to i
    until Ch is not a letter or i > the maximum word length
store spaces in the rest of Word

END OF ReadNextWord
```

We should also consider what happens when we reach the end of the document file. Does this algorithm have a smooth exit? The last item this module reads is the end-of-line character from the last line in the document file. Remember that end-of-line characters are read in as spaces. After reading this character, **eof** becomes true for the document file, and **ReadNextWord** is no longer called; the exit is smooth. If your implementation is not Standard Pascal and does not read the end-of-line character as a space, you may have to modify the routine to run on your system. This may be an implementation detail but it doesn't hurt to think ahead to the coding step.

InsertInList

The object of this module is to inspect an ordered list of words for a key word, and insert the key word in its proper place if it is not already in the list. We can use a modified insertion sort to do this.

Recall that the insertion sort begins with the second array element, because at that point the "list" consists of just the first element. In our case, the first element of the list will be the first word we read, which we will simply insert in the list. After that, we use a binary search to find the place where the new word belongs, and *only if it's not there*, make room for it in the array and insert it.

We pass the word by value to the module, and we pass the array itself and the array length by reference. Initially the array length is zero; in that case, we simply want to store the word in the first element of the array and increment the array length:

```
if ArrayLength = 0
    then
        store Word in WordArray₁
        store 1 in ArrayLength
```

If the array length is greater than zero, we perform a binary search to find where the word should be inserted, and insert it if it's not already there:

```
    ⋮
    else
        call BinSearch(Word, WordArray, ArrayLength, Place)
        if WordArray_Place is different from Word
            then
                loop for i going from ArrayLength down to Place
                    store WordArray_i in WordArray_{i+1}
                store Word in WordArray_Place
                add 1 to ArrayLength
```

That will take care of *InsertInList* except for the now-familiar *BinSearch*:

START OF BinSearch(Key, Array, Length, Place)
Passed by value: Key, Length
Passed by reference: Array, Place
Precondition: Array is in ascending order up to Length

store 1 in First
store Length in Last
loop
    store the number halfway between First and Last in Middle
    if Array$_{Middle}$ < Key
      then
         store Middle + 1 in First
      else store Middle - 1 in Last
    until First > Last
store First in Place

END OF BinSearch

This version of the binary search routine is slightly different from the version in chapter 9. This one keeps on searching even if it finds a word in the array equal to the key. Finally after *First* passes *Last*, it stores the value of *First* in *Place*. You should trace the algorithm and make sure you see that the index stored in *Place* is the place where *Word* is stored if it is in the array and the place where it should be inserted if it isn't in the array.

The completed algorithm for *InsertInList* is on the next page.

START OF InsertInList(Word, WordArray, ArrayLength)
Passed by value: Word
Passed by reference: WordArray, ArrayLength

if ArrayLength = 0
   then
      store Word in WordArray$_1$
      store 1 in ArrayLength
   else
      call BinSearch(Word, WordArray, ArrayLength, Place)
      if WordArray$_{Place}$ is different from Word
         then
            loop for i going from ArrayLength down to Place
               store WordArray$_i$ in WordArray$_{i+1}$
            store Word in WordArray$_{Place}$
            add 1 to ArrayLength

END OF InsertInList

ProcessWords

The only module that remains (besides the Upper function) is ProcessWords. When this module is called, we have a sorted list of unique words in the document, and we want to compare this list with another sorted list of words—the dictionary.

This can be done quite simply, and in one pass. Start by looking at the first word in the array and the first word in the dictionary.

If the dictionary word precedes the array word, then continue reading dictionary words until one is found that matches or follows the array word. If at this point the words are different, then write the array word out to the NotFound file and look at the next array word.

Continue the steps in the previous paragraph as long as there are words left in the array and in the dictionary. If you run out of dictionary words first, then the remaining words in the document must *all* be written to the NotFound file.

This is confusing, but a small example should help. Suppose the array contains the words:

    DOG
    FLEAS
    HAS
    MY
    ZEBRA

And, suppose the dictionary file contains:

```
CAT
DOG
FLEAS
FLIES
HAD
HAVE
MY
YOUR
```

At the conclusion of *ProcessWords*, the `NotFound` file should contain:

```
HAS
ZEBRA
```

Step through the routine described above and make sure it puts just those words in the `NotFound` file. You must also remember to handle the end-of-file condition properly.

The completed algorithm would look like this:

START OF ProcessWords(WordArray, ArrayLength, Dictionary, NotFound)
Passed by value: ArrayLength
Passed by reference: WordArray, Dictionary, NotFound

store 1 in i
if not at end of Dictionary file
    then
        read DictWord from Dictionary file
loop while i ≤ ArrayLength and not at end of Dictionary file
    loop while WordArray$_i$ > DictWord and not at end of Dictionary file
        read DictWord from Dictionary file
    if WordArray$_i$ ≠ DictWord
        then
            write WordArray$_i$ to NotFound
    add 1 to i
loop while i ≤ ArrayLength
    write WordArray$_i$ to NotFound
    add 1 to i

END OF ProcessWords

The Coding Step

We are now ready to begin coding our algorithms. We'll start with the lowest-level modules and build up, testing as we go. Let's assume the following global declarations for the program:

```
const
  MAXWORDLEN  = 15;
  MAXARRAYLEN = 1000;
  SPACE       = ' ';

type
  WordType       = packed array [1 .. MAXWORDLEN] of char;
  WordArrayType  = array [1 .. MAXARRAYLEN] of WordType;

var
  Dictionary, Document, NotFound : text;
  WordArray                      : WordArrayType;
  ArrayLength                    : integer;
```

Upper

The first module to be coded is the **Upper** function. It would be possible, although tedious, to code this function using a long ⟨*case statement*⟩. Fortunately, Pascal supplies some functions that make it a little easier to manipulate data of type **char** (or, as we'll see, any ordinal type).

Recall that characters are represented in the computer by numeric codes, and that the particular coding scheme (such as the ASCII code) may be different for different computers. Pascal supplies functions that find the next or previous value in the sequence, find the numeric code for a particular character, or find the character represented by a particular code.

succ **and** pred

The function that finds the next character in the sequence is **succ**, which stands for *successor*. The function that returns the previous character is **pred**, for *predecessor*. These two functions can also be used with other ordinal types, such as **integers** or **Booleans**. They always return values of the same type as their arguments. Here are some examples:

```
pred(5) is 4 and succ(5) is 6
pred('f') is 'e' and succ('f') is 'g'
pred(true) is false and succ(true) is an error
```

ord **and** chr

The function that returns the numeric code for a particular character is the
ordinal position function ord. This function actually works with any ordinal
type and returns an integer, which is the ordinal number of that value within
that type. These ordinal numbers start at 0 except for the type integer, in
which case each integer is its own ordinal position. For example, consider the
following:

        ord(6) is 6 and ord(-123) is -123
        ord(true) is 1 and ord(false) is 0

It is not possible to say what the ordinal position is for values of type
char, since the character set may vary from computer to computer. It will
always be the case, however, that the numeric characters are in order, the
lowercase letters are in order, and the uppercase letters are in order. We can't
be sure whether the codes for the uppercase letters are greater than or less than
those for the lowercase letters. Moreover, the numeric characters always come
together in the sequence, but the letters may not! This means that ord('9')
- ord('0') will always be 9, but ord('z') - ord('a') won't always be 25.
It *is* the case, however, that ord('A') - ord('a') is the same as ord('Z') -
ord('z'); that is, the code for a given uppercase letter differs from that of the
corresponding lowercase letter by a constant amount, a fact which will come in
handy when we write the Upper function.

In the case of characters, the ord function has an inverse, called chr. The
chr function takes an integer argument and returns the char value whose ordinal number equals the argument, if such a character exists. Again, the character
set may vary, but if ord('a') is the integer N, then chr(N) is the character 'a'.
In ASCII, for example, ord('A') is 65, and chr(65) is 'A'.

The Upper **Function, Finished**

Now we're ready to write this function in a much more efficient manner than
using a single ⟨*case statement*⟩. We pass the function a char value and it
returns a char. The code would begin:

```
function Upper(Ch : char) : char;

{ This function converts lowercase letters to uppercase. }
{ Other characters are unchanged.                        }
```

If the passed value is a lowercase letter, the corresponding uppercase letter is
returned; otherwise, the passed char is returned. We use the fact that the
code for the uppercase letter differs from that of the corresponding lowercase
letter by a constant amount. If the passed character is a lowercase letter,

we simply return the character whose code is that character's code plus the constant amount:

```pascal
begin
  if Ch in ['a' .. 'z']
    then
      Upper := chr(ord(Ch) + ord('A') - ord('a'))
    else
      Upper := Ch
end;
```

We'll leave it as an exercise to write a test program for this function. It should allow the user to type in various characters, each time calling the function and displaying the result.

The `ReadNextWord` Procedure

Having finished the `Upper` function, the code for `ReadNextWord` follows directly from the algorithm:

```pascal
procedure ReadNextWord(var Doc : text; var Word : WordType);

  { This procedure reads a word from the document file.  It      }
  { returns spaces if the first character read is not a letter. }
  { It converts all letters to uppercase.                        }

  var
    i, j : integer;
    Ch   : char;

    function Upper(Ch : char) : char;

      { This function converts lowercase letters to uppercase. }
      { Other characters are unchanged.                        }

      begin
        if Ch in ['a' .. 'z']
          then
            Upper := chr(ord(Ch) + ord('A') - ord('a'))
          else
            Upper := Ch
      end;
```

```
begin
  i := 1;
  repeat
    read(Doc, Ch);
    if Ch in ['A' .. 'Z', 'a' .. 'z']
      then
        begin
          Word[i] := Upper(Ch);
          i := i + 1
        end
    until not(Ch in ['A' .. 'Z', 'a' .. 'z']) or (i > MAXWORDLEN);
  for j := i to MAXWORDLEN do
    Word[j] := SPACE
end;
```

The test program for this module would look very much like the `ReadDocFile`
procedure, except that instead of inserting the word into the array it could just
print the word on the screen:

```
program Tester(input, output, Document);

{ Programmer:  Kevin Matsumura                    }

{ This program tests the ReadNextWord procedure.  }

const
  MAXWORDLEN = 15;
  SPACE      = ' ';

type
  WordType = packed array [1 .. MAXWORDLEN] of char;

var
  Document : text;
  NextWord : WordType;

  procedure ReadNextWord
    . . .
```

```
begin
  reset(Document);
  while not eof(Document) do
    begin
      ReadNextWord(Document, NextWord);
      writeln(NextWord)
    end
end.
```

Note once again that although this is Standard Pascal, the program would not run on any processor we know of. The Pascal file `Document` has to be identified to the operating system as some physical file.

BinSearch and InsertInList

The routines `BinSearch` and `InsertInList` don't involve any reading from or writing to files. We'll leave their coding as an exercise.

The ReadDocFile Procedure

There are two things to remember in writing the code for this procedure. First, the `Document` file must be `reset` before the first character is read from it. Second, in order to decide whether `NextWord` is blank, it is sufficient to look at the first character of `NextWord`. The complete `ReadDocFile` procedure would then be:

```
procedure ReadDocFile(var Doc : text;
                var WordArray : WordArrayType;
                    var Len : integer);

{  This procedure reads the textfile Doc and creates an array  }
{  consisting of the unique works in the file, arranged in     }
{  alphabetic order.                                           }

var
  NextWord : WordType;

  procedure ReadNextWord
    . . .
```

```
begin
  reset(Doc);
  Len := 0;
  while not eof(Doc) do
    begin
      ReadNextWord(Doc, NextWord);
      if NextWord[1] <> SPACE
        then
            InsertInList(NextWord, WordArray, Len)
    end
end;
```

The ProcessWords **Procedure**

We'll finish with the code for the ProcessWords procedure. Since we know the structure of the Dictionary file, we can simplify the process of reading words from it. There is one word per line in the file, so we can **read** characters until **eoln** becomes true (storing characters as we go), and then store spaces in the remainder of the characters. This is done in the procedure ReadDict. Also note the use of **reset** and **rewrite**:

```
procedure ProcessWords(var WordArray : WordArrayType;
                                  Len : integer;
                     var Dict, NotFnd : text);

  {  This procedure compares the words in WordArray with those  }
  {  in the file Dict.  Any words not found are written out     }
  {  to the NotFnd file.                                        }

var
  i, j      : integer;
  DictWord : WordType;
```

```
    procedure ReadDict(var Dict : text; var Word : WordType);

{  This procedure reads the dictionary file one word at a time  }
{  and returns the word read in Word.                           }

  var
    i, j : integer;

  begin
    i := 0;
    while not eoln(Dict) do
      begin
        i := i + 1;
        read(Dict, Word[i])
      end;
    readln(Dict);
    for j := i + 1 to MAXWORDLEN do
      Word[j] := SPACE
  end;


begin
  i := 1;
  reset(Dict);
  rewrite(NotFnd);
  if not eof(Dict)
    then
      ReadDict(Dict, DictWord);
  while (i <= Len) and not eof(Dict) do
    begin
      while (WordArray[i] > DictWord) and not eof(Dict) do
        ReadDict(Dict, DictWord);
      if WordArray[i] <> DictWord
        then
          writeln(NotFnd, WordArray[i]);
      i := i + 1
    end;
  for j := i to Len do
    writeln(NotFnd, WordArray[i])
end;
```

The Main Program

The main program for the spelling checker will look very much like the algorithm:

```
begin
   Introduce;
   ReadDocFile(Document, WordArray, ArrayLength);
   ProcessWords(WordArray, ArrayLength, Dictionary, NotFound);
   Conclude
end.
```

12.5   Other Types of Files

As we mentioned earlier, the components of a file can be of any type except `file`. The most commonly used files are textfiles but there's no reason not to have files that are, for example, `file of integer` or `file of real`. If you need to store a collection of `integers` in a file, and if the file is going to contain only `integers`, it's a good idea to make the file a `file of integer`. Then the `integers` can be written to and read from the file in a binary format. This will make I/O faster than with a textfile since no conversion from binary to a character representation and back again will be needed.

Be sure you understand that such files cannot be edited with a text editor. Only a textfile can be edited with a text editor.

Files of Records

To illustrate the use of files other than textfiles, we will consider a file whose components are records. Our problem will be to develop a program to keep track of the bank accounts for a tiny bank with 10 customers. The information relating to each account will be stored on an external file of records, each record containing the name of the customer and his or her account balance.

Even though the components of the file are now more complex, the file is still *sequential*, which means that in order to read the record of a particular customer, we have to read every record from the first one up to and including that customer's record. Furthermore, if we make a change to that customer's record (such as a deposit or a withdrawal), then we have to rewrite every record in the file.

As you can see, sequential files are quite cumbersome when it comes to manipulating the data in them. To avoid this, and still retain the advantage of an external file that exists independently of the program, we can simulate a direct access file by reading the file into an *array of records*, similar to the one we described in the previous chapter. This allows us to access each record directly, by specifying its index. The index, in effect, becomes that customer's "account number."

The Bank Teller Program

Let's refine the problem. We wish to develop a program that reads 10 records from an external file into an array, performs some typical banking transactions at the selection of the user, and finally writes the records back out to the file. For simplicity, our transactions will include only deposits and withdrawals. Each record will contain the customer's name and account balance. Since the records are stored in an array, the index corresponds to the customer's account number.

The main part of the program should present the user with a menu with three options:

```
(D)eposit to account
(W)ithdraw from account
(Q)uit
```

When the user chooses to make a deposit, the program should ask for the account number, then display the name and balance associated with that account, and prompt for the amount of the deposit. The account balance should then be updated accordingly.

When the user chooses to make a withdrawal, the program should again ask for the account number, then display that account's name and balance and prompt for the amount of the withdrawal. If the amount of the withdrawal is greater than the account balance, the program should display an appropriate message, otherwise the account balance should be updated.

Here's the top-level algorithm for the program:

> *Introduce*
> *ReadData*
> *MainMenu*
> *WriteData*
> *Conclude*

The modules *Introduce* and *Conclude* just display messages for the user; we can save those for coding time. Let's look first at *ReadData* and *WriteData*.

ReadData and *WriteData*

These modules are very similar, and the algorithms are straightforward. Each can be accomplished with a *loop for*:

> *prepare AccountFile for reading (or writing)*
> *loop for i going from 1 to the number of records*
> *   read (or write) record from (or to) AccountFile*

In order to code these algorithms in Pascal, we have to know how to prepare
the file for reading or writing, and how to read or write a record. In fact, we
already know how to do these things because the syntax is essentially the same
as for textfiles. The procedures **reset** and **rewrite** work exactly the same. The
procedures **read** and **write** are also the same, except that **readln** and **writeln**
are never used with non-textfiles—there is no end-of-line character because the
data is not arranged in lines. For the same reason, there is no **eoln** function,
but there is an **eof** function, which behaves the same as the one for textfiles.

The last thing we have to know is how to declare a variable whose type is a
file of records. Textfiles are predeclared types in Pascal. Other files have to be
declared in the usual way: a file type is defined, and then variables are declared
of that type.

The syntax diagram for the ⟨*type definition part*⟩ of the ⟨*definition/declara-
tion part*⟩ of the ⟨*block*⟩ is shown in figure 10.1. In defining a file type, the ⟨*type
description*⟩ consists of the words **file of** followed by the name of a previously
defined type. (Remember, the syntax diagram for a ⟨*type description*⟩ is in
appendix A.) Consider the following definitions and declarations:

```
const
   MAXNUM = 10;
   MAXLEN = 20;

type
   CharArray  = packed array[1 .. MAXLEN] of char;
   Account = record
       Name    : CharArray;
       Balance : real
     end;
   AccountFileType  = file of Account;
   AccountArrayType = array [1 .. MAXNUM] of Account;

var
   AccountFile  : AccountFileType;
   AccountArray : AccountArrayType;
```

We now have the two variables that will be passed to the modules that read
from and write to the file. As usual, since it's not legal Pascal to pass a copy
of a file, we have to pass the file by reference in both cases. We pass the array
by reference to the module **ReadData**, but by value to the module **WriteData**.
The modules would be coded as shown on the next page.

```
procedure ReadData(var ActFile : AccountFileType;
                       var A : AccountArrayType);

{  This procedure reads all the accounts from the account file.  }

var
  i : integer;

begin
  reset(ActFile);
  for i := 1 to MAXNUM do
    read(ActFile, A[i])
end;

procedure WriteData(var ActFile : AccountFileType;
                        A : AccountArrayType);

{  This procedure writes all the accounts to the account file.  }

var
  i : integer;

begin
  rewrite(ActFile);
  for i := 1 to MAXNUM do
    write(ActFile, A[i])
end;
```

MainMenu

As we mentioned before, the main part of the program displays a menu for
the user, and processes the user's requests until he or she wants to quit. The
MainMenu module will call submodules to process the transactions; these submodules will be *Deposit* and *Withdraw*. The *MainMenu* module must receive
as a parameter the array of account records, and in turn pass the array along
to its submodules. We'll leave the *MainMenu* algorithm as an exercise, and go
on to writing the algorithms for *Deposit* and *Withdraw*.

Deposit

The *Deposit* module is supposed to prompt the user for an account number
(a number from 1 to MAXNUM), display that account's name and balance, and
prompt for a deposit. It then updates the account balance and passes it back
to the calling routine.

The algorithm would be something like:

```
get valid account number
display corresponding name and balance
display prompt for deposit
accept deposit amount
add deposit to balance
```

Before we go any further we should notice that the *Withdraw* module is also supposed to get an account number from the user and display that account's name and balance. We might as well create another routine, say *GetAccount*, that can be called by both *Deposit* and *Withdraw*. This routine would be passed the array of records and will return the selected account number. If that's the case, then we could refine *Deposit* to:

```
START OF Deposit(AccountArray)
Passed by reference: AccountArray

call GetAccount(AccountArray, AccountNum)
display prompt for deposit
accept Amount
add Amount to Account Balance

END OF Deposit
```

Withdraw

The only difference between *Deposit* and *Withdraw* is that *Withdraw* has to check to see that the account has sufficient funds for the withdrawal.

Since it can call *GetAccount*, the algorithm would look like:

START OF Withdraw(AccountArray)
Passed by reference: AccountArray

call GetAccount(AccountArray, AccountNum)
display prompt for withdrawal
accept Amount
if Amount ≤ Account Balance
   then
      subtract Amount from Account Balance
   else
      display message to user

END OF Withdraw

Deposit and Withdraw in Pascal

Here is the code for the Deposit procedure:

```
procedure Deposit(var A : AccountArrayType);

{  This procedure allows the user to enter the amount of the  }
{  deposit and adds that amount to the account balance.       }

var
  ActNum : integer;
  Amount : real;

begin
  GetAccount(A, ActNum);
  write('Please enter the amount of the deposit: ');
  readln(Amount);
  A[ActNum].Balance := A[ActNum].Balance + Amount
end;
```

You may want this routine to check that the amount entered is positive before it updates the account balance. Notice that the last assignment statement is a bit cumbersome, since A[ActNum].Balance is such a long name.

This could be simplified using `with`:

```
procedure Deposit(var A : AccountArrayType);

{  This procedure allows the user to enter the amount of the  }
{  deposit and adds that amount to the account balance.       }

var
  ActNum : integer;
  Amount : real;

begin
  GetAccount(A, ActNum);
  write('Please enter the amount of the deposit: ');
  readln(Amount);
  with A[ActNum] do
    Balance := Balance + Amount
end;
```

We'll leave the `Withdraw` procedure as an exercise.

The `GetAccount` Procedure

The last module to write is the `GetAccount` procedure. The algorithm is:

START OF GetAccount(AccountArray, AccountNumber)
Passed by value: none
Passed by reference: AccountArray, AccountNumber

prompt for account number between 1 and the largest account number
accept AccountNum
loop while AccountNum is not between 1 and the largest account number
*   display error message*
*   prompt for account number*
*   accept AccountNum*
display account name and balance

END OF GetAccount

The code follows directly from the algorithm (note the use of with):

```
procedure GetAccount(var A : AccountArrayType; var ActNum : integer);

{ This procedure gets the account number from the user. }

begin
   write('Please enter account number (1 - ', MAXNUM : 1, '): ');
   readln(ActNum);
   while not (ActNum in [1 .. MAXNUM]) do
      begin
         writeln('Sorry, invalid account number.');
         write('Please enter a number from 1 to ', MAXNUM : 1, ': ');
         readln(ActNum)
      end;
   with A[ActNum] do
      begin
         writeln('  Name: ', Name);
         writeln('Balance: ', Balance : 10 : 2);
         writeln
      end
end;
```

That's the last of the modules to be written, except for those in the exercises. Of course, the modules that read and write information to the external file will have to be modified to run on your system.

Creating the File

There's one assumption we've been making all along that we have to think about now. Even if we were to write and compile the complete program, it would not run. It expects an external file to exist, so that it can be read when the program starts. This means that we have to create one before attempting to run the program.

We could add this as an option on the main menu, or simply write a little utility program to do the job. Since it's only going to be done once, it might make more sense to write a short single-purpose program. The main part of the program would simply be a loop where a name and an amount are accepted from the keyboard and written to the file each time through. As a final example of the syntax, we'll present the code for CreateFile; remember that it will have to be modified according to your version of Pascal. The const and type definitions are the same as those on page 422.

```
program CreateFile(input, output, AccountFile);

{  Programmer:   Colin McKinnon                        }

{  This program creates a file of records for the  }
{  Bank Teller program.                            }

const
  . . .

type
  . . .

var
  i             : integer;
  AccountFile   : AccountFileType;
  A             : AccountArrayType;


  procedure ReadName(var Name : CharArray);

  {  This procedure allows the user to enter a name. }

  var
    i, j : integer;

  begin
    i := 0;
    while not eoln do
      begin
        i := i + 1;
        read(Name[i])
      end;
    readln;
    for j := i + 1 to MAXLEN do
      Name[j] := ' '
  end;
```

```
begin
  rewrite(AccountFile);
  for i := 1 to MAXNUM do
    begin
      writeln('Account number: ', i : 1);
      writeln;
      write('Please enter the account name: ');
      ReadName(A[i].Name);
      write('Please enter the beginning balance: ');
      readln(A[i].Balance);
      write(AccountFile, A[i])
    end
end.
```

12.6 Using Textfiles—Once Again

Since this chapter has already covered several examples, we really don't need a "Once Again" section, but let's include one anyway.

Define the Problem

As an example of working with files and with counting, let's count the number of characters in a textfile. That is, the problem we'll solve is:

> Allow the user to enter the name of a textfile and then have the computer count the number of lines in the file and count the number of occurrences of each character in the file, drawing a histogram showing the relative frequency of each character.

For example, if we stored the above paragraph in a file and ran the program on that file, the histogram would look like the one shown on the next page.

```
      XXXXXXXXXXXXXXXXXXXXXXXXXXXXXXXXXXXXX
  ,   X
  .   X
  A   X
  a   XXXXXXXXXXXXX
  b   X
  c   XXXXXXXXXXXX
  d   XX
  e   XXXXXXXXXXXXXXXXXXXXXXXXXXXXX
  f   XXXXXXX
  g   XXX
  h   XXXXXXXXXXXXX
  i   XXXXXXX
  l   XXXXX
  m   XXXX
  n   XXXXXXXXXXX
  o   XXXXXXXXXXX
  p   X
  q   X
  r   XXXXXXXXXXXXXX
  s   XXXX
  t   XXXXXXXXXXXXXXXXX
  u   XXXXX
  v   XX
  w   XXX
  x   X
  y   X
```

As you can see, there was one 'A', one '.', several 'a's, lots of 'e's, and more spaces than anything else.

Since the number of occurrences of any particular character may exceed the number of columns on the screen, we should display a histogram that indicates the *relative* number of occurrences if the actual number exceeds the number of columns on the screen allotted for the histogram.

Solve the Problem

Before we can write an algorithm for the solution to this problem, we have to figure out how to count the number of occurrences of each character. We could use a separate counter for each character and a long *when* step to decide which counter to increment each time a character is read but there's a much better way: we can use a *counting array*. If we set up an array of integers with one cell for each character and start off with a zero in each cell, we can then add 1 to the appropriate cell whenever the character corresponding to that cell is encountered.

Consider figure 12.5. The figure shows just a portion of the array we're thinking of.

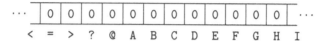

Figure 12.5 A Counting Array, Initialized to 0

At the beginning, each cell contains a zero, as shown. Then whenever a particular character is encountered, we go directly to that cell and add 1 to whatever is currently stored there. For example, if the first character in the file is an 'A', after that character has been counted, the array will look like figure 12.6.

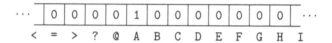

Figure 12.6 A Counting Array, After Counting One 'A'

When we reach the end of the file, the number stored in each cell will be exactly equal to the number of times the corresponding character occurred in the file. The advantage of using an array for this is we can go directly to the desired cell rather than having to search for the counter to increment.

It remains to determine the association between the cells and the characters. This turns out to be almost magically easy: just let the characters be the subscripts of the array themselves. Look back at figures 12.5 and 12.6. The character just below each cell is nothing other than the subscript of the cell.

Turn the Solution into an Algorithm

Now that we have a solution, we need to write the algorithms. A first cut at a top-level algorithm might look like:

display an introduction
initialize the filename and a counting array
open the file and count the characters
display the histogram
display a conclusion

Aside from the familiar introductory and concluding modules, we see that the solution depends on developing three lower-level modules:

- a module that prepares the file to be read from and initializes a counting array,

- a module that counts the characters in the file, and

- a module that displays the histogram.

As always, it is necessary to make decisions about the parameters and how they need to get passed to the modules. The following algorithms show the decisions we made. You should consider whether you would have done it the same way.

START OF Initialize(CountFile, Count, NumLines)
Passed by value: none
Passed by reference: CountFile, Count, NumLines

prepare the file, CountFile, to be read from
store 0 in each cell of Count
store 0 in NumLines

END OF Initialize

In the next algorithm, *CountChars*, we use a big *loop while* that continues until we reach the end of the file. Every time through the loop we either add 1 to *NumLines*, the counter for the number of lines, or we read a character and add 1 to the corresponding cell in the counting array:

```
START OF CountChars(CountFile, Count, NumLines)
Passed by value: none
Passed by reference: CountFile, Count, NumLines

loop while not at the end of CountFile
    if at the end of a line
        then
            add 1 to NumLines
        else
            read a character, Ch, from the file
            add 1 to Count_Ch

END OF CountChars
```

Now that we have counted the characters in the file, we want to display the histogram.

The larger the number of times that character appeared in the file, the longer the line of Xs in the histogram will be. As mentioned earlier, the total number of times a particular character appears in the file could well exceed the number of columns on the screen. If this happens we'll want to "scale" the numbers down so that they all fit. One easy way to do this is to choose a maximum length (call it *HISTLEN*) for the histogram, if the longest bar in the histogram would exceed this value, adjust each value in the counting array so that the largest becomes equal to *HISTLEN* and the rest are scaled accordingly. This is accomplished by making a pass through the array to find the largest value there and then—if necessary—making another pass, multiplying each element in the array by *HISTLEN* divided by this largest value. After this is done, another loop can display the corresponding character and the correct number of Xs.

Here's our algorithm:

```
START OF Histogram(Count, NumLines)
Passed by value: Count, NumLines
Passed by reference: none


store 0 in Longest
loop for Ch going through the printing characters
    if Count_Ch > Longest
        then
            store Count_Ch in Longest
if Longest > HISTLEN
    then
        loop for Ch going through the printing characters
            multiply Count_Ch by HISTLEN / Longest
loop for Ch going through the printing characters
    if Count_Ch > 0
        then
            display the character Ch
            display two spaces
            loop for i going from 1 to Count_Ch
                display 'X'


END OF Histogram
```

Notice that we decided to only show lines with at least one X. We'll leave the modules *Introduce* and *Conclude* as exercises.

Turn the Algorithm into Code

The code for this program is fairly simple. Once again we have the problem with associating the actual file with the Pascal file. We've written the code below, leaving out any lines that accomplish the task of associating the Pascal file, CountFile, with a physical file on the computer. You will need to add these lines, using whatever non-Standard features of your compiler that make it possible.

Our versions of Introduce and Conclude should be rewritten to reflect your own style.

In Histogram we didn't want to divide HISTLEN by Longest over and over so we used another variable to hold the result of the division. Also, notice that we wanted as accurate a result as possible so we used a real variable and then used round to change the value stored in Count. What would have happened if we tried to use an **integer** for HISTLEN divided by Longest? What if we had used **div**?

In the algorithm we used characters for subscripts of an array. We did this without ever asking whether or not this was possible in Pascal. The result was an algorithm that was easy to follow. Now we have to discover whether or not it is possible to use characters as subscripts in Pascal. Indeed, it turns out that it is possible. Pascal allows any ordinal type to serve as the index of an array. Since **char** is an ordinal type, any subrange of **chars** can be used as indices of an array.

Notice that we defined constants FIRST and LAST as constants of type **char**. Furthermore, FIRST equals a space character, the smallest printing character in ASCII, and LAST equals the tilde, the largest printing character. Then we defined the type of the counting array, CountType, as indexed from FIRST to LAST. This program works in ASCII but could be modified to work with a different coding scheme.

Here's the code:

```
program HistoCount(input, output, CountFile);

{  Programmer: Karl Takayanagi                          }

{  This program counts the characters stored in a textfile  }
{  and displays the relative frequencies in a histogram.    }

const
   FIRST = ' ';      { In ASCII, a space is the smallest printing }
   LAST = '~';       { character and the tilde is the largest.    }

type
   CountType = array [FIRST .. LAST] of integer;

var
   CountFile : text;
   Count     : CountType;
   NumLines  : integer;
```

```
procedure Introduce;

{ This procedure displays an introduction for the user.  }

begin
   writeln('This program counts the characters stored in a file');
   writeln('and prints a histogram showing the relative frequency');
   writeln('of the characters in the file.')
end;



procedure Initialize(var CountFile : text;
                         var Count : CountType;
                         var NumLines : integer);

{ This procedure initializes the counting array and the counter for
{ the number of lines in the file, and prepares the file for input.

var
   Ch : char;

begin
   {  add statements to locate file }
   reset(CountFile);
   for Ch := FIRST to LAST do
      Count[Ch] := 0;
   NumLines := 0
end;



procedure CountChars(var CountFile : text;
                         var Count : CountType;
                         var NumLines : integer);

{ This procedure reads the file and counts the number of  }
{ characters as well as the number of lines.              }

var
   Ch : char;
```

```
begin
   while not eof(CountFile) do
      if eoln(CountFile)
         then
            begin
               readln(CountFile);
               NumLines := NumLines + 1
            end
         else
            begin
               read(CountFile, Ch);
               if (Ch >= FIRST) and (Ch <= LAST)
                  then
                     Count[Ch] := Count[Ch] + 1
            end
end;



procedure Histogram(Count : CountType; NumLines : integer);

{ This procedure displays the histogram.  }

const
   HISTLEN = 70;

var
   Longest, i : integer;
   factor : real;
   Ch : char;
```

```
      begin
         Longest := 0;
         for Ch := FIRST to LAST do
            if Count[Ch] > Longest
               then
                  Longest := Count[Ch];
         if Longest > HISTLEN
            then
               factor := HISTLEN / Longest
            else
               factor := 1;
         for Ch := FIRST to LAST do
            Count[Ch] := round(Count[Ch] * factor);
         writeln;
         writeln('The file consists of ', NumLines : 1, ' lines.');
         write('It contains characters according to the following');
         writeln(' distribution.');
         writeln;
         for Ch := FIRST to LAST do
            if Count[Ch] > 0
               then
                  begin
                     write(' ', Ch, ' ');
                     for i := 1 to Count[Ch] do
                        write('X');
                     writeln
                  end;
         writeln
      end;



   procedure Conclude;

   begin
      writeln('That''s the end of the program.')
   end;

begin  { Main Program }
   Introduce;
   Initialize(CountFile, Count, NumLines);
   CountChars(CountFile, Count, NumLines);
   Histogram(Count, NumLines);
   Conclude
end.
```

For reference, here's a part of the output produced when we run this program and supply the name of the source code file as the file to be counted:

```
This program counts the characters stored in a file
and prints a histogram showing the relative frequency
of the characters in the file.

The file consists of 125 lines.
It contains characters according to the following distribution.

      XXXXXXXXXXXXXXXXXXXXXXXXXXXXXXXXXXXXXXXXXXXXXXXXXXXXXXXXXXXXXXX
  '   XX
  (   XX
  )   XX
  ,   X
  .   X
  :   XX
  ;   XXX
  =   X
  A   X
  C   XXXX
  F   X
  I   X
        . . .
  a   XXXXX
  b   X
  c   XXX
  d   XXX
  e   XXXXXXXXXXXX
        . . .
```

```
That's the end of the program.
```

Notice that those characters that either did not occur at all or occurred with a small frequency are not shown in the histogram. You might have wanted to show all the characters, even those that have a very small number of occurrences. Also, since the space character will nearly always dominate, an alternate version of this program might show only characters other than space characters.

Another modification of the program might show the numbers stored in the counting array as well as printing the histogram—in which case we would have to be careful not to change that number as we did. We'll leave these modifications for the exercises.

12.7   Summary and Review

- In this chapter we learned that a file is a collection of data. An external file is a data structure that exists independently of the program itself. In Pascal files are sequential, not direct-access.

- Files in Pascal consist of components of the same type. The supplied file type `text` is equivalent to a `file of char`. The files `input` and `output` are textfiles; usually `input` refers to the keyboard and `output` refers to the screen.

- We discussed the `read` and `write` procedures in detail. `read` and `write` can be used with any kind of file, but the `readln` and `writeln` forms can only be used with textfiles.

- We learned about the Pascal function `eof`, which returns `true` when the end-of-file character is about to be read, and the Pascal procedures `reset` and `rewrite` which prepare a file for reading from and writing to, respectively.

- We learned the Pascal functions `pred`, `succ`, `ord` and `chr`. The functions `pred` and `succ` can be used with ordinal types such as `char`s or `integer`s, and return the previous or next item in the sequence, respectively. `ord` is used to find the numeric code for a particular character, and `chr` is used to find the character represented by a particular code.

- We used these concepts to develop a simple spelling checker that works on documents of any size and uses a dictionary of any size. The only limitation is on the size of each word and the number of unique words in the document.

- As an example of a non-textfile, we considered a `file of record`. We developed a simple program to process deposit and withdrawal transactions for a small bank.

- In the "Once Again" section, we developed a complete program that read a textfile, counted the number of occurrences of each character in the file and displayed a histogram showing the relative frequency of these occurrences.

- We learned how to use an array for counting and we learned that an array in Pascal can be indexed by any ordinal type.

12.8   New Terms Introduced

binary file A file containing data stored in binary form. Not a textfile and not editable. The object file created by a compiler is usually a binary file.

chr function The Pascal function that converts an `integer` to a `char`.

counting array An array that is first initialized to zero and then a particular cell incremented by one each time that the subscript of that cell is encountered.

direct-access file A file created in such a manner that the operating system can read or write to any location in the file rather than only being able to access it sequentially.

end-of-file marker A special character used to indicate the end of a file.

end-of-line indicator A special character used to indicate the end of a line in a textfile.

eof function A Boolean-valued function used to indicate when the end of a file has been reached.

file of records A file where the components of the file are records rather than `chars`, `integers`, `reals`, etc.

histogram A bar graph showing relative frequencies.

ord function The Pascal function that converts a `char` (or another ordinal expression) to an `integer`.

Pascal file The file referenced from within a Pascal program.

physical file The actual file existing on the computer.

pred function The Pascal function that returns the predecessor of an ordinal argument.

reset The Pascal procedure used to open a file for input.

rewrite The Pascal procedure used to open a file for output.

sequential file A method of storing data where it can only be accessed by starting with the first component and accessing each component in sequence. It is not possible to move backward in the file nor to add data to the file other than at the end.

succ function The Pascal function that returns the successor of an ordinal argument.

textfile A file in which each component is a character. Textfiles can be created and edited by an editor. The source code for any Pascal program is contained in a textfile.

12.9   Exercises

1. Using the following lists of words, trace the *ProcessWords* algorithm (page 412). You should then modify the lists in various ways and trace it each way to test the algorithm as thoroughly as you can.

	WordArray	*Dictionary*
1	DOG	CAT
2	FLEAS	DOG
3	HAS	FLEAS
4	MY	FLIES
5	ZEBRA	HAD
		HAVE
		MY
		YOUR

2. Write a test program for the **Upper** function. Your program should repeatedly prompt the user for a character, call the function and display the returned value.

3. Using the given algorithms for the *BinSearch* and *InsertInList* modules, write the code for those modules and finish writing the code for the spelling checker program. You must determine what modifications are necessary so that the program will run on your version of Pascal. Test the program using a simple dictionary file and a short document created with your text editor.

4. Consider a textfile consisting of lines in the following format:

Characters	Contents
1 – 24	Name (in last name first format)
25	Sex (M or F)
26 – 49	Address
50 – 61	City
62 – 63	State abbreviation
64 – 68	Zip code
69 – 76	Phone number

   Write a program that creates another textfile consisting of mailing labels for all the females in the file. Your program should use the module from the "Once Again" section of chapter 11 to format the name. Create a test file using your text editor, and run the program. You'll have to be careful in creating the file so that each substring on a line is the right length. If it's more convenient on your system, direct the output to a printer instead of a textfile.

5. Write a program that will tally the frequencies of words which occur in a given textfile. The program can be modeled after the spelling checker program in the chapter. You will have to maintain an array of records, each element containing a word from the document and an integer representing the frequency with which the corresponding word occurs. After reading through the file and tallying frequencies, create an output file consisting of the words and their frequencies.

6. Modify the program from exercise 5 so that the output file is sorted by frequency, with the most frequently used words occurring first. You will have to sort the array of records based on the values in the integer field.

7. Imagine that you have created a `Dictionary` file for the spelling checker, and that you have run the program on a certain document file. You have corrected all the misspellings in the document, and you would like to add the words in the `NotFound` file to those in the `Dictionary` file. Write a program that will merge the two files into a third. (The old `Dictionary` file can then be erased and the new file renamed.) Don't use any large arrays in your program; it should be able to merge files of any size.

8. Modify the `HistoCount` program from the "Once Again" section so that it neither counts nor shows spaces. If your environment does not use ASCII, be sure to make whatever other modifications are needed to ensure the program will run in your environment.

9. Modify the program from the previous exercise so that is shows the actual number of times each character occurred, including those counts that are too small to cause a bar in the histogram.

Chapter 13

Two-dimensional Arrays

Time goes from instant to instant
in little "quantum jumps,"
sitting still for a minute, then jumping.
— Douglas R. Hofstadter

13.1 Overview of the Chapter

This chapter will discuss multi-dimensional arrays; in particular, two-dimensional arrays. The Game of Life will be used as the problem to be solved. A complete program that plays the Game of Life will be developed.

13.2 Introduction

The Game of Life was invented by the English mathematician John Conway in 1970. Since its invention, a great deal of work has been done on the problem by many different people. We use the Game of Life in this chapter as an example of how multi-dimensional arrays can be used. As you recall from chapters 9 and 10, a one-dimensional array allows us to work with a number of things at once, simply by changing the subscript. To implement a program that plays the Game of Life, we will use an array that has two subscripts rather than one. As in chapters 11 and 12, this chapter will include the Pascal implementation of the algorithm rather than leave the implementation for a separate chapter.

13.3 Two-dimensional Arrays

In chapter 9 we learned to picture an array as a row of places in memory all with the same name but each with a different number indicating which element it was. A two-dimensional array is very similar except that rather than picturing the array as a single row or column, we picture it as a series of rows and columns with each row and each column numbered. Of course, this picture is in *our* minds and not necessarily in the computer's memory. How the computer stores the elements of a two-dimensional array may not be like this at all.

As an example, let's assume there are 8 rows and 12 columns. The rows would be numbered from 1 to 8 and the columns from 1 to 12. Figure 13.1 shows how we picture the array.

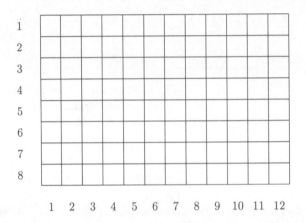

Figure 13.1 A Two-dimensional Array

Notation

A two-dimensional array is also called a matrix. Each element of a matrix is referred to by indicating the row and the column it's in. That is, the element in the third row and the fourth column is A_{34}. In general, to refer to the element in row i and column j, you would write A_{ij}. We could adopt this notation in this chapter for our two-dimensional arrays. However, as with one-dimensional arrays, we could also use the notation: A[3, 4] or A[i, j] rather than use subscripts. Since this is probably easier to read, and surely easier to type, we'll use the square-bracket notation.

It's important that you don't confuse A[3, 4] with A[4, 3]; remember that we always put the row number first and the column number second. A[3, 4] is the element in the third row, fourth column of the array; A[4, 3] is the element in the fourth row, third column.

We'll have several occasions where we need to access every element of a two-dimensional array and nested *for loops* will come in very handy.

For example, the following would initialize to 0 every element of a two-dimensional array with *NumRows* rows and *NumCols* columns:

```
loop for i going from 1 to NumRows
    loop for j going from 1 to NumCols
        store 0 in A[i, j]
```

Let's save further discussion of examples for our solution to the Game of Life.

13.4   The Game of Life

The Game of Life simulates the evolution of a society of simple organisms that inhabit a rectangular array of cells. The organisms live and die depending on the number of neighbors each organism has. If an organism has too many or too few neighbors, it dies from overcrowding or isolation. If an empty cell has just the right number of living organisms in its neighborhood, a new organism is born there. The set of organisms living at any instant is called a *generation*. The *neighborhood* of a cell consists of the eight cells next to it.

In figure 13.2, the cell in the center, marked with an asterisk, has the eight neighbors shown with numbers 1 through 8. You can see that a two-dimensional array is just the right thing to use to represent the world these organisms inhabit.

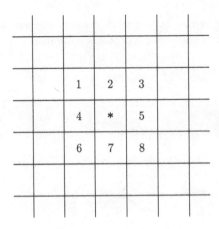

Figure 13.2 The Eight Neighbors of an Organism

Rules of Life

The evolution of one generation to the next is governed by three simple rules:

1. A new organism will be born on any empty cell that has exactly three organisms living in its neighborhood.

2. A living organism will die from isolation if there are zero or one organisms in its neighborhood, and it will die from overcrowding if there are four or more organisms in its neighborhood.

3. A living organism will survive to the next generation if there are two or three organisms in its neighborhood.

All births and deaths occur simultaneously so that organisms to be born in the next generation do not affect organisms in the current generation.

To guarantee that each cell has exactly eight neighbors—even those at the edge of the array—the world the organisms live on is assumed to be in the shape of a torus (a doughnut shape). This makes the array picture more complicated. To see how we can still use an array, imagine taking a rectangular array—a piece of paper will do—and "rolling it into a tube," joining the top edge with the bottom. Then—now pretend the paper is very rubbery—join the two ends of the tube to make a torus. Notice that when you do this, the bottom row of the array meets the top row and the far right hand column meets the far left hand column. Thus, the last row is considered to be adjacent to the first row, and the last column is considered to be adjacent to the first column; see figure 13.3.

If you were to carefully cut the torus pictured in figure 13.3 along the dark lines and flatten it out, you would get the array in figure 13.4.

The number of rows is 8, the number of columns is 12 and the name of the array is $World$. The eight neighbors of $World[3, 4]$ are $World[2, 3]$, $World[2, 4]$,

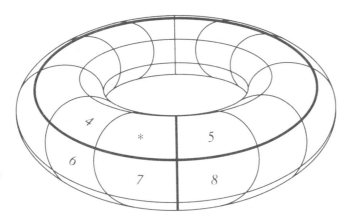

Figure 13.3 The World as a Torus

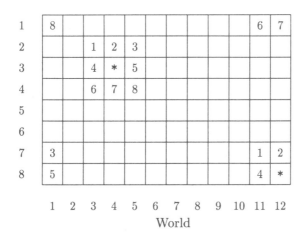

Figure 13.4 Two Organisms and Their Neighbors

World[2, 5], World[3, 3], World[3, 5], World[4, 3], World[4, 4] and World[4, 5].
The eight neighbors of World[8, 12] are World[7, 11], World[7, 12], World[7, 1],
World[8, 11], World[8, 1], World[1, 11], World[1, 12] and World[1, 1].

With these conventions out of the way, we are ready to state the problem
to be solved:

Write a computer program that plays the Game of Life.

13.5   Solve the Problem

A top-level solution for the problem would be something like: Explain the problem to the user. Allow the user to enter the initial data. Display the first generation. Compute and display the next generation, repeating this step until the user wants to quit. We can write the program so that the user can play repeated games until he gets tired.

The top-level solution suggests some modules that we will want: A module that displays an introduction, a module that gets the initial data, a module that displays the current generation, a module that calculates the next generation and, of course, the main program that controls the whole game.

Some decisions have to made concerning the display. If a cell contains a living organism, what should we display? A decent character might be an asterisk ('*'). How about cells where there is no life? We could display a blank space but then it's hard to watch things change. Let's agree to display a period ('.'), if a cell is empty.

The Module *Introduce*

The introduction should be straightforward. We'll leave it for you to write—and suggest that you wait until some decisions are made about how we'll write the program before you write it. It is normal for the introduction to the user to be the last module written even though it is the first module called by the program.

The Module *GetData*

Let's think about the module that gets the data from the user. What data has to be entered? We can allow the user to decide how large the array should be. A *display* and an *accept* for *NumRows* and *NumCols* will handle that. Since the size of the array must be determined in advance—at least in Pascal—we'll have to have a predetermined maximum for the number of rows and the number of columns. Let's suppose that these two values are *MaxRows* and *MaxCols*. The algorithm will have to insure that the number of rows accepted above is between 1 and *MaxRows*, and that the number of columns is between 1 and *MaxCols*. The real array will be *MaxRows* by *MaxCols* but the array the user sees will be *NumRows* by *NumCols*.

What else will the user have to enter? He will have to indicate the positions of the original organisms. How should this be done? There are several ways. We could have the user enter the row number and column number for each cell containing a living organism, entering some sort of sentinel when finished, we could write an interactive routine that allows the user to pick the initial places by moving the cursor around on the screen, or we could have the initial positions stored in a textfile.

While the second of these options might be the most fun, it would depend on the ability to move the cursor around on the screen and, although most

Pascals have the ability to do such things, it is not a standard feature of the language.

As you will see, the user will sometimes start with initial data that is interesting and sometimes not. Since it's rather tedious to enter a long list of row and column numbers only to create an uninteresting world, and since we'd like the user to be able to see the initial configuration again, possibly with minor changes, we'll store the initial array in a textfile. If you wish to, you can replace this routine with one of your own design.

This textfile should be created by the user before the program is run, and should consist of *MaxRows* lines of *MaxCols* characters each, where *MaxRows* and *MaxCols* determine the maximum size of the array. Notice that we are assuming the textfile contains *MaxRows* rows and *MaxCols* columns; the same textfile could be used for different sizes of *NumRows* and *NumCols*.

When you code this routine, if you use *NumRows* and *NumCols* in the loops to input the data, you'll have to put a **readln** after the inner loop to skip the elements on each line of text after you have read *NumCols* elements.

Anything else? Yes; we will want the user to be able to indicate whether the successive generations are to be displayed without interruption by the user or whether the user should be able to see each generation and press RETURN to get the computer to go on. In the former case we should let the user indicate how many generations are to be displayed. In the latter case we can let the user press RETURN or "Q" (for quit) before each generation is displayed.

So, we have to write *GetData* in a way that will return the following values: a number of rows for the array, *NumRows*; a number of columns, *NumCols*; the initial array of organisms, *World*; a flag, *Pause*, that indicates whether the successive generations should be displayed continuously or with a pause in between; and the number of generations to be displayed, *NumGens* (*NumGens* should be set to zero if *Pause* is true).

Since the routine is going to read the data from a text file, the file itself should be passed; as we mentioned in chapter 12, Pascal dictates that files be passed by reference. All this tells us that the first few lines of an algorithm for *GetData* would look like:

```
START OF GetData(NumRows, NumCols, World,
                                Pause, NumGens, InFile)
Passed by value: None
Passed by reference: NumRows, NumCols, World, Pause, NumGens, InFile
```

The steps in the algorithm should be easy to fill in. They just ask the user some questions and allow the user to enter some responses. Be cautioned that in order to implement the algorithm in Pascal you will have to include some non-standard code to handle the input from *InFile*.

The Module *DisplayGen*

We need a module that displays the current generation. (Displays it as a rectangle, of course. We're not going to try to draw it as a doughnut!)

Do we want to draw borders between the cells? You might, but then the time required to display each new generation is prohibitive, so let's just draw the organisms. So that we can keep track of where the organisms are and what generation we are looking at, let's display the generation number at the top, a row of column numbers at the bottom and a column of row numbers at the side.

Assuming that the user decided to have 8 rows and 12 columns, and entered the initial positions for the organisms in a text file read by *GetData*, the result of *DisplayGen* when sent the initial generation would look like figure 13.5.

```
Generation Number 1


    1   . . . . . . . . . . . .
    2   . . . ** . ** . . . .
    3   . . . ** . ** . . . .
    4   . . . . * . * . . . . .
    5   . . * . * . * . * . . .
    6   . . * . * . * . * . . .
    7   . . ** . . . ** . . .
    8   . . . . . . . . . . . .
                    1
            123456789012
```

Figure 13.5 The Initial World

We should be ready to write the algorithm. First, what are the parameters? We clearly need to send the *NumRows*, the *NumCols*, the generation number and the array *World* itself. Anything else? No, since the purpose of this routine is just to display the current generation, we don't want to have this routine decide how many generations to display or whether or not to pause. That should be done by the routine that calls *DisplayGen*.

So, the algorithm will look like:

START OF DisplayGen(World, NumRows,
NumCols, Generation)
Passed by value: World, NumRows, NumCols, Generation
Passed by reference: None.

display "Generation Number ", Generation
loop for Row going from 1 to NumRows
display Row
loop for Col going from 1 to NumCols
display World[Row, Col]
display a row of column numbers

END OF DisplayGen

The Main Program

Before we write the routine that calculates the next generation, let's look at the main routine and see how it will work. We will want to start by displaying the introduction and then getting the data from the user. The program should display the initial world, wait for the user to press RETURN, and then display successive generations until either the user says to quit or until it has displayed the number of generations indicated by the user. Then the program should ask the user if he wants to start with another initial configuration file or quit, and take the appropriate action.

An algorithm for the main program appears on the next page.

START OF The Game of Life

call Introduce
loop
    call GetData(NumRows, NumCols, World, NumGens, Pause)
    store 1 in Generation
    call DisplayGen(World, NumRows, NumCols, Generation)
    call NextGen(...)
    wait for the user to press RETURN
    loop
        add 1 to Generation
        call DisplayGen(World, NumRows, NumCols, Generation)
        call NextGen(...)
        if Pause
            then wait for user to press 'Q' or RETURN
        until user says to quit or Generation = NumGens
    display "Do you want to play the game again?"
    accept Answer
    until Answer is no

END OF The Game of Life

Notice that we still have to think about what will be sent to NextGen.

The Module NextGen

As you can see, the main program calls NextGen and we have to finish it before
we're done. There are some decisions that have to be made. First, how about
parameters? What do we need to send to this routine? Clearly we have to
send NumRows, NumCols and the current World. Does the routine return
anything? Sure, it has to return the next generation. How do we handle this?
We cannot use a function because functions only return simple types, not arrays.
Thus, we have to use a procedure and must pass the array by reference. Does
this mean we have to pass two arrays, one for the current generation and one
for the next generation? We could, but we don't really need to. After this
routine is finished, we don't need the current generation any longer; indeed the
next generation becomes the current generation. We can just have the routine
change the current generation into the next generation.

Will the routine need any local variables? Sure; it will need local variables
to loop through the rows and columns. But we will also need an array to hold
the next generation while we are calculating it. This can be handled in either of
two ways. We could have a local variable for the next generation and after it's
calculated, replace the original world with the elements of this one; or, we could
start by moving the original world into the local array and then calculating the

new elements and putting them right into the original array. We'll do it the latter way but you can do it the other way if you like.

Are there any preconditions? Only that each position in the array is filled with either an asterisk (living organism) or a period (empty cell).

Okay, then what does this routine do? It searches through the entire array and decides whether each position in the next generation should be empty or contain a living organism. This can be done with a pair of nested *loop fors*. Before we start, the original array is stored in the local array.

Let's write the algorithm:

```
START OF NextGen(World, NumRows, NumCols)
Passed by value: NumRows, NumCols
Passed by reference: World


store World in OldWorld
loop for Row going from 1 to NumRows
    loop for Col going from 1 to NumCols
        if OldWorld[Row, Col] = '*'
            then
                if the number of neighbors of OldWorld[Row, Col] equals 2 or 3
                    then
                        store '*' in World[Row, Col]
                    else
                        store '.' in World[Row, Col]
            else
                if the number of neighbors of OldWorld[Row, Col] equals 3
                    then
                        store '*' in World[Row, Col]
                    else
                        store '.' in World[Row, Col]


END OF NextGen
```

We wrote the above routine in a straightforward way, following the Rules of The Game of Life explicitly. You probably noticed that the algorithm stores an asterisk in World[Row, Col] if the number of neighbors is three—whether the current contents is an asterisk or not. Similarly, the only other time an asterisk is put into World[Row, Col] is when the number of neighbors is two and there is a living organism there already. You might want to rewrite the algorithm using this approach because it might be faster. We'll leave that up to you.

The Function *NumNeighbors*

Notice that we have yet another routine to write. We need to be able to calculate the number of living neighbors of any cell. That job can be done by a function called, say, *NumNeighbors*. This function is expected to return the number of living organisms in the neighborhood of the cell being looked at.

This routine is going to get called many times and each time it has to count the number of neighbors of a cell by looking at at least eight other cells. Consequently, this routine should be as fast as possible for otherwise the entire game may play very slowly.

There are several approaches to writing this function and you might want to write your own algorithm before looking at ours. You may very well find a quicker way to do it than we did.

It is clear that the function will have to have a copy of the old world. Also it will need to know the row number and the column number of the cell in question—*Row* and *Col*. None of these values are going to change so we can pass them by value as we normally do to a function.

One way to do the job would be to initialize a counter, say *Counter*, to zero, and have two nested *loop fors*, one that starts at *Row*−1 and stops at *Row*+1, and another that starts at *Col*−1 and stops at *Col*+1. Inside the body of the nested loops we would look at each of the *nine* elements these *loop fors* address. If the element at that location is alive (an asterisk) then add 1 to the counter. The cell *OldWorld[Row, Col]* would get counted too, so we'll have to subtract 1 if that cell was alive. As an algorithm, this would be:

```
store 0 in Counter
loop for i going from Row−1 to Row+1
    loop for j going from Col−1 to Col+1
        if OldWorld[i, j] = '*'
            then
                add 1 to Counter
if OldWorld[Row, Col] = '*'
    then
        subtract 1 from Counter
return Counter
```

That would be all there is to it except for the complication of what happens on the edges. Remember that the neighbors of a cell on the right edge of the array are cells on the left edge, and the neighbors of the cells on the top edge are on the bottom. Our function will have to take this into account. What we have works fine for all the cell locations except those on the edges. If *Row* equals 1, *Row*−1 equals 0 and there are no elements in row zero; in fact, there is no row zero at all.

We can write the function so that it handles the edges of *World* as special cases, using *if* ... *then* ... *elses* and maybe *div* and *mod*. The problem with this approach is that this routine is the bottleneck of *NextGen*; the function is called for every single cell in *World*. If it has to spend a lot of time testing for special cases every time it is called, it will run very slowly.

How can we handle the problem of *Row*−1 being 0 when there is no row zero, without testing for it every time?

That is, there is no row zero unless we make one and there are no elements there unless we put some there! That's the key to our solution to the problem. Rather than include a complicated decision to be made again and again on all the elements in the array, we'll add some rows and columns to the array *once*. We'll add an extra row at the top of the array and another row at the bottom. We'll add an extra column on the left side and one on the right side of the array. Then we'll put a copy of row number 1 in row number *NumRows*+1, we'll put a copy of row number *NumRows* in row number 0—yes, the new top row will be numbered 0—we'll put a copy of column number 1 in column number *NumCols*+1, and we'll put a copy of column *NumCols* in our new column 0.

We'll also have to fix up the new corners: What will *World*[0, 0] have to be? Take a look back at figures 13.3 and 13.4 and notice that the cell "above and to the left" of cell *World*[1, 1] is cell *World*[*NumRows*, *NumCols*]. What will the other three corners contain? You figure it out before continuing.

A Modified Algorithm for *NextGen*

We will not do all this "fixing" at the beginning of *NumNeighbors* each time, that would be too slow; instead we'll do it one time only at the beginning of the module *NextGen*.

All this will be easier to follow if we state it as an algorithm. On the next page we show an algorithm for *NextGen* with the necessary modifications.

START OF NextGen(World, NumRows, NumCols)
Passed by value: NumRows, NumCols
Passed by reference: World

store World in OldWorld
loop for Row going from 1 to NumRows
    store OldWorld[Row, 1] in OldWorld[Row, NumCols + 1]
    store OldWorld[Row, NumCols] in OldWorld[Row, 0]
loop for Col going from 1 to NumCols
    store OldWorld[NumRows, Col] in OldWorld[0, Col]
    store OldWorld[1, Col] in OldWorld[NumRows + 1, Col]
store OldWorld[NumRows, NumCols] in OldWorld[0, 0]
store OldWorld[1, 0] in OldWorld[NumRows + 1, 0]
store OldWorld[0, 1] in OldWorld[0, NumCols + 1]
store OldWorld[1, 1] in OldWorld[NumRows + 1, NumCols + 1]
loop for Row going from 1 to NumRows
    loop for Col going from 1 to NumCols
        if OldWorld[Row, Col] = '*'
            then
                if the number of neighbors of OldWorld[Row, Col] equals 2 or 3
                    then
                        store '*' in World[Row, Col]
                    else
                        store '.' in World[Row, Col]
            else
                if the number of neighbors of OldWorld[Row, Col] equals 3
                    then
                        store '*' in World[Row, Col]
                    else
                        store '.' in World[Row, Col]

END OF NextGen

We'll have to remember that the array we are using for a "World" really has
an extra row at the top and bottom and an extra column on both sides. When
we define the new type, we'll have to be careful to define the type to contain
these extra rows and columns. And, when we check the user's data entered in
the module *GetData*, we'll have to make sure the *NumRows* and *NumCols* are
within the proper limits. These are implementation details.

   If you add the customary words to the trial algorithm we wrote earlier for
NumNeighbors, it will now do what we want. You should finish it and finish
writing *GetData* before going on.

13.6   Implementation in Pascal

You should have a completed algorithm for the entire Game of Life and should be ready now to turn it into code. We'll leave most of that for you and will only mention the couple of new things about Pascal that you need to know.

First, we have to know how to define a two-dimensional array. As we did for one-dimensional arrays, we'll define a named type. What should we call the new type? Several names are possible but let's choose `Matrix`. A matrix is a rectangular array of things used by mathematicians and that name will remind us that our "`Worlds`" are two-dimensional. The syntax is very similar to that for a one-dimensional array. As before, we'll use named constants for the maximum numbers of rows and columns:

```
const
   MAXROWS = 21;
   MAXCOLS = 75;
type
   Matrix = array [0 .. MAXROWS, 0 .. MAXCOLS] of char;
var
   World : Matrix;
```

Notice that the dimensions start at 0 this time and that the component type is `char`. To refer to an element of the array, one simply uses two subscripts; i.e., the element in the third row and fourth column of `World` would be `World[3, 4]`.

We mentioned earlier that a two-dimensional array is an array of arrays. The above type definition is, in fact, an abbreviation of:

```
type
   Matrix = array [0 .. MAXROWS] of array [0 .. MAXCOLS] of char;
```

The element in the third row, fourth column would then be referred to as `World[3][4]`. The two-dimensional array notation seems easier to use and we'll stick with it from now on.

These choices of 21 and 75 were made to allow a `World` size that will allow the array to always fit on a standard 24 by 80 screen and will leave some room for numbering the rows and columns. We agreed to let the user choose the actual size at run-time. This will permit us to test it on smaller numbers but still run it with larger values after it's tested.

Moving an Entire Array

There are two places in the program where you want to move an entire array into another. Once in the main program and once again in the `NextGen` procedure. How can this be done in Pascal? Of course you could use a pair of nested for loops, but it is easier than that. If two arrays are of the same type, one can

be assigned to the other as a whole. For example, if in `NextGen`, you have
the parameter `World` and the local variable `OldWorld` and want to move all of
`World` into `OldWorld`, you can do it with the single assignment statement:

```
OldWorld := World
```

Notice that this works only if both arrays are of the same type. Indeed, any
time two things are declared to be of the same type—except for file types—they
can be assigned to one another.

Using Variable Parameters and/or Local/Global Variables

We are going to let you write the majority of the code, but for a reason that
will become clear in a moment, here is the code for the function `NumNeighbors`:

```
function NumNeighbors(Row, Col : integer;
                      var OldWorld : Matrix) : integer;
var
   i, j, Counter : integer;

begin
   Counter := 0;
   for i := Row - 1 to Row + 1 do
      for j := Col - 1 to Col + 1 do
         if OldWorld[i, j] = '*'
            then Counter := Counter + 1;
   if OldWorld[Row,Col] = '*'
      then Counter := Counter - 1;
   NumNeighbors := Counter
end;
```

Do you see anything funny in the way we wrote this function? Earlier when
we wrote the algorithm, we said that we would only need to send a copy of the
OldWorld to *NumNeighbors*. Yet, here we are treating `OldWorld` as a variable
parameter. Why? We are not changing `OldWorld` inside the routine and we are
not planning to send it back changed, so why pass it by reference?

In chapter 12 (page 406), we discussed the reasons for this departure from
the normal way of doing things. If we do send the array by value, the entire 22
times 76 elements of the array will have to be copied into another array each
time before the function can start counting. If we pass the array by reference,
only the address of the array in memory needs to be passed. Since this function
is called once for each cell in the `World`, this will amount to a significant increase
of speed.

That's a good trick to remember. Sometimes you should pass an array by
reference even when you don't plan to change anything in the array. This will
speed up your program and save on memory as well since you won't be storing
the array in two places.

The same savings can be accomplished by not passing the array at all. If you put `NumNeighbors` inside `NextGen`, you could simply treat it as a local/global variable inside `NumNeighbors`. (This is one of the valid exceptions to the Golden Rule of how to use global variables.) For the same reason, you might also want to pass the `World` to `DisplayGen` by reference rather than by value.

Pascal implementation note: If your system makes it easy, you might want to include a "clear screen" command at the beginning of the procedure that displays the next generation in order to erase the previous generation. On many systems, a call to the Standard Pascal supplied procedure `page` will clear the screen. The call would be: `page(output)`. This does not work on all Pascal compilers but when it doesn't, another procedure is usually supplied that will clear the screen.

13.7 Two-dimensional Arrays—Once Again

As we have done in this section in preceding chapters, we retrace the main points of the chapter with another example.

Define the Problem

The problem we want to solve can be thought of as a program that allows a user to practice building crossword puzzles, or, perhaps, as a program that allows a user to practice playing the game of Scrabble. We will draw a two-dimensional array on the screen and allow the user to fill it with words, either across or down, continuing until the user decides to quit. Since we'll not actually be displaying the entire array—we'll have to declare it to be quite large, probably larger than the user indicates—we'll refer to the array on the screen as a *board*. Every word the user attempts to add must fit on the board; i.e., it cannot be too long to fit where the user wants to put it and it must match any existing letters already on the board. The program will tell the user when words don't fit. So that a user can continue to add words to an existing board, we'll also want to allow the user to store and/or retrieve the current board in a file.

Solve the Problem

A solution to this problem is easy if we think of it in a modular manner:

> Explain the program to the user. Ask the user if he wants to retrieve a previous board, and if so, get it from the file. Allow the user to enter words to the board until he wants to stop, in each case telling the user when a word won't fit. When the user want to stop, ask if the current board should be stored in a file, following the user's wishes as indicated.

Turn the Solution into an Algorithm

The above solution suggests a top-level algorithm something like:

```
display an introduction
initialize the board either with blanks or with an board from a file
display the current board
loop
    get a word, the place for it to be put on the board, and
    its direction (across or down) from the user
    if the word fits on the board
        then
            add the word to the board
        else
            tell the user the word won't fit
    display the current board
    ask the user if another word is to be entered
    until the user wants to quit
save the board if the user wants to
display a concluding message
```

In addition to the customary modules *Introduce* and *Conclude*, this algorithm suggests several lower-level modules:

- *Initialize*: a routine that asks the user if the board should be read from an existing file or a new board started,

- *GetWord*: a procedure that allows the user to enter a new word, a place for it on the board, and an indication of whether it should go across or down,

- *Fits*: a Boolean-valued function that indicates whether or not a given word fits on a board,

- *AddWord*: a routine that adds a given word to the board,

- *DisplayBoard*: a procedure that displays the current board,

- *SaveBoard*: a procedure that writes the current board to a file if the user wants to save it.

Parameters

In each case the normal questions regarding parameters and how they should be passed have to be asked and answered. The following algorithms reflect our answers to these questions.

START OF *Initialize*(*Board, BoardFile*)
Passed by value: none
Passed by reference: Board, BoardFile

ask the user if an old board should be retrieved from a file
if the user says yes
    then
        prepare the file for input
        read the Board dimensions from the file
        read the Board from the file
    else
        ask the user the size of the Board
        initialize the Board to all blanks

END OF *Initialize*

Notice that we are treating the board as an abstract data type; it somehow consists of the array and the size of the board. Exactly how is not important at this point; we'll worry about the implementation details later.

The next module is *GetWord:*

START OF *GetWord*(*Word, Position, Direction*)
Passed by value: none
Passed by reference: Word, Position, Direction

ask the user for a word, making sure it contains only letters
ask the user for the position on the board where the word is to be placed
ask the user whether it should go across or down

END OF *GetWord*

In this algorithm we are making sure that the user enters a "real" word—that is, we want to make sure that the user enters only letters—and we are going to make sure that the user indicates whether the word is to go across or down. However, we are not planning to make sure that the word fits on the board at this point. We have decided to leave that job for another routine, *Fits*. This is not the only way the job could get done, just the way we decided to do it. If you prefer another way, go ahead and do it your way.

Here's *Fits*:

START OF *Fits*(*Word*, *Position*, *Direction*, *Board*)
Postcondition: *This function returns true if the word fits on the*
board at the indicated position going in the indicated direction
and returns false if it doesn't.

if Direction is Across and the word length > Board.Columns − Column + 1
or Direction is Down and the length > Board.Rows − Row + 1
then
return false
else
if any letters in the word fail to match the corresponding
non-blank letters on the board
then
return false
else
return true

END OF *Fits*

Notice that we are treating *Board.Rows* and *Board.Columns* as the dimensions
of the board, as well as treating *Row* and *Column* as the two components of
the *Position*. The details will have to be worked out when we write the code.
If the algorithm is understandable, that's all we need at this point. Of course,
if the algorithm is not understandable, we must work on it until it is. You'll
have to be the judge of whether or not the algorithm is understandable.

The next module is *AddWord*:

START OF *AddWord*(*Word*, *Position*, *Direction*, *Board*)
Passed by value: *Word*, *Position*, *Direction*
Passed by reference: *Board*
Precondition: *The Word is known to fit on the Board*
Postcondition: *The Word is added to the Board*

if Direction is Across
then
loop for i going from 1 to length of Word
store Word[i] in Board[Row, Column + i − 1]
else
loop for i going from 1 to length of Word
store Word[i] in Board[Row + i − 1, Column]

END OF *AddWord*

Notice how the column subscript changes when the word goes across and the row subscript changes when it goes down. When we wrote this algorithm, we had to draw a picture on a piece of paper to figure out which rows and columns on the board corresponded to the elements of the word array. The subscripts in the algorithm didn't just occur to us, we had to figure them out. There's nothing wrong with drawing a few pictures until you figure out the formula.

Next comes *DisplayBoard*:

```
START OF DisplayBoard(Board)
Passed by value: Board
Passed by reference: none

loop for i going from 1 to Board.Rows
    loop for j going from 1 to Board.Columns
        display Board[i, j]

END OF DisplayBoard
```

We'll leave it for the coding step to "pretty-up" the display.

Finally, here's *SaveBoard*:

```
START OF SaveBoard(Board, BoardFile)
Passed by value: Board
Passed by reference: BoardFile

ask the user if the current board should be saved in a file
if the user says yes
    then
        prepare the file for output
        write the Board to the file

END OF SaveBoard
```

Code the Algorithm

We are leaving out some of the detail in these "Once Again" sections, so we'll just present the code with very little discussion. Nevertheless, you should notice that the two types—WordType and BoardType—have been declared as records. WordType contains a one-dimensional array of characters and the length of the word, which is how we implemented a string in chapter 11. BoardType contains the number of rows and columns in the board as well as the array itself. These two numbers are needed so that the board can be read from and written to a file. Rather than define a new type to hold the position on the board where the word is to start, we've just decided to pass two integers.

Look carefully at the code in `GetWord`. To accomplish what we wanted and avoid a run-time error if the user enters non-letters, fails to enter any letters at all, or enters more letters than will fit in the word array, we had to use the flag `Done` and test for end-of-line. The `readln` after the loop gets past the end-of-line character. Do you think you can write this code without using a flag?

Notice that whenever we pass `Board` to a subroutine, we pass it by reference, even when it is not changed in that routine (see `DisplayBoard` and `SaveBoard`). This is another example of passing a large structure by reference to save time and space. As we've mentioned, passing an array by reference even when it's not getting changed can cause a significant increase in speed as well as a significant savings in storage requirements. We do not pass `Word` by reference except when it's getting changed; it isn't large enough to cause a significant savings.

Once again, this program will not run without change on any compiler we know of. We have made no provision for the user to indicate which physical file he wishes to store (or retrieve) the board in (or from). Every compiler does this differently; you will need to add the necessary code so that the program will locate the appropriate file on your computer.

Here's the code:

```
program CrossWord(input, output, BoardFile);

{  Programmer: Gerald DeGuzman II                                   }

{  This program allows a user to practice adding words to a         }
{  two-dimensional array, much like words are added to a            }
{  crossword puzzle.                                                }

const
   MAXROWS = 20;
   MAXCOLUMNS = 50;
   MAXLEN = 50;


type
   BoardType = record
         Rows, Columns : integer;
         Screen : array [1 .. MAXROWS, 1 .. MAXCOLUMNS] of char
      end;
   WordType = record
         Length : integer;
         Str    : packed array [1 .. MAXLEN] of char
      end;
```

```
var
   BoardFile    : text;
   Board        : BoardType;
   Word         : WordType;
   Again        : char;
   Row, Column  : integer;
   Direction    : char;

   procedure Initialize(var Board : BoardType; var BoardFile : text);

   {  This procedure either gets an existing board and its  }
   {  dimensions from a file or gets the dimensions from     }
   {  the user and initializes the board to all blanks.      }

   var
      Row, Column : integer;
      Answer      : char;

   begin
      write('Do you want to read an existing file for a board?  ');
      readln(Answer);
      while not (Answer in ['Y', 'y', 'N', 'n']) do
         begin
            write('Invalid answer, answer ''Y'' or ''N'': ');
            readln(Answer)
         end;
      if Answer in ['Y', 'y']
         then
            begin
              reset(BoardFile);
              readln(BoardFile, Board.Rows, Board.Columns);
              for Row := 1 to Board.Rows do
                begin
                  for Column := 1 to Board.Columns do
                    read(BoardFile, Board.Screen[Row, Column]);
                  readln(BoardFile)
                end
            end
         else
```

```
          begin
            write('How many rows do you want the board to have?: ');
            readln(Board.Rows);
            while (Board.Rows < 1) or (Board.Rows > MAXROWS) do
              begin
                write('Invalid answer, try again: ');
                readln(Board.Rows)
              end;
            write('How many columns do you want the board to have?: ');
            readln(Board.Columns);
            while (Board.Columns < 1) or (Board.Columns > MAXCOLUMNS) do
              begin
                write('Invalid answer, try again: ');
                readln(Board.Columns)
              end;
            for Row := 1 to Board.Rows do
              for Column := 1 to Board.Columns do
                Board.Screen[Row, Column] := ' '
          end
end;  { End of Initialize }



procedure GetWord(var Word : WordType;
          var Row, Column : integer;
            var Direction : char);

{ The procedure allows the user to enter a word (any sequence of     }
{ letters), the row and column where the word is to start, and       }
{ the direction (across or down) it is supposed to go on the screen. }

var
    Ch   : char;
    Done : Boolean;
```

```
begin
  with Word do
    begin
      write('Enter the word: ');
      Length := 0;
      Done := false;
      while not Done and not eoln do
        begin
          read(Ch);
          if (Ch in ['A' .. 'Z', 'a' .. 'z']) and (Length < MAXLEN)
            then
              begin
                Length := Length + 1;
                if Ch in ['A' .. 'Z']
                  then
                    Str[Length] := Ch
                  else
                    Str[Length] := chr(ord(Ch) + ord('A') - ord('a'))
              end
            else
              Done := true
        end;
      readln
    end;
  writeln;
  write('Enter the row and column (separated by a space): ');
  readln(Row, Column);
  writeln;
  write('Enter the direction (''A''cross or ''D''own): ');
  readln(Direction);
  while not (Direction in ['A', 'a', 'D', 'd']) do
    begin
      write('Invalid response, try again: ');
      readln(Direction)
    end;
  writeln
end;  { End of GetWord }
```

```
function Fits(Word : WordType;
        Row, Column : integer;
            Direction : char;
            var Board : BoardType) : Boolean;

{  This function determines whether or not the word fits on the board.

var
  i : integer;

begin
  with Board do
    if (Direction in ['A', 'a']) and (Word.Length > Columns - Column + 1)
        or (Direction in ['D', 'd']) and (Word.Length > Rows - Row + 1)
      then
        Fits := false
      else
        begin
          Fits := true;
          if Direction in ['A', 'a']
            then
              begin
                for i := 1 to Word.Length do
                  if (Word.Str[i] <> Screen[Row, Column + i - 1])
                        and (Screen[Row, Column + i - 1] <> ' ')
                      then
                        Fits := false
              end
            else
              begin
                for i := 1 to Word.Length do
                  if (Word.Str[i] <> Screen[Row + i - 1, Column])
                        and (Screen[Row + i - 1, Column] <> ' ')
                      then
                        Fits := false
              end
        end
end;  { End of Fits }
```

```
    procedure AddWord(Word : WordType;
            Row, Column : integer;
                Direction : char;
                var Board : BoardType);

    {  This procedure adds a word to the board.  A precondition  }
    {  for the procedure is that the word fits.                  }

    var
      i : integer;

    begin
      with Board do
        if Direction in ['A', 'a']
          then
            for i := 1 to Word.Length do
              Screen[Row, Column + i - 1] := Word.Str[i]
          else
            for i := 1 to Word.Length do
              Screen[Row + i - 1, Column] := Word.Str[i]
    end;  { End of AddWord }
```

```
procedure DisplayBoard(var Board : BoardType);

{ This procedure displays the board along with row }
{ and column numbers.                              }

var
  i, j : integer;

begin
  with Board do
    begin
      write(' ' : 7, '--');
      for i := 1 to Columns do
        write('-');
      writeln('--');
      for i := 1 to Rows do
        begin
          write(i : 5, ' | ');
          for j := 1 to Columns do
            write(Screen[i, j]);
          writeln(' |')
        end;
      write(' ' : 7, '--');
      for i := 1 to Columns do
        write('-');
      writeln('--');
      write(' ' : 9);
      for i := 1 to Board.Columns div 10 do
        write(i : 10);
      writeln;
      write(' ' : 9);
      for i := 1 to Board.Columns do
        write(i mod 10 : 1);
      writeln
    end
end;  { End of DisplayBoard }
```

```pascal
procedure SaveBoard(var Board : BoardType; var BoardFile : text);

  { This procedures writes the board to a file if the user  }
  { wants to save it.                                        }

  var
    Row, Column : integer;
    Answer      : char;

  begin
    write('Do you want to write the board to a file?  ');
    readln(Answer);
    while not (Answer in ['Y', 'y', 'N', 'n']) do
      begin
        write('Invalid answer, answer ''Y'' or ''N'': ');
        readln(Answer)
      end;
    if Answer in ['Y', 'y']
      then
        begin
          rewrite(BoardFile);
          writeln(BoardFile, Board.Rows, ' ', Board.Columns);
          for Row := 1 to Board.Rows do
            begin
              for Column := 1 to Board.Columns do
                write(BoardFile, Board.Screen[Row, Column]);
              writeln(BoardFile)
            end
        end
  end;  { End of SaveBoard }
```

```
begin  {  Main Program  }
   writeln('Crossword Program starts.');
   Initialize(Board, BoardFile);
   DisplayBoard(Board);
   repeat
      GetWord(Word, Row, Column, Direction);
      if Fits(Word, Row, Column, Direction, Board)
         then
            AddWord(Word, Row, Column, Direction, Board)
         else
            writeln('That word doesn''t fit.');
      DisplayBoard(Board);
      writeln;
      write('Add another word (Y/N)?: ');
      readln(Again)
      until Again in ['N', 'n'];
   SaveBoard(Board, BoardFile);
   writeln('Goodbye.')
end.
```

We had a little fun with DisplayBoard. We wanted to display a border
around the board and wanted some indication of the row number and the column number to be displayed so we could see where a particular word might
fit. There are lots of ways to make the output better but you might learn some
tricks if you look at what we did in DisplayBoard.

Here's an example of what DisplayBoard would display:

```
       -------------------------
    1  |                F        |
    2  |    PASCAL  D   UNTIL    |
    3  |    R     WRITELN        |
    4  | GLOBAL    S   C         |
    5  |    C      P   T         |
    6  |    ERROR    LOOPING     |
    7  |    D   E   A   O        |
    8  |    U    ARRAY   N       |
    9  |    R    D               |
   10  |    E                    |
       -------------------------
                 1         2
        12345678901234567 8901
```

The "Dangling Else" Problem, Again

We mentioned the "dangling else problem" in chapter 8. You might have noticed
that there was a potential for this problem to occur in the program. Here is a
part of the code from Fits.

```
if Direction in ['A', 'a']
  then
    begin
      for i := 1 to Word.Length do
        if (Word.Str[i] <> Screen[Row, Column + i - 1])
              and (Screen[Row, Column + i - 1] <> ' ')
          then
            Fits := false
    end
  else
    begin
      for i := 1 to Word.Length do
        if (Word.Str[i] <> Screen[Row + i - 1, Column])
              and (Screen[Row + i - 1, Column] <> ' ')
          then
            Fits := false
    end
```

The statements in the **then** and **else** parts of this ⟨*if statement*⟩ are only
single ⟨*for statement*⟩s and, therefore, the ⟨*compound statement*⟩s are not really
necessary. That's correct. However, if you then just go ahead and remove the
begin and **end**, and adjust the indentation, you'll have:

```
if Direction in ['A', 'a']
  then
    for i := 1 to Word.Length do
      if (Word.Str[i] <> Screen[Row, Column + i - 1])
            and (Screen[Row, Column + i - 1] <> ' ')
        then
          Fits := false
  else
    for i := 1 to Word.Length do
      if (Word.Str[i] <> Screen[Row + i - 1, Column])
            and (Screen[Row + i - 1, Column] <> ' ')
        then
          Fits := false
```

Which looks just fine and is valid syntax as far as the grouping of the statements,
but *it is not correct!* What you have is not the same as the earlier ⟨*if statement*⟩.

The `else` is a dangling else. Even though you've indented it to indicate what you mean, the Pascal compiler will interpret what you have typed as meaning:

```
if Direction in ['A', 'a']
  then
    for i := 1 to Word.Length do
      if (Word.Str[i] <> Screen[Row, Column + i - 1])
            and (Screen[Row, Column + i - 1] <> ' ')
        then
          Fits := false
        else
          for i := 1 to Word.Length do
            if (Word.Str[i] <> Screen[Row + i - 1, Column])
                  and (Screen[Row + i - 1, Column] <> ' ')
              then
                Fits := false
```

instead. This is completely different from what you intended; you wanted the second ⟨*for statement*⟩ executed when `Direction` is not in `['A', 'a']`. Instead the ⟨*for statement*⟩ is executed in the `else` part of the inner ⟨*if statement*⟩, inside the first ⟨*for statement*⟩—a drastically different meaning.

Remember what we said in chapter 8: whenever an `else` can validly be paired with more than one `then`, it will always be paired with the nearest one.

In this case, there's a good chance the compiler would complain about what you've typed. If the `else` is paired with the inner `then`, the second ⟨*for statement*⟩ will be inside the first ⟨*for statement*⟩. Since we used the same index, `i`, for both ⟨*for statement*⟩s, the `i` will be changed in the inner loop. This is not allowed and an error should be reported. You should be aware, however, that not all compilers will catch this.

Once again, watch out for inadvertent dangling elses. They won't all be caught by the compiler and they can be very hard to find when they aren't.

13.8   Summary and Review

- In this chapter we learned about a two-dimensional counterpart to the one-dimensional arrays of chapters 9 and 10. We learned how to visualize them and how to use them to simulate the Game of Life.

- We learned the rules for the Game of Life and we developed a collection of algorithms for its simulation. We treated the world the organisms live on as a torus and were forced to do some extra work to make an array act like a torus. We mentioned a couple of ways to handle the torus but decided on a scheme that added two extra rows and two extra columns to the array. Since the function that counted the number of neighbors of a cell gets called a large number of times, it was important to make this function as efficient as possible and we spent some effort on making `NumNeighbors` as fast as we could.

- We learned how to define and work with two-dimensional arrays in Pascal. In particular, we saw that we could define an array to start numbering the subscripts at zero rather than at one.

- We solved a crossword puzzle-like problem in the "Once Again" section that worked with a two-dimensional array of intersecting words.

- We saw a place where an inadvertant dangling else could occur.

- We learned an exception to the rules learned earlier about passing things by value versus passing them by reference; it might be wise to pass arrays by reference rather than by value even when they are not being modified by the routine being called. We also mentioned that there are exceptions to the rule on how to use global variables.

13.9 New Terms Introduced

The Game of Life A game that simulates the evolution of a society of organisms that inhabit a rectangular array of cells.

local/global variable A variable that is local to a routine but is treated as a global variable by the subroutines within that routine.

matrix A rectangular array. In mathematics, usually of numbers.

page procedure The Pascal procedure that causes a form-feed to be sent to a printer, or a "clear screen" command to the screen. (Not always implemented.)

torus A mathematician's name for a doughnut shape.

two-dimensional array An array with rows and columns, whose components are arrays.

13.10   Exercises

1. Write the code for the module `GetData`. You should decide what range of numbers is reasonable for each of the values being entered, and write the code so that these limits are not exceeded. Write a test program for the module that simply calls the routine and displays the initial values and the array on the screen. Remember to create the textfile with your text editor before running the test program.

2. Replace the *GetData* routine with one that allows the user to enter the positions of the initial organisms interactively. Suggestion: display the array as dots and allow the user to enter a row and column number for a cell and either an asterisk or a dot (to remove an asterisk entered in error). Redisplay the array and prompt the user again. Continue to enter and display initial positions until the user indicates that enough organisms have been entered. Test your routine by writing a test program like that in the previous exercise.

3. Write the code for the module `DisplayGen`. You may want to refine the algorithm a bit more. Notice in figure 13.5 how the row of column numbers is displayed at the bottom. How can this be done in Pascal? Expand on the test program from the first exercise so that it calls `DisplayGen`.

4. Write the code for the `NextGen` module. You can write it according to the given algorithm, or modify the algorithm to be more efficient if you can think of how to do it. Modify the test program from the previous exercise so that it calls `DisplayGen`, then calls `NextGen`, and `DisplayGen` again. You will have to include the code for the function `NumNeighbors` given in the chapter. You should create a textfile which has a variety of "clusters" of organisms in it in different combinations, and calculate the next generation with pencil and paper before running the test program. Make sure that the routine handles the edges of the "World" properly.

5. Finish coding the program `GameOfLife` by coding the `Introduce` module and the main part of the program. At this point the coding should be straightforward, since the other modules have all been coded and tested. As examples of patterns you might want to try, consider the following:

```
. . . . . . .        . . . . . . . . .        . . . . . . . . . . . .        . . . . . . . . . . . . . . .
. * . . * . .        . . ** . ** . .        . . . * . . . . * . . .        . . . . . . ** . . . . . . . .
. . . . . * .        . . ** . ** . .        . ** . **** . ** .        . . . . . . ** . . . . . . . .
. * . . . * .        . . . * . * . . .        . . . * . . . . * . . .        . . . . . . . . . . . . . . .
. . **** .        . * . * . * . * .                                . ** . . . **** . . . ** .
. . . . . . .        . * . * . * . * .        . . . . . .                . * . * . * . . . . * . * . * .
                     . ** . . . ** .        . . * . . .                . . . * . ** . . . * . * . . .
                     . . . . . . . . .        . * . * . .                . * . * . * . . . . * . * . * .
                                            . . . . * .                . ** . . . **** . . . ** .
. . . . . . . . . . . . . . . . .        . . . . * .                . . . . . . . . . . . . . . .
. . * . . . . . . . . . . . . . * . .        . . . . . .                . . . . . . ** . . . . . . . .
. ***************** .                                            . . . . . . ** . . . . . . . .
. . * . . . . . . . . . . . . . * . .                                . . . . . . . . . . . . . . .
. . . . . . . . . . . . . . . . . .
```

Each of these can be tried alone (and adding empty cells on all sides will help) or in combination with the others. You'll likely find others that are interesting. *Scientific American* and *BYTE* magazines have had several articles on the Game of Life over the years. The *Scientific American* articles have been collected in the book *Wheels, Life, and Other Mathematical Amusements* by Martin Gardner (1983, W. H. Freeman).

6. Find a way to write the algorithm for the Game of Life so that the program runs faster. (Check some of the references mentioned in the previous exercise if you can't think of a faster method.) Test your new version. Any increase in speed will show up most clearly when the program is run on a large array.

7. There is a number puzzle that consists of a square array of numbered plastic tiles with one empty space. Any tile adjacent to the empty space can be slid into the space, and the object of the puzzle is to put the tiles in numerical order. Write a program to simulate this puzzle. Use a 4 × 4 array of **integers** from 0 to 15, with the 0 representing the space:

1	2	3	4
5	6	7	8
9	10	11	12
13	14	15	0

The user moves by entering one of the numbers adjacent to the 0; in this case, 12 and 15 are valid moves. The user can also choose to quit by entering 0. Your program should allow only valid moves, and should give the user a chance to either start over or enter a 0 to quit.

8. Change the program in the previous exercise so that the computer scrambles the array before the user starts to move. A good way to scramble the puzzle is to have the computer make a given number of random (but valid) moves. The user can choose the number of moves to be made, and thus control the degree to which the puzzle is initially scrambled. This program should recognize whether the puzzle has been solved, and display an appropriate message if it is.

Chapter 14

Recursion

14.1   Overview of the Chapter

A function, procedure, definition or algorithm is *recursive* if it refers to itself. In this chapter we will introduce the concept of recursion and give a few examples of its use. The concept of recursion is as fundamental as that of branching or repetition, and just as important. Many routines in computer science are recursive; they can be explained and studied when they are stated in a recursive manner.

14.2   Introduction

The field of mathematics is full of recursive definitions, many of which are on a very elementary level and, as such, are often overlooked. Some of the simplest concepts can be explained better when viewed recursively. In this chapter we will look at a few recursive routines and implement them in Pascal. It should be mentioned that another reason Pascal is a language of choice for an introductory course is the fact that it fully supports recursion; languages such as BASIC and Fortran do not. Moreover, much of computer science is mathematics. A useful computer language needs to allow us to perform mathematical manipulations other than simple calculations and evaluations of formulas.

We should formalize the nature of recursion with a definition:

$$A \left\{ \begin{array}{l} \text{procedure} \\ \text{function} \\ \text{definition} \\ \text{routine} \\ \text{module} \\ \text{algorithm} \end{array} \right\} \text{ is } \textit{recursive} \text{ if it} \left\{ \begin{array}{l} \text{calls} \\ \text{refers to} \end{array} \right\} \text{itself.}$$

Read the definition using any one of the choices in the curly braces.

This is something we have not seen to this point. None of the modules we have written have called themselves. If they have called another routine, that routine has been declared separately. At first it may seem strange for a function or procedure to call itself. Don't worry about that; by the time you have seen some examples, it won't seem quite so strange.

In a sense, you have to learn to think recursively. We have looked at a number of problems in this text so far; we have learned to look for places where the algorithm branches or loops; now we have to learn to look for places where they *recurse*.

14.3   Factorial

Let's look at a simple example of a recursive function. You probably have seen the mathematical function factorial. A few examples will help you remember:

$$\begin{array}{lll} 3! & = & 3 \cdot 2 \cdot 1 & = & 6 \\ 5! & = & 5 \cdot 4 \cdot 3 \cdot 2 \cdot 1 & = & 120 \\ 6! & = & 6 \cdot 5 \cdot 4 \cdot 3 \cdot 2 \cdot 1 & = & 720 \end{array}$$

Similarly, $1! = 1$, and, by definition, $0! = 1$ also. Now, how would you define this notion of factorial? If n is a non-negative integer, what is $n!$? The definition seen in elementary math books is usually something like:

$$n! \equiv n \cdot (n - 1) \cdot (n - 2) \cdots 2 \cdot 1$$

with the "$\cdots$" representing all the integers between $(n - 3)$ and 3. This is an acceptable definition as long as you are willing to use your imagination to supply what's intended by the dots. One also has to define $0!$ to be equal to 1 as a special case.

So, what's this got to do with recursion? The definition is acceptable, as we said, but only in an elementary math class. It would not be acceptable to a mathematician; no mathematician would be happy with a definition that leaves something to one's imagination. Consider the following more precise definition:

$$n! \equiv \left\{ \begin{array}{ll} 1 & \text{, if } n = 0 \text{ or } 1 \\ n \cdot (n - 1)! & \text{, if } n > 1 \end{array} \right.$$

There are no dots to leave the meaning in doubt. You can determine exactly what $n!$ equals for any non-negative integer, n. Let's try one. What is 5!? According to our definition, 5! equals $5 \cdot 4!$. But what is 4!? Using the definition again, we see that 4! is $4 \cdot 3!$. Use the definition once again: $3! = 3 \cdot 2!$. You might be thinking this goes on forever but it doesn't; it is not necessary to apply the definition again after using it on 1! since $1! = 1$. No further recursing is needed. To summarize:

$$
\begin{aligned}
5! &= 5 \cdot 4! \\
&= 5 \cdot 4 \cdot 3! \\
&= 5 \cdot 4 \cdot 3 \cdot 2! \\
&= 5 \cdot 4 \cdot 3 \cdot 2 \cdot 1! \\
&= 5 \cdot 4 \cdot 3 \cdot 2 \cdot 1
\end{aligned}
$$

Do you see the recursion? Our definition defines $n!$ in terms of $(n-1)!$. Factorial is defined in terms of factorial.

That's fine, mathematically. However, we're talking about computer programming in this book, not mathematics. The point is, we can write functions in Pascal that call themselves; these are recursive functions. Indeed, we can also write recursive procedures in Pascal. We'll see this later in this chapter.

Factorial in Pascal

Let's write a recursive Pascal function for factorial. (Since it returns a value, it has to be a function, right?)

```
function Factorial(N : integer) : integer;

{ This function calculates N factorial, recursively.  }

begin
  if (N = 0) or (N = 1)
    then
      Factorial := 1
    else
      Factorial := N * Factorial(N - 1)
end;
```

The beautiful thing about this is *it works*! With no more code than this, we can write a Pascal function for Factorial. Do you see the recursion? Inside the function Factorial we *call* the function Factorial. You should type this

function up and surround it with a test program that calls it. Send it some
values (not too large) and see that it does produce the correct results for $n!$.

While we don't plan to get into it too deeply, let's try to imagine what the
computer is doing. Suppose we call this function from another routine and
send it the number 5. The computer puts 5 into the parameter N and looks at
N to see if it's equal to 0 or 1. Since it isn't, the statement in the `else` part is
executed. The function will attempt to multiply 5 times `Factorial(4)`. Before
this multiplication can be completed, however, the computer will have to know
what `Factorial(4)` is. All the current information—including the pending
multiplication—gets stored away somewhere in memory and the program calls
`Factorial`; this time sending it the number 4. Now N equals 4. Since 4 is not
equal to 0 or 1, the `else` part is executed once again. This time the program
has the computer try to multiply 4 times `Factorial(3)`. And once again the
multiplication has to be delayed until `Factorial(3)` is evaluated. Everything
is saved somewhere and the routine gets called yet another time.

This continues until `Factorial` is called with the value 1. This time it is
not necessary to recurse; the value of 1 is returned for `Factorial(1)`. This
1 is multiplied by the waiting 2 and the result (2) sent back as the value of
`Factorial(2)`. The waiting 3 is multiplied by the 2 and this result (6) is sent
back as the value of `Factorial(3)`. The waiting 4 is multiplied by the 6 and the
result (24) is returned for `Factorial(4)`. Finally the 5 that has been patiently
waiting for the value of `Factorial(4)` is multiplied times the 24 and the final
result of 120 is sent back to the routine that made the original call.

You don't have to be able to repeat that. You do need to remember that
you can write recursive routines in Pascal, and they will work.

14.4 Exponentiation

Let's try another operation from mathematics. In this example we'll consider
raising a real number to an integral power, that is, x^n, where x is a real number
and n is an integer. To keep things simple, we'll only consider positive integers
n in the text and leave negative and zero exponents for you.

Recall that 3^5 equals $3 \cdot 3 \cdot 3 \cdot 3 \cdot 3$ or 243, and that 2^7 equals $2 \cdot 2 \cdot 2 \cdot 2 \cdot 2 \cdot 2 \cdot 2$,
which you can multiply out to get 128.

How is x^n defined? In your math class you probably were given a definition
something like:

$$x^n \equiv \overbrace{x \cdot x \cdot x \cdots x}^{n \text{ factors}}$$

Again the "$\cdots$" imply some missing factors that your imagination has to
supply. We usually read the three dots as "and so forth." Your math teacher
probably persuaded you that it was okay, and it is, in an elementary math class.
But it really isn't good mathematics.

A recursive definition for exponentiation is possible:

$$x^n \equiv \begin{cases} x & \text{, if } n = 1 \\ x \cdot x^{n-1} & \text{, if } n > 1 \end{cases}$$

Remember, we are not worrying about zero or negative exponents.

What is 3^5? By the recursive definition, it is $3 \cdot 3^4$. And, by continuing to use the definition until we no longer need to recurse, we get:

$$
\begin{aligned}
3^5 &= 3 \cdot 3^4 \\
&= 3 \cdot 3 \cdot 3^3 \\
&= 3 \cdot 3 \cdot 3 \cdot 3^2 \\
&= 3 \cdot 3 \cdot 3 \cdot 3 \cdot 3^1 \\
&= 3 \cdot 3 \cdot 3 \cdot 3 \cdot 3
\end{aligned}
$$

Exponentiation in Pascal

Once again a Pascal function is easy to write. Before we write it for you, think about it a little. What should we call it? How many parameters are there? What are their types? What is the returned type of the function?

Here is a Pascal function that reflects our decisions to the above questions:

```
function Power(X : real; N : integer) : real;

{  This function calculates X to the Nth power, recursively.  }
{  Precondition: N is greater than zero.                      }

begin
  if N = 1
    then
      Power := X
    else
      Power := X * Power(X, N-1)
end;
```

How did your version compare to ours?

Exponentiation for Rational and Irrational Exponents

By the way, exponentiation is also defined for non-integral exponents. You will
likely remember what $2^{1/2}$ is. You might even remember what $6.2^{3.45}$ is defined
to be. It's less likely that you will know—or care—how 5^π is defined. Such
things are defined in mathematics, and raising a number to an irrational power
does make sense, but we won't get into that here. If you do need **real** numbers
raised to **real** powers in a Pascal program, there is an easy way to get them.
If you have had an advanced math course, you will remember that a^b equals
$e^{b \ln a}$. The Pascal supplied functions include ways to find e to a power (**exp**)
and the natural logarithm of a number (**ln**). Thus,

```
function RealPower(X, N : real) : real;

{  This function raises a real number to a real power.  }

begin
  RealPower := exp(N * ln(X))
end;
```

will return the right value.

We caution you not to use this function for simple exponentiations. There
is no good reason to use **RealPower** for simple integer operations like 3^4; the
result of 3^4 is an **integer**, not a **real**. Besides, you're likely to get something
like 80.99999973 instead of 81. Using **RealPower** to find the value of 3^4 would
be like using a buffalo gun to swat a fly!

14.5   Iteration vs. Recursion

You should write an iterative version for exponentiation (i.e., using loops instead
of recursion) and compare the iterative version with the recursive one. You
should provide for zero and negative integral exponents.

An iterative version of a function that returns n factorial should also be
easy to write. In fact, the iterative versions of these two functions (factorial
and exponentiation) would be more efficient than the recursive versions we've
been looking at. Just because recursion is available as a technique, that doesn't
mean that you must use it. When an iterative version is just as obvious, the
iterative version is usually more efficient than the recursive one since there is a
lot of overhead for a routine that repeatedly calls itself. However, that is not
to imply that there is always an iterative version that is just as straightforward
as a recursive one. In a few pages we'll look at some recursive solutions to
problems that don't have simple iterative solutions.

Inadvertent Recursion

You must be careful not to inadvertently combine recursion and iteration. The following Pascal function might look okay but it isn't!

```
function Power(X : real; N : integer) : real;

{  This function calculates X to the Nth power.  }
{  Precondition: N is greater than zero.          }

var
  i : integer;

begin
  Power := 1;
  for i := 1 to N do
    Power := Power * X    { Bugged!  Will not work. }
end;
```

At first glance this might look correct but it will *not* work. The occurrence of "Power" on the right side of the assignment statement amounts to a recursive call to the function. The compiler will think you are trying to call Power recursively and will complain that you failed to list the correct number of parameters. If you want to compute Power iteratively, you will need to use a local **real** variable to collect the product and then assign that result to Power just before the function is exited. We'll leave this for an exercise. Another way to inadvertantly use recursion is to try to display the value of a function inside the function. Consider the following skeleton:

```
function Foo( ... ) : ... ;
begin

   .

   .

   .

   Foo := ... ;
   writeln('The value being returned is ', Foo)
end.
```

The intention here is to put the **writeln** inside the function for debugging purposes but it won't work! When the compiler sees Foo as an expression in the **writeln**, it tries to *call* the function Foo recursively; you end up either with infinite recursion (see below) or an invalid call (no parameters). The name of the function cannot be treated as a normal variable.

14.6   Conditions Required for Recursion

Before we go onto another example, let's think about what must happen for
every recursive definition, procedure, function, etc.

- The recursion must get simpler; each time you recurse, you must recurse
  to a more elementary case. You could not define something recursively if
  each step got more complicated than the step before.

- The recursion must always end somewhere; there must always be a non-
  recursive case.

   For factorial, the non-recursive cases were 0! and 1!, and we found $n!$ by
recursing to $(n-1)!$. For exponentiation, the non-recursive case was x^1, and
we recursed from x^n to x^{n-1}.
   Every recursive procedure, function, algorithm, etc., must have a non-recursive
case. Otherwise, it will recurse forever—something known as "infinite recursion."

14.7   Combinations

The two examples of recursive functions were similar and, as a matter of fact,
could have been written using loops nearly as easily. Let's look at another
function that is not so straightforward and not nearly as easy to write with
loops. Consider figure 14.1, Pascal's triangle.
   There are several uses for the numbers in this famous triangle studied by
the man after whom the Pascal language was named. We won't discuss these

```
                          1
                      1       1
                  1       2       1
              1       3       3       1
          1       4       6       4       1
      1       5      10      10       5       1
  1       6      15      20      15       6       1
1       7      21      35      35      21       7       1
1   8      28      56      70      56      28       8       1
      . . .
```

Figure 14.1 Pascal's Triangle

```
1
1   1
1   2   1
1   3   3   1
1   4   6   4   1
1   5  10  10   5   1
1   6  15  20  15   6   1
1   7  21  35  35  21   7   1
1   8  28  56  70  56  28   8   1
    . . .
```

Figure 14.2 Pascal's Triangle, Redrawn

uses but will simply examine how the triangle is generated. If you look at any number in the body of the triangle—i.e., not on the edges—you'll notice that the number there equals the sum of the two numbers above it. For example, the 21 in the next to last row equals the sum of the 6 and the 15 above it.

To be able to refer to positions in the triangle, it is nice to be able to talk about which row and column a number is in. The rows are easy but it is a little harder to see any "columns". If we draw the triangle a little differently, the columns are easier to see; consider figure 14.2.

Now number the rows and columns starting at zero. The first row is row 0, the first column is column 0. The element in row number 6 and column 3 is 20. Let's adopt some notation. Because it's called this in other circumstances, we'll use the word "combination" to refer to the numbers in the triangle. So, for the number in row 6 and column 3, we'll use: "Combination(6, 3)". With this in mind, notice that Combination(6, 3) equals the sum of Combination(5, 2) and Combination(5, 3); that is, 20 = 10 + 10. Let's agree to use "Comb" rather than "Combination" from now on, since it's easier to write.

Try it again; look at the element in row 8, column 5. Comb(8, 5) equals 56. Look at row 7; the two numbers above and above and to the left of the 56 are 35 and 21:

$$56 = \text{Comb}(8, 5) = \text{Comb}(7, 4) + \text{Comb}(7, 5) = 35 + 21.$$

This is the recursive relationship we are looking for.

Now, to keep from having infinite recursion, we must determine a non-recursive case. When do we no longer need to recurse? On the edges of the triangle, of course. The numbers on the edges are always equal to 1. When does this happen? It's easy to see that the values are always 1 when the column number is zero. A little more thought reveals that the other edge occurs when the column number and the row number are equal. Thus, we can now state a recursive definition for Comb:

$$\text{Comb}(r, c) \equiv \begin{cases} 1 & \text{, if } c = 0 \text{ or } c = r \\ \text{Comb}(r-1, c-1) + \text{Comb}(r-1, c) & \text{, otherwise} \end{cases}$$

This definition can be written using the notation used in mathematics for combinations. You will see $\binom{r}{c}$ used for the number of combinations of r things taken c at a time. Using this notation, the definition becomes:

$$\binom{r}{c} \equiv \begin{cases} 1 & \text{, if } c = 0 \text{ or } c = r \\ \binom{r-1}{c-1} + \binom{r-1}{c} & \text{, otherwise} \end{cases}$$

Example of Combinations

As you will have concluded, this idea of combination is more useful than in just Pascal's triangle. Suppose, for example, you have five tennis players and want to know how many different matches are possible between them. Suppose the five people are Adam, Bill, Cathy, Denise and Ed. If you start listing possible matches, you'll see that Adam could play Bill, Cathy, Denise or Ed. Bill could play Adam, Cathy, Denise or Ed—but we already counted Adam playing Bill. Continuing without repeating, we'd have Cathy playing Denise or Ed, and, finally, Denise playing Ed. That totals to 10 possible matches. We call this number, "the number of combinations of five things taken two at a time." Look back at figure 14.2 and you'll see that the element in row number 5, column number 2 is indeed 10.

In general, if you have a set containing r elements and want to form subsets containing c elements, the number of different subsets containing c elements is known as, "the number of combinations of r things taken c at a time."

Combinations in Pascal

Once again it's easy to turn this into Pascal. Since it returns a single value, Combination is a function:

```
function Combination(R, C : integer) : integer;

{ This function calculates the number of combinations of }
{ R things taken C at a time, recursively.              }

begin
  if (C = 0) or (R = C)
    then
      Combination := 1
    else
      Combination := Combination(R-1, C-1) + Combination(R-1, C)
end;
```

Now you should write some more code in Pascal; write a complete Pascal main program that allows you to input some numbers for R and C, calls Combination with these values and displays the result. Even better, write a program that will display an arbitrary number of rows of Pascal's triangle. We should warn you that this routine, though elegant, is not very efficient. To calculate the number of combinations for values of R and C that are bigger than 10, or so, requires many many recursions. Watch your program slow down as it tries to print the first 12 rows of the triangle. By the way, shouldn't your program display the triangle as in figure 14.1, rather than as in figure 14.2?

In this case an iterative version of the program is not easy to develop. There are several ways to develop a function that will return the number of combinations of R things taken C at a time and not require recursion, but none of them are as "neat" as the recursive solution. Since our purpose here is to demonstrate recursion, we'll not spend any time looking for better ways to write Combination.

14.8   The Towers of Hanoi

The examples of recursion we have seen so far have been mathematical functions. Let's look at a different sort of example, one that's neither a function nor directly from mathematics.

The problem is known as "The Towers of Hanoi." Don't think of the modern city Hanoi in North Vietnam when you think about the problem; instead imagine a mysterious monastery high in some mountain range in Asia, a place where no person from the outside world has ever been.

At the dawn of time, the Creator of the universe established a monastery on this mountain. The Creator established an order of monks to live in the monastery and gave them a job to do. Three huge towers were created, made of pure gold with diamond needles standing in their centers. In the beginning, 64 golden discs were placed on the first tower; each disc on the tower was slightly smaller than the one below it. The discs, of course, are made of pure gold, are finely carved and are surely priceless. The monks were assigned the job of moving the discs from the first tower to the second. They were given two simple rules to obey:

1. Move one disc each hour from one tower to another.

2. Never place a larger disc on top of a smaller one.

When their job is completed, the stars will go out and the world will end.

Assuming that the towers and the monastery do exist, a couple of important questions come to mind. First, is it indeed possible to move the 64 discs according to the rules? Second, how long is it going to take?

Let's tackle the first question first. Rather than trying to move 64 discs, let's start by seeing if we can move three. Consider figure 14.3; it shows a simple example of three towers with just three discs on tower A.

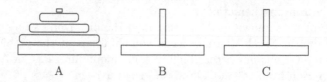

Figure 14.3 Three Discs

Suppose we want to move these three discs to one of the other two towers. How can it be done? Obviously there are only two moves at the beginning: move the top disc to either tower B or to tower C. It doesn't really matter which one we choose—except to determine which of the other two towers the three discs end up on. So, let's move the top disc to tower B. Then what? There are three legal moves at this point: (1) move the first disc back to tower A, (2) move the first disc to tower C, and (3) move the second disc to tower C. Only the last of these makes any sense, so let's do that.

Then what? We now have one disc on each tower. Again we have three legal moves: (1) move the second disc back onto tower A, (2) move the first disc onto tower A, and (3) move the first disc onto tower C. The first of these three just reverses the previous move and the second gets us nowhere. The third possibility, however, frees up tower B. Consider figure 14.4, which shows these three moves. The first two discs are on tower C and the third disc can now be moved over to tower B.

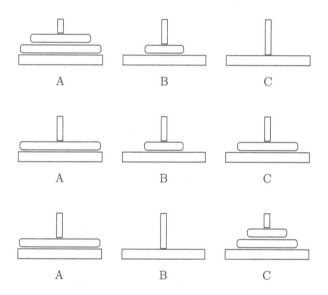

Figure 14.4 The First Three Moves

And now, using a similar strategy, we can finish moving the three discs, look at figure 14.5 for the next four moves.

We have shown that it is possible to move three discs, following the rules set forth by the Creator, and we determined the number of moves it would take: 7.

So, it was easy to move three discs; how about four? Can we move four discs? Sure; since we now know how to move three, it's easy to move four. Just move the top three out of the way, move the fourth disc to the free tower, and then move the three discs back on top of disc number four.

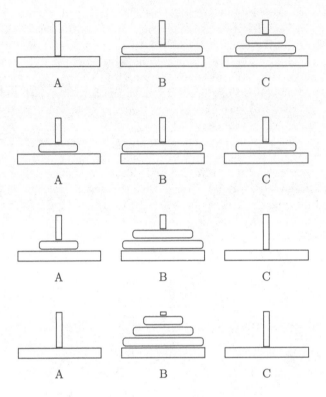

Figure 14.5 Moves 4, 5, 6 and 7

How about five? Again, since we are sure we can move four, it's clear that we can move five: move the top four out of the way, move the fifth one, and move the top four back on top.

Now we're thinking recursively! To move n discs, first move $n-1$ discs out of the way, move the nth disc to the free tower, then move the $n-1$ discs back on top. We have described the solution to the problem recursively; that is, we have described the solution to the problem of moving discs in terms of moving discs, but a smaller number of discs.

Let's make sure this is a proper use of recursion. As we mentioned above, we always have to recurse to a simpler case. Yes, that's okay. To move n discs, we recurse to moving $n-1$ discs, a simpler case. Also, there has to be a non-recursive case, a situation where no recursion is needed. Sure; when n equals 1 there is no need to recurse; just move the disc.

Let's make our solution a bit more formal; i.e., let's turn it into an algorithm:

START OF The Towers of Hanoi

To move n discs from one tower to another:
    if $n = 1$
        then
            just move the disc
        else
            move $n - 1$ discs from the given tower to the spare tower
            move disc number n from the given tower to the desired tower
            move $n - 1$ discs from the spare tower to the desired tower

END OF The Towers of Hanoi

Notice that we refer to the three towers as "the given tower," "the desired tower," and "the spare tower." Each time we move a given number of discs the "given tower," the "desired tower" and the "spare tower" will change, so they should be sent to the routine each time it is called; that is, they should be parameters. The number n will be needed each time so it too is a parameter. Let's rewrite the algorithm using these parameters:

START OF MoveDiscs(N, F-Tower, T-Tower, S-Tower)

To move N discs from one tower to another:
    if $N = 1$
        then
            just move the disc
        else
            call MoveDiscs(N−1, F-Tower, S-Tower, T-Tower)
            move disc number N from the F-Tower to the T-Tower
            call MoveDiscs(N−1, S-Tower, T-Tower, F-Tower)
END OF MoveDiscs

We are using F-Tower for "from tower" (the tower the discs are being moved from, referred to above as the "given tower"), T-Tower for "to tower" (the tower the discs are to be moved to), and S-Tower for "spare tower."

Do you see the recursion? The routine MoveDiscs calls itself.

Now all we have to do is call this routine and send it the number 64 for the number of discs and the names of the three towers.

The Towers of Hanoi in Pascal

Can we implement this algorithm in Pascal? Yes and no. We can write a program that implements part of the above algorithm but we'll have a hard time actually getting the computer to move the discs. You can imagine having a computer connected to a robot arm and directing the arm to pick up and move discs according to the commands issued by our program, and in some situations that would be possible. You can also imagine being able to simulate the movement of the discs with some fancy graphics on the computer screen.

Since we don't have a robot and Standard Pascal doesn't have any fancy graphics, what we'll do is print a list of instructions for the monks in the monastery. We'll tell them which disc to move each hour so that if they get confused, they can refer to the list. You can extend what we do to work with a robot arm or with graphics if your situation permits it.

Let's start with the routine MoveDiscs itself. Is it a procedure or a function? It does something and it doesn't return a value, so it is a procedure. How about the parameters? The parameter N is an integer, of course, but how about the towers? We can just let the towers be represented by single letters: A, B or C; their type would be char.

All we have to do now is replace the steps in the algorithm that say move a disc with a step that prints a message concerning which disc to move where. Here's the code:

```
procedure MoveDiscs(N : integer; FTower, TTower, STower : char);

{  This procedure prints a list of moves required to move N discs  }
{  from tower FTower to tower TTower, using STower as a spare.      }
{  The procedure is recursive.                                      }

begin
  if N = 1
    then
      writeln('Move disc #1 from tower ', FTower, ' to ', TTower)
    else
      begin
        MoveDiscs(N-1, FTower, STower, TTower);
        write('Move disc #', N:1,' from tower ', FTower);
        writeln(' to ', TTower);
        MoveDiscs(N-1, STower, TTower, FTower)
      end
end;
```

A complete program that uses the above procedure would be very easy to write. All it would do is ask the user how many discs to move, accept that number from the user and call the procedure.

Here's our simple version:

```pascal
program TowersOfHanoi(input, output);

{  Programmer:   Tim Wilson                            }

{  This program implements the famous Towers of Hanoi story.  }
{  It allows a user to enter a number of discs to be moved     }
{  and prints a list of moves required to move that many       }
{  discs from tower A to tower B using tower C.               }

var
  N : integer;

  procedure MoveDiscs(N : integer; FTower, TTower, STower : char);

  {  This procedure prints a list of moves required to move N discs  }
  {  from tower FTower to tower TTower, using STower as a spare.     }
  {  The procedure is recursive.                                     }

  begin
    if N = 1
      then
        writeln('Move disc #1 from tower ', FTower, ' to ', TTower)
      else
        begin
          MoveDiscs(N-1, FTower, STower, TTower);
          write('Move disc #', N:1,' from tower ');
          writeln(FTower, ' to ', TTower);
          MoveDiscs(N-1, STower, TTower, FTower)
        end
  end;

begin
  writeln('This program displays a list of disc moves to solve the');
  writeln('Towers of Hanoi problem.');
  write('How many discs would you like to move?  - ');
  readln(N);
  MoveDiscs(N, 'A', 'B', 'C')
end.
```

Let's test the program—but not with 64—let's start with our first example. When the program is run with N equal to 3, it produces the following output:

```
This program displays a list of disc moves to solve the
Towers of Hanoi problem.
How many discs would you like to move?  - 3
Move disc #1 from tower A to B
Move disc #2 from tower A to C
Move disc #1 from tower B to C
Move disc #3 from tower A to B
Move disc #1 from tower C to A
Move disc #2 from tower C to B
Move disc #1 from tower A to B
```

Number of Moves

Before you try running this program with the number of discs set to 64, we had better go on to the second question we posed earlier, namely, how many moves will it take? (It would, after all, be convenient to know how much time there is left before the monks finish their job. It might affect how we feel about other things if we know how much time there is left before the stars go out and the world ends.)

To move three discs, we needed seven moves. How many moves will it take to move four discs? Seven to move the first three out of the way, one move to move disc number four, and another seven to move the three back on top; a total of 15 moves.

How about five discs? Fifteen plus one plus fifteen: thirty-one.

We probably need a table to keep track:

Number of discs	Number of moves
1	1
2	3
3	7
4	15
5	31
6	63
⋮	

A little examination will reveal that each of the numbers in the second column is one less than two raised to the number in the first column. That is, it looks like the number of moves required to move n discs is $2^n - 1$. While a proof of this is beyond our purposes, let's accept the validity of the formula. Then, to move 64 discs, we will need to make $2^{64} - 1$ moves. We'll leave it for you to get out your calculator and determine how many hours that will require. We recommend that you do these calculations before you try running the program with N equal to 64.

14.9 Summary and Review

- We introduced the notion of *recursion*. Recursion is another fundamental technique used in computer programming. A routine is recursive if it calls itself or refers to itself. We saw that many interesting and seemingly complex things can be made fairly easy when viewed recursively.

- Pascal fully supports recursion. We can write Pascal functions and procedures that call themselves. (In fact, it is possible to have procedures and/or functions call themselves indirectly as well as directly. For example, procedure A might call procedure B, which then calls procedure A. This is also recursion and can be done in Pascal. The number of times such recursive calls are needed is much less than the straightforward recursion we have studied. Pascal does support indirect recursion too but we'll not consider the topic herein.)

- We've seen that many problems can be solved both iteratively and recursively. Whenever an iterative solution is just as "natural" as a recursive solution, the iterative one will almost always be more efficient. There are some problems, however, that just cry out for recursive solutions and for which iterative solutions are not at all easy to find.

- We learned that every recursive routine—or definition or module—must have two properties:

  1. The recursion must get simpler; each time you recurse, you must recurse to a more elementary case.

  2. The recursion must always end somewhere; there must always be a non-recursive case.

- We studied three mathematical functions that we defined recursively: factorial, exponentiation and the number of combinations of r things taken c at a time. We defined these functions recursively and wrote Pascal functions to implement them.

- We learned about the famous problem called "The Towers of Hanoi." The problem was solved recursively and a complete Pascal program was written that told the monks which disc to move each hour.

There are many other recursive relationships that are studied in computer science and mathematics; we have only examined a few. Others are mentioned in the exercises and you will see several others in more advanced texts that discuss things like binary trees and linked lists.

14.10   New Terms Introduced

combinations The number of ways that a certain number of elements of a set can be selected. For example, a set of five elements has ten subsets with just two elements.

factorial The mathematical function whose value is obtained by multiplying together the integers from 1 to n.

infinite recursion An incorrect recursive routine that never reaches a non-recursive step.

Pascal's triangle A famous triangle-shaped collection of integers, the elements of which are encountered in various areas of mathematics.

recursion A fundamentally important concept of mathematics and computer science where a function, procedure, definition or algorithm refers to itself.

Towers of Hanoi A famous mathematics problem where the goal is to move a series of different size discs from one tower to another without ever placing a larger disc on top of a smaller.

14.11 Exercises

1. Write a test program for the **Factorial** function. Test the function using numbers that are reasonably small. You may want to use a calculator to find out what values of N will yield an N! greater than **maxint**.

2. Write the **Factorial** function iteratively; i.e., *without* using recursion.

3. Write a test program for the **Power** function. Test the function, again using numbers which are reasonably small. Extend the function so that it handles zero and negative values for the exponent. How should zero to a negative power be handled?

4. Write an iterative version of the **Power** function (it should handle zero and negative exponents also). Compare the code for the two versions of **Power**. Which is shorter? Which is easier to follow?

5. Write a program that uses the function **Combination** to print the first N rows of Pascal's triangle, where N is input. Your program should print the triangle as shown in figure 14.1.

6. Think of the product of two numbers as the first number added to itself repeatedly. Using the **Power** function as a model, write the algorithm and then the code for a function, **Product**, that recursively calculates the product of two integers passed to it. Be careful to state any necessary preconditions.

7. Think of the sum of two numbers as the first number added to a series of 1's. Using the **Power** function as a model, write the algorithm and then the code for a function, **Sum**, that recursively calculates the sum of two integers passed to it.

8. A *Fibonacci sequence* is a sequence of numbers such that every number after the first two is the sum of the two previous numbers in the sequence. The first two numbers are arbitrary. For example, the Fibonacci sequence generated from 1 and 1 is: 1, 1, 2, 3, 5, 8, 13, 21, ... Write a recursive function that returns the Nth term in a Fibonacci sequence. What parameters must be passed to the function? Write a test program for the routine.

9. Type in the code for the Towers of Hanoi problem and make sure it works on your system. Is there a limit to the number of discs your system will allow you to use? Determine, either by using a calculator or by writing a simple program, the number of years the universe will last if it takes $2^{64} - 1$ hours to move the discs. If the monastery was built 5 billion years ago, how long do we have before the stars go out? You might want to use your function **Power** to calculate the number of hours.

10. Write the algorithm and the code for a recursive procedure that displays
    a given character string in reverse. Test the routine with a program which
    asks for a string and its length, and calls the procedure.

11. Write the *GCD* algorithm from chapter 5 (page 132) recursively. Write
    the code for the function and test it.

12. Write the *Binary Search* algorithm on page 285 recursively. Write the
    code for the procedure and a test program for it.

13. Write one of the *Bubble Sort* algorithms from chapter 9 recursively.

14. Write the *Selection Sort* algorithm from exercise 15, chapter 9, recursively.

15. Consider the *HeapSort* algorithm from chapter 9 (page 304). It is easy to
    view *Heapify* recursively:

    > *To heapify a subtree:*
    >   *if the data in the root node is greater than the data in either child*
    >   *then*
    >   *exchange the data in the root node with the data in the larger child*
    >   *heapify the subtree at that child*

    Write the algorithm for *Heapify* recursively (be careful to watch out for
    nodes which don't have children). Write the code for your new version.
    Replace the old version of **Heapify** with your new version and test it with
    the old version of **HeapSort**.

Appendix A

Syntax Diagrams

program:

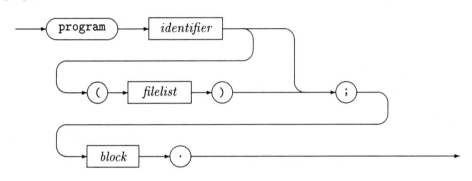

identifier:

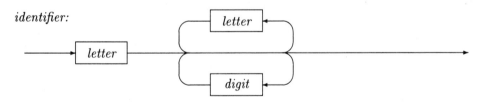

letter:

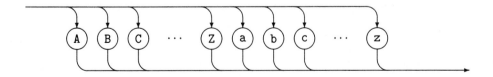

digit:

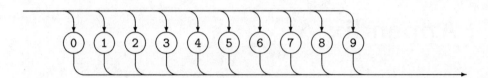

block:

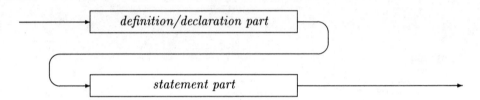

definition/declaration part:

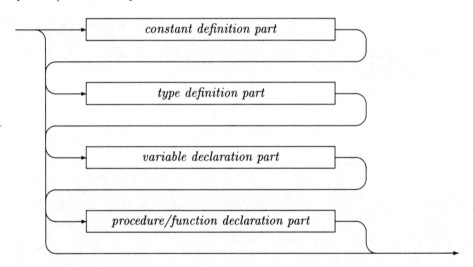

constant definition part:

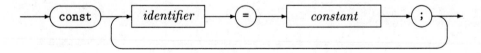

constant:

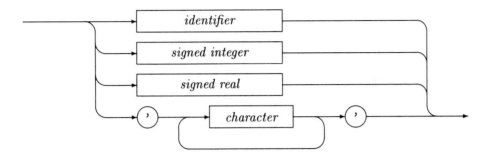

signed integer:

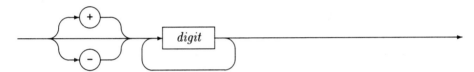

signed real:

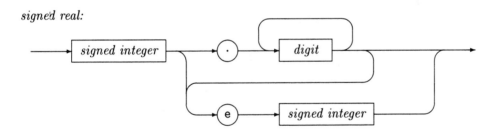

type definition part:

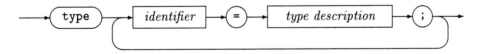

type description:

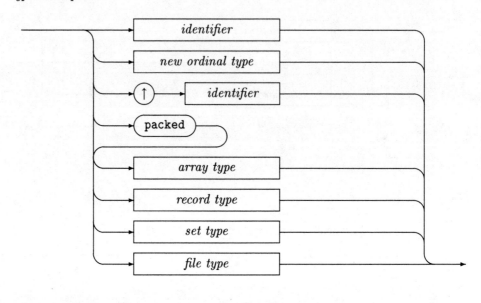

new ordinal type:

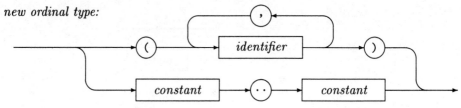

array type:

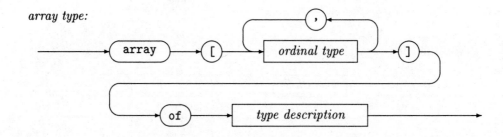

ordinal type:

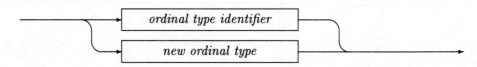

record type:

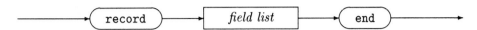

field list:

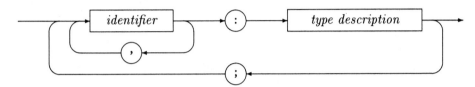

set type:

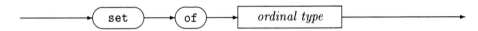

file type:

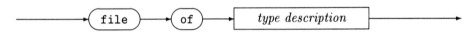

variable declaration part:

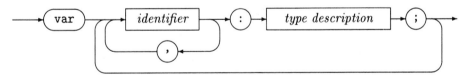

procedure/function declaration part:

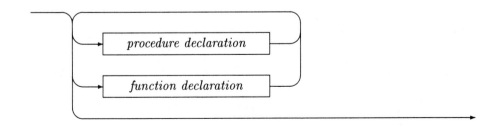

procedure declaration:

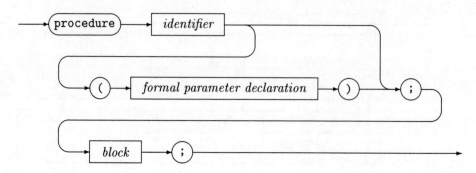

formal parameter declaration:

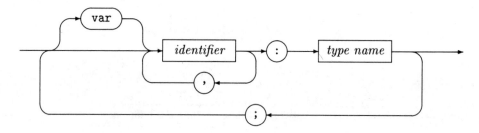

function declaration:

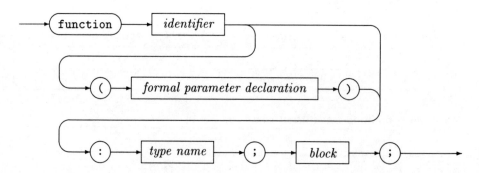

statement part:

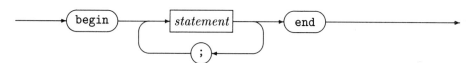

statement:

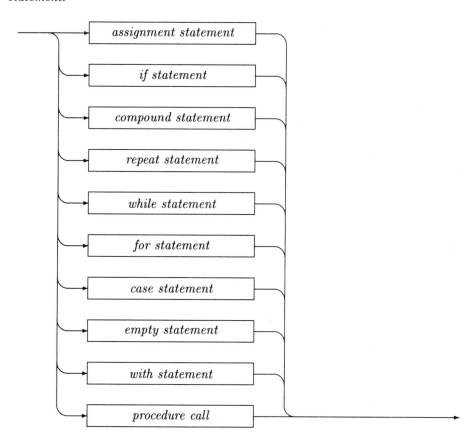

assignment statement:

expression:

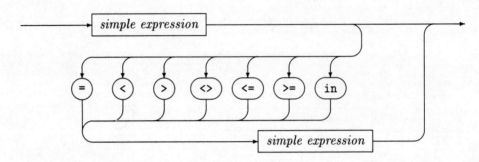

simple expression:

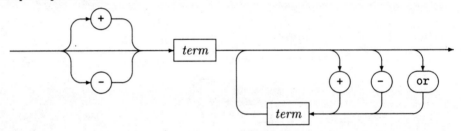

term:

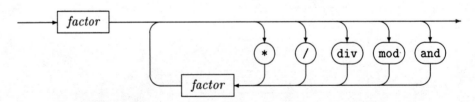

factor:

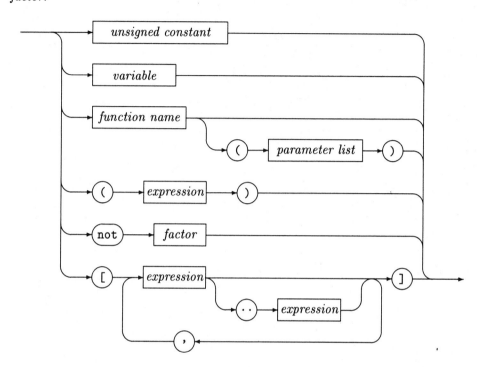

if statement:

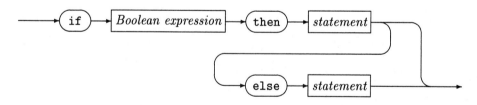

compound statement:

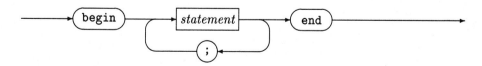

repeat statement:

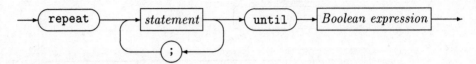

while statement:

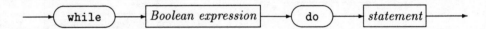

for statement:

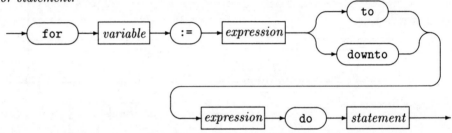

case statement:

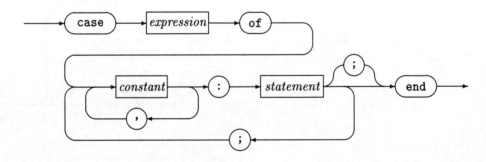

empty statement:

with statement:

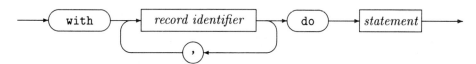

procedure call:

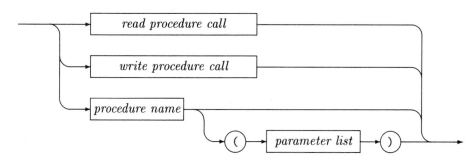

read procedure call:

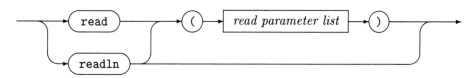

write procedure call:

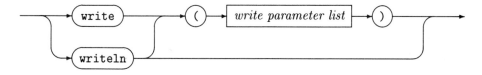

A.1 Index to Syntax Diagrams

Appendix B

Accessing Physical Files in Pascal

B.1 Turbo Pascal®

In Borland International's Turbo Pascal, the association between the internal file name and the physical file is made with a special non-Standard `assign` procedure. The physical file name is a string (either a string constant or a string variable) and the internal file name is, as usual, a variable name of type `text` or `file of` some component type. The `assign` procedure call must precede a call to either `reset` or `rewrite`. For example, suppose the MS-DOS file resides on drive B: and is named `SAMPLE.DOC`, and the internal file is `DataFile`. The following line of code would have to be added before the file can be accessed:

```
assign(DataFile, 'B:SAMPLE.DOC')   { Non-standard }
```

Then the file could be opened for input with `reset` or for output with `rewrite`.

File output is buffered in Turbo Pascal. This means that data are written to the file in big chunks, not character by character. If you write some data to a file (other than `output`), you must *close* the file when you are finished or some data that is in the buffer but not yet in the file might get lost. There is a non-Standard procedure, `close`, that does the job. If you have opened the file `DataFile` for output, using `rewrite`, you simply close it by typing:

```
close(DataFile)   { Non-standard }
```

Be sure this statement is placed after all `write`s to the file.

Also, in Turbo Pascal Version 3, the `read` procedure does not behave exactly the same as the Pascal Standard requires. To force `read` and `readln` to work as the Standard indicates, include the `{$B-}` compiler directive at the very beginning of the source code.

B.2   Berkeley Pascal, Apple Pascal and Light-speed Pascal

There are several ways to associate a physical file with an internal file name in Berkeley Pascal and Lightspeed Pascal. The simplest way is the same as the way it's done in Apple Pascal. You only need to include the physical file name—as a string constant or variable—in the call to either **reset** or **rewrite**. Suppose the physical file name is **triangle** and the internal file is **DataFile**. The file is prepared to be read from by:

```
reset(DataFile, 'triangle')    {  Non-standard  }
```

and it is prepared to be written to by:

```
rewrite(DataFile, 'triangle')    {  Non-standard  }
```

The string constant **'triangle'** could be replaced in either example with a string variable that was filled in by the user.

Berkeley Pascal does not require (or allow) a call to **close**. Apple Pascal and Lightspeed Pascal, on the other hand, have several variations on the **close** procedure call.

In Apple Pascal, to close a file opened by **rewrite** and to make sure the buffer has been written to the file, include:

```
close(DataFile, 'LOCK')    {  Non-standard  }
```

after all **writes** to the file.

In Lightspeed Pascal you can close a file by simply coding:

```
close(DataFile)    {  Non-standard  }
```

You need to be careful to open the file in a particular manner depending on the situation; i.e., how it was closed or is to be used. You should check the Language Reference Manual. Also, note that in Lightspeed Pascal, the file name is *not* included with **input** and **output** in the program heading line.

B.3   Pascal/3000

Pascal/3000 provides four different ways to associate an internal file name with a physical file. The first way is to just use the physical file name as the internal file name. In this case, the internal file name must be identical to the physical file name and, therefore, must be a valid name for a file on the HP 3000. Method Two is similar to that described above for Berkeley, Apple and Lightspeed Pascal; just add a string as a second parameter to the **reset** or **rewrite** procedure calls:

```
reset(DataFile, 'TRIANGLE')    {  Non-standard  }
```

or,

```
rewrite(DataFile, 'TRIANGLE')    {  Non-standard  }
```

You can check the Pascal/3000 Reference Manuals for details on the remaining two methods; essentially, they allow you to determine the physical file to be associated with the internal file when you issue the RUN command.

Pascal/3000 provides a close procedure that will close a file and, optionally, the programmer can choose the "disposition" of the file as it's being closed by specifying a second parameter to the close procedure call. If the programmer chooses not to close a file, the system will close it anyway so there is seldom need to use the close procedure.

B.4 PASCAL-20

PASCAL-20 uses an starting dialogue to associate files named in the program heading line with physical files. For each file mentioned in the program heading line, this dialogue asks for a name of a physical file to associate it to. As an example, if the program heading line was:

```
program test(file1);
```

When the program is executed the system would display a line like:

```
FILE1:  _
```

The user would be expected to enter the name of the physical file to associate with the logical file file1. If more than one file is mentioned in the program heading line, this dialogue would continue for each file listed. Indeed, the system even asks for the physical file to associate with input and output. For these files, you can just press the RETURN key.

Since the DEC-20 keeps track of a number of versions of the same file, this procedure can cause problems because the system may not know which version of the file is intended. Besides, it will not know whether to create a new file or not (if the file is used for output). For these reasons, the syntax of the program heading line has been extended to allow you to tell the system which version you want. In the program heading line, after the name of each file, you can type a colon (:) and either a + or a -. The - indicates the file is an input file; when the system asks for the physical file name, an error message will be displayed if the file does not exist and the user will be prompted for another file name. The + indicates that it is an output file. The user can specify a version number but if no version number is given, it defaults to create a new version of the file. Due to these extensions, the normal program heading line when no additional files are being used is:

```
program name(input:-, output:+);
```

The **reset** and **rewrite** procedures can have as many as six parameters; some of them assign protection attributes to the file. In the simplest case, you can give a name of the file as a second parameter by using a string literal or string variable; however, normally there is no reason to do this as the physical file name can be given via the dialogue described above. The dialogue will take place even if the file name is included as a second parameter, and, strangely, the file name used in the dialogue is not used.

All open files are closed whenever a program exits, so it is not absolutely necessary to close a file. However, it might be desirable to close the file while the program is running and not have to wait until execution of the program is complete (it might be necessary to allow other programs to use the file while your program is still running). In such a case, there is a **close** procedure that will close the file so other programs can use it. The syntax is simply:

    close(filename)

where **filename** is the logical file name.

Appendix C

Differences Between Compilers

In this appendix we will briefly discuss some well-known Pascal compilers and some of their differences as compared to the Standard. Most of the compilers discussed below allow for some sort of direct access file manipulation. This gets complicated; since Standard Pascal only supports sequential access files, and since we have not discussed direct access files at all in this text, we will not mention any of the methods these compilers use for direct access files.

C.1 Berkeley Pascal

Berkeley Pascal is used on computers running the UNIX operating system. This discussion will be concerned with version 3.0. We will not attempt to mention all of the differences between Berkeley Pascal and Standard Pascal, but will try to mention those that are most likely to be noticed.

The most obvious difference is the fact that Berkeley Pascal is case-sensitive. That is, identifiers typed in upper and lowercase are *not* considered to be the same. Were you, for example, to declare a variable `Flag` and attempt to refer to it as `flag`, you would get an "undefined variable" error message from the compiler. You can issue a "switch" to cause Berkeley Pascal to be case-insensitive. The switch amounts to telling the compiler to use Standard Pascal when it compiles.

There are a number of non-standard extensions in Berkeley Pascal. Among these are:

- String Padding: constant strings are automatically padded with blanks. That makes it possible to assign a string to a string variable without padding the to-be-assigned string with spaces. That is, using the example from the text on page 358, it would be possible to assign a value to S2:

  ```
  S2 := 'hacker'
  ```

  without padding `'hacker'` with blanks.

- A function can return structures (such as arrays, records, etc.) other than simple types.

- Comments can be delimited with either { and } or (* and *). If the character { appears in a comment delimited by { and }, or if the character (* appears in a comment delimited by (* and *), an error message is printed. This is a handy feature that will detect many hard-to-find errors.

- There are several non-standard procedures and functions. There are date and time procedures that will assign the current date or time to a variable and there are functions that will generate random numbers. Let's look at the functions that generate random numbers.

The function **random** requires a **real** parameter that is ignored; i.e., you must send it a **real** but it doesn't matter what **real** you send it. The function returns a **real** value x in the range $0.0 \leq x < 1.0$. The sequence of numbers generated will always be the same unless you change the "seed." There is a function, **seed**, that allows you to change the sequence by starting it with a seed of your choice. Here is a short piece of code that will accomplish the task of generating and displaying a new sequence of 100 **real** numbers:

```
write('Enter an integer:  ');
readln(Num);
Num := seed(Num);
for i := 1 to 100 do
   write(random(1.0) : 8 : 5);
writeln
```

The sequence of **reals** will begin at a different point every time a different **integer** is input. The same **integer** will cause the same sequence each time.

There are several other non-standard features in Berkeley Pascal. You are referred to the Berkeley Pascal User's Manual for further details.

C.2   Turbo Pascal

Borland International, Inc. developed a Pascal compiler for microcomputers in the early 1980s which has become immensely popular. Version 3.0 has been widely used since 1985. In 1987 they released version 4.0, and in 1988 version 5.0. These versions are rapidly becoming as popular as version 3.0. One of the nicest features of Turbo Pascal is the built-in editor, which is closely tied in with the compiler. If you use the editor to write your program and then compile it, whenever a syntax or run-time error is encountered, you are thrown back into the editor with the cursor sitting on the spot where the error occurred. We will not discuss the edit/compile process here; you should refer to your Turbo Pascal Reference Manual or Owner's Handbook for detailed instruction on how the process works.

There are several differences between versions 3.0 on one hand and 4.0 and 5.0 on the other. We'll first discuss features common to all three versions and then discuss those features that have been added in forming versions 4.0 and 5.0.

Turbo Pascal, Versions 3.0, 4.0 and 5.0

There are a number of non-standard extensions in Turbo Pascal and a few places where Turbo does not follow the Pascal Standard. We'll discuss these separately.

Turbo Pascal *vs.* Standard Pascal

In this section we'll discuss the ways that Turbo Pascal behaves differently than the Standard requires.

- The Standard procedures `Get` and `Put` are not implemented in Turbo Pascal. We do not discuss them in this book anyway. They are low-level I/O routines. We do all our I/O with the `read` and `write` procedures and Turbo Pascal does it much the same way. Further, Standard Pascal requires the reference to a "file buffer variable." Turbo Pascal does not allow such a reference.

- The `mod` operator works differently in Turbo Pascal. According to the Standard, `i mod j` is only defined if `j` is positive. Additionally, `i mod j` is positive or zero even if `i` is negative. In Turbo Pascal, `i mod j` can be negative when `i` is negative. The value of `i mod j` is `i - (i div j) * j`. So if `i` = -12 and `j` = 5, `i mod j` would equal 3 in Standard Pascal and -2 in Turbo Pascal.

- In Standard Pascal it is an error to "threaten" the index of a ⟨*for statement*⟩. This is not detected in Turbo Pascal.

- The `page` procedure is not implemented. To clear the screen, there is a non-standard procedure `ClrScr`. To advance the printer to the top of the next page, you can "write" a "form feed" character to the printer. For example, the following ⟨*write procedure*⟩ call will cause whatever follows to be printed on a new page:

  ```
  writeln(lst, chr(12))
  ```

  The `lst` is the file designating the printer, the "list device;" the `chr(12)` is the ASCII character for a form feed.

- The reserved word `packed` has no effect in Turbo Pascal, but you can still use it. Standard Pascal requires two supplied procedures, `pack` and `unpack`. Since `packed` has no effect in Turbo Pascal, these two routines are not implemented. We did not discuss these procedures in this text.

- Pascal allows a `goto`. We did not discuss it nor do we recommend it. Turbo Pascal has some limitations on its use that will not concern us.

- Standard Pascal allows you to pass procedures and functions as parameters; Turbo Pascal does not. We did not discuss passing procedures and functions as parameters in this text.

Turbo Pascal Extensions

As with all real-world implementations of Pascal, there are several extensions in Turbo Pascal. We do not plan to discuss them all. Rather, we'll just mention those that seem most useful or confusing.

- An identifier can contain the underscore character (_) after the initial letter. It is still a good idea to avoid this feature if there is any chance your code will be moved to another system.

- Strings are implemented in a very different manner than as indicated in the Standard; indeed, the word `string` is a reserved word in Turbo Pascal. There are built-in routines that delete and insert substrings from and into strings. String assignment is more flexible than allowed in the Standard. There are routines that convert a string to a number (`integer` or `real`) and *vice versa*. You can concatenate and copy strings; you can find the length of a string and determine the position of a substring within a string. All of these are similar in nature to those routines we wrote in chapter 11, but not the same. One nice feature is the ability to compare two strings using the "<" and ">" operators. Absolutely none of the string handling capability of Turbo Pascal is portable; if you use any of these features, your code will not run on a different compiler.

- The ⟨*case statement*⟩ in Turbo Pascal has been extended in three ways. First, if the value of the expression does not match the value of any of the constants, no statement is executed and no error is reported. Second, it is possible to include an "`else`" part. In place of a constant or list of constants, you can put `else` followed by a colon followed by a statement. This statement will be executed if the value of the expression does not match the value of any of the constants. Third, it is possible to include a range of constants as well as a list of constants. This is done using a form like `1 .. 20`.

- Turbo Pascal allows you to define *typed constants*. These are essentially variables that cannot be changed. They are not the same as constants in the Standard Pascal sense. In particular, a typed constant cannot be used where Pascal requires a constant, such as in the declaration of an array.

- Whenever a file is opened for output, using **rewrite**, it must be closed, using a call to the non-standard procedure **close**, or the data left in the buffer will be lost. This is discussed in more detail in appendix B.

- There are functions that will generate random numbers. The function **random** with no parameters returns a **real** value x in the range $0.0 \leq x < 1.0$. The function **random(N)** with one positive **integer** parameter returns an **integer** between 0 and N - 1, inclusive. The sequence of numbers generated will always be the same unless you include a call to **randomize**. Here is a short piece of code that will accomplish the task of generating and displaying a new sequence of 100 **real** numbers:

```
randomize;
for i := 1 to 100 do
   write(random : 8 : 5);
writeln
```

The sequence of **real**s will begin at a different point every time.

Here is a piece of code that will allow the user to enter an **integer** and will then generate 100 **integers** between 0 and the value entered by the user.

```
write('Enter an integer:  ');
readln(Num);
for i := 1 to 100 do
   write(random(Num) : 8);
writeln
```

Note that the number entered by the user is *not* one of the possible values. If you want **integers** between 1 and Num, just add 1 to **random(Num)**. Notice also that there is no call to **randomize** so that if these are the only lines of code in a program, the sequence of **integers** generated are supposed to be the same each time the program is run. In practice, however, it is not clear whether or not the same sequence will always be generated. It is suggested in the reference manual that you always begin with a call to **randomize**. Unfortunately, this makes it difficult to repeat an experiment with the same data.

- Turbo Pascal supplies functions that allow a programmer to get lower into the operation of a computer. For example, there are functions that look at the high order and low order byte of an **integer**. There are routines that allow for interrupt handling. Similarly, there are routines that allow graphics, turtle graphics, sound, color control and windowing on an IBM compatible computer.

- There are several compiler directives that allow for the setting of a number of things. These are beyond what we wish to discuss and you can consult the reference manual for the details.

Turbo Pascal Version 3.0

- Turbo Pascal version 3.0, in its default setup, handles the problems with interactive input differently than the Standard and differently than described in chapter 12. The following quote is from the TURBO Pascal version 3.0 Reference Manual:

> "When the *Read* procedure is used without specifying a file identifier, it always inputs a line, even if some characters still remain to be read from the line buffer, and it ignores Ctrl-Z, forcing the operator to terminate the line with RETURN. The terminating RETURN is not echoed, and internally the line is stored with a Ctrl-Z appended to the end of it. Thus, when less values are specified on the input line than there are parameters in the parameter list, any *Char* variables in excess will be set to Ctrl-Z, strings will be empty, and numeric variables will remain unaltered."

This can cause your programs to behave in unexpected ways if you write them as discussed in the text. Usually the differences are not noticed or don't seem to be a problem. When you do need to force Turbo Pascal to behave more like the Standard requires, you can give it a "compiler directive." Without going into detail, this amounts to putting the following comment at the very beginning of your program:

    {$B-}

You are once again referred to the reference manual for more details.

- If you are using Turbo Pascal version 3.0 in a CP/M environment, you have to be careful with recursion. You cannot pass a local variable to a recursive routine as a variable parameter. Further, the default setup of Turbo Pascal in a CP/M environment will not generate recursive code. If you write a recursive routine, you must include the compiler directive:

    {$A-}

Remember, this is only necessary in a CP/M environment using version 3.0.

- The evaluation of Boolean expressions is not done by "short-circuit evaluation." We discussed short-circuit evaluation in chapter 10, when we discussed the "and problem."

Turbo Pascal Versions 4.0 and 5.0

Versions 4.0 and 5.0 are considerably more powerful than version 3.0. These packages were designed to allow major programs to be written, programs that require more room than was possible in version 3.0. Many new procedures and functions have been added. Wirth's original design has been changed a great deal by the extensions in these packages. While the original intent was to provide a teaching language; i.e., a small compact language that would allow a user to learn the basic constructs of computer programming, Borland International has clearly designed versions 4.0 and 5.0 to be major production languages. We have no intention to discuss the full capability of Turbo Pascal versions 4.0 and 5.0. To do so would require a complete book. We will, however, mention some of the chief differences between the older version 3.0 and the new 4.0 and 5.0.

The first thing that you're likely to notice is the use of "units." To quote from the Owner's Handbook (Version 4.0):

> "Turbo Pascal gives you access to a large number of predefined constants, data types, variables, procedures, and functions. ... There are dozens of them, but you seldom use them all in a given program. Because of this, they are split into related groups called *units*. ... Each unit is almost like a separate Pascal program."

These units are available to you and you can pull them into your programs as you need to. There are units for screen-oriented routines; there are units that handle graphics and those that handle different printers. There are units that do system calls. Indeed, you can write and keep your own units.

Standard Pascal, as well as Turbo Pascal version 3.0, does not allow for the separate compilation of parts of a program; Turbo Pascal versions 4.0 and 5.0 do. Additionally, you can write programs that exceed to 64K byte limit imposed in version 3.0. Your programs are only limited by the amount of available memory in your computer.

Some of the other differences to be aware of are:

- The evaluation of Boolean expressions is done by "short-circuit evaluation." We discussed short-circuit evaluation in chapter 10. There is a compiler directive that will force non-short-circuit evaluation. Version 3.0 does not use short-circuit evaluation of Boolean expressions.

- The compiler directives in versions 4.0 and 5.0 are completely different from those in version 3.0. There are more of them and they all mean different things.

- In version 3.0 it was difficult to get a hard copy of a run of your program. There were some undocumented features that made it possible but it was never easy. In versions 4.0 and 5.0, you can simply redirect the output to a file and then dump that file to a printer. Caution: this won't work if you use the unit CRT. You can also echo everything that is sent to the screen to the printer by entering a control-P before and after the commands that run the program. (You will need to create an executable version of the program on disk to use these features. Just "Compile to Disk.")

- The `read` procedure modifications mentioned above for version 3.0 are not in force in versions 4.0 and 5.0. In particular, there is no {$B-} compiler directive. Actually, there is a B directive but it means something else. The `read` procedure in versions 4.0 and 5.0 work like the `read` procedure described in this text without any I/O directive.

C.3   Lightspeed Pascal

Lightspeed Pascal for the Apple Macintosh is a fast, friendly programming environment. It features a built-in editor that interacts closely with the compiler. We describe differences between Standard Pascal and Lightspeed Pascal first and then will describe a few of the extensions that have been added. The procedures `put` and `get` are supported in Lightspeed Pascal but since we have not discussed them in this text, we won't mention them in the following.

Non-standard Features

- In Standard Pascal, there must be at least one assignment statement in the statement part of a function block that assigns a value to the name of the function. This requirement is not enforced, for some reason, in Lightspeed Pascal. In practice, this will have little effect since you will always want to have such a statement in order for the function to work. It is nice when the compiler notices the absence of such a statement for debugging purposes.

- In Standard Pascal it is an error to "threaten" the index of a ⟨*for statement*⟩. This is not detected in Lightspeed Pascal.

- In Standard Pascal, all files used in the program must be listed in the program heading line. In Lightspeed Pascal, the only files that may be listed there are `input` and `output`.

Extensions

- An identifier can contain the underscore character (_) after the initial letter. It is still a good idea to avoid this feature if there is any chance your code will be moved to another system.

- In Lightspeed Pascal the ⟨*constant definition part*⟩, the ⟨*type definition part*⟩, the ⟨*variable declaration part*⟩ and the ⟨*procedure/function declaration part*⟩ may occur in any order and may be repeated more than once in the same ⟨*definition/declaration part*⟩.

- Lightspeed Pascal supports additional types that allow for longer `integers` and longer `reals`.

- Strings are handled quite differently than in the Standard. There are a number of procedures and functions that allow manipulations similar to those discussed in chapter 11. A string can be defined to have a particular "size" or a default size of 255 characters. The length of a string and the size of a string are not the same. The length of a string is, essentially, the number of characters that the string has at any moment while the size of a string is its maximum length. Strings can be handled as arrays of characters but care is required. For example, a string `StrVar` could be defined:

```
var
   StrVar : string[10];
```

and then assigned a value with:

```
StrVar := 'abcd'
```

It would then be valid to refer to `StrVar[1]` or to `StrVar[4]` but it would cause an error to refer to `StrVar[5]`. Notice that assigning something to `StrVar[5]` would even cause an error. You cannot refer to an element of a string that is beyond its length. There is a function, `Length`, that will return the length of a string. Individual characters may be referenced as if they are strings of length one.

- Functions can return values of any type.

- There is an "`otherwise`" clause for the ⟨*case statement*⟩. It must follow the last statement following a constant list. The `otherwise` is followed by a semicolon and a statement that is to be executed if the value of the expression does not match the value of any of the constants. Also, you can include a range of constants in addition to a list of constants. This is accomplished by using a form like 1 .. 20.

- Strings can be read with the ⟨*read procedure*⟩.

- Lightspeed Pascal supports the use of "units" to allow for constructing modules and for separate compilation. Additionally, Lightspeed Pascal supports all of the Macintosh Toolbox/OS constants, types, variables, procedures and functions. There are a number of procedures that support window manipulation.

C.4   Pascal/3000

Pascal/3000 for the HP 3000 computer follows the Standard fairly closely except in the area of I/O and provides a number of extensions. We discuss the differences between Pascal/3000 and Standard Pascal first, and then the extensions.

Non-standard Features

- Constants in Pascal/3000 may be specified with constant expressions, i.e., one may use the operators +, -, *, /, div and mod and other constants together to form a constant expression, which can be used anywhere a constant is required.

- In the ⟨*definition/declaration part*⟩ of the program or any procedure or function, you can repeat and mix the ⟨*constant definition part*⟩, the ⟨*type definition part*⟩ and the ⟨*variable declaration part*⟩. The ⟨*procedure/function declaration part*⟩ must still follow the other parts.

Extensions

- An identifier can contain the underscore character (_) after the initial letter. It is still a good idea to avoid this feature if there is any chance your code will be moved to another system.

- A function may return a value of any type (including structured types such as arrays, records, etc.) except for `file` types.

- The ⟨*case statement*⟩ allows an `otherwise` clause. The `otherwise` may precede a list of statements and the word `end`. If the expression evaluates to a value not specified in the constants, the statements following the `otherwise` are executed. Also, subranges may appear as case constants.

- There is an additional supplied type, `longreal`, which provides for `real` numbers with greater precision.

- You may indicate a non-printing ASCII character by typing a single letter after the sharp symbol; i.e., `#G` stands for a control G, the bell.

- Pascal/3000 supplies what it calls "constructors," which are also called "structured constants." These are essentially constants of types that are predeclared. This would allow you to construct a constant record or a constant set, for example.

- As you would expect, Pascal/3000 supplies several string-related procedures and functions. You can define strings with a particular maximum length; the word `string` is a reserved word. For example, you could define a new type by typing:

```
type
   StrType = string[10];
```

A variable of StrType could then hold up to 10 characters. Indeed, this is almost exactly the same as declaring StrType by:

```
type
   StrType = packed array [1 .. 10] of char;
```

However, the supplied routines only work for types declared with the word **string** and not on those defined in the standard manner. Some of the supplied routines duplicate those we wrote in chapter 11. Included are the functions strlen, strmax and strpos. Respectively these functions return the current length of a string, the maximum length and the position of one string within another. Included as supplied procedures are strappend and strinsert. The first appends (concatenates) one string onto another and the second inserts one string into another. There are others, check the reference manual.

String literals and string variables will be padded with blanks when assigned to strings that have a larger defined maximum length.

- The procedures get and put are supported. The get procedures uses what is called "Lazy I/O" so as to enable interactive input. In essence, this means that the ⟨*read procedure*⟩ will behave in a reasonable manner when used interactively.

- The ⟨*write procedure*⟩ may write enumerated types to a file, including the terminal.

- There are functions that will translate a string to an **integer**.

- Pascal/3000 supplies several "compiler directives." One of these directives, PARTIAL_EVAL, causes Boolean expressions to be evaluated by what we have called "short-circuit evaluation." We discussed short-circuit evaluation in chapter 10, when we discussed the "**and** problem."

C.5   PASCAL-20

PASCAL-20 (for the DEC 20, and hereafter called "Pascal-20") contains many features that make it a powerful language on the DEC 20. Many of these extensions are related to I/O and we'll not spend much time discussing them. Others allow a programmer to do monitor calls (i.e., operating system calls) and other low-level functions. You are referred to the Pascal-20 Hacker's Guide for help on these features.

We discuss Pascal-20 in two sections, one where we discuss differences between Pascal-20 and Standard Pascal and one where we discuss some of the extensions that Pascal-20 offers.

Non-standard Features

- The get and put procedures have been modified to allow you to work with files with variable-length records. Since we have not been concerned with get or put, we'll also not worry about these modifications.

- A comment can be enclosed in { and }, (* and *), /* and */, or % and \. In Standard Pascal { and (* are completely equivalent. That is, you could form a perfectly valid comment like:

```
{  This is a valid comment in Standard Pascal  *)
```

but this is not possible in Pascal-20 (nor in most other compilers). Pascal-20 uses the additional comment delimiters to form comments that nest. Consider the following sample of code.

```
{
  i := i + 1;   {  Add 1 to i }
  j := j + 1;   {  Add 1 to j }
}
```

The programmer was trying to remove the two statements (perhaps while debugging the program) but this causes a syntax error. The first comment is terminated by the first } (the second { is inside the first comment). Thus, the last } is not matched by a { and a syntax error results. In Pascal-20, you could rewrite the above code:

```
/*
  i := i + 1;   {  Add 1 to i }
  j := j + 1;   {  Add 1 to j }
*/
```

And no syntax error would result.

- An identifier can contain the underscore character (_). It is a good idea to avoid this feature if there is any chance your code will be moved to another system.

Extensions

- Apparently for compatibility with older versions, there are several alternate forms for Pascal's operators. For example, the operator >= can be replaced by a ". There's no good reason to use the alternate forms so we'll not discuss them further.

- Pascal-20 has added some string I/O features that allow a user to "read" and "write" to and from strings. You would use non-standard procedures StrSet and StrWrite in a manner similar to reset and rewrite to "open" the string. You are referred to the Hacker's Guide for more details.

- Pascal-20 uses "Lazy I/O" to read from the keyboard. This permits a programmer to put a prompt before a read call and not have the system lock up waiting for the input before the output is displayed. We have discussed this problem in some detail in chapter 12.

- The procedure page sends an ASCII form feed character to the printer.

- If a file is not mentioned in the program heading line but is used in the program, Pascal-20 treats it as a temporary file and deletes it when the execution of the program is completed.

- Pascal-20 does not detect the error of failing to assign a value to a function.

- Pascal-20 does not detect a reference to an undefined variable.

- The symbols : and .. are treated as equivalent. Don't use this feature!

- You may compile your program in pieces and include a piece compiled separately by use of the reserved non-standard identifier include. Moreover, you can access code written in other languages.

- In write and writeln, integers can be displayed in decimal, octal or hexadecimal. You would add an extra colon and either O (for octal) or H (for hexadecimal) after the integer expression.

- You can read into a string with the ⟨read procedure⟩.

- Pascal-20 has added several functions and procedures. There are inverse trig functions, hyperbolic trig functions, a random number generating function and a myriad of others. You should check the reference manual if you're interested. However, remember that the use of these functions and/or procedures make your code non-portable.

- The ⟨case statement⟩ allows an others clause. The others must be the last clause and must precede a statement and the word end. If the expression evaluates to a value not specified in the constants, the statement following the others is executed. Also, if the value of the expression fails to match any of the constants and the others clause is not present, an empty statement is executed and no error is reported.

- The index of a ⟨for statement⟩ can be a global variable if it is a local variable in a surrounding block. There's no good reason to use this feature, either.

- Pascal-20 has an additional looping statement that allows you to exit from the middle of the loop. While there are times that such a structure can be utilized, the same thing can always be accomplished with the standard repetitive statements provided and a flag. "Structured programming" philosophy would advise against a loop that can be exited in the middle.

C.6   Apple Pascal

Apple Pascal is an implementation of UCSD Pascal, which was developed at the University of California at San Diego. UCSD Pascal contains many extensions to the Standard, most having to do with string handling and graphics. The built-in string handling procedures and functions are similar to those developed in this book in chapter 11. The graphics procedures and functions are based on the "turtle graphics" developed by Seymour Papert of MIT.

Apple Pascal provides a complete programming environment based on its own unique operating system, including an integrated editor, compiler and linker. It was written so that it could run on early Apple II microcomputers with 40-column screens and a limited character set, as well as later models.

We will list some of the many non-standard features and extensions of Apple Pascal below; for a complete discussion refer to the Apple Pascal Language Reference Manual.

Non-standard Features

- Sets are limited to 512 elements, and a set cannot contain `integer`s less than 0 or greater than 511.

- The standard procedures `pack` and `unpack` are not provided. Packing and unpacking is done automatically.

- The standard `dispose` procedure is not provided. Memory that is dynamically allocated via the `new` procedure is returned to the pool of available memory through the use of procedures called `mark` and `release`. The memory used by a particular variable cannot be released to the system as with `dispose`; instead, the memory used by every dynamic variable created after a call to `mark` is released by a call to `release`.

- Some Standard Pascal mathematical functions are not built-ins in Apple Pascal, but are provided as library functions.

- There is a predefined type `interactive`, which is like the standard type `text`, but it is designed to relate to the keyboard. Some of the standard file I/O procedures and functions have slightly different behaviors when applied to an `interactive` file.

- The underscore character is allowed within identifiers.

- In the ⟨*case statement*⟩, there is no error if the value of the expression is not found on the case constant list. Execution continues with the next statement after the ⟨*case statement*⟩.

- The comment symbols { and (* match with } and *), respectively, allowing "nested" comments.

- The files listed on the program file list are ignored.

- The comparison operators = and <> work with arrays of exactly the same type and records of exactly the same type.

- Procedures and functions cannot be passed as parameters.

- The `ord` function will accept a parameter of type `pointer`. The `ord` of a `Boolean` value will not always return a 0 or a 1.

Extensions

- A predefined variable type `string` is included, as is a set of built-in string handling procedures and functions.

- An extension of the `integer` type, called "long integer", is supplied. Such an integer can be up to 36 digits long, and is defined by appending the length to the reserved word `integer`, enclosed in square brackets. For example,

```
type longint = integer[20]
```

- A procedure called `exit` is supplied that terminates the execution of a procedure or function.

- The `gotoxy` procedure positions the screen cursor at a place specified by the parameters passed to it.

- There is a set of byte-oriented built-in procedures and functions, and other facilities for dealing with memory or peripherals at a lower level.

- A group of procedures and functions can be compiled separately and called a `unit`. These `units` can then be included in a program by use of the `uses` declaration. Apple Pascal supplies some special `units`, most notably `turtlegraphics` for graphics modules and `applestuff`, a collection of utilities such as a random number generator.

C.7   Apple II Instant Pascal

Apple II Instant Pascal is very close in many ways to Macintosh Pascal, the precursor to Lightspeed Pascal for the Macintosh. It provides a complete programming environment for the Apple II modeled after the Macintosh interface, using pull-down menus and so forth. It runs under the Apple ProDOS operating system, and provides graphics windows for editing the source code, displaying the text output of a program and displaying graphics output.

One of the main differences between Instant Pascal and most others is that it is not a compiled language in the normal sense. Each statement is translated to low-level machine code as it is entered with the editor, and syntax is checked immediately. Instant Pascal also provides debugging tools that make it easier for beginning programmers to learn the language.

Instant Pascal claims to follow the ANSI Pascal Standard, with extensions some of which are listed below; for a complete discussion refer to the Apple II Instant Pascal Language Reference Manual.

Extensions

- The underscore character may be used in identifiers.

- `string` is a reserved word, since it is a predefined type. There is a set of string manipulation routines built in. `string` variables can be compared with variables of type `char`.

- There is an `otherwise` clause that is optional in a ⟨*case statement*⟩.

- A type `longint` is included along with addition types that represent reals: `double`, `extended` and `comp`.

- Various extensions for file I/O are included that allow for, among other things, direct access to files.

- `string` types and enumerated types can be read from text files using `read` and `readln`, and can be written to text files using `write` and `writeln`.

Appendix D

ASCII Table

Dec	Hex	Oct	Binary	Char			Dec	Hex	Oct	Binary	Char
0	00	000	0000000	^@	NUL		32	20	040	0100000	
1	01	001	0000001	^A	SOH		33	21	041	0100001	!
2	02	002	0000010	^B	STX		34	22	042	0100010	"
3	03	003	0000011	^C	ETX		35	23	043	0100011	#
4	04	004	0000100	^D	EOT		36	24	044	0100100	$
5	05	005	0000101	^E	ENQ		37	25	045	0100101	%
6	06	006	0000110	^F	ACK		38	26	046	0100110	&
7	07	007	0000111	^G	BEL		39	27	047	0100111	'
8	08	010	0001000	^H	BS		40	28	050	0101000	(
9	09	011	0001001	^I	HT		41	29	051	0101001	)
10	0a	012	0001010	^J	LF		42	2a	052	0101010	*
11	0b	013	0001011	^K	VT		43	2b	053	0101011	+
12	0c	014	0001100	^L	FF		44	2c	054	0101100	,
13	0d	015	0001101	^M	CR		45	2d	055	0101101	-
14	0e	016	0001110	^N	SO		46	2e	056	0101110	.
15	0f	017	0001111	^O	SI		47	2f	057	0101111	/
16	10	020	0010000	^P	DLE		48	30	060	0110000	0
17	11	021	0010001	^Q	DC1		49	31	061	0110001	1
18	12	022	0010010	^R	DC2		50	32	062	0110010	2
19	13	023	0010011	^S	DC3		51	33	063	0110011	3
20	14	024	0010100	^T	DC4		52	34	064	0110100	4
21	15	025	0010101	^U	NAK		53	35	065	0110101	5
22	16	026	0010110	^V	SYN		54	36	066	0110110	6
23	17	027	0010111	^W	ETB		55	37	067	0110111	7
24	18	030	0011000	^X	CAN		56	38	070	0111000	8
25	19	031	0011001	^Y	EM		57	39	071	0111001	9
26	1a	032	0011010	^Z	SUB		58	3a	072	0111010	:
27	1b	033	0011011	^[	ESC		59	3b	073	0111011	;
28	1c	034	0011100	^\	FS		60	3c	074	0111100	<
29	1d	035	0011101	^]	GS		61	3d	075	0111101	=
30	1e	036	0011110	^^	RS		62	3e	076	0111110	>
31	1f	037	0011111	^_	US		63	3f	077	0111111	?

Dec	Hex	Oct	Binary	Char		Dec	Hex	Oct	Binary	Char
64	40	100	1000000	@		96	60	140	1100000	`
65	41	101	1000001	A		97	61	141	1100001	a
66	42	102	1000010	B		98	62	142	1100010	b
67	43	103	1000011	C		99	63	143	1100011	c
68	44	104	1000100	D		100	64	144	1100100	d
69	45	105	1000101	E		101	65	145	1100101	e
70	46	106	1000110	F		102	66	146	1100110	f
71	47	107	1000111	G		103	67	147	1100111	g
72	48	110	1001000	H		104	68	150	1101000	h
73	49	111	1001001	I		105	69	151	1101001	i
74	4a	112	1001010	J		106	6a	152	1101010	j
75	4b	113	1001011	K		107	6b	153	1101011	k
76	4c	114	1001100	L		108	6c	154	1101100	l
77	4d	115	1001101	M		109	6d	155	1101101	m
78	4e	116	1001110	N		110	6e	156	1101110	n
79	4f	117	1001111	O		111	6f	157	1101111	o
80	50	120	1010000	P		112	70	160	1110000	p
81	51	121	1010001	Q		113	71	161	1110001	q
82	52	122	1010010	R		114	72	162	1110010	r
83	53	123	1010011	S		115	73	163	1110011	s
84	54	124	1010100	T		116	74	164	1110100	t
85	55	125	1010101	U		117	75	165	1110101	u
86	56	126	1010110	V		118	76	166	1110110	v
87	57	127	1010111	W		119	77	167	1110111	w
88	58	130	1011000	X		120	78	170	1111000	x
89	59	131	1011001	Y		121	79	171	1111001	y
90	5a	132	1011010	Z		122	7a	172	1111010	z
91	5b	133	1011011	[		123	7b	173	1111011	{
92	5c	134	1011100	\		124	7c	174	1111100	|
93	5d	135	1011101	]		125	7d	175	1111101	}
94	5e	136	1011110	^		126	7e	176	1111110	~
95	5f	137	1011111	_		127	7f	177	1111111	DEL

Index